Also available at all good book stores

9781785315510

9781908051776

9781785313264

9781785314278

9781785311840

9781908051509

9781909178694

9781909626560

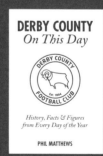

9781905411870

DAVE
MACKAY
Football's
Braveheart

The
Authorised
Biography

DAVE
MACKAY
Football's
Braveheart

Mike Donovan

Forewords by Derek Mackay and Denis Law

First published by Pitch Publishing, 2021

Pitch Publishing
A2 Yeoman Gate
Yeoman Way
Worthing
Sussex
BN13 3QZ
www.pitchpublishing.co.uk
info@pitchpublishing.co.uk

ISBN 978 1 78531 791 0

Typesetting and origination by Pitch Publishing
Printed and bound in India by Replika Press Pvt. Ltd.

Contents

Foreword by Derek Mackay 9
Foreword by Denis Law 13
Prologue 17
  1. 'Miracle Man' 21

PART ONE: BEGINNINGS
  2. Family and friendship 31
  3. These boots are made for football 42
  4. 'A wee guy who was a bit special' 53
  5. Rising Newtongrange star 63
  6. 'Hard but fair' 72

PART TWO: HEART OF MIDLOTHIAN
  7. 'Superman' in maroon 83
  8. Golden years 95
  9. Living for the weekend 106
  10. Auld Reekie 'blew its dignified top' 117
  11. A dream come true 127
  12. World Cup 143

PART THREE: TOTTENHAM HOTSPUR
  13. 'How would you like to live in London?' 159
  14. 'Transformed everything' 171
  15. 'The main man' 180
  16. Esprit de corps 190
  17. The Double completed 201
  18. Glade all over 211
  19. In his element 219
  20. 'My dad was always for the club, never himself' . . . 229
  21. Broken legs, broken hearts 239
  22. The second coming 250
  23. Fairytales can come true 258
  24. 'A born leader' 268

PART FOUR: DERBY COUNTY
  25. Brian Clough 283
  26. 'Exceptional player, exceptional human being' 298

PART FIVE: MANAGEMENT

27. Becoming a boss 311
28. Sowing seeds for Forest growth. 319
29. 'No other manager could have done it'. 325
30. The real deal. 334
31. Ken's Roller 346
32. The cradle of civilisation 357
33. Dubai to Doncaster 367
34. 'A strong character' 374
35. Pioneer's final frontiers 382

PART SIX: POST-CAREER

36. 'What more can a man ask?'. 391
37. 'Having a right good laugh' 400
38. 'Ninian Cassidy, ex-Hearts and Tottenham'. 408
39. Legend 416
40. The Banner Man 422
41. 'My best friend' 430
42. 'I was blessed' 438
43. Legacy 448

Postscript. 456

APPENDICES

1. Eulogy 458
2. Historians. 461
3. Fans 471
4. Poets 482
5. Quite interesting 486
6. Honours and career record 488

Acknowledgements 494
Credits 497
Bibliography 502
Index 507

DEDICATIONS

Author and Mum

Mims

Author's Mum by Georgia Rose Lucas

Mum, Kathleen Louise Donovan (10 October, 1930–13 April 2020): Forever a shining light

Dad, Maurice Donovan (15 October 1927 to 18 December 2000): Gave me my love of Dave Mackay, Spurs, football and a lot more

Mims (Sybil Lilian Leaver 22 April 1922–24 November 2020): Lovely and loved

Rosemary, Matthew and Benny: My foundation

Christine and Sean: Just the three of us

Mark, Tony and other mates who stood on the East Stand terraces at White Hart Lane with me watching Dave Mackay

Isobel and family

All supporters of the game

The NHS for all it does for us

Bobby Wishart: 10 March 1933–3 December 2020

Glenn Roeder: 13 December 1955–28 February 2021

Aunty June Perkins and family, thinking of you

Foreword by Derek Mackay

DAD'S PASSING turned all the family's lives upside down. We all miss him and always will. He's constantly in our thoughts and we gather on his birthday and the anniversary of the day he passed to remember him, together.

We are so proud of what he achieved as a footballer and, more so, as a father, grandfather, great grandfather, husband and friend.

We are grateful his legacy in the game remains strong. It's amazing. My son Daniel and I are Tottenham Hotspur supporters and read the online match programmes the club sent us during the 2020/21 season, with games played behind closed doors because of the coronavirus pandemic.

There was a feature in which Spurs supporters picked their all-time XI, and Dad's name was the first put down on the sheet by more than one. He is revered by young and old supporters for how he came to the club when they were close to relegation and turned it around to go on and win the Double and more in the club's Glory Years of the early 1960s.

It is fantastic when you think of all the great players the club have had. The fact his legacy has lasted all these years, I feel, shows you what sort of player and person he was. Even after all this time there's also loads of interest from Derby County, Heart of Midlothian, Scotland, wherever he played. And football supporters in general, I would have thought.

But Dad never spoke about himself as a great player. When he was growing up, Tommy and Frank, two of his brothers – the other one was

Ronnie – were with him at Hearts at one time. He would say, 'Tommy was a great player,' and, 'Frank was a great player.' Somehow they never made it but he never mentioned himself as a great player. Ever.

Lots of people such as team-mates, opponents, managers, supporters, analysts, whoever – with Bill Nicholson, George Best, Jimmy Greaves, Eusébio, Sir Alex Ferguson and Daniel Levy in the queue – have used the adjective or similar to describe him. They point out how he helped whatever club he was with to win trophies almost every season he played, and claimed a few as a manager. That he is a legend's legend.

What he did was incredible. He captained Scotland, and skippered Hearts to the title and cups. As well as the Double, he came back from a broken leg twice to lead Spurs to a third FA Cup in his time at White Hart Lane. He captained Derby into the First Division and also in the top flight, then managed Derby to the championship when the whole world was on his shoulders as he replaced Brian Clough with the players wanting their old manager back. But he left the judgements on his career to all those who made them. He had self-confidence but never bragged.

People said he was skilful and strong as a player. Hard but fair. He hated bullies, which was why he didn't like that famous picture of himself grabbing Billy Bremner by his shirt collar because it creates the false perception he was one, which, of course, he never was.

He always had a winning mentality. My uncle Pat told me he showed it when he saw Dad play Terry Venables at squash. Terry hit this ball which came off the wall dead low in the corner. Dad threw himself into it, sliding across the floor on his chest and got to it. It left him with red stains off the court markings all up his white tracksuit. He was so determined to make the shot.

Now and again you see on the internet how Dad loved Hearts. Of course he did. They were his first club. He supported them as a kid. But a lot of players have another team that they loved. He really loved Spurs – right to the end. He had great times there, and he also retained a love for Derby County.

Different times, of course. It is all corporate now for guests in the new Tottenham Hotspur Stadium when you go to matches. Lovely meals in a lovely place, but Mum said when she went to games at White Hart Lane she would go to a little tea room to get a cuppa and maybe a sandwich at half-time.

My earliest memories are sitting on wooden benches by the tunnel for a game at the Lane. The excitement was fantastic. My first memory was sitting on a bench and being absolutely amazed as I saw the top of my dad's head as he climbed the steps of the players' tunnel and fully emerged looking twice as big as he was, wearing his Spurs kit and thumping the ball he was holding high towards the goal where the team were to warm up. And there was this big, ear-splitting roar.

I also recall when I used to go to Derby County with Mum, my brother and sisters when he played there too and Dad's manager Brian Clough patted me on the head when I was introduced to him. He had an aura about him. I'll always treasure those memories.

He was a great dad and loved his family. He was fun to be around. He'd look out for all of us – even when we got older – to make sure we were all right. My mum was always supportive of Dad. They were devoted to each other for 60 years. It must have been hard for her when they moved down from Scotland when he was off with Spurs. They didn't know anybody and she had to look after us kids, but she did well. Our parents gave us a wonderful upbringing.

All of us children – David Junior, myself, Valerie and Julie – were born in Scotland.

At the time, if you wanted to play football for Scotland you had to be born there. Perhaps he was looking for at least one of us to follow in his footsteps, I don't know, but none of us became professional footballers. David Junior and I played for a while. We were captains at our junior school, Merryhills. David Junior was good and it was a shame the asthma he had held him back. I became disillusioned when the teacher at my secondary school, Enfield Chace, put me at full-back and told me not to go beyond the halfway line. I was an attacking midfielder! Maybe he just expected me to be brilliant in every game because I was Dave Mackay's son and didn't think anything of it when I played well.

Dad was so generous. My mum remembered a time when he was at Derby and the team coach driver, Eric, liked his expensive raincoat. Eric drove him and a friend to the races at Uttoxeter and he came home minus his coat. He said, 'Eric liked it so I just gave it to him.' Eric was so proud of it.

Dad always liked music. So did I. He loved the Beatles and David Bowie. I had a band in London with friends called Stroyd – we thought it was a trendy name as it sounded like asteroid – during the Glam Rock era of the early 1970s. Slade had made an album called *Slayed*. We called a cassette we made *D-Stroyd*. I had a snare drum and a cymbal and we played around each other's houses.

Anyway, I began to play the acoustic guitar years later for my own entertainment after the family had moved to Nottinghamshire. I wasn't that good, but played it more and more. My dad was starting to get ill and heard me playing in the hallway. It is said how people with dementia find music therapeutic and he asked me to play a few tunes. So I did and we'd have a sing-song. Together we'd sing Chas and Dave numbers, the Beatles' 'Yellow Submarine' and Nancy Sinatra's 'These Boots Are Made For Walking'. A nice memory for me.

I am glad our family have spoken to Mike Donovan about Dad for this book, and approved his efforts. I feel our involvement has provided deep, empathetic insights, and created a balanced, accurate portrait of my dad's life alongside other first-hand contributions from those who knew and admired him. We so appreciate his old pal Denis Law providing the other foreword. It is all a lovely remembrance for the family. The family thank everybody involved.

Derek Mackay
Burton Joyce
Nottinghamshire
April 2021

Foreword by Denis Law

DAVE MACKAY was wonderful. One of the best football players ever, by any standard. One of my favourite players and one of the best players for Scotland when we had a good side, which was unfortunate not to qualify for the World Cup. Could you argue he was the best Scotland player ever? Absolutely.

He was one of the best I've played with. I just loved playing alongside him and was very fortunate do so. He was a winner; so inspirational. He battled for 90 minutes every game. A complete player with skill and strength. He proved how strong he was by coming back from two leg breaks. The first was against my Manchester United and I remember being with him in the Old Trafford dressing rooms after it had happened.

I owe Dave a great deal. I was a bit younger than Dave and coming into the Scotland team, he was my captain. It was daunting when you hadn't played at that level but Dave took me under his wing. He was so supportive. I was with Huddersfield Town in the Second Division and he was in the big-time as a player during my first few games with the national side, moving from Hearts to Tottenham Hotspur. Spurs had a good side with some great players. As well as Dave, there was Danny Blanchflower, John White and Cliff Jones. I was at Huddersfield, thinking, 'It'd be nice to be in that Spurs team.'

Dave always helped all the young selected players who found it a bit too much being in the Scotland squad. A call-up to it meant so much.

After a while, we were able to settle and enjoy it thanks in part to the encouragement Dave gave us.

I hated playing against him. He shone in the Spurs team that developed into one that won the Double and, with Jimmy Greaves coming in, the European Cup Winners' Cup. Their fantastic manager Bill Nicholson made other great signings like Alan Gilzean, Alan Mullery, Cyril Knowles and Mike England to build another team which Dave captained to the FA Cup after those leg breaks. I had some big games against Dave when I was with Manchester United. Exciting games, big crowds. What a time!

He did okay as a manager – winning the league with Derby County after doing well for them as a player under Brian Clough and working in the Middle East – but I don't think he enjoyed it as much as playing. You can't replace playing.

We became great friends. Such a lovely guy, and I loved his company. We would always go out together after games and have a nice couple of beers. Wherever it was; in London and Manchester with our clubs or wherever we were with Scotland. We used to have nights out in Dave's home town of Edinburgh when we were younger.

We kept in touch after football and I went to Dave and his wife Isobel's ruby wedding anniversary party. Although I lived in Manchester and he was in Nottingham, he was still one of my best pals. Isobel sent me a lovely letter asking me to be one of the pallbearers at Dave's funeral in Edinburgh, but I was just getting over an operation on my arm and shoulder. I probably would have had the pain but I wish I had done it. I was disappointed not to have for such a great pal. It was such a sad day.

There were so many people there to pay their respects – lots of big figures in the game as well as family and friends. I remember Sir Alex Ferguson spoke. Sir Alex was a pal of Dave's and thought highly of him as a footballer as well as a person. If he had to pick the best ever Scotland team, Dave would be his first choice and captain. I would be the same as Sir Alex. Dave was a leader.

I have been asked if Dave Mackay compared to anybody playing in today's football. No, there is no one in the same class.

It is a different game today, of course. A different world. The pitches are so good. The passing is a bit boring because they pass across the field and give it back to the goalkeeper. When Dave and I played we tried to go and attack and score goals.

You can't tackle like you used to, either. These days they just pull shirts instead. I think if I played today I'd be sent off every couple of months! But Dave was not that type of player. He was hard but fair and was never sent off.

I was made a CBE (Commander of the Most Excellent Order of the British Empire) in the 2016 New Year's Honours List in part for my services to football. I think Dave should have had an honour for what he did for the game. I can't explain more than, as I've said, that he was one of the best players ever. I'm surprised he didn't get anything. When Dave and I played footballers didn't really get awards like that.

Should he have been Sir Dave? Absolutely. If he was living in today's world he would have definitely got one.

Dave is so deserving of a proper biography on him after what he did for football and the wonderful person he was. It is so good that he is still remembered, and it is lovely for his family to have a record of his life to pass down the generations. It ensures he will never be forgotten. That's the way it should be. I feel privileged to have known him.

I'm off to start another jigsaw while I keep myself occupied during lockdown because of the coronavirus pandemic!

Denis Law
Altrincham
Trafford
Greater Manchester
April 2021

Denis Law was an international team-mate of Dave Mackay in the late 1950s and during the first half of the '60s. Law was also a regular opponent of Dave's during his days at Manchester United and remains the only Scotsman to win the Ballon d'Or. And, with Princess Anne, presented the 2019 BBC Sports Personality of the Year award to cricketer Ben Stokes in Aberdeen (Law's home town).

Prologue

DAVE MACKAY figured in my life, indirectly, from birth.

The wife of ventriloquist Terry Hall, famed in the UK for his hand puppet Lenny the Lion, lay next to my mum in the baby ward of Middlesex Hospital in central London. No doubt discussing their respective births.

Fast forward a year or two and Dave and Isobel Mackay, with their children David Junior and Derek, move into the home vacated by the Hall family in Southgate, north London; something which coincided with the beginning of my love affair with Tottenham Hotspur.

Fast forward again and I am at the O2 Arena in Greenwich to report on the 70th birthday gig of Jimmy Greaves, the stand-up and fabled goalscorer who was a Spurs team-mate of Mackay.

I was in awe as I stepped into an elongated, crammed backstage room. I can cover a football match these days and interview 'celebrity' players without being overcome by the 'affliction' which makes you stumble over your words, feel awkward and struggle to resist the temptation to ask for autographs and thus break your mask of objectivity. Not here. Before me were England World Cup-winning heroes Martin Peters, Geoff Hurst and George Cohen, Chelsea pair Ron Harris and Peter Bonetti and a pantheon of Spurs legends including Cliff Jones, Bobby Smith, Terry Dyson, Pat Jennings and Martin Chivers, all former team-mates of Mackay, along with other N17 icons such as Steve Perryman and Ossie Ardiles. And, of course, Greaves. I was rubbing shoulders with football royalty.

One legend I didn't spot at first was Mackay himself. He sat quietly behind the door I'd entered, minding his own business, looking as humble as any individual could be. He had plenty to boast about as a footballer. I'd seen him play in his pomp for the Lilywhites. Jimmy Greaves was my hero, but Dave Mackay was the best player I had ever seen. He still is.

I spluttered a few words to him – I cannot remember what they were given my state – and was struck by his soft voice and friendly, easy manner, tolerant of the gibbering wreck in front of him.

Mackay popped into my mind after manager José Mourinho insisted his Tottenham side 'were not strong enough to cope with it psychologically' when they drew 3-3 with West Ham after leading 3-0 with eight minutes of normal time remaining in a Premier League fixture, held behind closed doors because of the coronavirus pandemic, at the Tottenham Hotspur Stadium on 18 October 2020.

It was all going so swimmingly for Mourinho's team. Gareth Bale, a former Spurs talisman, had made his return after seven years collecting European silverware with Real Madrid a mere ten minutes earlier. But the old one-two-three in the form of a header, an own goal and a last-kick wonder-strike denied Spurs victory.

Would that have happened if Mackay had been involved at his peak? To my mind, no, not if what he did for Spurs on his arrival from Hearts in March 1959 is anything to go by. Six months earlier, Spurs had defeated Everton 10-4. It was Bill Nicholson's first game as manager and the scoreline reflected the 'pretty but brittle' image of the side he inherited.

But Mackay injected the missing X-factors – primarily bottle, heart and a winning mentality – to turn the Lilywhites into the 20th century's first side to lift the Double of First Division and FA Cup just two years after his move south of the border.

He also supplied supreme ball skills, a tackle to be feared, attacking intent, an innovative long throw, goals and a work ethic without equal to make him the complete player; providing the beauty and the beast.

But it was his infectious, inspirational will to win which most inspired Tottenham to experience their Glory, Glory Days in the 1960s. And that's not just me, a first-hand witness to most of the on-the-field-goings-on at the Lane in those days, but team-mates, opponents and neutrals.

You look around for top leaders in the modern game and fall short. Yes, they exist or have existed. Steven Gerrard at Liverpool, John Terry at Chelsea, Patrick Vieira at Arsenal, Roy Keane at Manchester United and Vincent Kompany at Manchester City were examples in recent times. And Liverpool skipper Jordan Henderson has shown a less demonstrative form in leading Liverpool to the 2019 Champions League and 2020 Premier League titles.

But no one, to my mind, had the aura and self-confidence possessed by Mackay. No one with such a bloody-minded refusal to accept defeat. Sir Alex Ferguson, Mackay's friend and a managerial legend at Manchester United, revealed he would begin any Scotland Fantasy XI pick with Mackay as his captain.

Mackay was an icon with three clubs – which included his boyhood favourites Heart of Midlothian and Derby County, besides Spurs – and Scotland as a player. He is among the few people to win the English premier title as a player and manager, and was Footballer of the Year in Scotland and England. He was rated by Bill Nicholson at Tottenham and Brian Clough at Derby as their best signings as managers, and named by Nicholson in his best-ever Spurs side. And he was in Arthur Rowe's XI when the other great manager in the history of the London club was invited to make one up from his push and run back-to-back champions of 1950 and 1951 and the Double-winning side a decade later. George Best insisted Mackay was his 'hardest' opponent. Anyone who commands that kind of respect from these kind of people has something going for him.

What would Tottenham Hotspur, nay any club, do to have Dave Mackay now?

All this and more – not least for his family, especially his devoted wife Isobel, who shared 60 loving years with him – is why I feel this was an important book to write as it would provide a detailed document of the life and times of an individual, which could then be passed down the generations. It would be tantamount to criminal if researchers now and in the future were unable to glean a clear idea of his positive impact on the game – and indeed society – through his physical strengths and moral compass, while spreading his loving and personable manner away from the game to all he came across. He knew how to win on and off the field – the right way.

I have done my best to illustrate through the eyes of his relatives, friends, colleagues and neutrals – with the limitations imposed on the process through 2020 and 2021 by the coronavirus pandemic – and hope my efforts are, at least, partially worthy of such a figure. I also hope that you enjoy the read.

Mike Donovan

1

'Miracle Man'

THE SOUND of a chilling crack filled the air. Les Allen heard it. So did the rest of Dave Mackay's Tottenham Hotspur team-mates.

It reached the ears of the media and fans while eerily echoing around the sparsely populated White Hart Lane terraces and stands.

Aural confirmation that the left leg of Tottenham Hotspur's main man on the field, the team's heartbeat in the club's greatest era, had been broken for a second time.

Ten months earlier, another explosive, sickening noise reverberated around Manchester United's Old Trafford stadium housing close to 50,000 spectators to herald a similar outcome.

A ground either near-empty or near-packed, it made not a jot of difference.

Disaster had struck twice. It seemed to reflect for Mackay a line from the William Bell and Booker T. Jones blues track 'Born Under A Bad Sign', 'If it wasn't for bad luck I wouldn't have no luck at all.'

Eyewitness Ken Jones, who passed in 2019, was a cousin to Spurs' star winger Cliff, a team-mate of Mackay as manager Bill Nicholson's Lilywhites became the first winners of the Football League and FA Cup Double in the 20th century three years before.

Ken wrote in the *Daily Mirror*, 'It was like watching a re-run of a horror movie.'

The only person present who was convinced of the diagnosis initially was Mackay himself, who stamped his left foot into the turf to determine the verdict before accepting it.

It had been feared that Mackay's career might have been over following the first leg break. Would the second be a step too far even for the player perceived as the indestructible Iron Man?

It was Mackay's competitive comeback following a battle against the odds after the tibia and fibula bones in his left leg had been smashed in an horrific, violent collision with Manchester United's Noel Cantwell at the Theatre of Dreams the previous December as Spurs fell at the first in their defence of the European Cup Winners' Cup.

And the left-half stepped on to White Hart Lane's green sward champing at the bit to secure a return to the first team.

It followed a series of friendlies playing at inside-forward – 'to feel my way around' – which began against a Glasgow Select at Hampden Park 38 days earlier.

It was a dry, warm and sunny afternoon at the Lane on Saturday, 12 September 1964, and about 2.45pm. Mackay, in the dressing room, was pulling on the number six shirt for the first time in a competitive encounter since that fateful night in Manchester as Tottenham's reserves prepared to take on Shrewsbury Town in the Football Combination.

Spectators were flicking through the match programme, reading that the first of two dances would be staged by Mecca at the Lyceum ballroom in the Strand in London's West End to raise money for the John White Fund, which had been set up to benefit the family of the recently deceased member the 1960/61 glory team.

Mackay was named in the thin publication alongside goalkeeper Bill Brown, who was, with Allen, another Double-winning colleague, in the Spurs team line-up laid out in a 2-3-5 formation. As were debutants Roger Hoy (right-back), Steve Pitt (right-wing) and Neil Johnson (inside-right), plus Alan Dennis (left-back), Roy Low (right-half), Laurie Brown (centre-half), Derek Possee (left-wing) and John Sainty (centre-forward).

Sainty, a prolific goalscorer and reserve regular, said, 'There were a lot of good players around me. It made my job easy. It was a pleasure to play with these people. They made me look a better player than I was. It was a pretty useful reserve team. Those who had been in the first team, like Bill [who shared first-team duties with Pat Jennings that season], Laurie, a stopper who did the job, and Les Allen who was a great striker and used to give me a lift in from Essex.

'Alan I think was captain of the London Boys and Roy had a few tricks. Roger turned into a centre-half, Neil could run and Steve was a ginger-haired lad who could play when he got the ball and Derek on the other wing was as light and as quick as lightning.

'But the fact I was lining up with Dave Mackay was a major, major highlight for me. He was my hero. He could do anything as a footballer. I idolised him, so much so that I travelled up to Scotland on my own to attend his funeral.'

Tottenham had once been covered in woods in which Henry VIII was understood to have hunted while visiting a friend based on the High Road, when it was known as 'the highway'. But Spurs' home ground was in the middle of a setting now far from bucolic, more a man-made concrete and brick jungle. The nearest to what passed for rural England was a mile or two up the road in Epping Forest, believed to be the base camp of an uprising against the conquering Romans led by Boudica (aka Boadicea), the queen of a Celt tribe, another fearless British folk hero knocking about around 2,000 years before Mackay (pertinently, the royal's battle was in either 60 or 61 AD).

Sainty estimated the crowd was 3,000 to 3,500 in a stadium with a capacity about 20 times greater, attracted by thoughts of a relaxed afternoon of football-watching bathed in sunshine rather than experiencing the blood-and-thunder of the first team's derby against West Ham United six miles away at the Boleyn Ground. And, of course, the return of Mackay.

But any thoughts of having gentle fun in the sun were dispelled the instant those present had to listen to that sudden sharp sound of broken bone.

The moment came after 20 minutes, during which Mackay had displayed proof that he could be just *this* game away from a first-team return.

Ken Jones wrote, 'He looked fitter and faster. He was looking for work and finding it. He didn't shirk a tackle and his passes were beginning to have the old look of authority and precision.'

The fateful incident beneath the blue skies is clouded in contradiction.

It was reported that Mackay had moved into an attacking position on the edge of the Shrews' penalty area, anticipating a ball from the right, as visiting defender Peter Dolby came in to challenge. He shaped his body ready to pass the ball back before it whirled out of control as he clung on to his left leg.

Mackay said, 'I was holding up well when, when I stood like a stork on my left leg and played the ball with my right, the man came down on the back of my left leg and broke it again.'

Team-mate Allen, also on the way back from injury, saw it from close quarters.

The striker had finished second top scorer behind Bobby Smith in the historic Double campaign. Like son Clive, who donned a Lilywhite shirt two decades down the line, he had what the club's official website described as a 'natural eye for goal'.

Allen, living quietly in retirement with wife Pat in Essex, revealed he had 'one or two things I'm trying to get over' physically, but his mental marbles remained intact as he recalled the incident close to six decades after it happened.

Allen, who netted all four of Spurs' goals in a 4-1 win, said, 'I was about ten to 15 yards away from Dave when his leg went. I knew straight away that he'd done it again.

'It was frightening to hear it. You hear of people breaking their legs and you do hear of people hearing the cracking noise. When it happened we were more than aware that Dave had done it again.'

Shrews centre-half Dolby, en route to sealing a place in the hall of fame of his only league club, felt he might not have 'even tackled' Mackay and claimed the stricken Spurs player told him, 'It is not your fault.'

Dolby said to the national press on the day, 'He [Mackay] called for the ball, then rushed past me lunging out his leg. The next thing I know he is on the ground. I don't think I even tackled him. Dave shook his head and murmured, "I think it has gone again." He rolled down his socks and I could see he had broken his leg. I patted his shoulder and said, "Sorry, Dave." He looked up with tears in his eyes and said, "It can't be helped. It is not your fault. I can move my toes but not the rest of my leg."'

Mackay's mantra in the aftermath might have appeared conciliatory. But he reflected in his autobiography that Dolby had inflicted a 'diabolical' challenge on him, adding, 'I could not believe it. My first game back and crack! Utter bloody despair ... this man did not get booked, let alone sent off.'

Referee Peter Songhurst crouched beside Mackay and called for the trainer – understood to be Jack Coxford – and a stretcher. The trainer scampered on to inform that the leg was broken. That is when Mackay, despite the pain, tested the diagnosis by standing to stomp his left foot into the turf. Allen said, 'That's Dave all over. That was one of the things he would do. He was pretty fearless of pain.'

Mackay only recognised the reality as his cracked bone poked through his 'bloodied' sock. Even then he rejected the invitation of the four members of St John's Ambulance to hop aboard the stretcher they had carried out, determined to walk off, ideally without limping so as not to show weakness in front of the opposition, before finally accepting that would not be possible. Allen said, 'I wouldn't have been surprised had he walked off.'

A funereal atmosphere descended on the crowd.

Four male figures, each of a different generation, stood squeezed together on the thinly inhabited terrace, pressed against the players' tunnel wall where it met the metal ring-topped barrier, which stretched the length of the West Stand and separated the supporters from the pitch and surrounding area. A grey-haired senior citizen, a bespectacled middle-aged guy in a white shirt, a young, dark-haired adult in short sleeves with his left hand over his mouth and a diminutive child peeking over his left shoulder; each generation wore the same haunted expression, a mixture of shock, disbelief and concern. Less than a yard in front of them Dave Mackay lay flat on the stretcher carried by members of St John's Ambulance on each of its four corners, his face contorted in a grimace.

Thoughts might have been unspoken but it was clear the fans believed it was the last they would see of the marauding Mackay as a professional footballer. They felt they had borne witness to the end of a career of arguably the greatest Spurs player of them all at the age of 29.

Mackay, it seemed, was more concerned about the negative effect on morale the situation would have on his first XI team-mates taking on the Hammers (and losing 3-2), and manager Bill Nicholson in particular. After all, Spurs had had the triple-axis of their Double-winning team shattered over a nightmare seven months. First had come Mackay's first leg break in Manchester. Captain and on-field manager Danny Blanchflower retired in June 1964 and genius inside-forward John White was struck by lightning and killed during a round of golf in July.

Mackay told assistant manager Eddie Baily, who had sped down to pitchside from the stands, as he wrote in the *Daily Mirror*, 'Don't tell Billy Nick. I'll play again, don't worry about that.'

The Spurs players revealed to Ken Jones in the *Daily Mirror*, 'He just sat there saying, "It's gone again, it's gone again."'

Isobel Mackay, Dave's wife for six decades, said, 'I wasn't there because our youngest daughter Julie was only a couple of months old but I was floored when I heard the news. After all that he'd been through for it to happen again! I think it was Eddie Baily who phoned me.'

In the immediate fall out, Mackay said to the *Mirror*, 'It's rubbish to say I came back too soon. I'm sure that I would have been challenging for a league place inside a month.'

Nicholson added, 'It's a three-quarter fracture and we don't know yet how bad it really is. When I saw him he was happy and cheerful.'

In the meantime, Chelsea winger Frank Blunstone and Doncaster Rovers striker Alick Jeffrey offered words of advice and encouragement to the stricken wing-half, with both having come back from having their legs broken twice.

Blunstone said, 'I'm writing to Dave tonight. It's not easy to console him, but I hope my experience will help. It's really a mental barrier that stops most people coming back. An ordinary chap can go back to work with a plaster on. But a footballer, who is normally so active, finds it tough sitting around. But you MUST make up your mind to carry on playing come what may. Dave's a fighter – I'm sure he'll be back.'

Donny legend Jeffrey, who made his senior debut for the club aged 15, highlighted the role Mackay's family could play.

The frontman, who had agreed on a switch to Manchester United when suffering the first fracture, said, 'Watch as much football as you can. I know how depressed I felt the second time it happened, but I made myself watch as many games as I could. It's the only way to get the urge again.

'I also learnt how valuable a family can be at a time like this. Dave has a wife and children and it is easier to get over the shock if they are around to help take your mind off things and share the burden.'

Mackay was hospitalised at the Prince of Wales, just off the High Road in Tottenham, to discover the extent of the treatment required and whether he did indeed have a future in the game.

His spirits were lifted by sackfuls of letters from fans.

And they were boosted further by visits after he returned home from team-mates Terry Dyson and Bobby Smith, with whom, when mobile, he enjoyed nights out at London greyhound tracks.

Dyson said, 'We used to go round his house and played cards and whatnot.' But Mackay admitted to team-mate Jimmy Greaves that 'for a while it looked as if it was curtains' after the second break.

Yet Dave being Dave – football's Braveheart – you just knew a second coming from a broken leg would be a forgone conclusion if it was based on willpower, resolve and courage alone. The Scot might have been mortal and suffering physical afflictions, but he NEVER gave in. There would be no exceptions this time.

Isobel Mackay said, 'David wouldn't give up. That was the man he was.'

After he eventually came back, it could have proved third time unlucky when fellow Scottish international and Leeds fireball midfielder Billy Bremner – dubbed 'ten stone of barbed wire' – kicked him fiercely on his twice-broken leg in the opening game of the following season, which provoked an angry response from Mackay caught famously by photographer Monte Fresco's lens.

But 'Miracle Man' Mackay survived it all to provide a fairytale ending to a personal nightmare by lifting the FA Cup at Wembley in 1967 and gain further success later in his career. Isobel said, 'Fantastic how he came back twice from broken legs to win the cup? Yes, absolutely.'

Mackay even enjoyed sequels of glory beyond as he became a member of an exclusive club of individuals to secure the English title as a player and manager.

As Mackay said to Jimmy Greaves and Norman Giller in *The Sun* in the 1970s, 'Well it was something of a miracle really when you think of the mess my leg was in when Noel Cantwell did me at Old Trafford.'

Allen never had any doubt he would return. He said, 'Very few come back from one broken leg let alone two but I didn't think "that was it" for him, personally. Nothing seemed to hurt him. I never saw him shy away from anything. He was top dog.

'If people thought that maybe he was finished as a footballer, it made him even more determined to come back. It must have been gutting to have to come back from a broken leg twice. But he never complained about it. The treatment he had to have to get back, he just got on with it. He was the hardest man I ever played with or against as well as an exceptional player in my eyes.'

John Sainty was also convinced Mackay would bounce back. He said, 'Knowing Dave, he would have had the best chance in the world. It would have been really serious for him not to return. Anybody else it might be the case that having a cartilage out would finish their career. It was still guaranteed he'd get back even if he had had all his cartilage out and a broken leg.'

Cliff Jones hinted he felt the same. The superstar flanker returned from breaking his leg in an accident with team-mate Peter Baker in pre-season training for the 1958/59 campaign. He said, 'Dave had just got his eye in when he broke his leg again. Like the first it was a bad one. But he had enough desire and commitment to the game to get back. He'd already shown that when he fractured his skull in the European Cup in 1961.'

Terry Dyson said, 'Incredible that Dave's leg got broken again but he was hard, strong. It wasn't long before he was on his crutches and walking again. The fact he always used to come back is one of so many reasons why he was one of our key players.'

Jimmy Robertson, who was to be an FA Cup goalscoring hero for Spurs three years later, said, 'If it was possible to be done Dave would do it. I actually experienced the same thing because I twice had broken legs after leaving Spurs. And I always thought if Dave can do it then I can do it. And I did.'

Pat Jennings said, 'I was fearing the worst when I first heard he'd broken his leg again. That he wasn't going to come back. But he wouldn't give in on it.'

Phil Beal, who was to suffer a broken arm which put him out of the 1967 FA Cup-winning run, said, 'I was coming back on the coach from the first-team game at West Ham when I heard the news. Coming back twice after a leg break shows you what sort of person he was. Talk about tough.'

Joe Kinnear, who went on to work in management with Mackay, broke his leg against Manchester United in 1969 after shining alongside Mackay in the FA Cup Final two years earlier. He said, 'Is breaking a leg the worst injury you can get in football? Yes. It's bad. It's really difficult to come back from. And he came back twice!'

PART ONE: BEGINNINGS

2

Family and friendship

NINIAN CASSIDY was a close friend and hometown link for Edinburgh-born Dave Mackay since his first cousin Isobel met and fell in love with the late, lamented football legend in the mid-1950s.

Cassidy was instantly upbeat, cheerful, chatty and empathetic when he picked up my call and revealed exclusive insights into a 'fantastic, fabulous' individual.

'You can cover a lot of ground with that, Mike,' he said after being informed of my quest to write an authorised biography on his pal, who moved from his native Scotland and settled south of the border, bar two spells in the Middle East.

Not half. Mackay had a football career so glittering your optician would have recommended the darkest of shades to protect your eyes while viewing it. It had the pre-eminent telling you how pre-eminent he was as a player. Managers at his three major clubs considered him their number one signing. Team-mates Gordon Marshall, Jimmy Greaves and Roy McFarland, Scotland colleague Denis Law and international manager Matt Busby, who named him captain of his country, rated him among the best. Opponents including George Best and Eusébio uttered the highest praise, as did independent observers such as Sir Alex Ferguson.

And in this third decade of the new millennium, the respect, admiration and love for him from the football fraternity remains as strong as ever, a note to your author from Spurs chairman Daniel Levy being just one piece of evidence to prove it. We'll talk more about that later on.

Also, of course, there was Mackay's life outside football; his family, friends and battles with illness which eventually claimed his life aged 80 in 2015.

Businessman Cassidy had been there for his older friend ever since he was a toddler.

Tongue-in-cheek, Cassidy described himself as the 'Special One' in reference to his introduction into Mackay's orbit.

Portuguese José Mourinho gave himself the moniker when he entered English football management at Chelsea after winning the Champions League with Porto in 2004; proving he had a point as he became a serial trophy collector in England and back abroad before, in 2020/21, attempting to help Spurs lift the title for the first time since Mackay's side had done so 60 years earlier.

Cassidy said, 'Dave had not been long married when I first knew him. His wife Isobel is my first cousin, my mum and her mum being sisters. It meant I was a bit older than their children, although the same generation. I got looked after like a "Special One", as José would say! I was a special child!

'Myself and Dave and Isobel's children were close cousins. We went to the weddings together. Dave's wife and my mum might have been niece and aunty but they were also great pals. We'd go and see Dave and his family all the time.'

Cassidy – known to the Mackays as a baby – was just four years old when he first became aware of the fellow Scot's growing legend as a footballer. Typically Mackay – who won around 40 trophies – was holding a piece of silverware.

He said, 'Hearts won the Scottish Cup in 1956. I can remember being on my dad's shoulders at Tynecastle when Hearts came back with the cup from Hampden. Dave was coming on the coach and saying to me "here's the cup" as he held it above his head.

'Dave used to bring me along with him to Cheshunt – Spurs' training headquarters – for pre-season training every summer from when I was 13 to when I was 16.

'After Dave took me to the 1966 World Cup Final at Wembley and then to Cheshunt that year, I got to join in training. It was dreamland for a young boy, Spurs-mad because of Dave Mackay. They used to give me a strip and I'd supply my own footwear and train. I went on the road runs. Eddie Baily [manager Bill Nicholson's assistant] used to go round on a push bike checking players did them. I don't think Jimmy Greaves liked those runs! There was a big squad with the likes of Alan Gilzean, Alan Mullery, Joe Kinnear. Fabulous players. All brilliant to me.'

Cassidy was put up by the Mackays at their home in Enfield, north London, when he came down for a trial with Spurs shortly after his cousin's husband had departed for Derby County.

He said, 'I was down at Cheshunt and played in a training match when they were one short and Bill Nicholson said, "You've got to come back and play in a trial." I had a trial. It wasn't successful. I was there for a month. Graeme Souness was there at the same time.

'I played at The Den, different grounds, for Spurs youth and I got paired up with winger Roger Morgan when we trained in a big gym. We were the same height and build. One time we had heading practice, jumping together to head an imaginary ball and I accidentally knocked Roger for six and he cut his knees on the tarmac, poor bugger.

'I remember there was a run-in with Graeme Souness. We used to get a job every day after training. One was to sweep the gym. It was Graeme's turn this day. I was in the dressing room waiting on him to have a game of snooker on the table near the manager's office.

'He finished but Johnny Wallis [physio, former player, reserve manager and future kitman] came up behind him and told him to sweep it up again. Souness said, "No, I'm not doing it. I've done it." Johnny went off, came back and said, "You've got to go and see Mr Nicholson." I went with Graeme as backing. Bill Nicholson said, "What is this all about?" I said, "Well, Mr Nicholson, I've had a look at it [Souness's gym sweep] and I think it is fine." Bill Nicholson said to me, "It's got bugger all to do with you, get out of this office right now." That was me outside. I shut the door and I could see Bill Nicholson lecturing Souness, and heard him say to him, "If a job's worth doing it is worth doing properly. Get back and do it again."

'I think it was Dave Mackay who had given Spurs the heads up on Souness. He saw him in a schoolboy international at Wembley and said to Bill Nicholson, "You should really go and see this boy. He's really good."'

But as Cassidy grew up, the boy–man friendship between him and Mackay became one of man to man.

Cassidy said, 'Dave was nothing but fantastic with me. Fabulous. When I became older I became his friend. I was a boy growing up with a man. He still looked after me and made sure I was okay when I became a man.

'But Dave would give me stick in a friendly way. I used to see him regularly. Every time I saw him for a drink or a meal after he'd retired I asked for a laugh, "Are you Dave Mackay, ex-Hearts and Tottenham?" You see I was on S [schoolboy] forms with Hearts. And he used to smile and reply, "Are you Ninian Cassidy, ex-Hearts and Tottenham?" And then he would add with a smile, "How many f*****g games did you play?" You see, I'm the ex-Hearts and Tottenham player who never played, and I replied, "Not as many as you." Eventually I'd say, "None." He said, laughing, "Yeh I've got that." He used to recite how many games he played for Spurs and Hearts. Always a great laugh.'

Cassidy was, though, exposed to his friend's competitive nature. He said, 'We used to play golf, table tennis and snooker together. He would not accept defeat. Hated it. I could beat him at snooker but he would not shake my hand after I beat him. He used to say "you were lucky" and call me everything and then five minutes later you were having tea with him and you'd be best pals again. Defeat wasn't even on the menu. Dave wanted to win.'

Cassidy revealed how Mackay continued to display his caring side as the football legend's pal moved into adulthood, 'He remained fantastic to me. I remember when he became Derby manager in the 1970s and they played Real Madrid. He gave us all the hospitality you could get and would take us anywhere. He wouldn't say "wait there", he'd take you with him and made sure you were looked after. He was just fabulous.

'He would have given you anything to help you. A generous man, funny and loving. Loved a carry-on, a laugh. He'd host the parties the Spurs boys had and was in charge of the entertainment. Never wanted or looked for special treatment – but got it. He just loved talking about football. A people person – happy to sign autographs for anybody and happy to talk to anybody.'

Cassidy fondly remembers Sunday, 21 December 2008, when Dave met Harry Redknapp, by now Spurs manager.

Redknapp's side had just endured a setback to a revival. He had taken charge of Juande Ramos's League Cup holders after his Spanish predecessor had guided them to six losses and just two draws at the start of the league campaign. But Newcastle United put their spoke in by overcoming Redknapp's visitors 2-1 at St James' Park. Spurs had Gareth Bale on the bench and Luca Modrić, soon to move to Real Madrid, on the scoresheet.

But Redknapp's mood picked up when he visited the office of Magpies boss Joe Kinnear, Mackay's former team-mate who had become a management partner at Doncaster Rovers.

There was Mackay, with Cassidy and Isobel's brother Tom Dixon, and Kinnear.

Cassidy said, 'Dave, Tom and I had been invited to attend the game. Harry made a beeline for Dave when he spotted him, coming across the room, giving him a big hug and saying, "Great to see you, Dave. Do you ever come down to the Lane these days?" Harry is told by Tom that Dave gets the odd invite. He couldn't believe it and said to the rest of the company, "An invite?! He's Dave Mackay – he doesn't need an invite!" Harry held him in such esteem.'

* * *

Ninian Cassidy also remembers turning up at Dave Mackay's doorstep in the Nottinghamshire village of Burton Joyce on a 'terrible night' in the middle of winter. The snow was perhaps deepish, crispish and possibly uneven.

Cassidy, now a close pal for six decades, had driven close to 300 miles from his home near Edinburgh, his window wipers working overtime, on a mission to get the individual he first met as a four-year-old in the mid-1950s to sign 100 Tottenham Hotspur shirts, replicas of the ones worn when his fellow Scot captained the club to the 1967 FA Cup after coming back from his two broken legs. The trip was linked to a business venture.

Cassidy rung the doorbell and Isobel answered.

They had had a phone conversation to confirm the arrangement before Cassidy had set out on the drive.

Cassidy said, 'Isobel invited me in and added, "I don't think he'll be able to sign the strips." Dave was sitting in the living room watching football on the TV. So I was thinking, "I've done a wasted trip." I went in the living room. Dave looked at me and said, "What are you doing here?" I said, "I'm here to see you." He said, "What do you want?" I said,

"I want you to sign some strips." Dave started signing them but stopped after about ten and put down the pen. I thought he wasn't going to do any more. And he looked at me and said, "Amazing. You never forget your own name!" He had the onset of dementia but he knew how to sign "Dave Mackay". He signed all 100 and I put £300 in his hand and said, "That's for you, Dave." He had never asked for money. He said, "What's that for?" And I said, "That's for signing the strips." He looked at me and smiled, "Have you got any more strips?!" That was Dave Mackay. Even though he was ill, he still had a sense of humour. He was really, really sharp.'

Cassidy also recalled when Dave and Isobel visited his home a year or so later. The pair were sitting upstairs watching Manchester United in a Champions League tie on the television and sipping rosé wine. I said, "Do you think Manchester United will win?" He said, "Yes. It'll be comfortable." The game just started and they lost a goal. I said, "Do you still think they'll win?" I think they lost another goal ten minutes later and he said, "F*****g rubbish."'

Cassidy revealed Mackay's attention drifted away as he looked out the window at the hills in view, which triggered a childhood memory.

Cassidy said, 'His memory was foggy and he said, "What are those?" I said they were the Pentland Hills. He asked me this question five times and I repeated my answer each time. Then he said, "I could see the Pentland Hills from our home in Glendevon Park [the Edinburgh street in which he grew up]." I said, "No you couldn't! I've spent £500,000 building this house, you can't see what I can f*****g see." He said, "I could." My wife and I got in the car the next day and drove to Glendevon Park and sure as God you could see the Pentland Hills. He was absolutely right – and I was doubting him because of his memory.'

* * *

David Craig Mackay was born at 56 Montpelier Park in Edinburgh 10 on Wednesday, 14 November 1934, 'a matter of weeks' before the family moved to 18 Glendevon Park in Edinburgh 12.

Isobel said, 'Dave shared his birthday with Prince Charles and got time off school when Charles was born. David was 14 when that happened and joked it was in celebration of his birthday, not Charles!'

Dave was the second of four sons to mum Catherine and linotype operator dad Thomas. His elder brother, named after their father, had come along a year earlier. Frank, son number three, was born the following year and Ronnie on 14 February 1940.

On the day of Mackay's birth, south of the border England had come through a bruising encounter to beat Italy in the 'Battle of Highbury'.

It was a year that saw a 'surgeon's picture' of the Loch Ness Monster published in promotion of a fable which has been a boon to Scotland's tourist industry. Elsewhere, the Cunard liner *Queen Mary* launched on the River Clyde.

Around a few corners from the Mackay clan's household, the Palladium Theatre, which was to provide a venue for the early incarnations of the Edinburgh Festival in the 1950s, saw comic actor John Le Mesurier tread the boards for the first time.

Further afield, notorious American criminals Bonnie and Clyde and Baby Face Nelson met their fate, French actress and animal activist Brigitte Bardot, famed for her role in the film *And God Created Woman*, was born, while Alice Liddell, linked as the inspiration for Lewis Carroll's *Alice's Adventures in Wonderland*, passed.

And Winston Churchill, who was to lead Britain in the Second World War, warned that Germany under new chancellor Adolf Hitler, was re-arming itself 'secretly, illegally and rapidly' two decades after the Great War.

Scotland's capital itself was and remains packed to the gills with enough history and culture to satiate the appetites of the most demanding tourist in its centre. It is home to Holyrood Palace, the monarch's residence in Scotland, and Edinburgh Castle, the two venues connected by the Royal Mile, plus the Scottish Parliament. And, of course, there is the annual international arts festival. It is the birthplace of poet Sir Walter Scott, also a novelist, who mentioned the city's nickname Auld Reekie (Old Smoky in reference to soot which covered much of its Old Town), in *The Abbot*. Most pertinently to the subject of this book, he wrote *The Heart of Midlothian*, which it is thought influenced the naming of Mackay's first professional football club.

Glendevon Park is in a popular area on the edge of Edinburgh, three miles south-west of the centre, and was originally built up to re-house re-located inner-city families. Less than a mile to the north-east is Murrayfield, the home of Scottish rugby, and to the south-east is Tynecastle, the stadium housing Heart of Midlothian Football Club.

Double Scottish title-winning footballer Bobby Wishart, a Mackay contemporary who lived in nearby suburb Corstorphine and got to know the young fellow Scot and passed on 3 December 2020, said, 'It was a buffer housing estate with a mixed population situated between the upmarket Murrayfield area and Whitson/Stenhouse Housing Estate.'

House prices in the street these days are a far cry from when Mackay's parents paid, as our subject remembered from a conversation with his dad, less than £750 for their two-bed home in the 1930s.

They peaked at close to £200,000 in 2007 before dropping to an average of close to £180,000 in 2020, according to property dealers Rightmove. And number eight, with its kerb appeal – a well trimmed hedge, loft extension and bright red door – would seem an easy sale for an estate agent.

It appeared it would have been – for those who could afford it, of course – when the Mackays were resident.

Mackay recalled the street where he grew up with great affection. He said, 'I come from a nice home and my father's wages always enabled us to have everything we wanted in Edinburgh. We were a tight-knit community … everyone knew everyone else. We were all in the same boat and there was no question of keeping up with the McJoneses. Nobody's parents had a better car because nobody's parents had a car. Dad's printer's wages were enough to enable him to buy our home. Glendevon was a mixture of corporation and privately owned houses, although there was no way of telling from the outside. It was not an issue.

'Glendevon Park … was working class, but I don't think it was particularly poor … I never encountered abject poverty. I know of no kids that had to steal to eat, or of drunken or abusive parents, street gangs or prostitutes … I was not scarred by any horrific early experience. Sometimes today, when I see or read about childhood memories, I think I must be the only person who had a happy and fulfilled early life. But I did. We all did.'

Mackay, with brothers Tommy and Frank, shared a passion for playing football either on the street or in a small park – a grassed area – close by.

The boys might have been able to read Churchill's concerns – which were to prove justified when Hitler began country-gathering – via each day's edition of *The Scotsman* their dad brought home following his night shift at its city centre print works. But it seems they were too pre-occupied with their *fitba* to much notice anything else; a blessing for their father, as he could get some sleep during the day without his energetic offspring bouncing around indoors.

Dave, Tommy and Frank (and, later and more occasionally, Ronnie) maintained their routine through the Second World War with their dad called up by the RAF to combat German *fuhrer* Adolf Hitler's megalomania.

It seemed nothing disrupted the Mackay boys' street and park *fitba* schedule.

Even when their father returned home with a bag full of confectionary, they were back outside to play at the first opportunity, said Mackay's son Derek.

Even when bombs twice fell on Edinburgh Zoo just over half a mile away the Glendevon Park Gang's schedule remained uninterrupted.

It seemed the blinkered focus on the ad-hoc sport on either tarmac or turf – along with a lack of a television, telephone and, probably, radio, with Mackay writing 'if we had a radio we boys never listened to it' – made it easier for their mother to keep such matters away from her kids so they could remain in 'the bubble' of childhood. In fact, the bombing raids on the zoo did little damage, bar killing a giraffe on the first in 1940. Mackay believed they were 'probably intended' for the Forth Bridge across the Firth of Forth, a cantilever railway construction nine miles west of the city centre and voted Scotland's 'greatest man made wonder' in 2016 and a UNESCO World Heritage Site.

Mackay said, 'From the time we could walk, our lives were out in the fresh air, in the road, or under the bridge and into the park. That was our world.'

The *fitba* sessions could be mammoth.

Numbers could drift up to 20-a-side with changes made to the teams as they went along. Someone might wander off home or one group would unexpectedly prove too strong, so the sides were shuffled around to correct the imbalance.

They would carry on for hours, but the Mackay brothers knew to be in for tea at 8pm or when the light began to fade as the nights drew in so they could be in bed by 9pm. They had no wish to risk the wrath of their mum who, Dave revealed, would give them a clip on the ear – or even a punch. He said, 'None of us resented it, either then or now.'

Mackay was small for his age and fancied himself as a bit of a winger, with a weaving run, a cut inside and a blast at goal. However, all involved in the sessions, it seems, focused on the arts of a forward.

There was a railway bridge close to the family home under which he attempted to hone such skills.

Conversely, he speculated in his autobiography that the rough, jagged edges of a stone wall which helped make up the structure might have been of more benefit to developing defensive attributes. The ball rebounded at all angles, so concentration, anticipation and judgement – the cornerstone qualities of any defender – were sharpened.

He said, 'Perhaps then I did identify with midfield and defensive players more than the average boy.'

The smaller one in the swarm of boys wafting up, down and around Glendevon Park – trying to score between the lampposts or jumpers for goalposts – might have been overpowered and perhaps flattened. Not Mackay. He knew what it took to survive and thrive with what seemed an innate competitive gene. He battled. He sweated. He tackled. He hustled, unafraid to inform slacking team-mates to buck their ideas up. Even if those team-mates towered over him.

He said, 'Certainly, I was conscious of my lack of height and build, and tried to compensate for this ... I never shirked from a tackle, sometimes with boys twice my size, and ran for almost every ball. I could not stop myself harrying, encouraging and sometimes b******ing my team-mates. I'm sure those who didn't take the game quite as seriously as me found it over the top and annoying.'

His outlook served him well in a beyond-glittering career. It seemed the only thing that scared him was the prospect of that 'clip' from mum.

Football, without the distractions of today's sedentary interests of youngsters such as computer games, smartphones and satellite television, was all-consuming for Mackay and his brothers.

The *fitba* in the park or street remained a daily routine, even when the Second World War started in 1939. Mackay and Tommy also found time to practise further afield while getting paid.

With their father away, the loss of his income from his job 'in the print' forced the family to pull in their horns.

Catherine Mackay, along with other wives who had husbands in the fighting forces in the UK, was given a 'status of dependency on the state' which meant she would receive financial benefits from the government.

It was something but not as much as Thomas Mackay, away with the RAF, would have brought home from *The Scotsman*'s printworks on Market Street. And the fact she had four boys meant Catherine was unable to become a 'war worker' in a factory or similar.

In short, money was tight, although Mackay insisted in his first autobiography *Soccer My Spur*, 'We always had clean clothes, never went short of food.'

Mackay's eldest sibling Tommy hit on an idea to supplement the family income by taking on milk and newspaper delivery rounds before and after school.

And he invited 'David' to assist him. Mackay said in *Soccer My Spur*, 'I felt it would be nice also to assist Mother.' And Catherine was given ten bob (50p) a week from the 'Mackay Brothers Organisation'.

But the enterprising duo devised a way of improving their football abilities with a tennis ball while making deliveries.

They would each take one side of a street. In turn, one of them guided the ball across the road before rushing up to a door to put the bottles of milk on its step or stuff either *The Scotsman* or an *Edinburgh Evening News* through its letterbox before racing back to stop the return ball hitting the kerb.

Mackay said, 'In cold print it may seem very uninteresting, but in reality it was great fun, and for my brother – later to sign for Hearts – and yours truly it laid the foundation of our ability to pass a football accurately and quickly.'

3

These boots are made for football

DAVE MACKAY'S interest in football was increased being brought up in an area with a professional football club at the hub of a community, which also included a golf club and a prison. Heart of Midlothian provided one of his earliest memories, if not his first. In his autobiography, he revealed that he was 'yet to reach five years of age' when he visited Hearts' Tynecastle ground and 'rolled under the gate' and 'stood absolutely alone on the empty terrace for a few breathtaking seconds' before 'swinging my little body under a crush barrier' and exiting back under the gate and on to Gorgie Road and home.

That gap in the gate later provided his entrance as a pre-teen to watch matches, telling old Spurs team-mate Jimmy Greaves in *The Sun* in the 1970s whether he always wanted to be a footballer, 'Not just a footballer, a *Hearts* footballer. They have always been my favourite club. When I was just a kid I used to walk three miles there and three miles back to get to watch them play at Tynecastle, and I was so small I could nip under the turnstile and get in without paying. My one dream was to play in the maroon and white shirt.'

And it seems the fact he disclosed an awareness of Bobby Baxter, the centre-half who joined Hearts around the same time, underlined the start of his obsession with the Maroons.

Starting school provided another opportunity to indulge his developing passion for the national sport.

His fellow pupils at Balgreen Primary were, like him, dotty about it. At break times he was one of up to 100 trying to control one tennis ball or, by hook or crook, gain possession of it in a seemingly otherwise aimless game which drifted around the playground. It was another way for Mackay to develop his skills. He became adept at playing the ball with either foot and revealed the tenacity and precision of his tackling which he had begun developing around Glendevon Park.

Mackay earned a spot in the school team as a centre-half. That was all very well and good but if he wanted to do himself justice, he was short of a vital piece of equipment – a pair of football boots.

Either rubber-soled trainers in the dry or everyday shoes in the wet had sufficed. But donning the school's shirt was different to anything else he had experienced.

Fortunately for Mackay, there was a class-mate who had a pair of boots for sale. Jim Hutton said to Mackay between lessons, 'I've grown out of my boots, Dave and, although I haven't worn them very much, you can have them for seven-and-sixpence [37.5p].'

It was a miniature fortune back in the early 1940s for a youngster like Mackay, not far off the combined weekly wages he and Tommy collected for doing the milk and newspaper rounds. And a pound back then would be the equivalent of close to £60 today.

Mackay approached his mum to see if the boots could be a Christmas present for him. He caught her on a good day.

He said, 'It was a look of love and understanding as she said, "It so happens, David, I've been given three half-crown savings stamps as a Christmas box. If you go to the post office and cash them you'll be able to get those boots off Jim Hutton."'

Mackay hugged his mum in gratitude as she gave him the stamps. The flush of excitement, evident in his face at the prospect of being able to represent his school in proper boots two days later, was soon replaced by a panic-stricken expression.

He initially stuffed the stamps into his trouser pocket, walked to the bus stop and hopped on the bus to the Post Office.

When he arrived, Mackay fished in his pocket for the stamps to hand over the counter in return for 7s 6d. It was empty. That's when his visage turned pale. It was a nightmare. He retraced his steps, first the bus stop where he had alighted. No sign. Tearful and distraught, he walked on. That was it until he reached the stop where he had got on the bus close to the family home. On the pavement by it rested the three stamps, where they had fallen out as he had boarded earlier, unnoticed by passers-by.

He raced back to the Post Office. And, after collecting the money, he exchanged the 7s 6d for the boots within the half-hour.

His elder brother, though, added perspective if Mackay was getting ideas above his station just because of the footwear he now had at his disposal. Tommy said, 'Now you'll find yourself playing with greater confidence, but don't think you're Gordon Smith.'

Smith, a Hearts fan as a youth, was establishing his career at Hibernian where he went on to lift the first part of an historic treble as the only player to lift the Scottish title with three different clubs, going on to complete the hat-trick at Tynecastle and Dundee. And he was fast becoming an idol to those kicking a ball about in the streets and parks of his native Edinburgh after scoring a hat-trick on his first-team Hibs debut against his boyhood heroes on 28 April 1941.

The winger was also part of the most feted forward line, the 'Famous Five', in the history of the Easter Road club – alongside Bobby Johnstone, Lawrie Reilly, Eddie Turnbull and Willie Ormond – before eventually switching to Tynecastle.

But Mackay's feet were clearly kept on the floor by his elder brother. Yet younger brother Frank was convinced of Dave's potential. He said, 'He was a WINNER from primary school age. The small primary school we all went to won a premier competition while he was there.'

Balgreen might have helped Mackay improve his football techniques. But an incident in his penultimate year there also helped spark a lifelong hatred for bullies.

He was joining in the chaotic playground game of hang-on-to-or-get-back-the-tennis-ball one lunchtime. A fellow pupil considered a hard nut and in the year above was in possession, chased by the pack. Mackay managed to get across him and trap the ball but the older boy fell across his body and ended up grounded and decidedly unamused. Mackay uttered an apology which went unaccepted as the bigger boy challenged him to a fight on the Saughton Park field opposite and away from interference by teachers after school. Brother Tommy was nearby wondering what his sibling would do about it all.

Mackay feared he would be 'bashed to a pulp' and felt 'sick to his stomach' as he sat back in class. Gradually the fear was replaced by hostility.

He said, 'I had done nothing wrong. It was an accident. Everyone could see that. I was younger and smaller with no appetite for fighting, therefore the older boy was a bully and I have never been able to abide bullies. There is nothing worse.'

Mackay decided to face the boy up. With other pupils forming a human ring, he stepped into it and struck the pose of a boxer obeying the Marquess of Queensberry rules with his arms up, one covering his chin and the other forward, both fists clenched.

His challenger seemed to be bemused as Mackay attacked and rained around ten blows on him with the human ring moving to maintain the rectangle. The older boy soon crumpled to the ground as the contest ended.

He immediately acquired a reputation as a 'tough wee laddie' and was left alone and occasionally came to the aid of the bullied.

Mackay said, 'That was my first real fight and, as far as I can recall, my last during my school days. I found out later that my older cousin Andrew Walker was in the throng and he told me that if I had started to take a hiding, he would have stepped in and sorted it out. Fortunately, that didn't happen. I think I would have been mortified if it had.'

Mackay mused whether his by-the-rules performance was inherited from his dad and uncle Louis, who both dabbled in the sport in the 1920s. And his dad's brother had a son of the same name who became the Scottish flyweight title-holder in the 1950s and 1960s.

His dad even taught the noble art at a school. And there was a bit of home tutoring with Mackay revealing how it led to him having the tooth next to his front gnasher knocked out, leading to a trademark look through his playing career.

Mackay said, 'Living with Dad could be likened to Peter Sellers [as Inspector Clouseau] living with Cato [in the comedy film series *The Pink Panther*]. He liked to keep us on our toes and would often appear from behind doors or out of the pantry and start bobbing his head from side to side and shadow boxing.

'"Keep your guard up, son," he'd urge. In fact, I owe my trademark missing tooth to one of these surprise attacks when he whipped his fist across the space in front of me and, unprepared as usual, I walked right into it. He was mortified, poor man.'

Mackay's youngest brother Ronnie passed away but his two others survived him – Tommy, the eldest, and Frank, the third in line, both of whom had spells with Hearts.

The pair recalled memories of growing up with their famous sibling with warmth and affection. Your author caught up with Tommy, who signed for Hearts before Dave, at the home he shared with his wife Maureen in Fife on the north side of the River Forth with Edinburgh on the south.

His gentle manner and humour shone through besides his humility and positivity, qualities also accredited to the second child of Thomas and Catherine.

It would have been understandable had there been a tinge of negativity, telling me he had just learned of problems with his sight.

He said, 'I've lost some of my eyesight. Not entirely. I just can't read newspapers or anything like that, or do emails. My wife actually bought me a used laptop for my 87th birthday [on 19 October 2020]. And two days after it arrived I couldn't use it because I couldn't see enough to use it. It happened kind of overnight. She's just said to me she's going to buy me a radio.'

He had, up until a year before, played golf as his 'main hobby'. Yet, although he revealed he did not 'get out much', he had no cause to complain.

He said, 'All you can ask for is to be happy and healthy? Exactly. We often say that. We often say how lucky we've been. To have got to this age still reasonably healthy. I feel fine.'

Mentally he was in fine fettle when talking about growing up with his younger brother and the rest of the family. He spoke with clarity.

Tommy said, 'Dave was my best pal. Simple as that. There was only a year between us. We more or less did everything together when we grew up.

'David and I used to get the tram right down to my dad's mum in another part of town to pay her a visit on a Sunday or whenever. She was bed-ridden virtually from when we were very young. We didn't know my dad's parents that well but we knew my mum's parents reasonably well.

'Football, though, was our main attraction. Even from an early age. David and I just used to play football all the time. I can recall maybe from the age of seven or eight, and going on from that.

'We used to play outside on the street, down the stairs in the hallway, and a local park and golf club. Where we lived it was private houses. But on the other side of the street it was council houses. So it was a mix of all types.

'I can't recall all four of us playing together. As far as I'm concerned, it was just David and I playing together, we were about a year apart. And David would play with Frank.

'I can't really recall playing with Frank because the three-year age difference between us was a lot at the time.

'We used a tennis ball and played out on the road, no problems. There was very little traffic as it wasn't a through road, it was one which led to the golf course. A lamppost and pavement each end of it were our "posts". We had games with other children who were neighbours. We also used to run with the ball along the pavement down to the golf course, and play in a small park nearby.

'From then on, mainly as we grew older, David and I played football together more or less all the time through school, youth and juvenile levels. Eventually we were both signed provisionally by Hearts, but never played together with them. Hearts put us out on loan, David to Newtongrange Star and me to Edinburgh City. David and I had a good understanding when we played. Surprised they didn't keep us together? Well, I think David showed more prowess than I did! I was only at Hearts a year and didn't make it.

'Our dad went away to the air force in 1939 and these war years were pretty difficult for Mum. Mum and Dad had met in a dance hall. Mum was in service at a household and Dad was a printer, which I went into. But she then didn't work until Dad went off to the forces and went to work in a local baking factory from nine in the morning for a few hours.

'She did very well to bring four boys up, looked after us and made sure we had the fundamentals. I wouldn't describe it as a poor upbringing.

'Big treats came when bananas arrived at the Co-op. Our mum used to love coming back to the house to show us the bunch of bananas she had got. Sweets were rationed as well, but I don't think any of the brothers were bothered by that, to be honest with you.

'David and I would be playing head tennis in the hallway much to the annoyance of our mother, I think. I don't think she was too pleased about it. We did it anyway.

'The four of us brothers used to share two double beds between us in our ground-floor bedroom. We used to nip out of the window, on a Sunday especially to go and play football on the 18th fairway of the local golf course.

'But before football that day – we're talking about when David and I were around the ages of nine or ten – we used to go to the club to collect golf balls to sell. You see, the first five holes of the course was sectioned off for wheat fields during the war and we used to go along the rows to pick up the balls and flog them to the guys as they came in for the golf. We only sold them for about a tanner [sixpence, now two-and-a-half pence] each.

'The wheat field was there until a year or so after the war when the course was able to reclaim its first five holes.'

Tommy also recalled those other money-making exercises, in which Thomas and Catherine's eldest sons boosted the family coffers delivering milk and newspapers – earning ten bob a week – while sharpening their football skills.

Tommy said, 'Yes, we'd pass a ball between us across the road in between running to each house on opposite sides to make the deliveries. We were never without a ball. All the time it was football, football, football.

'There's no doubt that work with the tennis ball developed the skills he would show later on. No doubt about it. David was just a natural with a ball and good at anything. He played cricket, golf and even tennis. In the summer holidays we'd go to a park which had tennis courts, and hire rackets and balls and play for a couple of hours. He was better than me at it.

'I'm not so sure about David or Frank, but I was aware of the war going on. I used to look at the newspapers – how the advance in France was going and things like that. In those days they used to give you a map of how far into France the Allies had gone.

'I remember one bomb being dropped on Edinburgh Zoo, which wasn't far from where we lived. We joked in the air raid shelter about hearing lions and tigers roaring and hoping they hadn't escaped the zoo as a result of the bomb.

'I don't think any of us were that brilliant at school. We all managed to pass our 11-Plus equivalent for secondary school. That was about the level we got to.

'There's been a lot said about David being the hard man and all that jazz. He was NOTHING like that as a youngster. Growing up he was still very much a gentlemanly type of person off the field, and remained so.

'I really don't know whether he took after our mum and dad. Mum provided discipline and Dad more easy going? Yes. A mix of the two in a way. Dad was a footballer [playing for non-league Portobello Thistle in the 1920s] so in that respect he would take after my dad. I wouldn't have said he took after anybody overall. He was his own self.

'Did he have the will to win he was known for as a professional footballer as a boy? Oh yes, aye. He had that will to win. No doubt about it. No other way to describe it without being over the top with it. He just wanted to win. Reflected in his life generally? Yes, absolutely. I think we were all like that. I think it is most people's nature to be a bit that way.

'We were close as brothers, and protective of each other. David could look after himself but there was a boy in our area who was trying to bully him. He was a lot older than David. I sorted him out. I can't remember how – but I stopped him in his tracks.

'The youngest brother, Ronnie, was six years younger than me but he did play football with us for a wee while. I remembered he was a bit too heavy as a youngster. When he did play, he played in goal. We used to kid him on that he was too heavy to reach a high ball. Sadly, he passed when he was about 40.

'I remember Ronnie coming along one time to watch us play when David and I had two matches in one day. David and I got a couple of buttered rolls made up in the dairy where we worked [Dumfrieshire] after our milk round. They were for our lunch. We gave them to Ronnie to carry. We came off the pitch after the first game and discovered Ronnie had bloody eaten the rolls! So we had no lunch that day! Ronnie only did it the once, mind!'

Frank Mackay, the only brother who remained in Edinburgh, revealed to your author that he shared the friendly, witty dispositions and football obsessions of his siblings. But he also remembered how serious Dave in particular could be when it came to the welfare of his brothers.

Speaking from his home in the Scottish capital, Frank, who trialled for Manchester United and played for Everton, said, 'Being two years older, he [Dave] was very supportive to the younger ones. We had a railway bridge just at the entrance to the golf course about 200 yards from our house and we used to play football down there, under the bridge. There was one occasion where I was playing football under the bridge with a friend, one other lad. And this guy – about David's age then, two years older than us – came along and he had a knife and was threatening us with it. We were both terrified.

'I saw David coming along the street after finishing his work – he was an apprentice joiner at the time – and shouted. He came down, took the knife off the guy, gave him a couple of clips on the jaw and told him, "I never wants to see you in the area again." We never did. He was fearless, David. That's what he was like as a person? That's right.

'For another example, at school, the third-year boys used to have a "welcoming system" where everybody that was new had their heads put down the toilet as it was flushed. David totally refused to have it done. And he said, "I'll fight anybody that you pick, your strongest, before you'll push me in that toilet." They decided not to bother. So it never happened to him, although it happened to everybody else. It happened to me.

'He would never bully anybody. Never. But he would never take it from anybody that gave him trouble. He'd sort it. He had this total confidence in his own abilities. He was one of these guys who was a winner, even from primary school age. He helped Balgreen win one of the premier titles.

'Yes, I think he had the best of both of our parents too with Mum the disciplinarian. Strict. With four boys she had to be, especially during the war when my dad was away. She wasn't five-foot tall but by God she could discipline us. She kept us on the straight and narrow. We were thoroughly kept in line and had to behave ourselves.

'I remember our mother coming in to *scatterer* the four of us for making too much noise in our crowded bedroom with the double beds which pretty well filled the room.

'Mum used to stand on the doorstep and call you in when we were out playing football. If we were at the park she would say "be in by five o'clock for your tea". And if you weren't in by five o'clock you were in trouble!

'Dad – who we all missed when he was away in the war – really left the discipline to my mother. She was strong enough to keep us all in check.

'It gave him an easier life, I think! He was easy-going. He worked at a private school outside Edinburgh at Bonnyrigg teaching boxing. So he used to go to work as a linotype operator at five o'clock in the evening and come home at three in the morning. Have a sleep and then he'd go out to Bonnyrigg.

'My father was I think a local boxing champion. David actually was interested in boxing at one stage, but my mother put that down very quickly!

'During the war we had a little government support but were short of finances with my dad away and Mum did a great job. She fed and clothed us.

'She had a system. She was a member of the Co-op and every 16 weeks she would get out money, almost like a loan, and get us whatever was required. She would pay that off over 16 weeks and immediately take out another over 16 weeks. We lived all through the war that way.'

There was no heating in the family home, with Frank remembering frost on the windows when it was cold, or a telephone 'until well after the war'. But the four boys kept warm and communicated through the national game.

Frank said, 'Growing up it was all about football really. David played football in the street, all the way to school and back as well as at school. It was never-ending. During the six weeks of the school holidays he literally spent most of his time playing in the park near the house. My mother used to despair the amount of times she had to go out and buy shoes for David because he went through a lot!'

Two of Mackay's children, Valerie and Derek, like their oldest sibling David Junior and youngest Julie, were born in Edinburgh, and were fond of relatives associated with their dad's upbringing.

Valerie said, 'Dad's middle name, Craig, was Nana's maiden name. It seems to be the thing they do in Scotland.

'Dad was named after his uncle David, who was killed in the war. Dad told the story where he had a sip of Uncle David's beer as a joke. Dad said he absolutely hated it! He thought it horrendous but pretended otherwise. "I'll have a sip of that," kind of thing.

'I do remember he went on holiday. It was to our aunty Annie's, but he got homesick. He said to us he had a tear in his eye, but told them he had a stone in it. He was missing his folks.'

Derek, Mackay's second son, living close to his mother Isobel in Burton Joyce, also revealed he gleaned positive insights into his dad's early life from the horse's mouth. And had his own memories of the cast of characters and the environment.

He said, 'I learned a few little bits and bobs about Dad's early life. Not that much really, but he did tell of how he used to play football in the street with a tennis ball and his brothers. And the milk and paper round routine of kicking a tennis ball across the street to each other with uncle Tommy.

'I reckon that played a big part in how he got his skills. It helped there were no – or at least only a few – cars in those days.

'Grandad and Nana – his parents – were lovely. Grandad used to save up ration slips he got from being in the RAF in the war to bring back chocolate bars for the kids. He was kind and attentive. Their home was nice for that era.

'My elder brother David Junior and I lived in Scotland for a couple of years when we were little but I've got no memory of that. Nor moving to our next home which was in Southgate, north London, when Dad joined Spurs. My earliest memories are from when we lived at Enfield. It was in a bungalow in a street called The Glade.'

In the meantime, Dave's future wife Isobel was growing up to the east of Edinburgh.

Isobel said, 'We lived in a coal mining village outside Musselburgh [Whitecraig]. My dad Patrick was a miner and mum Annie worked at a farm. We were lucky food-wise. My mum's mum was from Musselburgh and ran a fish business and helped us out, treated us well. I remember going with her to supply Edinburgh hotels near the end of the war. My mum's brother drove a van delivering fish to the local villages like Dalkeith.

'Like a lot of the other children we didn't have toys. We made our own and played out practically all day. We entertained ourselves, playing things like rounders and, when the snow came, sledging. We were happy. Never wanted [for anything]. We had a healthy lifestyle and a great time as kids.'

4

'A wee guy who was a bit special'

CARRICK KNOWE, an Edinburgh suburb built on the site of a bog and loch, has a municipal golf course 'with gentle contours' made up of mature parkland; each hole framed by trees with a 'grand' backdrop of Edinburgh Castle three miles to the east and in the shadow of Murrayfield, the home of Scottish rugby. The course is home to two golf clubs, one named after the area and the other called Carrickvale.

But Dave Mackay and his pals wanted to take part in another sport on it one Sunday just after the Second World War.

As we know, Mackay and Co. regularly played football in the street or park. But the Sabbath provided limitations as the public parks were closed.

This day wee, slim Davie – all 4ft 6in of him – and his pals thought they would see if they could surreptitiously turn the course into Tynecastle for a few hours, at least in the mind's eye.

Coincidentally, another group of youngsters had also turned up at the same venue in the hope of doing the same. Among them was Bobby Wishart.

Wishart was to attend coaching sessions for juniors with Mackay at Hearts not long afterwards and go on to win the Scottish title with Aberdeen in 1955 and, alongside Mackay's future Spurs team-mate Alan Gilzean, with Dundee in 1962.

But this day he was just another *fitba*-daft kid delighted to have come across like-minded contemporaries.

And eight decades later, Wishart revealed how he instantly recognised the talent of his temporary team-mate – before officialdom intervened.

53

Wishart, who passed on 3 December 2020, said, 'I grew up in a village [Corstorphine] that had grown into a fashionable suburb of Edinburgh, 20 minutes away from Dave.

'Most young boys there were members of a youth organisation. We played marbles and "kick the can" [a mix of tag and hide and seek involving a can. Someone is designated 'it' and covers his eyes while the others hide. When 'it' tags someone they are captured. Then someone has to nip out of hiding unnoticed to kick a can, which had been placed on the ground]. The billiards hall was popular for the 14 to 18-year olds in our village.

'The football sessions we played in Corstorphine at the local grounds or parks were like chalk and cheese to the ones Dave had at Glendevon Park. In Corstorphine you had all types of lads playing together. Guys from comprehensive and fee-paying schools, trades people, younger lads serving apprenticeships. They had "village values". Dave's football upbringing was in a tougher area where you learned to look after yourself.

'On my first visit to play at Dave's park, our team changed at the side of the pitch before the game. No changing rooms in those days! After the game I discovered my shoes had gone – a lesson in life.

'On this day I first played with Dave, a few pals and I had decided – as it was a Sunday – to try our luck at the municipal golf course for a game of football.

'When we got there, there was another bunch of young lads in their early teens with a similar idea. We picked two teams. It didn't take me long to realise I was playing with a wee guy who was a bit special. That was Dave Mackay. But our partnership didn't last long as someone policing the course got on a bike and chased us off.'

Wishart also revealed Mackay had a close friend called George McDonaugh. He said, 'Dave and George McDonaugh were great pals. They went everywhere together. They were part of a group of young guys who were friends who had nicknames for each other. George called Dave "The Marquis" and Dave called George "The Laird".'

Derek Mackay said, 'George and Dad stayed pals for life. George played for Hibs as a youth player but didn't get any further. Andy Bowman, a Hearts team-mate of Dad's, was part of the gang with George and Dad and also had a nickname, "The Bow".'

Isobel Mackay said, 'George was an old friend. He would say how he played for Hibs and David would joke, "You never played anyway." George didn't play much for Hibs, you see.'

Tommy Mackay, Dave's eldest brother, remembered the golf course 'jackets for goalposts' matches.

He said, 'The greenkeeper could see us from his house. We used to keep an eye open to see when he was coming out of it, getting on his bike and chasing us. When he did we'd lift the jackets we had down as posts and nip over the adjacent railway. Never once did he catch us. We were too smart for him.'

Frank Mackay, Dave's third sibling, said, 'He [the greenkeeper] was forever chasing us off!'

Dave's interest in football was an obsession which developed swiftly when he switched from Balgreen Primary to secondary education, attending Saughton school. The 7s 6d second-hand boots purchased from Balgreen school-mate Jim Hutton helped him step up a level, hardly surprising given his reliance on those well-worn rubber shoes on hard ground and his 'everyday' pairs when the surface was soggy.

Mackay might have imagined himself as a winger when he first took to playing on the street or in the parks, darting and slaloming his way through defences before unleashing a power drive. But at Balgreen he first made the school team as a centre-half due to the accuracy of his tackling, aided by being smaller and thus closer to the ball than the other boys.

In his single-figure years he also played as an inside-forward, largely a maker of goals, and at full-back. In fact he lined up in most positions, including in goal if you factor in his love affair with street football, dodging the odd vehicle.

His improvement was noted by Saughton masters George Newlands and Willie Moyes, who ran the school's games section and selected its team. The erstwhile science and technology teachers spotted how Mackay loved a tackle and could distribute the ball effectively and decided his best position was left-half where he could exploit those attributes to break up play and set off counter-attacks.

Mackay was delighted. He said, 'I was able to use to the full my enthusiasm for tackling bigger and tougher opponents.

'I was always like that [competitive]; that's just my nature. I want to win at everything I play: pool, football, even in the gym … it doesn't matter to some players but it does to me. As a kid I was very small; slim, as well. So at school I had to be a tackler to get the ball. That's how I became such a good tackler. I wanted to play, and to play, you have to have the ball. As a slight kid, I had to learn how to tackle, and tackle well.'

Sibling Frank, two years his junior, said, 'Did it help him grow up quicker in football terms? Oh, aye. He was absolutely relentless. He would take on guys twice his size without any problem. He was never short of courage.'

Mackay was convinced he had found his true position and was improving several aspects of his game such as ball control and, by heeding the cautionary words of his dad, exercised greater self-control which enabled him to keep his temper under lock and key.

His first season in the school team in the number six spot proved a success. His elder brother Tommy played up top on the wing. And he linked up well with John Paterson and Mackay pal Terry Tighe in the middle of the park, while second-hand boot entrepreneur Jim Hutton was also in the line-up. The team proved almost invincible, losing just once.

Tommy Mackay, Dave's eldest brother, said, 'I've read a Graeme Souness book and he tells a story of how sick of he was of hearing how good Dave Mackay was when he got to the school a few years later, by which time it, like with our Frank, had changed its name to Carrickvale. It cheesed him off. He could have been a successor to David at Spurs? Aye.'

Our subject even caught the eye of the Edinburgh Schools under-15s selectors. Mackay, who had reached the age of 13, Tighe and Paterson earned a trial at Meggetland. The venue is now an international sports complex since redevelopment in 2006, playing host to rugby [Boroughmuir, Edinburgh's premier club], cricket, hockey [CALA] and football [Tynecastle, Brommuir Thistle], even gridiron [Edinburgh Wolves], and it boasts 3G, Astroturf and grass pitches with an impressive pavilion.

But, although there were pitches when Mackay, his mates and other expectant trialists arrived, not all of them had nets. Also, there was a diminutive clubhouse in the middle of the site where the selectors gathered the hopefuls after a series of concurrent small-sided matches.

Just 11 names were read out. Mackay's mates Tighe and Paterson were among them. Mackay, usually a wing-half, thought he might have missed out before it was revealed he would be wearing number 11.

He said, 'Although I was surprised to hear the news, it did not shock my colleagues, or my schoolmaster, when it was announced I had been chosen to play ... at outside-left, a position I disliked and one in which I did not shine at all.'

The Edinburgh selectors seemed oblivious to Mackay's preferred position and he remained in the number 11 shirt for the next match.

He said, 'I had a shocking game ... kicked the ball only four times. As the entire family had turned up to see me on parade, I felt like this was the end of the world.'

Mackay had put in the hard yards to show he had enough talent and self-control to command a place in a team at left-half and eventually convinced the individuals who decided on such things when chosen at number six for the city schools' senior side.

Messrs Newlands and Moyes gave Mackay the platform to show off his half-back skills nationally by entering Saughton in the Scottish Schools Under-16s Shield in the 1948/49 season. It was the first time that Saughton had competed in the country's most prestigious schools' competition since Mackay's arrival.

And it followed an impressive run by the team in the previous campaign, Mackay's first in organised league football. Saughton only lost one game and won the other 24. The school finished it only three short of the century of goals scored while letting in a meagre 21. No doubt such stats and performances persuaded the team's joint managers that it was worth giving the national competition – which would have eaten through the school's budget – a bash.

Saughton faced up to the challenge and charged through the rounds into the final to face Glasgow's Kings Park at Hampden Park in May 1949.

Mackay had been disappointed and embarrassed that his family and friends had witnessed those less-than-memorable outings for the city under-15s. He was determined there would be nothing but pride in achievement for his nearest and dearest to bathe in.

And he would have his brother Tommy alongside him to ensure the team came through. And, as a bonus, Hearts stopper Jimmy Brown, who had played for Scotland in a North American tour the year before, announced he would coach them in the decider.

The encounter was big news and attracted in excess of 10,000 fans to the home of Scottish football, where local Hearts heroes past and present such as Barney Battles Junior and Tommy Walker had strutted their stuff and record goalscorer Willie Bauld was to net his first full international goal for Scotland against Switzerland 12 months later.

It proved to be an evenly matched encounter which ended in a thrilling goalless draw. But the good news for Mackay was that the replay would be staged at Tynecastle Park. It would be the first time he would tread the hallowed turf of his heroes. School was shut for the midweek date as its pupils, their relatives, members of staff, friends and others made up a crowd of 5,370.

The nerves of Mackay and his brother Tommy jangled as they sat in the dressing rooms where such fabled Hearts performers as Battles Junior, who claimed the club record number of goals in a season in 1930/31 (44) and overall (151 goals in 162), had once changed.

As, no doubt, were those of their team-mates and the guys across from the west coast of Scotland in the other changing room.

But the siblings from Glendevon Park ensured their team rose to the occasion, Davie laying on the winner for Tommy.

Mackay said, 'My chest fills with pride when I think of Mum's and Dad's faces as they hugged Tom and me after the game. It was, up to that point, the best day of my life.'

There was a taste of the sort of thing that was to come in his career as the community came out of their houses to applaud Dave, his brother and the rest of his team-mates as they paraded on foot along Gorgie Road for the two miles back to school led by a bagpipe band. They celebrated with fizzy drinks and cake on their return to the school.

Mackay's efforts earned him his first newspaper write-up. An Edinburgh publication stated, 'D. Mackay was the match's personality and helped immeasurably to weld the Saughton boys into a hard-hitting and solid defensive side.'

Tommy said, 'Playing at Hampden Park in the first match was marvellous. I was a "flashing" right-winger! David was at left-half. I scored the winning goal and David crossed the ball. A bit of glory? Yes. Then there was the piper leading back down the Gorgie Road from Tynecastle back to the school. It was a terrific occasion.'

Frank said, 'It was an incredible thing. Unheard of. At secondary school you finished aged 15 but the tournament included those up to 17.'
The day convinced Dave that he could legitimately believe he could play

for Hearts one day. He said, 'I played because I loved it and because that's what us kids did. I also loved Hearts … and dreamt that one day I might play for them. After collecting my medal against Kings Park, there were no mights … an ambition formed … to break through at Tynecastle and then lead them to glory … I was never one to be afflicted by self-doubt.'

It seems Mackay, who also played for the trophy-winning Gorgie Road Boys' Brigade team, was not the only person to feel that way. He impressed Bauld, who was at the start of his glittering Tynecastle career. Mackay said, 'The great Willie Bauld … was at the match and at the end of the game had turned to Hearts trainer John Harvey and said, "We'll no start winning anything until that wee laddie is playing for Hearts."'

In the meantime, Mackay's success on a national stage prompted an international call-up. The Scottish Schools FA selected him for their under-14s to face Northern Ireland at Kilmarnock's Rugby Park. He felt he did not play well but received another encouraging write-up in the *Edinburgh Evening News*, which insisted that he was one of three Scottish players who had 'compared favourably against smarter Irish opponents' despite a 3-2 defeat for the hosts.

Such was his pride in coming into the fold, Mackay wore the scarf and tie he received in recognition of his selection 'on every possible occasion' in the wake of his international debut.

Mackay earned his second selection for his nation's schoolboys the following season, for a big game against the so-called Auld Enemy at Wembley Stadium.

It would be Mackay's first visit to England. And his family had a pow-wow on just how they could support him, even though it was understood the Scottish Schools' FA were covering all expenses. It was decided they would give him a ten-bob note – in pre-decimal times half a pound sterling and then worth the equivalent of about £16, a sizeable sum considering the average weekly wage in the UK was £7.08 in 1950.

Wide-eyed Mackay peered out of the train as it trundled from across the border into London.

He admitted to thinking he had 'already arrived in Heaven' as he settled into the squad's 'beautiful' hotel, with its 'soft lights, sweet music and luxury'.

The following morning he was joined by a couple of squad-mates for a walk near 'Heaven' and a spot of shopping, spending the money given him by his family on presents for his parents, which he said was, 'a habit I had developed whenever I played away from Edinburgh'.

The reconvened squad ate a 'light' lunch before stepping on to the team coach bound for the world-famous stadium in Wembley, in north-west London. The size of the occasion hit home as their vehicle turned on to what was then Olympic Way.

Mackay said, 'Most Scots will tell you that their greatest ambition is to play at Hampden Park, but if they are honest with themselves they'll add "and Wembley". That's how it was with me.'

It had been 'an enormous thrill' to play at Hampden for Mackay, but he felt the pitch 'wasn't good' while the home of English football's had a 'lush green turf'.

But he was only named reserve with his brother Frank saying, 'They never picked him [for the starting XI] because of his height, he was not very big. Ludicrous.'

Yet Mackay said, 'Although named only as a reserve, I got as big a thrill as if I'd been chosen to play as our coach edged up Olympic Way towards the Twin Towers of the famous English showpiece stadium.'

But he was 'jealous' of the 11 chosen to kick off as he changed alongside them in the dressing rooms been used by football legends of club and country since 1923.

He had to put three pairs of socks on his feet to ensure his 7s 6d too-big-for-him second-hand boots did not slip off should he be required.

Finally, donning a tracksuit, he took his place on the bench with the team trainer. He watched an exciting encounter but with increasing concern as his team struggled to contain their talented opponents – which included future England senior captain Johnny Haynes – with the scoreline at 1-1.

Substitutes were allowed up until a minute before the interval, and shortly before the break Scotland needed one due to injury. Mackay unzipped his tracksuit and prepared to step into the action.

Mackay recalled the 'ironic cheers' which greeted his entry from the home supporters who, naturally enough, made up the vast majority of the 60,000 spectators.

But he was unaffected by the crowd reaction, captivated by the 'velvet' surface that, in another setting might have had 'keep off the grass' signs posted on its edges; the 'thick lush turf' was 'like a billiard table'.

The Three Lions were revelling in the playing conditions, and in particular Haynes. It was 'Go Johnny go', to borrow a line from rock 'n' roll legend Chuck Berry, as the 15-year-old starlet bamboozled Mackay and his mates with precise passes long and short which jetted to all sections of the field and put a strain on their muscles and stamina, exacerbated by the depth of the thick grass. Mackay tried to nullify Haynes personally but admitted the player destined to be the first £100-a-week footballer with Fulham made a 'monkey' out of him. And Haynes's team-mate Ray Parry, later to become the youngest First Division footballer with Bolton aged 15 years and 267 days, also aided and abetted Haynes's virtuoso display.

Mackay admitted that Scotland were 'given not only a football lesson, but a hammering' as the hosts romped home 8-2, a humiliation that was to be repeated in a full international and, again, orchestrated by the 'boy genius' Haynes, born just up the road from White Hart Lane.

Haynes said, '[It was] great fun and a thrilling overture to a match at Wembley, against Scotland, one week ahead. With this single match, I was made. There were more than 60,000 people at Wembley. The match was televised. The date was 15 April 1950, the most important day of my life, the day on which for the first time I became a national figure. The England boys played brilliantly for a huge 8-2 win and I had a marvellous match. I was said to be the smallest boy that Wembley had ever seen in action but I do know that as soon as I set foot on that splendid turf I felt I could do no wrong. All the dribbles, all the passes, all the shots seemed to be just right. I even scored one of my two goals with a "one-step-and-shoot" penalty effort.'

Mackay, who vied with Haynes for the 'smallest boy' crown, said, 'I was crushed and ashamed. I was also depressed, having brutally realised that there are levels in football and we were on a lowly rung compared to these English boys.'

And a colleague added salt to the wound when he quipped to Mackay as the teams trooped off the field, 'And to think it was only 1-1 when you came on, Dave.'

The remark cut the Glendevon Park *fitba* graduate to the core. He became lost in his thoughts as he climbed the 39 steps to the Royal Box to receive a consolation plaque from Prime Minister Clement Attlee. There was no consideration of how his team-mates were feeling equally bad.

He was taking the total blame for the loss, feeling that he had let his country down. And he considered giving up the game.

Mackay's family tried to lift him out of his funk. And it was his dad, especially, who succeeded in doing so. It was a turning point.

Thomas Mackay gave his second-eldest some blunt home truths, and was able to instil in his offspring perspective and principles.

Mackay said, 'Dad gave me a bit of a talking to and told me that football, like life itself, is full of ups and downs and I should take it on the chin and not be so sensitive.

'He advised me that if I felt I was not good enough, I should make myself good enough and not just accept it. He also mentioned he'd noticed I had made some bad tackles under pressure and had argued with referees.

'He told me to accept defeat graciously and never stoop as low as arguing with officials, or deliberately or carelessly hurting another. They were principles I attempted to abide by all of my playing career.'

But Mackay admitted he needed a reminder of a few of them when he progressed to grown-up football at Scottish Junior level with Newtongrange Star.

5

Rising Newtongrange star

DAVE MACKAY'S first official 'link' to his beloved Heart of Midlothian came when he and a few Saughton school team-mates were offered the opportunity to attend coaching sessions at Tynecastle.

The Scottish Shield triumph must have helped put Mackay's school on the club's radar. But Mackay believed the invitations probably came as a result of a recommendation to Hearts by the Jambos groundsperson Matt Chalmers, who lived four doors down from him and his family. Chalmers had borne witness to the development of the youngsters first hand as they played *fitba* around Glendevon Park.

It was a two-way arrangement, of course. The youngsters experienced professional training to aid their development and the club could keep their eye on their potential.

Mackay said, 'I told people I was "attached" to Hearts FC. It was still a great mark of status.'

When the Saughton contingent – with Bobby Wishart – arrived they discovered the sessions were run by the colourful Bobby Flavell, to start with, and Charlie Cox.

Charlie Cox was the first team's right-half, one shirt Mackay was to occupy at Tynecastle.

Centre-forward Flavell had guested for Spurs in the war and was to be considered a 'soccer outcast' when he signed for Millonarios to play alongside future icon Alfredo Di Stéfano in Colombia in June 1949, earning a Scottish record fine of £150, a ban and transfer-listing on his return from South America the following December. He also went on to score in successive Scottish League Cup Final triumphs for Dundee and became a manager at Ayr, St Mirren and Albion Rovers. Mackay's time with Flavell might have been brief but the striker and Cox both made a positive impression on the youngster from Glendevon Park.

Mackay said, 'They were grand men and intelligent coaches, who taught me far more than I appreciated at the time, although Bobby Flavell may recall the answer he received from me when he asked, "And what do you want to do when you leave school?"

'"I want to play for Hearts, and for Scotland," I replied. "Good luck," said Bobby Flavell, adding with a smile [while ruffling Mackay's hair], "And there is nothing like ambition."

'In due course, I was to become a Hearts player, like Flavell, play for Scotland, like Flavell, and, again like Flavell, play for Spurs.'

He was also fortunate that Davie McLean and his then assistant Tommy Walker, who was to take over following the sudden passing of the Jam Tarts manager, spouted upbeat noises about Mackay's progress during the coaching courses. Wishart said, 'Dave was always a lad, and always there for his football. He always wanted to win and always gave 100 per cent. He was always full of fun when off duty.

'There were about half a dozen youngsters in a small gym at Tynecastle. But remember no clubs were organised with a junior policy at the time following the war.'

It was a case of first things first for Mackay. Shortly before his 15th birthday and leaving Saughton at the end of the school year, Mackay had sat down with his parents to discuss how he intended to earn a crust outside an educational environment which he found protected him from such responsible decision-making.

Mackay had loved school as it allowed him freedom to mix with his mates and provided plenty of sports games to play.

Thomas Mackay puffed on a cigarette as his son rejected his dad's suggestion that he follow in his footsteps in the print trade, with its job security and decent wage. His offspring wanted employment which allowed him time off on a Saturday to play football. Thomas said to Dave, 'That rather limits the field but I'll have a word with your uncle [Louis] to see if he has any ideas.'

Thomas's brother came up trumps. He sung Mackay's praises to his boss at Laurence McIntosh Limited, an Edinburgh joinery and cabinet-making firm and the youngster became an apprentice joiner, despite having found woodwork at school 'boring'. And the £5-a-week job left his Saturdays free.

Mackay gave it his best shot and didn't want to let his uncle down as he got on with his role, which included assisting joiners to fit shops and construct cabinets and shelves for customers and tidying up.

Laurence McIntosh himself spoke his mind and Mackay was on the receiving end as his boss called him out for leaning against the nearest wall and making a racket while moving about work sites. It cured Mackay of habits which he admitted must have been 'maddening' while making him 'appear slovenly'.

Mackay was also grateful to his old-school boss – whose company now claims to be a 'byword' in its field – as it indirectly helped him as an individual and a footballer.

He said, 'He taught me there was an urgency about life ... McIntosh, in being firm but fair, sharpened me up, and as I grew a little older I found my football getting an edge on it which had been missing.'

In Mackay's favour was the fact he was linked to Hearts, albeit only through the coaching courses. McIntosh was a Jambos fan.

Incidentally, though, Tommy Mackay was to be grateful for the skills his brother developed as a joiner.

Tommy said, 'When my wife and I married we moved into an old-fashioned tenement block and after our first child was born he made us a pram box at the bottom, to save us going all up the stairs with it, so his skills weren't wasted!'

And, fast forwarding to 2013, the then chairman of the Royal Mail, Donald Brydon, revealed how his family benefitted from Mackay's joinery skills.

Mackay attended the launch of stamps – featuring himself and ten other players – to commemorate the 150th anniversary of the Football League with his family.

And Sir Donald told them how his fellow Scot came to his family home to complete a repair over half a century earlier.

Isobel Mackay said, 'The chairman lived in Edinburgh when he was young and his father was a staunch Hearts supporter. They were needing some garage doors at their house and David was sent to do the job. His dad couldn't believe that David Mackay the Hearts player was still being a joiner. After that, David gave the "wee boy" – which was Donald – a programme after each game. He's still got those programmes. And the doors are still there!'

Derek Mackay said, 'The "wee boy" and his dad were Hearts regulars and were thrilled after Dad fitted them garage doors. From then on, they would wait at a given time outside the players' entrance at Tynecastle before kick-off and Dad would nip out and hand them a programme, also the latest away match programme too. Interestingly, the "wee boy" grew up to be the chairman of the Post Office, and mentioned the story in his speech at Wembley at the unveiling of the stamp collection. The stamp thing was going to be a big occasion in the media, but on that very day Sir Alex Ferguson announced his retirement! And that was it! Barely any coverage at all! Would Sir Alex have delayed his announcement if he'd known his pal was to be commemorated on a stamp? I'm sure he would have!'

Near-neighbour Matt Chalmers continued to have an influence on Mackay's nascent football ambitions.

Chalmers was on the committee of Slateford Athletic, a juveniles football club, and had been impressed so much with the youngster's footballing ability that he hooked him up for those courses at Tynecastle.

Slateford, an Edinburgh suburb and former village a mile and a half south-east of Glendevon Park and across from Gorgie Road, is the birthplace of Sir Chris Hoy, the serial Olympic cycling champion.

Mackay was only too pleased to get on his bike to accept another invitation from the Hearts groundsperson and sign on for Athletic.

He said, 'Matt Chalmers was forever encouraging and pushing me in my football.'

Mackay was joined by several other members of Saughton's national glory boys – his elder brother Tommy, school captain Eddie Kelly, Terry Tighe and John Paterson.

They also had Willie Duff, who was to become a team-mate of Mackay at Hearts, in goal. Former Slateford left-back Duff, brought up near Wishart in Corstorphine, found he was better as a stopper, having pulled on the then-green jersey when the regular custodian failed to turn up for a game.

Familiarity with his team-mates, and growing ability while adapting successfully to the higher level, made Mackay 'enthuse' about his time with Slateford.

And, together with Duff, they helped guide Chalmers' charmers to five juvenile prizes over two years.

The following two years were pivotal in the launching of one of the most legendary of football careers. Hearts, who had kept tabs on Mackay, signed him on provisional and then permanent forms, while the player himself revealed the Jambos 'opted to send me to Newtongrange Star' – a leading Edinburgh and District Junior League club – to pick up experience at a level one below the Football League south of the border in the 1951/52 and 1952/53 seasons.

Hearts managed to secure Mackay's services despite interest from Edinburgh rivals Hibernian. Mackay was convinced he would join his family and community's club and help turn it into a 'great' one ever since his Saughton side won the Scottish Schools Under-16s FA Shield.

But it appeared that Hibs had stolen a march. The Easter Road outfit, it seemed, were looking for a hat-trick of old boys from his alma mater after giving deals to Eddie Kelly and Terry Tighe. They approached Mackay, who had begun his joiner apprenticeship after leaving school. He was offered the opportunity of an interview with Hibs manager Hugh Shaw.

Mackay was conflicted as he wanted to carve out a career in professional football with the Maroons. The possibility that the Jam Tarts might not even want him crossed his mind. He said, 'Just the thought broke my heart.'

Mackay added, 'I had attended many of their coaching courses for schoolboys and there was in my heart a great love for the Tyneside club.'

He explained the mental torture to his dad who advised him that if Hearts were not interested he should link up with a club that was.

Mackay said, 'My dad decided he wanted to go for a walk. He never told me this and I never asked but I do not think he walked very far. I believe he walked straight into Matt Chalmers' house, four doors down, and told him that his Davie was about to be offered terms with Hibernian and if Hearts wanted him they needed to act fast.'

And act fast they did. A letter popped through the Mackay family door the following day from Hearts manager Tommy Walker, inviting Dave for an interview at Tynecastle just 30 minutes before he was due to sit down with 'Mr Shaw', who had played for both Edinburgh giants as a left-half and was in the Jambos' 1928 title-challenging outfit which eventually finished fourth. Mackay said, 'I'm pretty sure Matthie [Chalmers] tipped them [Hearts] the wink.'

Mackay met 'the quietly spoken and kindly' Walker, who swiftly offered him a part-time deal; a weekly wage of £10 during the season, £8 in the off time, with a £20 signing-on fee. The player asked if he could mull it over and talk to his family before making a decision.

Mackay agreed to sign for Hearts but believed Junior football experience would benefit him before becoming a 'league professional'. Walker went along with it, seemingly confident he would get the player in the end and clearly a believer in the value of the Junior set-up, having loaned Mackay's eldest brother Tommy to Edinburgh City. Hearts, though, were keen to guarantee Mackay would put pen to paper on a provisional deal, believed to be similar to today's pre-contract arrangements. In a questionnaire for *The Recorded History of Newtongrange Star FC: 1890 to 1987* by A.C. Smith, Mackay revealed he did just that on 13 September 1951 (although Hearts club historian David Speed understood the signing was on 22 November).

The impressive Mackay had just helped the Star to a 2-1 Scottish Junior Cup first-round win – with Alex Hope and Bobby Kinghorn on target – at Armadale Thistle.

Returning from the West Lothian mining-turned-modern-day commuter town 25 miles west of Edinburgh, Jambos scout and coach Duncan McClure accompanied Mackay on one of the player's last legs home, down Dalry Road leading into Gorgie Road.

Former full-back McClure was a one-club man who played more than 400 times for Hearts and took part in a wartime international for Scotland, and he was to help bring Alex Young to Tynecastle in 1954.

This evening, as they walked, McClure asked Mackay, 'Why not become a professional with us at once? You can continue your job as a joiner, and in every way the money will come in useful. What do you say?'

Mackay kept his counsel for a minute as the pair continued to wear leather from their shoe soles, admitting he was 'playing hard to get' before replying, 'When do you want me to sign?'

McClure said, 'Right now.'

The loyal Hearts employee dug into the right-hand pocket of his overcoat and pulled out a signing-on form, retrieved a fountain pen from an inside pocket and said, 'Now for somewhere to rest the form.'

McClure guided Mackay to a tenement entrance, handed him the form and the youngster propped it up against a staircase wall and, when the scout passed him the pen, scratched his signature on it.

Mackay insisted he never regretted the decision and went on, Hearts revealed, to make it a permanent professional arrangement on 26 April 1952.

Would he have joined Hibs if that letter from Tommy Walker had not come through? He said, 'Yes, I would have done but not once I knew Hearts wanted me. I was desperate to sign for Hearts and would have done anything to play for Hearts.'

His younger brother Frank was also to link up with Hearts. So with three Mackay siblings linked to Tynecastle and the fourth, Ronnie, skippering the Saughton school team, the footballing Mackays provided a decent feature for any media outlet and hosted several visits from the fourth estate at 18 Glendevon Park.

Dave said, 'We were always on our best behaviour as we sipped tea with the reporters, dressed in our shirts, ties and woollen V-neck jumpers.'

The Saughton contingent, including a 16-year-old Mackay, pal Terry Tighe and Eddie Kelly, attracted the attention of Newtongrange Star, a leading club in Scottish Junior football, while Duff went off to Star's Junior league rivals Easthouses Lily.

Nitten could boast the likes of 'King' Willie Bauld, Jimmy Murray and Freddie Glidden, who were to become Hearts championship-winning team-mates of Mackay, among its former players and Alex Young, another member of the Jambos title team, joined him at Victoria Park in 1952.

The Star had won a multitude of glittering prizes since its formation in the then mining village in 1890. They could also tell Mackay they were in good current shape. They had secured the Edinburgh and District League title for the first time in 18 years in 1950/51 with the ill-fated Charlie Elms shining in the play-offs. Star had topped the Mid/East table and overcame West champions Camelon Juniors 3-1. Inside-right Elms scored and played most of the game with a head bandage after a collision and he also netted while the Star totted up a club record 11-2 victory over Fauldhouse United en route to winning their group in the St Michael's Cup, while lifting the Murray Cup and Thornton Shield outright.

Rival player Jim Kelly remembered playing against Mackay when our subject shone for Newtongrange Star.

He said, 'I was part of the Lochee Harp team which was invited through to Newtongrange Star in 1955 to open their new stadium, and the game was played under their state-of-the-art floodlights ... We were asked to take part in the game through a mutual connection with both clubs and remember it as a great occasion, even having a meal in an Edinburgh hotel prior to the game.

'In the Newtongrange line-up that night was a young Dave Mackay, who would, of course, go on to play for Hearts, Tottenham Hotspur and Scotland, Tommy Preston, who would later join Hibs, and a goalkeeper called Marshall, who signed for Rangers.

'We beat them 3-1 and our defence included myself at right-half ... One of our frontmen, Billy McLardy, later went down to Manchester City.'

Tying himself to the Star began a two-year period which Mackay felt was 'the most important of all' in his career, when he looked back having completed the historic Football League and FA Cup Double with Tottenham Hotspur in 1961.

Initially, Mackay confessed, perhaps with his tongue in his cheek, that he might have been influenced to hook up with the Star because they offered him a pair of boots and 'gear' as much as the opportunity to play at the higher level.

But he soon discovered the positive benefits to his game that his switch into grown-up football provided.

Mackay believed that he and his friend Terry Tighe, 16 and fresh out of full-time education, were only 'filling in' and were 'not expected' to get into the team regularly because of their age following their debut, a 2-1 loss against hosts Arniston Rangers at Gorebridge on 6 August 1951, but 'excelled to the extent they could not be kept out'.

Scottish Junior football provided him with experience playing with up and comers like himself and canny performers who have been round the block in the national professional league. He felt it gave him the chance to 'notice how they [the canny performers] approached various problems', and that the experience was 'invaluable to me'.

He was asked by the club later, 'Was there any player around at my time with the Star that influenced you in any way?'

Mackay said, 'All the older players, particularly Alex Mann, Fee Ferguson and Alex Skinner. Remember Terry Tighe and I were only teenagers at the time.'

He continued, 'On the field itself I learnt far more in 90 minutes than I could at coaching classes in 90 days. And I say this without in any way decrying the value of coaching. At Slateford we were basically the Saughton school side growing up together. Juveniles becoming men. At Star … we were suddenly amongst the men.'

The 'shocking' pitches provided another 'invaluable' learning curve for Mackay. He figured if he could put on a decent display on a poor surface it augured well for when he strode around a good one.

There were also the experiences of playing at a proper ground in front of 'fanatic' supporters. Opponents always knew when they visited Victoria Park that they would be facing a 'small' but 'raucous' home following with which Mackay and his team-mates became acquainted on an individual basis.

The Star often brought with them up to 1,000 vociferous supporters for away games. Fans boarded coaches and trains to follow their Junior favourites, eschewing the top league clubs in Edinburgh like Hearts or Hibs, and further afield in Glasgow with Rangers and Celtic.

Mackay was only too aware of what Star's one-eyed loyalists expected. He said, 'Believe me, we had to justify their faith in us, otherwise if we didn't they told us a number of home truths … genuine supporters of the team.

'I learned to appreciate just how enthusiastic women supporters can become. When they follow a side they really let their hair down, and there have been occasions, especially when I've played away from home, when I've expected to see them invade the pitch and show us how to play the game they loved.'

6

'Hard but fair'

THE NEWTONGRANGE Star loyalists caused referees who had given controversial decisions to be advised to stay in the dressing room post-match. Mackay admitted that although they were 'genuine supporters', they were 'at times rather violent'.

The opponents certainly got to know Nitten when they came calling in their backyard. One such host was Edinburgh and District Junior League (Mid/East) rivals Bonnyrigg Rose Athletic.

Mackay admitted Rose's New Dundas Park was 'one of the most exciting grounds to play on'.

He said, 'The crowd were enthusiastic, the local side never gave anything away, and I was a fellow who liked to put everything into a game.'

He got over-excited in one league fixture against what were title rivals at the Park in his first season, which saw the hosts pip the visitors with the only goal of the game. And it taught him an invaluable lesson in self-control.

He lost his rag with an opponent and earned himself a booking, something a lot rarer then than now.

Mackay said, 'I lost my temper for the first time. I was a very foolish lad, for I allowed a trivial thing to develop into something out of all proportion and quite rightly the referee took my name.'

That was not the worst of it for this budding wing-half. He took his place in the team coach along with his father for the 30-minute return journey home. Thomas Mackay, described by his son as 'quiet but very firm', turned to his offspring and gave him a 'verbal lashing', part of which was the reminder of the advice his dad had offered following the humiliating defeat with Scotland schoolboys against a Johnny Haynes-inspired England at Wembley.

Mackay said, 'Father pointed out to me not only the disgrace of having my name taken but how I was letting myself down by losing my temper … he handled me in the right way at the right time and made me realise my mistake. I made up my mind to avoid at all costs a repetition of that loss of temper.'

It largely worked as he was never sent off in what would become a 19-year professional playing career.

Bonnyrigg's Nat Fisher, a former player, kitman and, in 2017, club historian, remembered Mackay at the Star, even prior to his eventful visit in the 1951/52 campaign.

Fisher said, 'I played against Dave Mackay … but before he was a Junior. I was at Heriot-Watt school of printing during my apprenticeship and … filled in for an under-age team against Slateford Athletic. Mackay was playing. A great, great player but hard. We bounced off him. He went on to play for Newtongrange Star but everyone knew he was going to the very top.'

Fisher also revealed his connections with John White, who was to become a Scotland and Spurs team-mate to Mackay and was tragically killed by a lightning strike on Crews Hill golf course in north London in July 1964.

Fisher said, 'I did play for Bonnyrigg A. They were short of a player for a game at Musselburgh, so I borrowed boots and during the shooty-in I saw a player on the other side I thought I recognised from school.

'He worked for a builders but John was dead keen for the training. If he was working up this way, he came to the ground afterwards, put his tools and his piece-box in the pavilion and went to get chips. Then he was ready for the training. There was nothing on him, too.

'I remember a goal he scored at Penicuik, big rivals. He was standing on the 18-yard line and saw the keeper was off his line. A free kick soared towards him and he just glanced it over the goalie's head. Simple. Beautiful. He was the best.'

Fisher was also friendly with Edinburgh-born Sean Connery, who played for Bonnyrigg the year Mackay joined Nitten Star.

The knighted, Oscar-winning actor known by his middle name and sharing his first with Mackay's dad and eldest brother (Thomas) is most famous for playing James Bond in the movie franchise, and appeared on Rose's right wing, although not with 007 on his back. And it is unlikely Connery, who passed aged 90 on 31 October 2020, faced Mackay as he 'didn't play a lot', according to Fisher.

Fisher used to chat to Connery while sorting the kit, and recalled, 'He was in and out of the team [for about six months]. He played outside-right and most people in Bonnyrigg remember him for scoring a wonderful goal from 30 yards against Broxburn in the Scottish Cup. It nearly took the net off but we still lost 3-1.'

He added in an article for the Scottish Junior FA website, 'Playing-wise … well, Sean didn't play a lot, as far as I can remember. The team was pretty rubbish back then anyway, and when Connery was released [after two seasons], three other right-wingers were released too. It was suggested Connery had trials at Celtic and Manchester United.'

Connery, who earned five shillings (25p) a week plus travel expenses and trained twice a week, once said, 'I played for Bonnyrigg Rose and I was offered a trial by East Fife. That's the truth. Celtic, no.'

But the rumour mill has it that United manager Matt Busby, a fellow Scot, offered him a £25-a-week contract having been impressed by the actor's performance representing the *South Pacific* touring musical team against a local outfit.

Connery said, 'I really wanted to accept because I loved football. But I realised that a top-class footballer could be over the hill by the age of 30, and I was already 23. I decided to become an actor and it turned out to be one of my more intelligent moves. Perhaps I'm not a good actor, but I would be even worse at doing anything else.'

William Shakespeare, the most famous of English playwrights, split his canon into tragedy, comedy and history. And apart from the learning process linked to his football, Mackay's time at Newtongrange Star reflected all three elements.

Tragedy first. He learned how tough life, let alone football, could be when he experienced the prelude to the death of a team-mate. It was also in his first season at the club, and the feeling stayed with him.

Charlie Elms was an inside-right and one of the 'canny' players Mackay relied on to soak up his football nuances.

Mackay had, understandably, no social interaction away from the club with the thoughtful, amiable and supportive Elms. His team-mate spent his working week as a miner, one of around 5,000 who used to go down one of about five major pits in the area.

The mining community were big supporters of the area's football club in a village 14 miles south-east of Mackay's Glendevon Park home. It is understood that each miner had a penny deducted from their wage by the National Coal Board to help support the Star. And it was fitting they had a representative on the field.

Elms was part of a striking threesome – which also included Rob Kinghorn and Johnny Slater – and managed 20 goals in that productive 1951/52 season, which also went well for Mackay and his team overall.

But the inside-forward passed away after being taken ill during a match in the 1952/53 season.

Mackay revealed that Star's number eight told him as he left the field, 'I'll have to go off, son. I feel pretty groggy.'

Mackay acknowledged Elms's remark as he processed how his team-mate appeared. He said, 'I remember thinking, I'd never seen anyone look so grey; a short time before the end of the match he had died.

'At half-time, he was not in the changing room and, as it was not my place, I did not ask where he was. I thought that maybe he felt so bad he might have taken the bus home. We played out the second half with ten men and when we came back into the changing room the manager and a few club officials and helpers were standing there.

'"I have some bad news," said one of the men, blinking back tears. "Charlie died 15 minutes ago in hospital. It must have been his heart."

'I was dumbfounded and tears welled in my eyes … I had not experienced death yet. Only old people died in my book. Or soldiers. Or miners in pit disasters. Not strong men playing football. As young lads engrossed in our own lives, we got over this tragedy reasonably quickly, but I still think of Charlie to this day and can only imagine the grief felt by his wife and family.'

Mackay rated Elms as one of the three best players he performed with for the Star, along with winger Alex Hope and Johnny Slater.

It was recorded in A.C. Smith's Newtongrange Star centenary year publication in 1990 that the fatal match was against Ormiston Thistle in the Thornton Shield on 22 April 1953.

Star historian Andrew Hickie said, 'The date for this match is difficult. Star played Loanhead Mayflower four times that season. Elms was last mentioned on the scoresheet on 14 February 1953 against Thorntree United. There was only one of the Loanhead matches that took place after that date but it was on 9 June 1953. So it's not entirely clear.'

Mackay's team-mate Andy Morris remembered the opposition as Loanhead. Morris said, 'I … played in a game v Loanhead when Charlie took ill. It was not v Ormiston as the history says. We beat Loanhead, which was unusual. A real bogey team. I was outside-right. Charlie headed the new ball, which had the red-painted logo on it. He fell and it was thought he was cut … it was all go in the dressing room until Jimmy Kirkwood stood on a chair and said, "Charlie is dead, a burst ulcer." Alex Young and I never said a word on the bus to Dalkeith.'

The comedy came as soon as Mackay arrived – and it emphasised the age difference between he and Tighe, and their team-mates.

He said, 'At the end of the game when the older players were having a drink, Terry Tighe and I would go for an ice cream.'

Laughter also arrived inadvertently. There was the time Mackay injured his own goalkeeper as a match was about to kick off. He said, 'By accident I caused our team to start off with ten men against Ormiston Primrose. It was quite a silly happening. Before the kick-off I collided with Jimmy Dalglish, our goalkeeper, while we were shooting in at goal and he had to receive treatment from the trainer just as the referee started the game. Fortunately for me, we did not concede a goal while Dalglish was receiving "running repairs".'

Mackay recalled another occasion that provoked smiles after the event, and again it was against Primrose.

He upset a female follower 'letting her hair down', although this one was supporting the opposition and in a 'brolly' rather than jolly mood.

The wing-half was presented with a questionnaire by Nitten and it asked whether he had any controversial or embarrassing moments that happened with the Star to recall.

Mackay said, 'The one I remember happened at Ormiston in a Star v Ormiston game. After a heavy tackle on an Ormiston player I was threatened by a lady Ormiston supporter who was brandishing an umbrella, and coming out with unladylike language.'

Mackay helped create history for Nitten, who collected trophies for fun with him, providing copper-bottomed proof he was a winner at grown-up level following the successes at school and youth/juvenile levels.

He was considered 'one of the cornerstones' of a 'remarkable' season rated 'probably the finest in the club's history' despite his tender years.

Mackay helped inspire the retention of the Edinburgh and District League title, topping the Mid/East table by six points and netting 119 goals in 30 Mid/East fixtures after the opening-day blip in front of 2,000 in the Glendevon Park prodigy's first appearance.

And he netted in the 6-2 play-off win against Broxburn Athletic, along with Elms, two-goal Morton-bound Hope, free-scoring Kinghorn who ended up with 78 goals overall to make it 210 in three seasons, and Slater.

Mackay was also central to the lifting of four other trophies – the Brown Cup and St Michaels Cup, plus successful defences of the Thornton Shield and the Murray Cup.

His development continued apace in his second and what would prove his final season at Victoria Park.

He helped rampant Star complete a successive hat-trick of Mid/East titles, improving on their effort of the previous season with 133 goals and an unbeaten home record, although they were pipped 5-4 in the play-off final against Armadale Thistle. Mackay was on target in a 3-0 Brown Cup Final victory and he netted en route to a successful retention of the Thornton Shield. Time after time he was there for the team and, appropriately, was, along with the other players, presented with a watch as the side totted up seven trophies in total for the season.

Mackay's international career received the boost of a win-double during his time with Nitten. Having had mixed experiences representing his country as a schoolboy, his two appearances for Scotland's junior side provided a confidence boost. He was part of the team that pipped Wales at Hibernian's Easter Road on 7 March 1953, and one day short of a month later he helped secure a victory against hosts Republic of Ireland at Dalymount Park in Dublin.

Mackay recalled the win in the Irish capital. He said in A.C. Smith's history, 'The match ended up in a win after a twice-taken penalty.'

Journalist Laurie Cumming wrote Mackay was the 'top architect in Scotland's success, his grand positional play and strong tackling had the crowd voting him the best youngster they had ever seen in a junior national side'.

Newtongrange Star appreciated what they had and paid tribute to the player who moved on to Scottish league football with Hearts for the 1953/54 season and eventual football immortality. The club stated, 'He had been a powerful influence during a golden spell for the Star and his contribution would be greatly missed.'

Nitten historian Andrew Hickie praised the legacy Mackay left. He said, 'Dave Mackay is still a figure that commands respect and admiration at Newtongrange Star. His photo still adorns the club lounge wall and whenever his name is mentioned it is with a sense of deep pride that he once played for the club. There is even a respect amongst those who are too young to remember him playing, myself included. I remember only last year before a match, an opposition player was in the social club and saw the photo. He asked, "Did Dave Mackay play here?" He was told he did. In that moment it was interesting to see the respect that was still there. Even though Dave had passed away a few years beforehand and the player was in his 20s, Dave Mackay was clearly still held as a figure of respect and admiration. He will continue to do so by those associated with Newtongrange Star.

'We had a former player, Davie Pryde, who continued to support the club in later years. He often said jokingly that the reason he left Star was because Dave Mackay took his place. Sadly he passed away a couple of years ago.'

Neil Martin, the Scotland international striker who would work with Mackay in the 1980s, said, 'I remember Dave as a wee laddie. My oldest brother played in the same junior team as him, Newtongrange Star. I used to go with my brother [Tom] on the team bus. I was only about eight. Tommy Preston, who played for Hibs, was also on the team. They had a brilliant team. Dave was signed for Hearts but loaned out to Star. And he was the same player then.

'Later, Dave used to say, "How's your brother?" My brother had gone to Australia. Tom was an inside-right. The club produced a few players. Hearts, especially, and Hibs, if they had any top young players, they loaned them out to Newtongrange Star to harden them up a bit, like. Junior football then, you played against some experienced players. That's where I started, with my local team Tranent when I was 18 and we played a team called Bowness and they had a few hard cases. They flattened me in the first five minutes and they just said, "Welcome to the Junior game, son. You'll have to learn to take what you get."

'Same thing happened when I signed for Sunderland. I forget the centre-half's name. A big boy, crew cut. First five minutes he flattened me. I just looked at him and looked away again. Not like nowadays. They roll over about ten times. He hit me again five minutes later and he bent over and said, "Welcome to England you Scottish bastard." So I thought, "Oh well, it's a long way to go, mate." I got him back a few times!'

Mackay has remained unforgotten by Star fans. Supporter Harry Powell said, 'Having been brought up in Nitten … I remember watching players like Dave Mackay and Alex Young. I met a couple in Munich recently who know Freddie Glidden [who played with Mackay at Hearts].'

In turn, Mackay always remained grateful to the club for what it did for his career. To prove it, he returned to Victoria Park for a testimonial match on 15 May 1973. It was for the benefit of club official Jimmy Kirkwood and trainer Jock Denholm. Mackay, naturally, was on the winning side as his Old Star XI defeated the current one 2-1. His team-mates that day included Alex 'Golden Vision' Young and Tommy Preston.

Hickie said, 'He didn't forget about those who had influenced his early years.'

It might have seemed that Mackay did well at Victoria Park. But the boss of the then apprentice joiner was less than impressed when he popped along to see how his employee was progressing in his alternative career.

Laurence McIntosh was proud of the fact his employee was being earmarked by his beloved Hearts. Yet Mr McIntosh was, as we have discovered, a no-nonsense individual who believed in plain speaking.

He told Mackay, 'I don't think you'll ever make the grade, Davie – and that's being blunt.'

Mackay confided the utterance to his dad who said, 'Don't worry son, but only you can prove him wrong.'

And the youngster worked tirelessly to do just that during an ever-improving and glittering junior career. It was clearly part of what readied him for the professional game.

He said, 'For two seasons I studied the football business in Scottish junior football … it provided me with the kind of education I could never have secured anywhere else, for not only did I learn the soccer arts and the tricks of the trade, but it also impressed on me that … you have to take the hard knocks as well as give them.

'I met some of the greatest sportsmen in my life and for the most part everyone played it hard but fair.'

In a Hearts tribute programme of 14 March 2015, Mackay was quoted, saying, 'I was playing against grown men. I was just a boy. I supposed it toughened me up a bit because you were playing against guys who were much older than you … I don't think it was a huge advantage to sign for the club [part-time] so young. I don't think it made me any stronger. I was already pretty tough having played for Newtongrange Star.'

PART TWO:
HEART OF MIDLOTHIAN

7

'Superman' in maroon

CLUB OWNER Ann Budge revealed that there are words by Dave Mackay displayed on the wall of the Heart of Midlothian dressing room at Tynecastle to inspire the club's players of today.

They are, 'For as long as I can remember all I wanted in my life, nothing else, was to play for Hearts, which is my dream team. And to play for Scotland. I had no ambition for anything else. Always Hearts.'

He uttered similar sentiments to Jimmy Greaves in *The Sun* in the 1970s. His old Spurs team-mate asked him, 'Did you always want to be a footballer?' And he replied, 'Not just a footballer, a *Hearts* footballer. They have always been my favourite club.'

The fact that the Jambos have selected Mackay's message to motivate is indicative of the greatness the local lad achieved at the club. That 'football immortality'.

Another is reflected in the memories of Craig Brown. Brown became a wing-half who helped Dundee lift the Scottish title with Mackay's future Spurs team-mate Alan Gilzean before going on to manage Scotland in Euro 96 and the 1998 World Cup finals and receive the CBE for his services to the game.

But he was transported back to his teenage childhood in his mind's eye as he recalled the day he 'patted Dave Mackay on the shoulder' as his 'boyhood hero' prepared for a long throw.

The Brown family lived in Hamilton on the west coast of Scotland, 12 miles south-east of Glasgow. Craig had pretensions of becoming a professional footballer and informed his dad Hugh ('who was a keen football guy') about the ambition. He said, 'My dad wanted to try and make me into a footballer, a midfield player. So he took me not to see Hearts but to see Mackay.'

Hugh Brown would take his son to see Mackay live so he could learn from 'the best in the business' just 'any time' Hearts were playing nearby at the likes of St Mirren, Motherwell and Hamilton Academical – Tynecastle on the east coast of Scotland would have been a stretch – in the 1950s.

One day, with Mackay in his pomp, father and son stood on the Fir Park terraces to see hosts Motherwell take on Hearts.

Brown said, 'He was a Superman. My favourite player. One of my earliest memories as a young boy was in the enclosure at Motherwell FC this day. Dave Mackay was captain of Hearts. And in those days the players used to go out separately. One team would run out and then the other team. Now they do it hand in hand. The Hearts team didn't jog out, they ran. And Dave Mackay was in front with the ball. They ran right into the centre circle. The rest of the team drifted into one half. Mackay ran right into the circle and threw the ball right in the air and back-heeled it on the drop – a half-volley back-heeler – right into the goal his team-mates were moving towards. I've never seen anything like it in all my years in football. The Hearts keeper hadn't got to the goal yet and the ball bounced into the net. Maybe Dave wanted to show the opposition what they were about to face? Exactly.

'When he took a throw-in he used to go back to the wall, hitch up his shorts and take a long throw. I was desperate to pat him on the shoulder when he did. I said to my dad, "Take me down so I can just touch him." And I did. Then I stood behind him to watch his long throw. It made it the most memorable game for me as a boy. Honestly, that was my feeling about Dave Mackay.

'I also watched him play from the Hampden terraces for Scotland. And then, so many years later, I was working with Billy Davies at Derby County, when Derby got into the play-off final against West Bromwich. I was the football consultant at Derby with Billy as manager. I was overawed when he said Dave Mackay was coming! I was starstruck. You cannot speak to anyone who has more admiration for Mackay.

'He combined great skill, terrific ability, with being aggressive, oh aye. A competitor. A warrior. A leader.'

Bobby Wishart, who trained with Dave at Hearts after playing with him on the golf course close to Glendevon Park, believed he was fast-tracked and an 'instant hit' at Tynecastle.

Wishart said, 'He was an immediate hit with the players and fans. That was a unique feature of Dave. I don't remember Dave Mackay ever being a reserve player. His arrival at Tynecastle meant he moved into the first team straight away. Dave had the ability to play on the right or left side of the team. He was very versatile. His natural ability, coupled with his drive, and the ability he had to get the best from his team-mates, were his best qualities.'

Mackay took a step closer to achieving his boyhood dreams as the 1953/54 season unfolded. Newtongrange Star was in the past as he combined his fledgling professional football career with Hearts and work as an apprentice joiner.

The Hearts bug might have begun to bite as he ducked under that gate at an empty ground shortly after starting school. It spread through the early 1940s when, with brother Tommy on packed terraces, he watched the likes of Tommy Walker, his future Tynecastle boss, a rookie Alfie Conn, one of the Terrible Trio and father of former Spurs player Alfie Junior, Bobby Baxter and Alex McCrae put him through agony and ecstasy, even in just one game, which he left before the end believing his favourites had lost 2-0 only to discover they had won 3-2.

And he might have begun to believe the fairytale of playing for his favourites would come true after that famous day he had marched behind the bagpiper following his school's national triumph at Tynecastle.

That fairytale, of course, included leading the Jambos to glory – which is what eventually happened – but for the time being he had to adapt to the reality of being a raw Hearts recruit.

The feeling was epitomised when he began training with the first team. The youngster felt confident and thrilled to be among those watched rather than the watching as he first reported to Saughton Enclosure for the session under trainer John Harvey.

He was given a kit consisting of shorts, vest, sweater, rubber-soled shoes and spikes before receiving a spot of coaching from Willie Bauld and Alf Cox, first-teamers whose extra duties included passing on the wisdom of their experience to young players.

Mackay, again, struggled after an upgrade. There was no laxity allowed. Everything seemed to be done at twice the intensity to what he was used to. He was in awe of the effort the experienced players put in, the level of fitness and the company he was keeping.

The players, as they are wont to do, took advantage of the freshly arrived, slack-jawed youngster by performing a practical joke on him involving Bauld one day.

Mackay told a tale in his autobiography of how he was preparing to take part in a five-a-side with the first team and was short of footwear. He espied a pair of plimsolls which he was 'advised' were 'spare' and put them on and ran out on to a concrete pitch for the small-sided encounter.

The next thing he knew Bauld turned up to inquire, 'Which one of you buggers stole my plimsolls?'

Mackay, who had struggled to banter with players who were his heroes since that initial training session, said, 'I did. I'm sorry Mr Bauld. I didn't realise they belonged to you.'

Bauld gave him a grave look and said, 'Remember one thing young Davie.'

Mackay said, 'Yes, what is that?'

Bauld said, 'The name's Willie.'

Mackay's anxiety evaporated as all the players fell about laughing, and from that point onwards he felt more relaxed and at home.

Mackay said, 'I thought it was a big step up in quality especially from the Juniors but I think I fitted in pretty well. It was wonderful for a young man like me because I was earning £20 a week from Hearts and £5 to £10 as an apprentice joiner for Laurence McIntosh, who was a big Hearts fan ... he loved to have a Hearts player working for him. He used to love to say, "Davie Mackay works for me."

'We had a pitch at the back [of Saughton Enclosure] which was kept for us. Tommy Walker would come and watch us training, and take notes, but it was Johnny Harvey who took training. He was Tommy Walker's right-hand man. Donald McLeod came along later. We would play a lot of games. Sometimes ten v ten and things like that. And we would practise free kicks and set pieces as well.'

The sports science that has revolutionised modern football was underdeveloped in the game as a whole when Mackay was getting used to methods of match preparation.

He said, 'No one ever told us what to eat. But you knew you had to look after yourself. You couldn't afford to get fat and the guys were all very fit.

'I think there were one or two who smoked, but I never did … The players would socialise after a game. We'd go for a drink after the game but we didn't drink a lot. And the night before the game I was always in my bed early. I was always good for that right through my career.'

There were a few question marks hanging over Mackay – ones he was asking himself – when he made his Hearts debut.

It came in a reserve match against Montrose after a near 200-mile round trip to the east coast of Scotland, north of Dundee and close to Arbroath, on Saturday, 8 August 1953.

It was a goal fest as Hearts bagged six with Scotland international Eddie Rutherford firing a hat-trick. It has been recorded as a 6-5 win by the club in front of 3,000 on a blazing hot day, but it certainly wasn't six of the best for Mackay as far as his own performance was concerned.

Mackay described his display as 'terrible'. The self-critical wing-half said, 'I played like a schoolboy, had about as much stamina as a retired carthorse, and, at half-time, I was literally out on my feet.'

It was a better but similar experience when he made his home debut in a 2-1 reserve victory over East Fife four days later.

He received positive media coverage for his performance and one journalist was impressed, feeling that Mackay's tackling and passing showed 'great promise'.

But Mackay said, 'I disappeared from the game after 35 minutes … I became exhausted. My legs felt like a couple of leaden weights and I would have been just as useful to my colleagues had I gracefully retired to the dressing room after half an hour.'

He might have had his eyes opened by the endeavour and expertise shown by his colleagues in training, but the experiences against Montrose's Gable Endies and back in the Gorgie District proved to him how far he had to go physically and mentally to bridge the gap as he attempted his latest jump in class.

Mackay internalised, declining to tell the non-playing staff how he felt because he was 'too frightened' and pledged to himself to double the amount of training he was doing to make up for what he perceived as a lack of fitness.

But eventually he did open up to colleagues who had witnessed his opening performances in maroon. They told him he had spent too much time wasting his energy on chasing players who couldn't be caught and passes that could not be reached.

He took their advice on board and listened closer to the sage coaching comments of Bauld and Cox. Mackay, automatically, stopped chasing lost causes on the field and developed a positional sense to block passes. He also worked on improving his stamina and speed through a 'severe course of exercises'. Hearts fan and employer Mr McIntosh was understanding as Mackay took time off to focus on slimming down, taking off the bulk he carried around his hips. Rome wasn't built in a day. Nor was a professional footballer.

Mackay said, 'I learned by using my head how to save my legs.' He also developed attacking tendencies to complement the defensive qualities he possessed as a wing-half. And he was convinced it all helped him shine as Hearts' reserves progressed in the Scottish Cup, through their section and to ultimate glory, with Mackay netting both goals as the Maroons overcame Rangers 2-1 in the last four.

Mackay said, 'I like to think, because I took the trouble to try and learn my business thoroughly, that I played a part in our reserve team's progress. What tickled me most was that [in the semi-final] I twice beat Bobby Brown, the Scottish international keeper who for so long had been among my heroes.'

Mackay remained part-time as he began his first full season of devoting his football solely to Hearts. He was named first-team reserve several times and impressed in the reserves for the opening months of the 1953/54 campaign, but Davie Laing, the player he shadowed, maintained fine form for the main side looking to improve on a fourth-place finish – and a run to the last four of the Scottish Cup – the previous season.

Mackay, though, earned his call-up to Walker's main team by default when Laing was sidelined by injury. It was against Clyde at Tynecastle in the league, seven days short of his 19th birthday. His parents were there among the 16,000 gathered. Two-thirds of the Terrible Trio – Alfie Conn and Jimmy Wardhaugh – were alongside him, and so was John Cumming, a half-back destined to form a formidable partnership with Mackay in the title-winning season four years away.

He lined up with Watters, Parker, Adie, Armstrong, Dougan, Rutherford, Conn, Wardhaugh, Cumming, and Urquhart.

That Saturday afternoon produced disappointment in terms of the result as Wardhaugh scored Hearts' only goal and the Lanarkshire visitors scored twice.

For Mackay, it was a personal disappointment as it exposed his shortcomings in the 'nuance' department; that like a chess master you needed to be many moves ahead of the opposition to avoid a checkmate.

He said, 'I played a shocking game, and, as had happened on every occasion in the past, it had stressed to me that I was never fitted to step automatically from one grade of football to the higher grade.'

Mackay was immediately dropped after his 'league flop' and considered 'making my first season as a league player my last'. He said, 'I made the decision I would quit Hearts at the end of the season.'

Mackay did not feel he was worth the money he was being paid. And combining football and joinery wasn't helping. Part-time training was 'getting on my nerves'. He said, 'I felt washed out and ready for bed, rather than serious training when I reported in the evening for training … after a hard day's work as a joiner.'

Mackay was in a mental funk as far as his football ambitions were concerned. He was replaced in the Hearts first team by John Cumming at number six and felt his career was going nowhere as he became a fixture in the reserves without a glimmer of a recall. He had no quibble with Walker's decision to keep him out of the league line-up. He respected his manager's opinion.

The limbo period in Mackay's career also produced a change in his personal life. He met the love of his life at the Palais de Danse in the Fountainbridge district of Edinburgh; the iconic venue living up to its reputation as the place where 'countless married couples met their future partner on the sprawling dance floor' with junior footballer and future James Bond actor Sean Connery reported to have worked there as a bouncer.

Mackay was on a Saturday night out following an outing with the reserves at Tynecastle that February 1954 afternoon. Mackay had lived a largely male-orientated existence through football, McIntosh's and home. A visit to the Scottish capital's niterie was his way of discovering how to link up with females. He had stuck on his only suit, travelled to and entered the dance hall featured on TV's *Come Dancing* before the 'Strictly' moniker was added on in its 2000s revival and stood around the periphery of the floor watching girls dancing to a live band, not daring to get involved. Suddenly it was the 'ladies' choice' where the females present could select a dance partner.

Mackay claimed that he normally went to the loo for the duration of the ritual because he feared the embarrassment of not being picked. But on this night he stood where he was, lost in thoughts about his next game when a member of the opposite sex said to him, 'Would you like to dance?'

He looked to where the voice had come from and espied 'the most beautiful young girl smiling sweetly at me'. He blustered something in the affirmative and danced with her, confessing his concerns over being ignored by the populous of single females present. Isobel Dixon pointed out that the situation was more difficult for the females running the risk of their request being rejected. It was, he insisted, love at first sight.

Isobel, Mackay discovered, had journeyed to the hall from where she lived with her family in the mining village of Whitecraig, eight miles east of Edinburgh, and that all of her family supported Hibernian. Mackay kept his own counsel about his Hearts affiliations, introducing himself as a joiner. He thought playing in the reserves for Hearts would not be of interest. Besides, of course, he was, at the time, unsure whether he had a future career at Tynecastle.

She said, 'Why did I ask him to dance? I think I liked him straightaway! His friends had all been up dancing and he was just standing there and I thought "mmm, he looks nice". I suppose it was love at first sight.

'He mentioned he worked as an apprentice joiner with McIntosh's in Drummond Street. He also asked me where I came from. I told him it was a little village away in the outskirts, that he wouldn't know where it was. When I told him, he said, "I know Whitecraig. We used to go through there on a Saturday to pick up our goalkeeper Bobby Ross when I played for Newtongrange Star." I couldn't believe it as Edinburgh people were so different from country people. And I knew Bobby Ross!'

Mackay – who helped Hearts' reserves beat Rangers 2-1 in the Second XI Cup semi-final on 13 March 1954 – had not had a sniff of first-team action for three months but it all changed for the better a few weeks after he met Isobel.

Coincidence? Kismet? You judge for yourself, although the romantic in me prefers the second theory, despite Isobel only receiving news that her new beau was a professional player AFTER his positive change of football fortune.

On Wednesday, 17 March 1954 – St Patrick's Day – Mackay finished a hard shift at his joiners and, still in work togs and carrying his tools in a haversack over his shoulder, made his way to Tynecastle. It was a club rule all players had to turn up to the ground on a matchday – or in this case evening – whether or not they had been selected. The Maroons, with a title challenge fading, were facing Hamilton Academical.

As Mackay walked across the tennis courts close to the ground, he bumped into first-team centre-half Freddie Glidden who informed him that John Harvey was looking for him.

He hurriedly found the trainer who told him he had been selected to play for the game, which was kicking off in just under an hour's time. Mackay hadn't a clue. Why should he? After all, his previous appearance had been in a 2-0 League Cup defeat for the reserves against Dundee seven days earlier. He put it down to an 'oversight', otherwise he would have got an early cut from McIntosh's.

The fact he had no time to think about returning 20 games after his disappointing debut seemed to work in his favour. Playing alongside King Willie Bauld for the first time, he impressed as the 'monarch' found the net in a 3-0 victory.

The media declared, 'It will be hard to keep Davie Mackay in the reserves.' And that was, not withstanding injury, how it turned out.

Three days later he was in the side pipped 1-0 by Aberdeen at Pittodrie, a result which ended any faint hope of championship success.

But that Saturday was also significant, personally, for Mackay. Isobel said, 'We had started seeing each other at the Palais on a Saturday night, and had made an appointment to meet there this particular Saturday. I was waiting outside for him and he didn't turn up. There were no mobiles or house phones in those days. My mum and dad didn't even have one. So I went in as my best friend May – we used to go together – was there. During the night this boy [Mackay's friend and Hearts team-mate Bobby Blackwood] asked me to dance, saying, "Are you Isobel?" I said yes. He says, "I've got a message for you. You know David Mackay? You were to meet him?" I said, "Yes, I was but he didn't turn up." He said, "Well actually, he's away with the Hearts team." I said, "Whaaaat! Are you kidding me? All our family are Hibs supporters!'"

She saw the funny side. And as she was from a Hibs-supporting family, the irony of introducing her relatives to a Maroon was not lost on her.

Isobel said, 'I said to my friend, "I can't believe that! Playing for Hearts. Can you believe that?" So when we got home, we got a copy of the *Pink*, the Saturday sports paper, and found the match report. There was his name. Playing for Hearts! He hadn't told me.

'I don't think he liked being a joiner. He preferred football. But he was quite a good joiner. He ended up doing quite a few jobs for our mums. He used to say, "When we get our permanent house I'll do 'this and that'." But he never did.

'I remember when we eventually lived at The Glade in Enfield after he had moved to Spurs. We had this massive window one of the kids had damaged. He got John White, his team-mate who was also a joiner, to come in and fix it. I said to John how cheeky I thought that was but John just laughed and said, "Oh, I wasn't doing anything."'

Mackay completed his season with the first team in the penultimate fixture, again replacing Laing as he moved to right-half with Cumming back into the line-up at number six.

It was the first time he had played with the entire Terrible Trio, and hosts Clyde were pipped 1-0 with a Jimmy Wardhaugh goal.

But he had to sit out the final game, a 2-1 reverse at Patrick Thistle, with top scorer Wardhaugh bagging his 34th goal of the season as Hearts finished a creditable runners-up, although seven points were dropped in the final six games.

Mackay had sustained a severe knock on his right knee at Clyde – a side which seemed to be jinxing him – jeopardising his place in what was to be on an end-of-season South African tour.

But he was given the green light. Life was on the up for Mackay as he took off with the rest of the Hearts party for the republic, 8,500 miles away.

He was in love with a girl who was to become his life partner and had secured a place in a Hearts team that seemed to have the potential for glory.

Any thoughts of quitting football were banished as he planned for a bright future, professionally and personally.

The trip provided an opportunity not available to most 19-year-old Brits of his time, such as visiting countries beyond their home islands, for instance.

To start with, how would they have been able to afford it if they had had to provide the dosh themselves? The transportation, accommodation, and sundry expenses all had to be financed. Knowledge of the republic would have been limited to geographical text books and travel brochures for the majority.

It also provided the chance for Mackay to get to know his fellow Hearts players better, having only been in their company either on a matchday or training night. And the fact his team-mates immediately made him feel like 'one of the lads' enabled him to swiftly lose the diffidence which had formed his outward appearance in company since childhood.

Furthermore, the multi-match tour forced him to grow up and self-improve. He had to adapt to a new world, and develop decisiveness and social graces. He was emboldened.

He said, 'In a matter of a few weeks [the trip] taught me far more than all my years studying at school … Football, without many of us realising it at the time, offered far more to young men than mere pounds, shillings and pence.'

Everything was new to him. Foreign travel – a plane journey out there, a ship trip on the return – led to experiencing an alien culture on a continent with multiple ethnic groups.

Mackay's new adventure saw his club's hosts lay on visits to reserves, diamond mines, vineyards and significant monuments.

But football-wise, he spent the opening three matches on the bench to ensure he was fully recovered from the injury sustained at Clyde's Shawfield Stadium.

Mackay was in line for his comeback in the next match but a day before it stubbed his toe in training on a bone-hard surface; the digit forced through the cap and broken by its jarring collision with the top. Mackay had to withstand a ribbing from his fellow players for this clumsy incident.

But he finally started to play and helped the Jambos beat Orange Free State 4-0 with manager Tommy Walker opting for a defensive line-up which showed plenty of attack.

Unfortunately, Mackay was in the wars again in the next match – the big one, against the South African national side, at a fine, packed stadium with a superb pitch in Durban.

He believed the fact he had added a powerful, extra edge to his game by now secured his spot, but he ended up in hospital. The hosts' goalkeeper caught him in his left ear with his fist as they both went for a high ball after the interval, and blood oozed out. He carried on but when another bash in his shell-like perforated its drum and more of the red stuff spurted out it was time to begin three days of treatment as Hearts lost 2-1 and finished the tour without him.

He said in the Edinburgh press, 'I spent three days in hospital. My right ear is perfectly all right, but the left is practically useless.'

8

Golden years

DAVE MACKAY always remembered the day the post-war Golden Years officially began for Heart of Midlothian, and why it resonated with him.

On Saturday, 23 October 1954, his Maroons were singing in the rain. They had secured their first big trophy in 48 years by defeating Motherwell 4-2 in the Scottish League Cup Final before 55,640 at Hampden Park in the afternoon and Edinburgh came out in force to celebrate in the evening.

Mackay said, 'The League Cup win was very special because it was the first trophy the club had won in years. I remember coming back to Princes Street and it was awash with Hearts supporters. The number of fans was just incredible.

'Most of the players, including myself, were supporters as well, so it was a double victory. As a player, I had won the cup. As a supporter, my team had won its first trophy in half a century. I had never experienced such bliss.'

Freddie Glidden, the number five alongside him and who passed on 1 January 2019, said, 'To become part of the history of the club is really great because it goes on forever.'

John Robertson hailed Mackay's part in helping to spark the 1954 success which 'was the catalyst for a period in the history of the Heart of Midlothian which is unlikely to be repeated'.

Robertson was a pallbearer at Mackay's funeral and Hearts' all-time top league goalscorer netted in a seven-goal 1996 League Cup Final thriller which saw the Jambos pipped 4-3 by Paul Gascoigne's Rangers.

The striker passed the club's league scoring record of 206, held for almost 40 years by Mackay's Hearts team-mate Jimmy Wardhaugh, in 1997. The following year he was an unused substitute as the Jam Tarts stuck it on Ally McCoist's Rangers in the Scottish Cup Final.

He also managed Hearts to the League Cup semi-finals in 2004.

He recalled his own father's tales of 'Mr Mackay'.

Robertson, three times a Scottish Premier Division runner-up with Hearts, said, 'My dad was also called John – and to be fair he was running out of names when it came to me. I was the seventh of eight children my mother had!

'He was a big Hearts man in the Golden Years of the 1950s leading up to the 1960s with Dave Mackay, the Terrible Trio of Conn, Wardhaugh and Bauld, eventually Alex Young. It was inarguably Hearts' greatest ever time.

'Unfortunately for me I didn't get to hear all of the stories because I lost my dad when I was 14.

'In those times when I was a young lad in the 1970s, it coincided with Hearts' worst in terms of teams and players. They didn't do too well, overshadowed by Hibs who took control of the capital. My dad would hold on to the fact he had seen the greatest Hearts team ever. A huge part of that was Dave Mackay.

'While most of the headlines were about the Terrible Trio for the goals they scored, my dad waxed lyrical about the industrial side of the game perhaps a bit more. He liked the guys who got stuck in. One of Dave Mackay's big traits was the fact that he could win the ball and, more importantly once he got it, could play it as well, and feed these other wonderful players. My dad's two favourites were Dave Mackay and Freddie Glidden. Freddie was a central defender. He didn't run, he glided. That's how my dad saw him. I spoke at Freddie's funeral. I had visions of Freddie as a swan that glided across the pitch.

'Mr Mackay – if my dad was alive he'd slap me around the ears for daring to call him Dave – was the ultimate iron fist in the velvet glove, my dad used to say.

'My dad instilled an appreciation of Mr Mackay, his team-mates and other players of the time.

'My dad was a footballer. Many people of that generation saw some really great teams and players. He would tell stories of his admiration of the way they all went about it. Working-class guys who had got lucky and got into football and did really well for themselves, achieved, but never lost that sense of where they came from.'

It was a time of optimism for Hearts going into the 1954/55 season after decades without any major silverware to fill the Tynecastle Park trophy cabinet.

Their second place in the league and a respectable run to the quarter-finals of the Scottish Cup the previous term – as Mackay experienced a rollercoaster baptism in his first full campaign at a Scottish League club – was indicative of the progress the club had made since Davie McLean took over as manager in 1941.

McLean, described as 'quiet, contemplative and pipe-smoking' by Albert Mackie in *The Hearts*, worked hard at developing a robust youth policy. He would develop full-time footballers with cash incentives, high-class coaches and trainers, and not with 'expensive transfers'.

McLean said presciently, if understatedly, in *The Hearts*, 'It may take a little time to succeed with the policy I suggest but I am confident that, though you may not get to the top of the league or win cups, the Hearts will have a good team, and it will last for years.'

The first fruits of it were sown when he selected the soon-to-be dubbed Terrible Trio together for the first time against East Fife in the League Cup at Tynecastle on 9 October 1948. Willie Bauld hit a hat-trick and Alfie Conn netted twice in a 6-1 win. The threesome were to go on and score more than 900 goals between them – Wardhaugh 376, Bauld 355 and Conn 221 – for Hearts.

An assistant manager was also part of McLean's plan. The person he had in mind was Tommy Walker. Hearts' inside-right was described as, 'shy', 'self-effacing', not 'the bossy type' or, as a player, an 'aggressive individualist' on the field. But McLean was convinced Walker was the right fit. Even after Walker stunned Tynecastle by leaving for Chelsea after leaving the army in 1946, McLean remained confident Walker would return to become his deputy, which he did at Christmas in 1948. The pair guided Hearts to third in 1949/50.

When McLean passed on 14 February 1951, Walker was appointed manager and destined to oversee the most successful period in the club's history, having inherited the foundations of a decent side in the shape of the Wardhaugh, Bauld and Conn strike force, full-backs

Bobby Parker and Tam McKenzie and half-backs Davie Laing and Bobby Dougan.

And in the build-up to the 1954/55 campaign the wisdom of the McLean-Walker blueprint was ready to prove profound. Mackay, Freddie Glidden and Cumming were capable of providing a formidable defensive threesome in the middle. The Terrible Trio had developed into the strike force they'd threatened to be, the full-back partnership of Parker and McKenzie had flowered and Jim Souness, formerly of Hibs, was showing himself to be a wizard on the wing. And Mackay's former Slateford youth mate, goalkeeper Willie Duff, was on the verge of a breakthrough into the club's main team.

Mackay's Hearts were ready to kick off what would prove to be the most successful era in their history with Walker swift to recognise McLean's role of 'fatherly interest in the welfare and development of the players'.

And it seems it was Mackay who threw the final switch, just as he was to do at Tottenham Hotspur and Derby County.

Gordon Marshall, who was a Tynecastle team-mate for a title and another League Cup success down the line, said, 'Hearts were a really good team but when they got Davie, they got someone who made the team win.'

Pre-season training for 1954/55, after the summer exertions in Africa, helped ensure the players would be in peak physical condition and tougher. Trainer John Harvey said to the media, 'We plan to build them up, make them more rugged ... we seek determination, fitness, agility and skill at Tynecastle.'

Walker said, 'We hope naturally that we can do better than last season when we finished second in the league. We are hoping we are able to go one better this time.'

Sadly, the passing of Jimmy Wardhaugh's 11-week-old daughter Hilary, 'suffocated by a pillow in her pram' shortly after the striker's return from the tour, must have cast a dark cloud over preparations.

But the sky, at least, would clear and the sun would shine on a professional front for Wardhaugh, Mackay and the club.

The League Cup was in its ninth year and provided an early-season opportunity to collect a pot, with quarter-final qualifiers before the league programme started.

Mackay, 19, displaced experienced Dave Laing as the regular right-half for the dawn of the new campaign, and the sun rose swiftly for him. After helping the Jam Tarts kick off the momentous campaign with a 3-1 win over Dundee at Tynecastle on 13 August, he scored that first senior goal with the Terrible Trio sharing the rest in a 6-2 dismissal of hosts Falkirk in the second match.

He completed an impressive winning hat-trick in his first season as a first-team regular in professional football as he helped Hearts defeat Celtic 2-1 at Parkhead. Hearts had to complete what would prove to be the formality of qualification – given their flying start – with Mackay sidelined and Laing restored. After a 4-1 loss to the Dee at Dens Park, Walker's team moved into the last eight with home wins over the Bairns of Falkirk (4-1) and the Bhoys of Celtic (3-2).

Mackay returned for the rest of the run. He was present as Hearts eased through to the last four against St Johnstone 7-0 on aggregate with the half-back line made up of the Pride of Glendevon Park, Freddie Glidden, and number six John Cumming showing how swiftly the crucial partnership was melding.

And an 'outstanding' Mackay performance was backed up by Jimmy Wardhaugh who brought his goals total to seven in the campaign with a double to help see off Airdrieonians 4-1 at Easter Road and secure the Jambos a final spot.

What a difference a year had made to Mackay. The potential was there for him to go from feeling a zero to hero as he prepared for the biggest football day of his life.

The weather in the afternoon of Saturday, 23 October 1954 in Glasgow could be described as *dreich*, revealed to be Scotland's favourite word in a government poll by *The Scotsman* in 2016. The esteemed newspaper told us the word means Scottish weather 'at its most miserable … wet, dull, gloomy, dismal, dreary or any combination of these'.

But the folk on the terraces and in the stands of Scotland's national stadium resplendent in maroon could care not one jot as they stood cheering and applauding their heroes with the 48-year wait for a major prize over.

Mackay, half-back pals Glidden and Cumming, skipper Bobby Parker and Tam Mackenzie, who passed a late fitness test, were all in front of a second 19-year-old in goalkeeper Willie Duff.

In front of them, wingers Jimmy Souness and Johnny Urquhart were flying and the Terrible Trio, marauding down the middle, combined to give the collective from Scotland's capital what they wanted.

'King' Willie Bauld wore the biggest crown in the eyes of the fans – who also numbered Mackay and his family – for scoring a hat-trick, completed with a late header from a cross by Conn, whose son Alfie was Bill Nicholson's last signing at Spurs and a performer for both Old Firm clubs. It was fitting Wardhaugh, with the personal trauma he had endured, scored the remaining goal for the history-makers.

Bauld headed the first from a Souness cross in the drizzle after nine minutes. The slick conditions favoured Hearts' style of moving the ball around smoothly and searching out wide balls, and Bauld made it 2-0 from a Conn ball in the 16th minute as the Maroon version of the Hampden roar echoed over the vast stadium.

Motherwell's Willie Redpath, who played with Glidden and Conn for Stoneyburn village school, reduced the arrears from the spot after a Conn foul on Wilson Humphries on 28 minutes. The match was developing into a thriller and Wardhaugh made it 3-1 when nodding home a Souness cross just before the interval.

Motherwell, who had stunned the strongly fancied Rangers in the last eight, battled back in a pacy encounter but Mackay, Glidden and Cumming helped stonewall them.

And Bauld recovered from a knock to complete his trio in the 87th minute before Motherwell pulled back a consolation through Alex Bain less than 60 seconds later.

Motherwell boss George Stevenson offered his congratulations to Tommy Walker in the dressing room corridor at the whistle as hundreds of Maroon followers ran on the field, avoiding the attempts of members of Glasgow's constabulary to restrain them from entry. Nobody but perhaps the Hampden groundsperson would have denied them their moment of undiluted rapture.

Walker said, 'I'm a happy man.' And skipper Bobby Parker added, 'We're delighted but it is just so hard to take it all in.'

The intensity of the outpouring of endorphins was more than prevalent in Auld Reekie as Mackay and his conquering team received a heroes' welcome with the light fading into night and the wee small hours of Sunday morning.

The players, all in shirts and ties and blazers and, mostly, overcoats to protect from the cooler weather, poked the top halves of their bodies out of the opened glass roof of the team coach, clutching the cup and acknowledging the jammed, cheering crowds who had waited hours in the city centre to receive them.

Mackie described the scene colourfully at length in *The Hearts* after the team had switched to the coach on the west edge of Edinburgh with an official bus having ferried them in an 'endless stream' of vehicles from Glasgow.

He said, 'A spotlight on the roof was trained on the shining trophy which meant a new era in Tynecastle football … veteran sports reporters … likened the reaction of the townsfolk to "citizens welcoming a liberating army."'

At 'a leisurely pace in their triumphal chariot', the players journeyed close to the Mackay home at Glendevon Park.

Mackie wrote, 'Edinburghers who sit on their hands in theatres went crazy with cheers. Motor horns joined in fanfaronade that would have drowned Louis Armstrong. Double-deckered buses nearly keeled over as passengers on top rushed to one side to see the juggernaut carrying their idols.

'At Saughton Park, nearing the club's home at Tynecastle, which is in the populous district of Gorgie … a district with a friendly heart, and it certainly showed it that night … fireworks were going like Chinese New Year. People went frantic when Bobby Parker … stood out to raise the cup for all to see.

'Naturally in the surrounding crowds maroon was the predominant colour. Maroon scarves, maroon berets, banners inscribed in maroon letters. The noise was like Hell let loose, but this was Gorgie in Heaven.

'On the coach rolled, between the rows of tenements. Many Edinburgh people live "up the stair". It is a city which, in its oldest part of town, pioneered in skyscrapers of 11 storeys or more, and in which four-storey tenements have remained common. And among its tenement-dwellers there has grown up a pastime of '*hingan oot windae*'. This means hanging out over the windowsill to obtain a grandstand view of what is going on. There are even, in Gorgie, windows so strategically placed that it is possible to 'hing' and view from them the game at Tynecastle, and you can imagine what a treat that must have been for a Scotsman!

But never before – not even when Burke the murderer was hanged in the Lawnmarket within full view of the Royal Mile tenements – was there such a feast of '*hingan*' as on that October evening of 1954. Every window was crammed.

'The old grey-stone walls, the smoke-blackened walls, reverberated with the wave after wave of cheering. Women threw maroon rosettes to the team as if to Spanish toreadors. At McLeod Street, where part of the Saturday crowd surges into Tynecastle, there were crowds of people singing outside the public house where the fans have their last hurried pint on the way to the match, and their first to celebrate victory or drown their sorrows afterwards. This time it was undoubted and crowning victory, and the foaming pint tumblers of good strong Edinburgh ales slopped over as they were raised in salute.

'But the singing was not left to these secular roisterers. Gorgie boasts a first-class Salvation Army band, and a Salvation Army choir which vies with it in talent, and the men in braid and the bonneted belles who peddle the war-cry among us Saturday sinners raised their voices bravely in hymns of praise over the confused shouting of the crowd. And some of these local Salvationists would, I am sure, be forgiven if their religious fervour was not unmixed with pride in the achievement of Bobby Parker and his merry men.

'So the team passed on towards the city, beneath the smoke-caked railway bridge which is a welcome landmark to fans trudging out to Tynecastle from town. Up at the parapets of the bridge the railwaymen crowded, waving their peaked caps.'

The procession went past the memorial to Hearts' war heroes on Haymarket. Mackie wrote, 'It was difficult to move an inch in that closely packed concourse, loud with cheering, drums, bells and ratchets, and bright with banners, flags, painted slogans, coloured balloons.

'At the Caledonian Hotel, Princes Street Station, and at some other West End hotels and clubs, diners in evening dress and dinner jackets stood up at the windows to join in the cheering and such scenes continued along what we locals boast is the "Street of Streets".'

Everywhere was crammed and 'a vast crowd had gathered' outside at the Northern British hotel over Waverley station where the celebration party was to be held. A cacophony of whistles, bells, bugles, ratchets and cheering greeted the team's arrival. Fans climbed up the statue of the

Duke of Wellington. Mackie wrote, 'Waterloo, even Bannockburn, had faded into insignificance beside this victory.'

Mackay soaked up the experience. He said, 'My euphoria was increasing by the minute. As we pulled into Princes Street, the most amazing sight greets us. Even though the night was cold, thousands of people wrapped in heavy overcoats and scarves were cheering us on and filling the road.'

Mackay, who had only ever had a couple of pints, recalled in his autobiography how he became increasingly tipsy as the evening progressed, and admitted to 'light-headedness'. He sampled beers at a pub as the players waited to board their 'triumphal chariot' and at the party he was 'plied with celebratory champagne'.

Mackay was brought down to earth with a bump when he and Isobel joined younger players for a post-party at the Palais. The commissionaires refused to let them in.

Mackay said, 'The commissionaires told us we were too late to be allowed entry. "We've just won the cup with Hearts," I explained. "We're all footballers."'

But the retort from one was, 'I don't care if you are all escaped prisoners of war, there's no entry after 9pm.'

But Mackay and his team-mates found a private party going on next door. Mackay said, 'My next clear memory is of waking up on the settee at Glendevon Park. Beside me was a bucket. An unpleasant smell pervaded the air.'

Isobel Mackay said, 'I wasn't at the game. In fact, David didn't like me going to see him. I had NEVER been to Hearts to see a game. But he invited me to the reception in the evening. I couldn't get near the hotel. You should have seen the fans. It was 48 years since Hearts had won something major. So I thought, "How am I going to get in there?" I got near the door and managed to get in, and his dad was there. It was the first time I'd met him if I remember correctly. I met the Hearts players. That was my first encounter [with them]. There were a few of the younger ones who said, "Let's get out of here and go to the Palais." The hotel said, "Well, you'll not get out the back door because there were still supporters celebrating." Three players – Bobby Blackwood, Jimmy Mullen and David with me – got out and went to the Palais. It was after ten and they wouldn't let us in!

'We were standing about. These Hearts supporters came along, going crazy and they were having a party near to the Palais. And they said "come on". I remember going up some stairs into an apartment in a block of flats. They were giving David whisky – and he didn't drink. He also had a big cigar. We had to get a taxi home. That was the first time I went home to his mum's. She was mortified because he was drunk. Jimmy Milne came with us in the taxi which dropped us off at his mum's. David was so drunk, he was sick. He never drunk whisky again after that.

'David came from a lovely, lovely family. His parents, brothers. All his aunts and uncles. But we never spoke about Hearts and Hibs as my family were all Hibs. Another thing was I was Catholic and David was Protestant. Religion was never really spoken about. We got round it.'

The only downside to the day for Mackay was that his mum wasn't at Hampden with the rest of his family to see his first moment of triumph.

He said, 'Once I graduated to senior football she said she could not watch anymore. She was fearful of what might happen to me. She said it made her feel ill and that when she saw me sliding in for a tackle, she was scared I would break my leg or worse. I imagine by worse she was thinking of my neck. "I'm a footballer not a boxer, Mum," I would say. Later in my career I would discover just how well founded her fears were.'

Mackay, whose brother Frank became the third of his siblings to sign on at Tynecastle in the November, made 25 appearances (with two goals) out of a possible 30 as Hearts finished fourth in the league, and he played in all of the ties as Hearts made the quarter-finals of the Scottish Cup. He curried further favour with those from Gorgie by helping his side inflict five-goal thrashings of Hibs in both competitions.

His efforts attracted the attention of the Scottish selectors that term. He linked up again with Bobby Wishart after their time together on the municipal golf course and attending Hearts' coaching sessions for kids. Wishart was en route to helping Aberdeen to the Scottish League title that season when the pair turned out for their country's first under-23 international against England at Shawfield Park in Glasgow, on 8 February 1955. They were part of a 6-0 reverse, with Duncan Edwards (three), Mackay's schoolboy nemesis Johnny Haynes, John Atyeo and Frank Blunstone netting for the Auld Enemy managed by our subject's future boss at Spurs, Bill Nicholson.

Wishart said, 'I had high hopes that we would establish a powerful midfield superiority. One [midfield] was, unfortunately not by Dave but by a young Manchester United midfielder, Duncan Edwards. We were well beaten.'

Nonetheless, Mackay had begun to prove his worth as a player and, more fancifully I guess, a lucky mascot for his club with his involvement in the historic League Cup triumph.

9

Living for the weekend

DAVE MACKAY was, of course, not only a player, but a Heart of Midlothian fan and would have, like the rest of the club's supporters, known about its history and, for at least a chunk of that time, experienced first-hand the long wait to find its place in the sun once more.

The celestial body had shone in the club's early years as its colours changed from red, white and blue to maroon.

There were different stories of how the Hearts came to be. One was that young members of a dance club named after the old jail were encouraged to take up football by a policeman disparaging of their attempts to move rhythmically to music. Another was via a group who played in a street close to the place of confinement hauled down in 1817.

Either way, Mackay's proud club were named after a razed Edinburgh jail which gave its moniker to the classic historical novel by Sir Walter Scott familiar to its founders.

Hearts were productive in the collection of shiny trophies following their official formation in 1874 (although their first captain Tom Purdie and inside-right John Cochrane claimed it was a year before).

Purdie led the Jambos to securing an early – probably first – member of the collection. It was won by overcoming neighbours Hibernian, skippered by their first captain Michael Whelahan, to secure the Edinburgh Cup after four replays. And it was indicative of a rivalry which has lasted to this day. Legend has it that Purdie was chased from the field at the end of the encounter by a 'mob of roughs' upset by the result. There has also been a hint that Purdie eventually defended himself with a 'cabby's whip'.

Purdie was 'stoned' and kicked by aforesaid 'roughs' at the finish after guiding Hearts to a repeat victory over Hibs in the competition the following year.

After ground-hopping, they earned more local bragging rights by overcoming Hibs in the Rosebery Charity Cup in 1886, the year they moved to their current Tynecastle site. Mind you, there did not appear to be much charity as hooliganism reared its head again before the destination of the trophy was decided after three matches.

Mackay said, 'The first match was stopped when enraged Hearts fans invaded the pitch because one of the players had his leg broken in a tackle. In the second, the Hibs fans stopped the game when they went 2-0 down. And, finally, in the third match Police Inspector Mackay of the Edinburgh force marshalled a strong police presence to ensure the game could be played, and Willie Mackay scored the winning goal. You see, it takes a Mackay to sort out Hearts!'

Hearts soon earned national recognition. They lifted the Scottish Cup for the first time in 1891 which sparked a treasured era after an incident-packed journey.

They defeated Methlan Park at Meggetland inside the grounds of the Electrical Exhibition, a first for the competition. Hearts full-back Jimmy Adams sparked the introduction of the penalty kick in the Scottish FA rulebook by handling a goalbound shot as the Jambos saw off East Stirlingshire. A strong Third Lanark were dismissed on a boggy pitch to set up a final clash with Dumbarton who were pipped 1-0 thanks to a Mason goal, with the majority of the Jam Tarts' line-up being from Edinburgh.

Four years later, Hearts won their first Scottish League title despite the decimation of their cup-winning side thanks to shrewd signings such as future Scotland international full-back Barney Battles from non-league neighbours Bathgate, who helped maintain the local character of the Hearts. Battles sadly died of pneumonia aged 30 and his son Barney junior played for the Jambos in the 1920s and 1930s.

The club's second Scottish Cup triumph came the following season, and it was all the more satisfying as it was completed by defeating Hibs on a national stage at Logie Green in Edinburgh rather than Glasgow, the competition's traditional home. It was a second cup success for Isaac Begbie, David Russell and Davie Baird, who were in the line-up in 1891 – and Purdie was on the club committee.

Hearts completed a successive hat-trick of prizes by taking the league for a second time in 1897 with the help of Edinburgh-born Bobby Walker, who was to become a club legend, rivalling Mackay in the debate to conclude who was the best of all.

Right-winger Walker, who hailed from Gorgie, was in the side which sealed the crown by two points from Celtic with a 5-0 crushing of Clyde at Tynecastle, a week after a 5-1 win to overcome the club which proved so troublesome as Mackay first blinked into the sunlight of Scottish League football.

And Walker shone as the Jambos lifted their third Scottish Cup in 1901, the same year Mackay's second club Tottenham Hotspur lifted their first FA Cup south of the border. It is recorded Hearts beat Spurs for the World Championship the following season. The 1901 showpiece has been recalled as 'Walker's Final', and his inside-right and fellow goalscorer, Charlie Thomson, told him after the game 'Bobby, you are the best player in Europe.'

Walker netted as the Bhoys, who included former Jambos defender Battles, were edged out 4-3 at a muddy Ibrox, where he played for Scotland against England 12 months later and witnessed the crumbling of a stand which killed 25. And he figured in the Hearts team which closed its first Golden Era by claiming its fourth Scottish Cup in 1906, defeating Third Lanark 1-0 in the decider.

His obituary in *The Scotsman* stated, 'The Hearts never had a more brilliant forward than Walker. He was amazingly clever in manipulating the ball, and it was on skill alone that he relied, for he was never favoured with physique. With the ball at his feet he could turn on his course elusively, and in such little space, that he could often put a whole defence out of position with his deft movement.'

The *Football Encyclopaedia* from 1934, edited by Frank Johnston, referred to him simply as 'Bobby Walker, the greatest natural footballer who ever played'. Mackay said, 'He ... was still talked about in referential tones when I was a boy.'

Mackay's Hearts came close to emulating the feats of their forefathers. The Jam Tarts might have begun a second Golden Era with their third title in 1914/15, having won their opening eight fixtures with a side built up by manager/secretary John McCartney. The replacements for the war heroes maintained a title charge until two weeks before the end of the season.

But there were more important considerations with the First World War under way. With the first Battle of Ypres ongoing and the horrific loss of UK lives, McCartney was encouraged by the government to help recruitment through Tynecastle. It was announced by Sir George McCrae, colonel of the 16th Scots Unit, at the club on 25 November 1914 that 11 Hearts players had voluntarily enlisted for service, making the Jambos the first British club to be involved in such a gesture *en masse*.

Two followed the next day to bring the total of Hearts' 'soldier footballers' up to 16. They were largely all in Colonel McCrae's battalion, which was mainly made up of sportsmen. Seven Hearts players died in service during the conflict – James Boyd, Duncan Currie, Ernest Ellis and Henry Wattie on the Somme, Jimmy Speed at the Battle of Loos, John Allan in action in the French village of Roeux, and Tom Gracie passed of leukaemia in 1915. Several survivors were unable to resume at the level they had reached due to physical and mental ailments.

The memorial clock tower was unveiled in Haymarket, Edinburgh, on 9 April 1922 with Robert Munro, the Scottish Secretary of State, telling over 30,000 in attendance, 'Hearts had shown on the battlefield that courage, resource, skill, endurance, dash and daring that made them famous on the football field. Thank God for men like the Hearts players who fell in the morning of their days and saved the British people from destruction.' The battalion was inducted in the Scottish Football Hall of Fame in 2014.

The volunteers from Tyneside provided the ammunition for British Prime Minister Lord Asquith to put down an anti-football body in Parliament seeking to suspend the professional game. As the McCrae's Battalion Trust stated, 'Hearts, most notably the Hearts *players*, had saved their sport. The slings and arrows directed at football were always undeserved; but Tynecastle enlistment was the blow required to silence the critics, ensure continuation and preserve the game's good name.'

These wartime heroics were close to Mackay's heart and another reason to be proud of his club. He said, 'In the history of Hearts, the club's brave act of patriotism is considered by many to be their finest moment.'

All the on-field triumphs in the last decade of the 19th century and the first of the 20th had been the last occasions Hearts had won the league and the Scottish Cup – or anything of national significance – until Mackay happened along.

The proud headed for a fall for the Hearts, as the man himself referred to the club he loved, as it became the butt of music hall jokes due to its inability to add major silver pots to its trophy cabinet between the world wars. The closest they got to the title was in 1938 when finishing as runners-up. In the Scottish Cup they had reached the semi-finals in 1921 and 1935.

In the meantime, they built a reputation for entertaining and nuanced, if not winning, football. It helped develop a devoted fanbase for a club, comforted by the glories of the late 1800s and early 1900s. Albert Mackie said in his superb 1959 tome *The Hearts,* 'I do not believe any other football club in the world can lay claim to have aroused and retained such warmth of affection, and this from a people who do not make a practice of displaying their emotions.

'There have been seasons dispiriting enough, but the followers have always remembered the past greatness of Heart of Midlothian and been convinced that what has been can be again.

'Hearts fans take their football seriously, but not simply. They have an appetite for the subtleties of the game and do not demand that every game should have some facile "happy ending". Addicts of the "happy ending" need not follow such a club, for it is a sporting club and often unpredictable. There have been times when to follow it was as quixotic as following Bonnie Prince Charlie, and when the outsider sought an explanation in a Scotsman's romantic addiction to a lost cause.'

It appeared to some that winning wasn't everything. Mackay might have had a strong appreciation of the niceties and idealism expressed in that view, although, as we will increasingly discover, he would have zero tolerance for anything other than winning.

And it became clear even to the lovers of the beautiful game referred to by historian Mackie – both players and supporters – wouldn't mind a cup of two to go with the aesthetics.

Mackie said, 'If it is a club of players rather than pot-hunters, of sports not spoilers, neither the men on the field nor their ever-loving fans would deliberately turn their backs on the glittering prizes.

'In recent years there has been a renewed will to win, and the breaking of a 50-year hoodoo by the winning of the Scottish League Cup ushered in a series of marvellous years.'

And that taste for sweet success was illustrated in the manner of the celebrations that sparked the endorphins rushing through Mackay, his team-mates, club officials and fans.

Mackie said, 'When the League Cup came back east in October 1954, I do not think the *douce* citizens of Edinburgh had been so demonstrative since they lynched Captain Porteous of the City Guard as described in Sir Walter Scott's *Heart of Midlothian.*'

The banks had broken the day the League Cup was lifted after half a century of hurt – and water flooded the plain of glory left barren for so long.

It proved the hors d'oeuvre with number four Mackay centre stage for the second appetiser, the main course and dessert.

It was all go for Mackay on the home and professional front. And a further element was thrown in the mix when he got his call-up papers to join the army in July 1955. His country needed him, to paraphrase Lord Kitchener's First World War message heeded so bravely by Hearts' football heroes turned war heroes. It was time to do his National Service, a compulsory conscription system for physically fit UK males aged 17 to 21 to complete 18 months in an armed force. It remained in place from 1949–60 in the wake of demobilisation after the Second World War when it was deemed there was an 'urgent need to keep up high levels of military manpower in parts of the world where Britain had strong ongoing commitments – in Germany, Palestine, and India'. Not ideal for a teenager in love and trying to making his way in top-flight Scottish football.

Mackay, it was believed, might have escaped National Service altogether. He had reported to the services for a medical in June 1955 and its doctors 'wouldn't grade him' due to the ear problem sustained in South Africa in the summer of the previous year. Instead he was referred to an Edinburgh ear expert.

The following month, his call-up papers arrived and the British War Office assigned him to the Royal Engineers, so Sapper D. Mackay 23162786 reported for duty at the army's Worcester barracks on 4 August 1955, ten days before the start of the football season.

He said to the Edinburgh media, 'I didn't think I was going to be called up at all. I have a slight defect in one of my ears which made me Grade 3. But I might as well get it over with now. If I got another deferment I would just have to go at the end of the season.'

It would be the first time he had lived permanently away from 18 Glendevon Park. And 300 miles away at that. He said, 'For eight weeks I had to slog away with a number of other young men. At the time I hated it.'

But he was more fortunate than many as Hearts came to an arrangement with the government for Mackay so he could play for them at the weekend. This had the added bonus for the reluctant soldier of being able to see Isobel on Saturday evenings and have lunch at either of their family homes the following day.

He would then catch the 10pm train for an eight-hour journey to Birmingham, changing for Worcester and 'a frantic dash' to be back in camp for Monday at 8am. Mackay said, 'I lived only for the weekend. It was great because I'd miss out on all the army stuff every weekend.'

The trips to home and back were made more bearable with the company of Celtic player Eric Smith, who was stationed in the same barracks. From home, Smith, already on the train which he had picked up in Glasgow, used to tie a scarf in his club's green and white colours around the door handle of his compartment so Mackay could find him after getting on at Waverley Station, Edinburgh.

Isobel said, 'They used to get money to pay for a sleeper, but could sleep on the long seats in their compartment and keep the money they had saved.'

The routine was maintained for the 14 months he spent in the West Midlands cathedral city of Worcester before he finished his military stint in Hampshire at Farnborough, close to the home of the British Army in Aldershot, over 400 miles from the Scottish capital.

Mackay looked back appreciatively on his army experience. He said, 'The war was finished so the only fighting I did was to get home at weekends to play for Hearts. The forces used to help. I enjoyed it. You're not fighting so there's nothing to worry about; you ain't going to get killed. But you get the same discipline and treatment as everybody else, footballer or not. Do something wrong, you get the same stick and have to abide by the same rules. I was always frightened to go out of line in case they said, "Hey, you ain't going home this weekend." That would have killed me. I've never been a rebel.

'I got off lightly. There was no war to worry about and I had a sergeant major in the Royal Engineers who was a football nut. He used to make sure I got home every weekend to play for Hearts, provided I got him a ticket. I also played for my regiment in midweek and was as fit as a fiddle. I did more running about on the pitch than square-bashing.'

And he kept some company on those army pitches. There was Cliff Jones, a Welsh winger from Swansea who was to play alongside Mackay in Spurs' Double-winners in 1961.

Mackay said, 'I can remember thinking he would undoubtedly break through in the game … Cliff played dazzlingly.'

The feeling was mutual. Jones said, 'The first time I came across Dave was in the army when we were doing our National Service. Straight away I thought "what a player, what a character".'

Manchester United trio Duncan Edwards and Eddie Colman – along with future Old Trafford skipper Maurice Setters – were also team-mates in the forces.

Edwards and Colman were two of the much-lauded Busby Babes who made up much of a young, talented team put together by United manager Matt Busby, who was to be knighted for his contribution to the game.

Edwards, only 18 and already an England international, was reckoned to be destined to develop into the greatest player Britain had ever produced, and Colman seemed on a similar journey. But they both lost their lives with 21 others in the 1958 Munich air disaster, when the United party's plane crashed on a third attempt to take off from a slush-covered runway while returning from eliminating Red Star Belgrade and reaching the semi-finals of the European Cup.

Mackay said, 'For people of my generation, it is one of the tragic public events that form desperately sad milestones along the path of our lives. Munich, Kennedy, Aberfan, Dunblane – the names themselves are enough to re-ignite the emotions felt at the time.

'Duncan was an exceptional talent. He displayed a football talent beyond his years … He [Colman] was flamboyant and full of confidence, and he was only a boy.

'As a very raw Scottish footballer, I used to admire them all; but it was Eddie Colman who impressed me most. But for the Munich air disaster

I think Colman would have rated among the finest footballers of his time. I consider myself fortunate that I once played with so distinguished a player.'

Jones added, 'What a team we had. Bobby Charlton [a "Babe" who survived Munich] was also with us.'

Mackay believed his time in the forces was 'among the more important moments in my life'. He said, 'A footballer has to discipline himself … In the army, although I possibly did not like it at the time, I learned to appreciate the true value of tidiness, planning, and discipline, and I like to think my two years in the services weren't a waste of taxpayers' money. It taught me too the true value of comradeship and team spirit in a world where so many people prefer to think only of themselves.

'I do believe that National Service made a man of you; if we still operated such a system today, I think we'd have far fewer problems than we currently do. Besides all the discipline stuff – and people react to that in different ways – if nothing else it took young men off the street at a time when their physical and mental development dictated they would be most predisposed to getting themselves into trouble. It was a mistake to abandon it. Such an opinion is generally scoffed at nowadays, but just because a view is not fashionable or politically correct, does that mean it should not be aired? I hope not.'

In the meantime, love was in the air. Mackay and Isobel had taken a break in the Channel Islands in July 1955, just before he began National Service. It was a learning-about-life experience for the couple.

They booked a hotel on Jersey. Mackay might have become more worldly on the South African tour after completing his first full season as a first-team regular with Hearts, but he was still inexperienced in how certain things were done. Neither he nor Isobel had dealt directly with hotels. The Scottish Schools' FA and Hearts – in St Pancras, north London, and South Africa respectively – had organised such accommodation for him on the only previous times he had stayed in one. On this occasion, the 'item' discovered budgeting for their two rooms could present problems. They appreciated that money was tight so opted to stay in on their last night on the holiday island rather than splash out on seeing a show. But they didn't appreciate how tight. The few shillings saved from their parsimoniousness was needed to complete payment of the bill when they reported to reception the following morning. It was all they had, bar four shillings put aside for food on the return journey to Edinburgh.

It left them with empty pockets on arrival by train – and they still had a taxi ride to complete the journey. Mackay hit on the idea of persuading the driver to stop off at Glendevon Park so his mum could pay the fare. He said, 'As this happened in the early hours of the morning, you can imagine she did not feel altogether pleased with me.'

Isobel said, 'Mum had to pay the taxi driver! Ran out of money? Yeh, well, he was buying presents for everybody to take home. He bought me – I've still got some of it – a necklace, earrings, brooch, bracelet and a ring all to match. When we got to Kings Cross eventually we had a packet of crisps each and two oranges. That's all we had from Kings Cross to Edinburgh.

'He treated me well. I never had that much money. He was always treating me.'

Mackay stepped the relationship up to its most committed level after beginning his basic training with the army, and he proposed to Isobel outside Murrayfield.

Isobel said, 'I met David at the station after he'd done his first weeks of National Service. He was in his army uniform. We walked home to where we were staying and were passing Murrayfield when he stopped and said, "I think we should get engaged."'

The wedding took place at the City Chambers Registrar's Office in the central Haymarket district of Edinburgh on 12 December 1955. Isobel said, 'It was close family. Not a big wedding.'

Dave's brother Tommy was best man. Tommy agreed that Dave was a 'snappy dresser' and it is understood our subject looked smart on his big day, although the wedding pictures which would prove it have remained under wraps, with Isobel far from impressed with them.

But Tommy remembered when he once had to help his brother out in the clothing department. He said, 'It was when we were both signed at Hearts. I was invited to a Hearts dance. I'd signed ahead of David and been earning a wage of £3 a week with them for about six months – which was a lot of money then. David hadn't done so I bought him a suit so he and Isobel could come to the dance. Quite amazing when you think about it. They met at a dance, of course, and so did our parents.'

Hearts' annual ball doubled as a wedding reception in the evening. It was a union blessed at Our Lady of Loretto in Musselburgh, near Isobel's home village of Whitecraig. Dave said, 'It was a wonderful day that we will always treasure.'

The couple saved up for a deposit to buy a property, while also going on Whitecraig council's housing list. When they reached the top of the list they opted to rent a place in Whitecraig, prompting Mackay to splash out on a new car. He said, 'I think it may have been the first time that Isobel worried about my impetuousness.'

Isobel said, 'We were looking for a house in Edinburgh near to David's mum and dad in Glendevon Park. In the meantime, our name came up for a brand new council house in Whitecraig. I thought, "David will not want to live here." But he said, "Well, why not?"

'We had lived with my mum after we got married, with David still doing his National Service. When he came out he had four driving lessons, passed his test and bought a brand new car, a pale blue Hillman Imp RSS 168. Not many people had new cars in those days. Was it with the money we were saving up for deposit for our own house? Probably. We'd have bought a flat probably. But it solved a lot of problems as he was able to drive to Tynecastle from Whitecraig [close to a 15-mile trip]. And we stayed at Whitecraig until we moved to Tottenham.'

Isobel, who gave birth to the couple's first two of four children, David and Derek, while living in the house, added, 'The natives all took to him. David was like one of them. Our house was right next to a bowling green. He was made honorary president of the Whitecraig Bowling Club! He used to go down occasionally. It was all good.'

Derek said, 'We were in Scotland when we were little but I've got no memory of that. My earliest memories are from when we moved to London, living at Southgate and then Enfield.'

10

Auld Reekie 'blew its dignified top'

DAVE MACKAY missed the opening five matches due to his army commitments as Hearts began their defence of the League Cup in the 1955/56 season.

He eventually got his campaign going in the last qualifier, which produced a 4-0 victory over East Fife, although he could do nothing about the ending of his side's hold on the crown in a two-legged quarter-final loss against reigning league champions Aberdeen, who went on to lift the trophy with Bobby Wishart in the side as they defeated St Mirren in the final at Hampden.

Hearts had strengthened with the £2,500 signing of Raith Rovers full-back Bobby Kirk, who initially replaced Tam McKenzie.

But it was wingers Ian Crawford, a free transfer from Hamilton Academical in 1954, and Johnny Hamilton, signed from Junior football, plus reserve and ex-Newtongrange Star forward Alex Young, who gave the first team bigger shots in the arm as Mackay and Co. cranked up a league title challenge. Hearts were joint second with Rangers and two points behind leaders Celtic with a game in hand by the turn of the year.

Mackay was certainly taken with Young, who went on to glories with the club and then Everton, where he was dubbed 'The Golden Vision' by Mackay's Tottenham captain Danny Blanchflower.

Mackay said, 'Alex Young, a waspish centre-forward, bagged his first hat-trick in only his third first-team appearance [in the 4-0 win over East Fife in which Mackay began his season]. Like me, Alex had served his apprenticeship with Newtongrange Star and had done his time in the reserves. For a centre-forward he was small, but I've seen him out-jump centre-halves who had nearly a foot on him, and then there was the uncanny way he would hang in the air and wait for the ball to come to his head rather than the other way round. It was almost supernatural. With hair like flakes of gold pasted to his head, his sparkling eyes and classic bone structure, there was something of the Roman emperor about him.'

Unless Tommy Walker could accommodate him and the Terrible Trio in the same forward line, Alex threatened the status quo.

Hearts' unbeaten 1955/56 league run extended to 18 in the new year to give a real hope of the championship trophy ending up at Tynecastle.

But by then the Jam Tarts had twin targets for the year with an historic campaign in the Scottish Cup running alongside their title dreams.

The double proved illusory as the wheels came off their league campaign and they had to settle for third, although a 7-2 win over Raith Rovers in the final fixture brought their total goals to just one short of three figures, reflecting the eye for goal which would help the side succeed two seasons later.

But the shiny cup ended up making its way into the Gorgie trophy room; the domestic knockout prize that mattered the most in Scotland, like the FA Cup in England, for its tradition.

It was like that old adage, 'You wait ages and then two come along at once.' Yes, it is most related to buses, albeit in Edinburgh, London, Derby, Swindon or wherever else Our Hero ended up being based, but it was applicable to Hearts and their 'lucky mascot' Mackay in 1955/56 when the oldest national football trophy in the world was captured for Tynecastle.

The League Cup at the beginning of the previous season was the first major prize won by Hearts since the Scottish Cup in 1906. And just one campaign later the knockout cup presented to the winners of the competition since 1874 was back in their possession.

And the displays of Mackay, named man of the match in the decider, were big reasons why 50 years of hanging about ended.

He was being developed as a future captain by Tommy Walker, and was leader in all but name, and displayed maturity beyond his years as he became an integral part of the half-back engine room, sticking out his chest and helping roar Hearts to cup glory throughout the campaign.

The first steps were comfortable as they dismissed Forfar Athletic and Stirling Albion, amassing eight goals without reply at Tynecastle.

But the next – for a place in the semi-finals – was a big one and perhaps the biggest on current form, in the shape of Rangers.

Their mighty opponents from the west of Scotland had been unbeaten in 15 league matches, while they had also defeated a powerful Aberdeen and seen off Dundee to earn their visit to Tynecastle. The Ibrox outfit were rated by the bookmakers as favourites to take the trophy but Hearts were no shrinking violets themselves having gone 14 league games on the bounce with a reverse when they entertained the 'Gers on 3 March 1956.

Jambos followers were concerned that the draw had produced such opposition. But Tommy Walker was not. His attitude was simple – to be the best you have to beat the best.

And it proved to be a beating beyond the ken of those worried Hearts fans in front of almost 50,000. Mackay, alongside Freddie Glidden and John Glidden 'rolled back the [Rangers] forward line'. Young and Crawford were a constant threat out wide with the former laying on the opening goal of a 4-0 win for the latter. Equally menacing were the Terrible Trio of two-goal Willie Bauld, Alfie Conn, who netted one, and Jimmy Wardhaugh, who made merry against their stunned visitors.

The pulling power of the competition was reflected as Hearts were held to a goalless draw by Raith Rovers in the semi-final on 24 March before Kirk's former employers were dismissed 3-0 in the replay thanks to goals from Wardhaugh (two) and Crawford. The two encounters at Easter Road over just four days attracted a total of 112,681 spectators. In both games, the Mackay–Glidden–Cumming axis was solid as Wardhaugh (two) and Crawford were on target in the second, while the lively Hamilton, in for the injured Conn, laid on two.

It was estimated that as many as 60,000 Hearts supporters journeyed by road, rail and tram from east to west for the final against Celtic on Saturday, 21 April 1956. The efforts of the Maroons had excited Edinburgh and an astonishing 132,840 packed out Hampden Park that sunny day; a number that included survivors of the club's 1896 cup winners in Alex King, who had scored two in that Victorian-era triumph, left-back James Mirk and right-winger Bob McLaren. Mackay described the figure as 'incredible'.

It was more than attended arguably the greatest match of all time when Real Madrid defeated Eintracht Frankfurt 7-3 to lift the 1960

European Cup in front of a UEFA final record attendance 127,621 at the ground; more than the official attendance of 126,047 for the first FA Cup Final at Wembley in 1923, featuring Bolton Wanderers and West Ham United plus a policeman on a white horse clearing pitch invaders; more than a third greater than when England defeated West Germany at Wembley to lift the World Cup in 1966.

Mind you, their opponents had played in front of more in 1937 when Celtic pipped Aberdeen 2-1 before 147,365 in the Scottish Cup Final at Hampden. And furthermore their manager Jimmy McGrory, the leading top-flight British goalscorer with 550 career goals, played at centre-forward on that pre-war day which set attendance records as the biggest for a domestic match in Europe and a national cup final in the world.

Interestingly, though, Hearts manager Tommy Walker played at inside-forward for Scotland when they defeated England 3-1 in front of Hampden's attendance record of 149,547 just a week earlier.

Hearts, clearly buoyed by the upcoming cup decider, had been able to boost the confidence of the faithful as well as themselves by sinking Falkirk 8-3 at Tynecastle five days earlier.

Mackay felt his team had stability and an 'elusive' blend of youth and experience playing an attractive, all-action style, with the likes of the Terrible Trio having reached their apogee. Moreover, it was the wing-half's belief his outfit had an indefatigable faith minus overconfidence in themselves and each other that had been instilled by Walker.

He also drew strength from the fact the Jambos had beaten and drawn with Celtic earlier in the season, plus their opponents had been in erratic form coming in to the final. Mackay considered them less of a threat than Rangers. He said, 'We were the underdogs, but we knew we shouldn't be. Our team had reached a wonderful stage.'

Overall, he was in a positive mood. He said, 'We were always confident of winning when Conn, Bauld and Wardhaugh were playing. With those three playing, you knew you were going to score goals and that gave you confidence.

'It didn't matter whether you were playing Rangers or Celtic or Hibs.'

He added to Mike Aitken in *London Hearts*, 'Alfie was a brilliant player with a powerful shot who could score goals for fun. He was a member of the Terrible Trio and you couldn't ask for a better threesome

… Alfie was a good pal of mine and used to visit me in England when he moved into sales after he gave up football.'

And Mackay had an extra motivation to be on the winning side as his squaddie friend Eric Smith, stationed with him in Worcester, was in the Celtic line-up.

He said, 'I was too scared of losing the '56 cup final because I didn't want to go back to camp and listen to Eric!'

Celtic, it has been suggested, inadvertently helped their opponents in the eyes of their supporters. Out injured were Jock Stein, who became the club's most famous manager, and key midfielder Bobby Collins, in at the start of the Don Revie revolution at Leeds United. And it was considered that McGrory's final selection produced 'unexpected changes' with 'several players being played out of position'.

But Hearts were aware of their rivals' battling spirit to do well in the competition but even so, the Jam Tarts, unchanged from their previous two matches, had plenty of reasons to be cheerful.

Bobby Parker had been troubled with a cartilage problem in the second half of the season. But Tam Kenzie, one of the League Cup heroes, provided more than just reliable cover for the captain's absence. The 33-year-old came in at left-back as Bobby Kirk switched to Parker's right-back spot with goalkeeper Willie Duff behind them and the steel of the half-back line of Mackay, new skipper Glidden, and Cumming immediately in front.

Mackay, who had lost half a stone in getting fitter and fitter, developed a full-blooded wing-half partnership with Cumming. It might have differed from the one he was to have with Danny Blanchflower at Spurs, with his Irish captain providing a cerebral rather than physical foil, but it was nonetheless effective. In fact, he revealed the extent of the pair's preparation which provided a daunting physical presence to opponents with the temerity to challenge them.

He said, 'In training we endeavoured to toughen up one another further by charging at each other from a distance and then colliding with our shoulders and chests. There was not a ball in sight. The other lads said it was like two fighting stags locking horns.'

Ian Crawford, the former Hibs youth player, and the fast-developing and versatile Alex Young provided the youth and zip out wide with that Terrible Trio a three-pronged strike force in their prime, with Conn having had the opportunity to build up his match fitness after missing the semi-final replay with a shoulder injury.

The Hearts party was given a stirring send-off by fans as they boarded the midday special to Glasgow at Waverley Station, named after the Sir Walter Scott novels with a 60m monument of the writer towering over it.

The players received a sprig of 'lucky' white heather from Tommy Walker – given to him by a group of blind Aberdeen supporters at Pittodrie a fortnight earlier – before crossing the barrier on to the platform.

And when seated on their train they were presented with maroon carnations for each of their button holes. The flowers had been donated by the Former Hearts Players Club, who had to sort an 11th-hour mix-up with the florists who had originally delivered a spray rather than individual blooms.

And for extra good fortune there was a human-sized teddy bear called Davy Crockett, which was a mascot loaned to them by a guest during a recent holiday break in Crieff, a market town in Perth and Kinross.

Fellow passengers lined up to cheer them out of Queen Street Station on their arrival in Glasgow before they boarded a coach with police motorcycle outriders to Hampden and the sanctity of their dressing room.

And the *Edinburgh News* revealed how the players relaxed there before kick-off. Groundsman Matt Chalmers, so influential in Mackay's formative football career, and injured captain Bobby Parker entertained them with a double act. Chalmers donned an old frock coat, a bowler hat and a false nose and glasses while Parker, who lifted the 1954 League Cup, wore an Hawaiian dancing female's hula hula skirt.

Then it was showtime on the field as Mackay and his mates in maroon got the call to emerge from their Hampden House of Fun to the deafening roar from those who had travelled from *Auld Reekie*.

It was in the day when football shirts looked like everyday shirts. Hearts' maroon tops had white collars – worn unbuttoned to the chest – and cuffs and white shorts. Their socks, of course, were maroon and topped off with white. Mackay's shirt had the number four emblazoned in white on his back.

How proud Isobel, his mum – braving it this time – and dad, must have felt as they caught sight of their chief focus of attention. He was one of five Newtongrange Star graduates, along with team-mates 'King'

Willie Bauld, Freddie Glidden and, of course, Alex Young, plus Celtic's Mike Haughney.

And their pride and joy did not let them or anyone else connected with him down on a bright afternoon in stark contrast to the *dreich* conditions on the team's visit to the home of Scottish football the previous season. He earned the man of the match tag by spreading his influence between the attack and defence; stonewalling Celtic and marauding forward when the occasion demanded in harness with Glidden and Cumming.

The final sprung into life after a scrappy start when Crawford had a drive from a Wardhaugh pass kept out by Celtic stopper Dick Beattie after 17 minutes. Then the lively Crawford put Hearts ahead with a 20-yard angled blast from a ball by Conn – 'full of dash and dazzle' – three minutes later.

But Mackay and his team-mates were forced to defend as Celtic, despite having the wind in their faces, twice went close through Neil Mochan and Haughney. And when the Jambos went forward they came up against a solid rearguard organised by skipper Bobby Evans, the Scotland international. Young struggled to get on the ball.

To make matters worse, Cumming was left with blood dripping from a cut left eyebrow in a clash of heads with Willie Fernie, as they jumped for the ball with Mackay just before the interval. The left-half nicknamed Iron Man had to be helped off by Hearts trainer John Harvey and assistant Don McLeod, with his arm around each of their shoulders as his prone opponent received on-the-pitch treatment after being knocked out. A minute later, referee Bobby Davidson blew the half-time whistle.

It might have been a temptation for Hearts to abandon their on-the-floor, attacking, passing game and concentrate on building an impenetrable wall and settle for what they had. But Mackay disclosed that Walker was having none of that as he spoke to the players at half-time in measured tones. Mackay said, 'Tommy Walker [was calm and] told us not to make the mistake of just defending. I expect we had been doing this subconsciously. I, for one, was terrified at the prospect of losing our lead.'

It was a well-founded fear – and not just because of the sledging he would get from Eric Smith – with just a goal separating the teams and Cumming injured in an era when no substitutes were allowed.

But brave Cumming resumed a minute after the interval, sporting a plaster after having three stitches inserted into the wound and carrying a sponge.

Cumming performed as stoutly as ever, even when his plaster came off and the stitches loosened, forcing him to stem the blood flow down his face with the sponge following each 'coming together'. He remained unbowed despite a couple of 'hard knocks' and continued heading the ball to the end without any outside sign of discomfort, a quality reflected by Mackay later in his career, although Cumming confessed in the *Edinburgh News*, 'The final whistle was never such sweet music.' As Mackie, emphasising Cumming's courage, put it in *The Hearts*, 'Blood doesn't show on a maroon jersey.'

Hearts, heeding the words of their manager, got on the front foot and doubled their advantage. Crawford, with the aid of Bauld and Young, gave the Jambos breathing space when he netted his second three minutes after the restart.

Celtic halved Hearts' advantage after 53 minutes when goalkeeper Willie Duff was unable to retain the ball after a Haughney shoulder charge – another thing you were able to do back then – and the Bhoy scored despite an effort from Mackay to block. Any jangling nerves in the Maroons' camp were settled when Bauld headed on to Conn who thumped the ball into the top of the net ten minutes from time.

Hearts had matched their opponents' revered fighting qualities and displayed their ability to play the beautiful game beautifully. The Jambos had secured revenge after Celtic had defeated them in their last Scottish Cup Final appearance 49 years earlier.

The inspiration of Mackay, with his surging runs forward which saw him fizz one effort inches wide, Cumming, and the two goals by Crawford were fundamental to the success.

Mackay said, 'It was a great day. John Cumming went off when he split his head and these days players would stay off but John was a hard man and he came back on and just carried on.

'Not many harder than John Cumming, believe me. He's still hard to this day. And against Celtic he split his eye open. Just got it stitched up. Come back and he was the first one to get up and head the ball. There's others who think, "I can't head it, I've split my eye open." He didn't care. He was up there. A brilliant player, he was.'

Perhaps Mackay had a crystal ball and was thinking about how he would come to play on despite a fractured skull. But there was no question how high he estimated Cumming's display that day. Mackay, who played in a testimonial for Cumming at Tynecastle on 11 May 1980, said, 'I was happy to see that a number of national newspapers had named me as man of the match, but I felt that honour should have gone to John Cumming, who cut his head badly in the first half after a clash of heads … He had continued to play [with] blood streaming down his face … after the wound opened up again.'

Mackay was also relieved that Celtic winger Charlie Tully had a quiet game. He said, 'Outside of Hearts, he was my hero … a legend at Parkhead … giving value for money with his impudent play and a wonderful box of tricks … similarities to Jimmy Johnstone.'

But Mackay was unequivocal about the result. He added, 'The reality was that Celtic did not play well and were never a serious threat.'

Celtic captain Bobby Evans said at the time, 'I'm disappointed, of course, but I'm glad Hearts have broken their duck.'

Edinburgh 'blew her dignified top' and 'her reserved citizens flipped their immaculate lids', to quote Mackie, as an overall estimated 150,000 in Scotland's capital celebrated the iconic achievement. The outlying towns and villages joined in as the team coach detoured – after being given a sporting send-off from Celtic supporters lining the streets outside Hampden – to where the players grew up en route to *Auld Reekie*. One visit saw it turn off the A8 main road from Glasgow to Edinburgh for Blackburn, a small West Lothian town for the sake of former resident Freddie Glidden, the team captain.

Mackie said in *The Hearts*, 'His [Glidden's] mother came out to the cottage door to see the cup held proudly by her son, and his father threw a sprig of heather into the vehicle.'

Eventually Mackay, the other players, Walker and the remaining staff, swapped vehicles on the western outskirts of the city at Maybury for a floodlit, open-topped double-decker supplied by Scottish Omnibuses, decked out in maroon with the legends 'Hearts Special' on its front and 'Hearts are trumps' and 'Well done, Hearts' on its sides for the final leg of the journey into the city centre lined with thousands. Glidden held the cup aloft and Crawford its lid as Mackay and the others smiled and waved at the well-wishers. It was a more orderly procession than the previous season due to the police having learned from the more 'chaotic' scenes after the League Cup win by putting extra bobbies on shift.

With the floodlit Edinburgh Castle providing a dramatic backdrop, the crowd greeted them on their arrival in the city centre's West End as the bus crossed the North Bridge on to Princes Street and into South Charlotte Street for the victory dinner at the Charlotte Rooms, taking a couple of bows from its balcony to the baying crowd. Mackay said in his autobiography, 'The crowd cheered us as we crawled into Princes Street again but this time there were even more people and they were even more jubilant … this time I was careful with my alcohol intake.'

It was in the week that American actress Grace Kelly married Prince Rainier in Monaco. And the Lord Provost, Sir John Banks, the guest of honour, said in the media, 'This has been a great week for big events. There was the Grace Kelly wedding and now Hearts have won the cup. I leave it to you to decide the most important.'

Hearts manager Walker said, 'It was the greatest day of my life.' And, like the celebrations the season before, Hearts were also given a civic reception. Edinburgh had cup fever.

Congratulatory messages poured in but Walker selected one which 'probably touched' Mackay and all involved in the triumph the most. It was from the Hearts FC Blind Party – and sent, with a translation, in Braille. Walker, a spiritual individual, said in the media, 'Maybe we should do what we did before with the League Cup – invite them to come along and handle it by just tracing the markings on it with their sensitive fingers.'

Hearts reached out to their supporters in several ways, including paying a visit to fan George Scott, who had been at Hampden to ensure he had seen all five of the club's Scottish Cup wins.

The future looked very bright. Former Hearts and Scotland goalkeeper Jack Harkness said in the media, 'Never was it brighter with peace and dignity reigning in the boardroom [the lack of which was one reason proffered for the long wait for trophies]. With reserve power equalled by no other club in the country. With a wages scale and an automatic benefit system … which would guarantee a most contented atmosphere among the players.'

11

A dream come true

DAVE MACKAY was making a big impression at Hearts. He had already developed a list of positive characteristics which had coalesced to provide the X-factor in turning a team of nearly men into winners. They were recognised by Scottish Cup-winning captain Freddie Glidden, his half-back partner on the road to back-to-back trophy successes in consecutive seasons.

Glidden said, 'You would never know when Davie was hurt as he kept going all the time. He was non-stop and quite a character. He was always there to help. When Davie wasn't playing, you often wondered what was wrong with the team as he was such a huge asset. Playing alongside him was just great.'

But the best was yet to come. The 1956/57 season might not have produced more silverware to dust and polish for the Tynecastle trophy cabinet but the team proved not too dusty as their potential glared in the faces of those who viewed the Old Firm of Celtic and Rangers as the only clubs in Scotland worthy of consideration. Hearts were no support act to the Glasgow giants.

Mackay might have been a two-time cup winner but was still only 21 going into the season. Yet, despite his lack of experience in terms of the number of matches played, he was at the root of the Jambos' growing confidence that they could dominate their domestic league, a vine to strangle the life out of rivals with their solid defence and free-scoring attack while putting on an overall style which entertained. The former Glendevon Park street footballer could already dip his toe into either area of the pitch, provide steel at the back and panache further forward, at the appropriate time, while helping his side thrill its support.

He was part of a flying start in the league with the nine remaining outfield players from the Scottish Cup triumph, with Wilson Brown replacing goalkeeper Willie Duff, who had National Service duties to fulfil. The Maroons sealed nine out of a possible ten points in their opening five fixtures after a disappointing League Cup exit in the qualifying group.

The Jambos lost Alfie Conn to a broken jaw and Duff, who returned for four games, went back to the services then signed for Charlton Athletic. But with promoted reserve Brown and 17-year-old Gordon Marshall sharing goalkeeping duties they were able to sustain decent league form and with it a title challenge from October to April.

They were top with 13 points from eight, one ahead of Motherwell, and extended their lead to three by the end of the year. The Steelmen's challenge softened as Rangers threatened Hearts' dominance.

The Jambos entertained the 'Gers on what was billed as a virtual championship decider in front of 49,000 at Tynecastle on 13 April 1957 and were pipped 1-0 by a team who had also ended their Scottish Cup defence in the fifth round two months earlier. It left Rangers just two points down on front-running Hearts with two games in hand.

The Jam Tarts finished their season with two clean-sheet victories, with Mackay netting their final goal of the campaign against Aberdeen, but Rangers won their final four matches to claim the crown by two points. Yet it had been Hearts' best season since they had last finished top 60 years earlier.

Mackay said, 'The season was not a disappointment, though. Morale was still high. We had played great and rewarding football. We had nearly won the championship by playing high-scoring, high-octane football. The forward line of Wardhaugh, Young, Bauld, Conn and Crawford was irresistible. Tommy Walker explained calmly that patience is a virtue and that the championship would surely come.'

* * *

Mackay's increasing influence on the Hearts team caught the eye of the Scottish selectors. He was named captain of his country for an under-23 international against England at Ibrox on 26 February 1957 and again he was up against his nemesis Johnny Haynes, who had become a full international.

Mackay had mixed feelings. He said, 'This was a tremendous honour although I must admit a slight shiver went down my spine as I contemplated meeting Johnny Haynes again.'

His side, which also included club-mates Alex Young, goalscorer Ian Crawford and Johnny Hamilton, battled to a creditable 1-1 draw against a strong England outfit which also included his future Derby manager Brian Clough at Ibrox.

But Mackay was upset when described in sections of the press as being 'dirty' in marking Haynes. He said, 'The match was a hard, physical one. I had stuck to Johnny like glue and was uncompromising in my tackling generally. But then I always was. The referee had seen no reason to caution or discipline me in any way. I was upset by the coverage, having only experienced thus far a sympathetic, supportive and appreciative press in Scotland.'

But Haynes defended Mackay. He stated, 'I wish every player I met tackled as fairly as Dave Mackay. I thought he had an excellent game. He got stuck in but always went for the ball. I am amazed that there should be any quibbling about his play. For my part, he is a hard tackler who sets out to give everything he has got. That's his job and he did it without the slightest suggestion of unfair tactics. Anyone who says anything else is talking nonsense.'

The fourth estate has a reputation for 'building up and knocking down' public figures and Mackay clearly did not enjoy his first taste of it. Yet the call-up gave Mackay justified optimism that he might join Haynes as a full international in the not too distant future. He admitted part of that feeling was thanks to his Hearts team-mates.

Mackay said, 'When a footballer is playing for a successful side he invariably produces soccer of a higher standard even if he may not be quite as good as his colleagues. That possibly applied to me, inexperienced as I had been.'

The end result was his inclusion in the senior Scotland squad for two World Cup qualifiers with a friendly squeezed between the two.

Mackay made up the numbers as he watched Jackie Mudie and Bobby Collins score as their country overcame Switzerland 2-1 in the first in Basel on 19 May 1957.

Three days later he played the same supporting role as Collins with two and Mudie were again on target as Scotland secured a 3-1 friendly victory over West Germany in Stuttgart.

But on 26 May 1957 he got his opportunity to pull on his country's shirt in a full international for the first time. And he was in at the deep end against a Spain side featuring Real Madrid duo Alfredo Di Stéfano and Francisco Gento, two of the original Galacticos, in a World Cup qualifier in front of 90,000 at the Bernabéu.

Forward Di Stéfano, rated the best player in world football by Geoffrey Green, the esteemed football correspondent of *The Times* who was to rate Mackay 'a giant at Spurs', and flying winger Gento were en route to turning Real into serial European Cup winners. And on their home patch, with the assistance of Barcelona superstar Laszlo Kubala, it all underlined the task was a daunting one for a 22-year-old Mackay and his team.

There were two trains of thought over his selection. One was he was being thrown in over his head, given his inexperience against continental opposition, although he had home international experience. Another theory was that Scotland needed to blood their promising youngsters to enable them to have a better chance of coming good in the 1958 World Cup finals in Sweden the following summer.

Mackay and Bobby Evans came in for the legendary George Young and fellow stalwart Ian McColl as the only changes from the side that rolled over the Swiss.

It was the omission of captain and centre-half Young, the first Scot to secure 50 caps and understood to be on his final tour with his country, that got folk hot under the collar.

It mattered little that Mackay was effectively replacing McColl at number four while the experienced Evans was taking over the number five shirt from Young.

It was enough to be involved in a decision which ended a great career prematurely, albeit by just one match.

Mackay needed to pull at least a couple of rabbits out of the hat to appease Young's supporters. Unfortunately, he was unable to produce one with a disappointing full international debut as his side slumped 4-1 against the hosts with future Hearts winger Gordon Smith providing the lone consolation goal for the visitors. Even the encouragement and advice of the sporting Young failed to help his performance.

Mackay was stunned to be picked, despite showing promise in the Scotland under-23s and an appearance, in March, in a 3-2 win for the Scottish League XI against an English League team containing Duncan Edwards and Tom Finney at Ibrox. He dreamed like every other Scottish footballer of playing for the senior international team but thought he had been taken on tour purely for the experience.

But the dream became a reality when Evans conveyed the news after knocking on the door and then entering Mackay's room at the Phillip II Hotel in El-Escorial as the young player soaked in a soapy bath.

In an instant he realised the shock decision by a faceless committee – with no manager to take the buck – to exclude a 'genuine Scottish hero' would go down like a lead balloon.

His own touring party were divided on the wisdom of tinkering with a winning formula. If it ain't broke don't fix it seemed to be the mantra. After all, Scotland had won two qualifiers on the bounce, starting with a 4-2 home win over Spain, with an unchanged line-up.

Some felt it reckless, and disrespectful to both Young and McColl, while others ascribed to the long-term view of getting a young player ready for Sweden. The media and the fans were generally not best pleased.

It was the selectors rather than Mackay who got the flak from the fourth estate. Under the headline 'This wasn't fair to Dave Mackay', a scribe wrote, 'The dice was loaded against Mackay, particularly when he entered the arena in the company of mates downcast by the omission of their captain. Mackay had a poor game but was that not to be expected? I accuse the selectors of making a first-class blunder in playing Mackay after dropping Young. If they had included the Ranger [Young] they could have trusted him to advise the Tynecastle youngster. Instead we found Davie on the day, because of the circumstances, out of his depth and swimming in a sea of bewilderment. But I don't blame him for the failure. The responsibility for that lies solely with the selectors.'

Mackay himself was self-critical after ignoring the advice of Bobby Evans prior to kick-off. He said, 'Bobby Evans, a football-wise character, knew that I enjoyed nothing more than a hard sliding tackle, so he warned me that such tactics would be asking for trouble against the Spaniards. "Keep on your feet all the time, Dave," he said, but once out on the park, with 100,000 Spaniards roaring their heads off, I forgot all about Evans's advice, and not for the first time, played very badly indeed.

I couldn't have tackled a hot dinner on that showing … I put my whole heart into the game, but against magnificent footballers of their calibre it was not good enough.

'The fact I was remotely connected with the affair [Young and McColl's axing] embarrassed me, and what should have been a dream match became something of a nightmare, with people on either side constantly making remarks which I thought were in bad taste, no matter what one felt about the unsatisfactory ending of George Young's wonderful international career. It was typical of George that, just before I went on to the field, he should draw me to one side, wish me luck and pass on advice he thought would help me in my hour of trial.

'Jimmy Greaves has a record of scoring on all his debuts. I seemed to have a record of marking my debuts by playing poorly. I was terrible.'

Mackay said to the press, 'When you're capped you really think you've made the big time, that you're at the top. Well, I learned my lesson that day. I was never in the game. The speed of Di Stéfano and Kubala was fantastic. Di Stéfano is the greatest footballer I've ever seen.'

Tommy Docherty, who was to become a friend and whom he was to get the better of as Spurs captain against the Doc-managed Chelsea in the 1967 FA Cup Final, assured his team-mate he would get another opportunity.

But Mackay did not get another call for Scotland's senior side for another year – and it would come at the 1958 World Cup finals.

He managed to occupy his time in between, a period which proved among the most momentous of his long and illustrious career. Any shortcomings that he and the Scottish selectors had perceived were not in evidence as he helped Hearts to their first Scottish title in 61 years.

Mackay entered his club manager's office on Thursday, 8 August 1957. Tommy Walker had called for him. He was about to tell his young wing-half that he had appointed him team captain, making him among the youngest ever Hearts skippers.

Mackay's barrel chest was fit to burst with pride. Still three months off his 23rd birthday and only demobbed from National Service as recently as 31 July, Mackay had already reached and passed a series of unforgettable milestones in a few short years. He had signed pro for his boyhood heroes then made his first-team debut, helped the club lift its first major trophy in 48 years then end a 50-year wait to win the Scottish

Cup, while also being a part of the team that secured Hearts' best league season in six decades. He had also represented his country in a World Cup qualifier.

But being told he would skipper his beloved Hearts – by a manager building his reputation as the most legendary of Tynecastle bosses – topped the lot.

Mackay said, 'This made me more proud than anything that had gone before. Even being capped by my country. Wee Davie Mackay, captain of Hearts. Can you believe it? This was real *Roy of the Rovers* stuff and I became doubly determined to help supply the perfect ending to my personal fairytale.'

The Scottish selectors might have had their doubts about the Glendevon Park graduate after Spain rained on his and his country's parade in the World Cup qualifier. But Walker had no such qualms. He had, of course, earmarked Mackay as skipper from the beginning. Now he felt the time was right to finally give him the armband.

An Edinburgh newspaper reported the following day, 'It is a responsible position for one of his years – the wing-half indisputably has the temperament for the job. There is no inferiority complex about David who has it in him to supply urge to the more seasoned campaigners.'

Two weeks earlier the publication dismissed the championship hopes of Hearts, even though they had run Rangers so close in the previous campaign.

It stated, 'Who is going to be second to Rangers? I say Hearts. They are indeed a more attractive team to watch than the dour men from Ibrox ... but they suffer from the artistic temperament. Neither do they have yet the 'killer' touch ... Hearts won't reach the peak of success ... until they realise they have to *go go go* all the time. Until they get more steel in the team ... Miles and miles of heart trumps miles and miles of smart technique.'

Permanent get up and go, steel and heart were precisely the qualities Mackay would bring to the team that season. Qualities, if the reporter had been studying the player closely up to that point, he already possessed.

The published words, though, must have at least added one more log to the fire in the collective bellies of the Hearts. And the fire raged so fiercely that almost exactly a year after becoming his side's leader Mackay was able to experience something even more special to him, taking part in the ceremony to unfurl the championship flag at Tynecastle at the first home game of the following season, a 3-0 League Cup victory against Third Lanark. He said in *Hearts' Greatest Ever Season*, 'My finest moment yet.'

He added in *Great Tynecastle Tales*, 'I played for Scotland in vital matches and won trophies with Spurs but the greatest thrill of my professional career was unveiling the league flag at Tynecastle … more than 30,000 people were there for the final match of the season against Rangers, which we won 2-1. It was a great occasion. I remember I was lifted up on someone's shoulders and the Tynecastle crowd roared. We had a great team.

'It really was the stuff of dreams and I had been the 23-year-old skipper of the team that had done it. Wise, kind Tommy Walker said some lovely things to me; my local community made such a fuss; the supporters idolised us and the press saluted us. Everywhere I went people stopped me and shook my hand or asked for an autograph or just said, "Well done, Dave." Whoever complained about the pressures of fame? I loved every minute.'

Goalscoring prowess and flair mixed with a solidity and nerve proved vital ingredients in the trail-blazing, title-winning league campaign of 1957/58. Mackay's Hearts were close to invincible, losing just once in 34 games. Record after record was smashed as 132 goals were scored and just 29 conceded as they totted up 62 points, 13 more than dethroned Rangers.

And Mackay, leading from the front, matured sufficiently to help harden up the soft underbelly often cited for the long gaps between Hearts winning silverware. He also provided fast-developing skills on the ball and a taste for goals, bagging an impressive 12 from midfield in an impact and influence that helped earn him Scotland's Footballer of the Year award for 1958, chosen by the *Sunday Mail*'s Rex Kingsley, for his efforts.

Kingsley wrote in the 16-page programme for the event, which saw Mackay collect the Rex Statuette at the Usher Hall in Edinburgh on 15 February 1959, 'Mackay – the human football bomb – the dynamo who exploded the new Hearts into life – the youngster who snatched up the torch set alight by Bobby Parker and raced round the ranks with it until the last tatters of the old namby-pamby Hearts disintegrated and the death-or-glory Hearts burst upon the scene. The spirit of Mackay was the spirit of Hearts who took the three great honours of our game in succession – the League Cup, the Scottish Cup and the Scottish League championship.'

Tommy Walker said Mackay's 'greatest asset was his capacity for the game he loves' and 'which is much better for his being in it' as he and the other players were mentioned on a commemorative pennant for winning the championship and the subject of photographs in the *Edinburgh Evening Dispatch*'s Football Stars series.

Mackay said, 'A prestigious accolade at the time … That was a great honour and totally unexpected. I still viewed myself as a new kid on the block.'

It was clear that Hearts' championship-winning goalkeeper Gordon Marshall would agree the recognition was well deserved. Marshall said, 'We had quality through the team but Davie inspired everyone around him. He could make people play.

'I was only a youngster and Davie was a senior player, a wee bit older than me. You looked up to people like him. That's what made it so good for me, being a goalkeeper as well. He gave me advice, although we all gave each other advice.

'I remember we were a good defensive team. Only conceding 29 goals shows that. It was a side which had a good balance and good players throughout the whole of it. Jimmy Murray, Alex Young and Jimmy Wardhaugh were the main "up front" men. Alex was a good player who went to Everton and won trophies with them. But, as I said, the players who were there were quality players. It was good. Happy, happy days. Probably the best Hearts team ever? Yes, I would say that.'

It wasn't just an individual or team achievement, it was a squad achievement. Walker utilised the strength in depth of the playing staff, emphasised by the reserves helping Hearts lift their national title.

Mackay and Marshall, along with Jimmys Wardhaugh and Murray, full-back duo George Thomson, largely replacing Tam McKenzie, and Bobby Kirk, plus Alex Young who hit 24 goals, were the most regular performers. Wardhaugh and Murray top-scored with 28 and 27 goals respectively.

But half-backs John Cumming and Andy Bowman, centre-halves Freddie Glidden and Jimmy Milne, wingers Bobby Blackwood, on his return from National Service, and Ian Crawford, had a fair few outings.

Willie Bauld and Alfie Conn were limited to just 14 league appearances between them but managed a nine-goal return in a season that spelt the end of the Terrible Trio. Other supporters' favourites such as Bobby Parker, who skippered the 1954 League Cup-winning side, and Johnny Hamilton also did their bit, as did Danny Paton, another Newtongrange Star graduate, Wilson Brown, and Willies, Higgins and Lindores.

Debate was lively as Walker pondered on his team selection choice to kick off the season at Kilmarnock in the League Cup at Rugby Park on 10 August 1957. There was talk – some would say 'treasonable' talk – that the Terrible Trio were past their best and that Alex Young deserved a spot. After all, he had displayed his ability to fill in for each of them the previous season when he also wrestled Johnny Hamilton for the outside-right role. Was Gordon Marshall, at 18, too wet behind the ears to be the number one? Was the more experienced Thomas Wilson Brown a better option? John Cumming was fit after being sidelined through injury for the last few months of 1956/57, while centre-half Jimmy Milne had impressed as deputy for Freddie Glidden.

Walker decided on the team of Gordon Marshall, Bobby Kirk, Tam McKenzie, Dave Mackay, Freddie Glidden, John Cumming, Johnny Hamilton, Alfie Conn, Willie Bauld, Jimmy Wardhaugh and Ian Crawford.

The thunder rolled and the lightning flashed at Killie's Rugby Park during the cup encounter as if to announce the arrival of Mackay as the captain who would lead Hearts to the promised land.

But the powerful, showy-offy display by the elements was in stark contrast to the anti-climax of Mackay's Maroons finishing the tie sodden wet – due to the second-half rain – and beaten 2-1, underlining the theory 'Davie' had of his debuts being washouts. There was even a call in the *Edinburgh Dispatch* for the new skipper himself to be axed – along with Jimmy Wardhaugh, John Cumming, Alfie Conn and Bobby Kirk – in its wake. The judgement, it seemed, was based chiefly on 90 minutes of football. What did Tommy Walker decide for the second tie against Queen's Park at Tynecastle? He kept the same line-up as the first and Mackay's home debut as skipper was celebrated with a 9-2 romp against the oldest club in Scotland, clearly going against the Mackay Debut Nightmare scenario.

Overall, the cup campaign disappointed as the Jam Tarts failed to qualify for the knockout stage, with the Terrible Trio taking their final bow together in the third tie, a 2-2 draw at Dundee. Mackay said, 'The only slight sad note for me was that this 1958 triumph also marked the end of the Terrible Trio.'

The disappointment of the cup exit at least paved the way for a greater concentration on the league programme. By then, Tommy Walker, normally calm and measured, had given his side the 'hairdryer treatment', which helped put the players consistently on the 'goal' standard.

He lambasted them for missed chances after a 1-1 draw with eventual section winners Kilmarnock in their fourth League Cup tie. One newspaper printed, 'A fumbling *footery* maroon-clad forward line made a complete hash of dozens of good chances.'

Walker reportedly said to his team, 'What were you dreaming about? You tip-tapped about as if you were frightened of hitting the ball in case it burst. Cut it out. Open up the play. Don't shoot when you see the whites of the keeper's eyes. Shoot when you see the whites of the goalposts.'

Another day that again defied Mackay's negative 'opening night' thoughts gave cause for optimism in the tenements of Gorgie as far as title aspirations were concerned.

Mackay led his team out of the dressing room on to the Tynecastle pitch tended by his Glendevon Park neighbour Matt Chalmers for the first time in a league game on Saturday, 7 September 1957. It was against Dundee. He was followed by the likes of Alex Young, who had come in for Hamilton after the opening four games, wing-half partner Cumming, recovered from a knock, and debuting inside-right Jimmy Murray, a replacement for the injured Conn and the first indication that the Terrible Trio were not to figure as a unit throughout the campaign and forever more.

And Mackay's responsibilities as captain did not detract from his personal performance, especially when linking up with Young, who was outstanding, and Ian Crawford as the predatory home front line plundered five goals while defender Kirk converted a penalty. As Mackay and his troops shook hands with the opposition and took the applause from the 19,000 fans present and returned to the dressing room, they could reflect on a 6-0 win. 'Dee stopper Bill Brown, soon to link up with Mackay at Spurs, must have wondered what hit the visitors.

Hearts scored for fun as they won the away fixture 5-0, crushed Airdrie 7-2 at home, overcame East Fife 9-0, Queen's Park 8-0, Falkirk 9-1 and Third Lanark 7-2. They completed win doubles against neighbours Hibs and the Old Firm. The lone fly in the ointment for the buzzing Jambos came against Clyde, who seemed to have the Indian sign over Mackay when you add his poor first-team debut against them to the argument.

But Mackay proved he carried no mental scars as he netted a hat-trick in that 9-1 annihilation of the Bairns of Falkirk, who were to employ his future Spurs team-mate John White the following season, seven days later.

It was a similar story as Mackay scored in an emphatic 4-1 win over Queen's Park at Hampden as third favourites Hearts bounced back from having their hopes of a double ended by Hibs a week earlier. The Jam Tarts' neighbours had beaten them 4-3 in a third-round Scottish Cup derby epic in front of 41,668 at Tynecastle; perhaps the Hibees were still smarting from a Mackay goal sealing a 2-0 league win at Easter Road on New Year's Day?

Mackay's free-scoring Hearts put on a late show as they hit their 100th league goal of the season when Conn ploughed through the falling snow to drive home his second of the game to complete a 4-0 defeat of Motherwell at Fir Park on 22 February 1958, with all the strikes coming after the interval.

Hearts were charging away with it in the run-in but Mackay began to suffer injury woes. The wing-half scored and picked up a foot knock along with barracking from the home support for what they considered 'dirty play' in a 4-1 victory at Queen's Park on 8 March, yet was fit enough to guide Hearts to another win – at home to Queen of the South – two days later.

He then helped the Jambos complete the league double over the Bhoys in a thrilling 5-3 victory at Tynecastle on 14 March. But he suffered a thigh injury and was sidelined for the next game, which saw Clyde steal a point from Gorgie.

Mackay returned for the following fixture against Falkirk at Brockville and was troubled by his right foot, which had caused him discomfort at Hampden. He played on after treatment as the Hearts completed another 4-0 triumph, but an x-ray revealed he had cracked a bone in his foot and broken a small toe. It was the end of the season for Mackay, who had been in line to represent the Scottish League a few days later and to earn a Scotland recall back at Hampden the following month while also being all set to seal the title with his club.

But Mackay believed 'the Championship was as good as won' – with the Hearts well ahead of second-placed Rangers – as he was forced to sit out the final five fixtures.

In the first, Hearts levelled and passed Motherwell's 26-year-old record number of league goals scored in a Scottish season in a 4-1 win over Raith Rovers at rain-lashed Tynecastle on 29 March. Just 9,000 braved the wet conditions as Jimmy Murray equalled the top total of 119 after just two minutes, then Wardhaugh, with John Cumming one of two survivors of the players Davie McLean handed over to Tommy Walker, created a new high mark with a header five minutes later.

The opportunity to seal the crown was missed as the Jambos drew 2-2 at Kilmarnock on 5 April but seven days later they were champions. Love was all around in the Jam Tarts camp as they overcame St Mirren 3-2 at Love Street.

Mackay was disappointed not to have been on the pitch as his side completed a history-making season, although he joined in the post-match celebrations. He insisted that missing the final matches 'did not detract too much, such was the excitement … I knew the rest of the lads would not trip up'.

Chalmers had provided a pitch 'fit for heroes', Walker a team of heroes and Mackay an heroic captaincy. Mackay believed victory was 'pre-ordained'. He said, 'We just knew we'd score a lot of goals that year … [we] had the Terrible Trio and Jimmy Murray scoring goals for us. Willie Bauld was the perfect centre-forward and Alfie Conn had an incredible shot on him. I even scored a few myself that season. I don't think it was a surprise that we won the league … we just had so many good players. Normally you might have a team with one or two weak links; they were all brilliant players.'

Mackay earned praise for his goalscoring feats that season, topping the charts among wing-halves in Scotland. One newspaper described him as being the 'sixth forward' in support of the front five. But Mackay insisted he never went out looking to get on the scoresheet. He said to the media, 'I take it as the game runs. There were times when John Cumming and I must think only of defence. But when we get the chance to move up, well, I naturally have a go.'

Mackay insisted he loved being the captain, even though it was felt in sections of the fourth estate that he wasn't enjoying the role. The responsibility was cramping his playing style early in the season.

He said at the time of the observation, 'Definitely not. I like the job. I believe the trouble may have been the change in my way of living. I was just out of the services. I was probably feeling the effects of all that travelling. Now I'm used to all the full-time training again. I'm feeling 100 per cent.'

Walker told the press, 'David is a very young man to have such a responsibility thrust upon him. But he accepted it readily and has given the team a lead and set an example to which they have all responded.'

Pundit Tommy Muirhead said, 'Was it a wise choice? The 22-year-old human dynamo … did not seem to have the stature or composure for the job. But Tommy Walker knew his player.'

Another commentator also concluded that Walker's decision to install Mackay as his skipper was vindicated, saying, 'It was a decision that must have taken a lot of courage … Mackay was young, impetuous and sometimes in trouble because of his too-emotional tackling. [But] he had the drive, the will to win, the hatred of defeat that marks every champion.'

Mackay proved he did have the sort of fire that Hearts – with that long tradition of 'casual' football –needed so badly.

The fact he became the leading scorer among wing-halves in the Scottish League also impressed. But the feats of Mackay and his Hearts did not escape criticism. The steely edge the skipper provided could, it was felt, on occasion, turn their play from fair to unfair.

John McPhail, a former Celtic player writing in the *Daily Record*, sparked controversy when he blasted Mackay for aspects of the wing-half's performance against Queen's Park which got the home boo-boys hot under the collar. Mackay was verbally slaughtered and McPhail insisted the critical fans had a point when it came to a tackle he made on Queen's Park player Malcolm Darroch. McPhail wrote, 'In 18 years of professional football experience, I've never heard such merciless barracking of any player – the boo boys panned Dave – they panned him hard. AND I THOUGHT THEY WERE RIGHT.

'In fairness to Mackay though I should point out that the referee did not award a foul. But I give this advice to Mackay – a player I particularly admire, a player whom I rank as the finest Scottish wing-half potentially for years – cut out this too-tough tackling.

'I know that under Mackay's captaincy and inspiration Hearts have lost their traditional softness and been transformed into a hard-hitting trophy winning outfit … For the first time ever I heard words of bitterness in reference to the manner of Hearts' victory.

'I would suggest that he controls his exuberance and cuts out the crude tackles. Hearts have a good name to uphold.'

Mackay hit back in the same paper. He wrote, 'Why don't they come straight out with it and say I'm a dirty player? What really made me maddest was what John McPhail wrote in the *Record*. He was the hardest of the lot and I didn't expect that from someone who was a famous player himself. Maybe it looks different from the spectators' point of view but I know I'm not a rough player and if I tackle hard I tackle fairly. My boss has never said a word to me on the subject and that's good enough for me.

'I've always been a fairly small fellow. At school against the bigger lads I just had to find something else to be any good against them. That's where I started being a hard tackler. Even now I'm only 5ft 8in and weigh 11st. I'd be a fool to pretend that I take it easy but I'm sure I don't deserve all these veiled threats. I'm certain that Hearts don't always get the praise they deserve.'

And McPhail responded, 'I took in my time an awful lot of criticism. I got – as we used to say at Parkhead – a lot of stick.

'But one thing I learned in my football career was that the men who sit in the press box and in football judgement have a job to do … as I had a job to do on the field. I have also learned early in my newspaper career that you can get stick too, from footballers, from football fans, from sports editors. I hope I can still take it. Now to you David, I suggest you should take it. From now you are going to get it.'

Tom Nicholson, another journalist, weighed in to defend Mackay and Hearts. He said, 'I like him the way he is and I like him the way he represents Hearts. Mackay has had his say. John McPhail has had his say. They are both absolutely straight and sincere but now let me put the point of the ordinary Hearts fan. What they say is simple, "This lot get the results." And who can blame them.

'It's all right giving us the Gentleman Jim stuff. All the time Hearts were building up their reputation as classy footballers and fine footballers and fine sportsmen, Rangers and Celtic were regularly running off with the honours. And don't tell me that either of these clubs don't believe in carrying player who could mix it.

'Others in the Tynecastle rearguard tackle just as firmly but it is in the constant urgings and the untiring effort of Mackay that Hearts of late have found so much of their inspiration.

'Lay off him I suggest … let him carry on learning in every game as he is young and sensible enough to do. But don't try and damp down the fire that has made him one of the most wholehearted Hearts of this generation.'

It was also observed by another pundit, 'I've heard in the last few weeks you'd think it was a crime for any club other than Rangers or Celtic to do that sort of thing. It now transpires you were only everybody's darlings so long as they weren't winning anything. Malcolm Darroch gets carried off following a tackle by Tynecastle skipper Davie Mackay. It was "BRUTAL MACKAY". Four days later Davie Mackay himself is carried off in the game against Celtic and it was "PURELY ACCIDENTAL".'

12

World Cup

DAVE MACKAY'S fast-tracked career picked up further momentum when he was recalled after a year's absence to the Scotland squad for the 1958 World Cup finals in Sweden; his country successfully completing their qualifying programme without him following his forgettable debut in Spain.

He had impressed in trials at Easter Road and Ibrox, making two goals in the first match and scoring twice in the second, and capped it off in the third by scoring a last-minute winner playing for Hearts against a Scotland Select at Tynecastle.

It had seemed his broken foot would scupper his chances of selection but it healed in time for him to board the plane with club-mate Jimmy Murray to, first, Poland for a warm-up game and, then, on to Stockholm.

But any hope the biggest tournament on the planet would provide warm memories into his dotage were swiftly dispelled.

Matt Busby had been appointed national manager early in 1958, combining the role with the same one he had at Manchester United.

But Busby suffered bad injuries in the tragic Munich air disaster on 6 February 1958 which claimed the lives of eight United players.

He was still in recovery for the finals and Scotland opted to put coach Dawson Walker in, ostensibly, caretaker charge rather than name a replacement manager for the stricken Busby, although Mackay revealed fellow midfielder Tommy Docherty 'filled the vacuum as best he could … with no official sanction', adding, 'In times of crisis, leaders emerge.'

Mackay was left to kick his heels as Jimmy Murray scored his country's first goal in the finals to earn Scotland a point in a 1-1 draw in their opening group game against Yugoslavia in Arosvallen, Vasteras.

Mackay was again kept on the sidelines for the second game, which saw his side pipped 3-2 by Paraguay in Norkopping.

But Walker included Mackay, alongside Murray and future Spurs team-mate Bill Brown, in Scotland's last qualifying match against France. It took place in Orebro, 120 miles west of Stockholm, on 15 June.

It was the wing-half's one and only appearance in a World Cup finals and Scotland were edged aside 2-1 by a strong French team, whose goals came through superstar forwards Just Fontaine and Raymond Kopa before Sammy Baird halved the deficit after the interval. Defeat ensured Scotland finished bottom of their group and out of the competition.

Mackay said with a smile when asked how Scotland would have fared if he had played all the group games, 'A lot better! But I don't pick the team; that's the manager, or back then the selection committee with all their different views.'

Yet overall the experience left him dissatisfied.

He said, 'The preparations were shambolic … Why the authorities did not replace him [Busby] is beyond me. Can you imagine an international side being allowed to travel to the World Cup finals without a manager nowadays?

'We were not shamed in the tournament. We played some good football and in some of the matches were unlucky not to win or draw, but we were just not good enough.

'My point earlier about the poor preparation and lack of guidance was not by way of an excuse. It is a fact that we went in with no manager and only 13 players! Had we taken a squad, had we employed a manager and invested in some weeks of preparation, it is hard to believe that we would not have done better than we did.'

* * *

Mackay had things other than football on his mind.

Wife Isobel said, 'He came back laden with presents as usual. I remember when he was away I got badly bitten by mosquitoes. I had to have poultices on. My mum did it. The heat from it before it touched my leg made me go, "Oh no no, don't put it on." She said, "When David

Mackay comes back from Sweden I'm going to tell him you are such a baby!"'

Busby resumed his role of Scotland manager at the Home Internationals a few months later – and named Mackay as his captain prior to the opener against Wales; perhaps taking a leaf out of Tommy Walker's decision to name the young midfielder as Hearts skipper.

Mackay said, 'My chest swelled with pride. Captains are normally senior in years and have been long established in a side. I was just 23 years old and playing only my third international game. Matt could see what I was thinking. Tommy Docherty, then playing at Arsenal, and Bobby Collins, were both in the team and far more experienced and respected than I was.'

Walker told a newspaper the appointment would not change things for Mackay at his club, 'We know Dave's style of play. At Tynecastle we give him his head. If we ask him to change his ideas, we might not be left with the Dave Mackay we admire so much.'

It was, as it happened, the same with Scotland. Busby vowed then, 'You can take it from me, I have no intention of curbing Mackay's natural brand of play. Anyway, since when was enthusiasm considered a fault in football?

'Mackay has now had nearly two years of experience of captaining his club side. Age doesn't enter into it. A player either has what it takes to be a skipper or he hasn't … whether he is 21, 31 or 41 doesn't alter that fact.'

Busby told Mackay, 'Davie, you are the man for the job. Be in no doubt. You are hungry. You never admit defeat. You inspire those around you and you have many years left ahead of you. You are an old head on young shoulders.'

Busby also told him prior to taking on Dave Bowen's Red Dragons on 18 October at Ninian Park to smash any penalty he took and to go in goal if the stopper was injured, catching high balls and not fisting them away.

Mackay led his side to a 3-0 victory, but had a side-footed penalty saved and debutant Denis Law saved his blushes by clearing the ball he dropped having replaced the injured Bill Brown.

Mackay said, 'I strongly feel that Matt somehow watched that match before it was played and had run through it in advance.'

Law said, 'It was the first time I'd played with him [Mackay]. I just loved it. An inspirational figure; I cannot think of many better players than him who played for Scotland and, of course, Hearts in the early days.'

Cliff Jones, sidelined with a broken leg, was a club-mate of Wales duo Terry Medwin and Mel Hopkins and would play with Mackay at White Hart Lane.

Jones said, 'What a player Denis Law was. Can you imagine a team with Dave Mackay and Denis Law in it? The players they had [going into the 1960s]. How they didn't win the World Cup, I do not know.'

Mackay also skippered Law and Scotland a second time in a 2-2 draw with Northern Ireland at Hampden the following month, where he was impressed by future Spurs team-mate Danny Blanchflower's performance for the opposition.

He said, 'He [Blanchflower] reminded me of a continental, like those I had seen on my debut against Spain. His penetrating passing and his ability to slow or speed up again was breathtaking. He saw space before it was there.'

Mackay and Hearts dipped their toes into the European Cup for the first time on 3 September 1958.

Edinburgh neighbours Hibs had been the first British team to play in the inaugural competition for the champions of countries affiliated to UEFA in 1955/56. The Greens, although only finishing fifth in their domestic league, accepted an invitation to take part after title winners Aberdeen declined to enter.

And they reached the semi-finals before exiting to Reims who were defeated by Real Madrid in the decider; a run which might have made the Jambos 'green' with envy. But the difference between the city rivals' participation, of course, was that the Hearts were there by right.

And Mackay and Co. were determined to make their mark for Scotland and themselves in the globe's premier club event after Rangers had failed to make a significant impression in the two campaigns following Hibernian's run.

It was to prove a competition in which the midfielder enjoyed relative success down the line with Spurs but, backing his negative perspective on his debuts, it proved the shortest of campaigns with Hearts falling at the first hurdle, against Belgian club Standard Liege.

Walker decided to play Mackay at inside-right in place of Jimmy Murray rather than in his customary midfield position for the first leg at their opponents' Sclessin Stadium. John Cumming switched from left-half to the former Newtongrange Star graduate's usual right-half berth with Andy Bowman at number six.

Their hosts provided a rock-hard surface and Mother Nature an uncomfortable humidity by a river.

Mackay was missed at half-back as Cumming and Bowman were 'overrun', especially by the hosts' star player, Congolese Paul Bonga-Bonga, the first African chosen for *World Soccer* magazine's world XI in 1962.

Ian Crawford put Mackay's boys in front but the attacking visitors were vulnerable to the counter-attack and conceded three in the last 18 minutes as they slumped to a 5-1 defeat.

'Mackay, as always, worked like a Trojan,' wrote one newspaper of the player who forced a couple of saves and tackled like a tiger. It could be speculated Hearts must have felt they would need a team of Trojans to overcome such a deficit as they sat back in their 'rustic' dressing room post-match.

Even so, almost 40,000 turned up at Tynecastle – an attendance perhaps swelled by a derby league thumping of Hibs at Easter Road in between, with Mackay on target – for the second leg, most hoping against hope. Mackay, moved back to number four, made a Willie Bauld goal which put the Jam Tarts ahead ten minutes into the second half. And, although Josef Givard levelled two minutes later, Bauld bagged his second to complete a 2-1 victory amid complaints about the continental referee's performance – something Mackay would come across again with Spurs in the same competition.

There was, as the *Daily Record* headlined, 'smash ... but no grab' and, according to another journal, a lack of guile by Hearts.

Mackie said, 'Hearts at once cheered and exasperated their fans by winning 2-1, proving that they need not have gone down to the Belgians in the first place, but falling out of the running with an aggregate of three goals for the two legs against six for the champions of Belgium.

Goalkeeper Gordon Marshall said the European experience was a 'culture shock ... I remember Hibs being our [Britain's] first team to go into Europe and get into the semi-finals, with the English clubs coming later. I was a boy and used to go and watch them.

'But Hearts didn't do that great in Europe. That was a whole new ball game. What a player Bonga-Bonga was. The football wasn't that different to what we were used to but going to Belgium we discovered differences in what you eat and other things. It was a culture shock.'

Mackay viewed the exit as being 'dumped', but at least a victory to appease home fans was a small compensation.

Mackay took part in the ceremony to unfurl the league flag for the first time in 61 years at Tynecastle prior to the Jambos kicking off their first competitive home match of 1958/59 with a comfortable 3-0 League Cup group win over Third Lanark in front of 18,000 on 13 August.

But he did not return to action until his club's final group game due to a stress fracture of a bone he had broken in his right foot in March. He reportedly expressed a hope the foot would 'not be permanently weak', thus avoiding question marks over his future, and said he would 'make sure' he was 100 per cent fit before playing again. Trainer John Harvey struck an optimistic note when he declared that Mackay 'was a quick healer'.

The injury ruled him out of a loss and a win against Rangers in front of a crowd total of 107,000 and a 5-4 victory against Third Lanark which sealed a last-eight League Cup spot, along with a league defence-opening six-goal dismantling of Dunfermline at Tynecastle.

He made a goalscoring return at right-half in a 3-1 victory against Raith Rovers to underline qualification before the Gorgie faithful on 30 August. It was rated an 'inspiring' display, in which he was 'urging the team on in his usual true captain's way'.

Mackay's comeback added to a developing feel-good factor domestically in what was to prove another glittering cup campaign which ended with the skipper lifting another piece of silverware, his club's fourth in four years.

But they were forced to start their bid for a League Cup semi-final spot just a day after the second leg of their European Cup tie, and they had to make a 160-mile round trip to the west of Scotland for their encounter with Ayr United for the first leg.

Mackay, Marshall and the rest of the back six from the previous day remained in place, but Walker made three changes up front, with Danny Paton, Alex Young and Jimmy Wardhaugh in for Bobby Blackwood, Willie Bauld and Ian Crawford.

And the captain helped Hearts reproduce the scoreline in Liege – this time in their favour. Formalities concluded with a 3-1 second-leg win at Tynecastle seven days later, and a final place was assured for his

Jambos with a convincing 3-0 victory against Kilmarnock before 41,000 at Easter Road.

Mackay led the Maroons out for the League Cup decider against Partick Thistle in front of close to 60,000 at Hampden Park on Saturday, 18 October 1958 with most of their fans gathering on the west bank terracing, holding banners such as one stating 'Heart of Midlothian South Side' and another a silver-coloured cup replica, while directors sat in the stands sporting maroon carnations and sprigs of white heather (the wearing of which had brought them luck in the Scottish Cup Final). He was one of five survivors of the team which triumphed four years before, with fellow half-backs Freddie Glidden and John Cumming and forwards Willie Bauld and Jimmy Wardhaugh. Alex Young was travelling reserve.

Mackay believed his outfit were clear favourites – although some pundits, much to his bemusement, held the opposite view – with the Jambos having made an unbeaten start in their bid to retain the league title.

Hearts justified Mackay's faith and roared into a 4-0 interval lead with Willie Bauld and Jimmy Murray each netting a double. In fact, one young supporter thought his side had done enough to warrant the presentation of the 'trophy' at half-time. The *Evening Dispatch*'s Jimmy Cowe reported, 'A little laddie decked out in a maroon tammy and tracksuit expressed the thoughts of the crowd when he toddled on to the field to present Gordon Marshall a replica of the cup.'

Partick, forever in the shadow of Rangers and Celtic in Glasgow and without injured top scorer Andy Kerr, had the temerity to launch a comeback by reducing the arrears through George Smith. But Mackay was his swashbuckling self and, along with Glidden and the outstanding Cumming, helped Tynecastle's finest nip such attempts in the bud before right-winger Johnny Hamilton made it 5-1 to complete the scoreline. Hearts, it was reported, 'outclassed' their Firhill opponents in yellow and red hoops and were lauded 'Scotland's most accomplished team'.

Marshall, still only 19, had one smart save to make but was otherwise relatively untroubled.

Marshall, who must have enjoyed the mock presentation mid-match, said, 'Davie was one of some good players I had around me. I was new still, just breaking through myself. I had two bad kicks and let in a goal. Had a quiet day that day.'

It would prove to be the last moment of glory he shared with Mackay, but far from the last he himself experienced with the Jambos; helping them to another league title in 1960 and League Cups in 1959 and 1962.

Mackay was buoyed by being a part of a fourth trophy-winning team in as many years. So buoyed, in fact, that when the team arrived for their celebratory dinner in Charlotte Street in Edinburgh's city centre he held the cup aloft and declared to the estimated 25,000 fans gathered in their maroon favours, as quoted in *Gritty, Gallant and Glorious*, 'I was really proud of the boys today and now we are going all out for the treble [adding the title and Scottish Cup].'

He said, 'As captain, I lifted my second cup and drank in the atmosphere as we drove down Princes Street on the victory bus which was now becoming a familiar route. We were playing well enough to retain the championship. There was the Scottish Cup coming up. I could smell a treble. I wanted to be the captain of not only the finest Hearts team in history, but also the finest Scottish team in history. There was still much to go for.

'I would never have dreamt it then as I stood on the bus waving and cheering with the people of Edinburgh, but other people had different plans.'

But the wheels soon came off Hearts' treble hopes, starting with an unwanted early Christmas present on 6 December. Mackay injured his foot again – splitting a bone – and limped off six minutes from time during a 5-1 defeat of Aberdeen at Tynecastle. He was sidelined until 4 February when he returned for a 3-1 league victory at Queen of the South.

Rangers dislodged and removed the second 'wheel' in two stages. They thumped Hearts 5-0 in the league at Ibrox on 13 December and, with Mackay back, unromantically knocked the Maroons out of the Scottish Cup on Valentine's Day, in front of 53,000 at Ibrox.

Four days later, a third wheel came off when hosts Partick Thistle exacted revenge for their League Cup final defeat to put a further spoke in Hearts' title challenge in an encounter which was to prove the last time Mackay played alongside hero 'King' Willie Bauld.

Three days later, Mackay scored his 29th competitive and what would be his last goal for Hearts in a 2-1 win against Raith Rovers, with the final wheel about to come away. He also helped the Jambos pip Queen of the South 2-1 at Tynecastle.

Mackay considered himself at the core of the developing new side with the era of the Terrible Trio et al coming to a close.

He said, 'I identified as strongly with the future as I did with the past.'

Yet the fourth and final wheel had, indeed, broken away. Mackay had made in fact his final appearance before being sidelined with a recurrence of his foot problem for a win over St Mirren on 9 March and a draw at Clyde on 14 March. He then signed for Tottenham Hotspur on 18 March 1959.

Whether Hearts would have won the title had he stayed for the remaining seven fixtures will forever remain moot. They were six points down on rivals Rangers when he went south of the border to White Hart Lane and they did end up just two behind the Ibrox giants. But with Mackay they might have finished up two to six points clear at the top.

There have been theories about why Hearts decided to sell their most prized asset. One was that the board might have given up on a title challenge and were in need of money to help offset outlays on installed floodlights and a covered enclosure for 15,000 fans (estimated at a total of £37,000). Yet it would have appeared the books might have been balanced from the money – collectively estimated at £38,000 – raked in from the title-winning season, the 1958 Scottish League Cup triumph and European Cup excursion.

Another suggested the club directors were concerned about Mackay's injury record and wanted to cash in with the player still considered a 'key man' in a golden period for the club.

Isobel Mackay received a letter from the then chairman of Royal Mail, Donald Brydon, who she revealed told her his father was friendly with Nicol Kilgour, the Hearts chairman, at the time. His dad had told Kilgour, 'What on earth have you done?!' and the head of the Jambos board replied, 'We think David was going to struggle with his foot.' The communication came as a result of Brydon's involvement in the 2013 issue of stamps to commemorate the 150th anniversary of the FA, with Mackay one of 11 subjects chosen. Isobel said, 'It was a bombshell when Hearts sold David to Tottenham.'

Either way, the player himself did not want to leave. He said, 'I would have been very happy to stay with Hearts for the rest of my career … I was very disappointed that Hearts were prepared to sell me. It didn't change my attitude towards Tommy Walker but I was very disappointed the club sold me.'

Mackay's departure was a bolt from the blue.

There was no inkling when the player accepted his Scottish Footballer of the Year statuette from Rex Kingsley at a packed Usher Hall in Edinburgh's West End on Sunday, 15 February 1959. He said in the tribute programme that receiving the award was 'great'.

When his departure became a reality, the club and the city were dumbfounded.

Kingsley wrote, 'Just before we stepped on to the Usher Hall platform to face nearly 3,000 of his fervent admirers he told me he was Hearts daft and had no other time for any other club … "I'm the happiest player in the country. Not only playing for Hearts but actually captain of Hearts." And now … He didn't ask to leave. He must have been as astonished as we are. Maybe Hearts need the money. I'd have thought they needed Mackay more.'

His team-mates were also left reeling. Gordon Marshall said, 'It was a shock. We were all out golfing that day and when we got back the trainer [John Harvey] came in. I thought he was going to burst out in tears. He said, "Davie's just signed for Tottenham."'

The tributes have flooded in ever since for a player rated the greatest Heart of all.

Marshall said, 'Dave Mackay was the best player I ever played with. I cannot praise him enough. He could play football and mix it as well; a good all-round player. He could inspire everyone around him and make people play. He had a big reputation at a young age. A great player for Hearts, and for Tottenham, and after for Derby and all that as well.

'Tottenham paid £30,000 for Davie. What a "steal" that was. England poached all our good players. Alex Young eventually went down to England as well.

'It felt like we had sold half the team. He was a class act. Davie was a real bouncy character and a winner. When [the team] got Davie, they got someone who made the team win, even at five-a-sides. He just loved playing football. He was also very fit. I remember I was at the ground on a day off – we'd had a night out – and heard someone running around the gymnasium. I went up and had a look and there was Davie running around with three jumpers on sweating like anything. He was hammering the ball off the four walls and really putting himself through it. That was the dedication he had.

'He was Hearts-daft and there was no doubting Hearts was his team.

'We won things even though Davie left. I mean we missed Davie but Andy Bowman was a good replacement. Didn't let anybody down.

'Maybe Andy was not as good a player but he was every bit as hard. He could mix it as well. He was a good man for the club, for the team.

'Winning the championship a second time was a high point. We should have won it in 1958/59. We got beaten by Celtic in the last game of the season. If we had won it that day we would have won it three times in a row.

'Then Hearts were a team, a club, that was invited all over the world. Twice we went out to America. We even went to Australia on tour. It was unbelievable.'

Mackay's Scottish Cup-winning captain Freddie Glidden, his half-back partner on the road to back-to-back trophy success, recognised the qualities of the individual who had come a long way from being one of the banes of the Carrick Knowe municipal golf course greenkeeper's life during impromptu football sessions close to his Glendevon Park home.

Glidden, who passed aged 91 on 1 January 2019, said of Mackay, 'He made quite an impression during his time with Hearts and was someone everyone looked up to. People talk about him being Hearts' greatest player and it is hard to argue against that.'

Jimmy Murray, his club and international team-mate who passed aged 82 on 10 July 2015, said, 'He was a true legend and a great ambassador for the club …He was never beaten – even playing snooker … A wonderful footballer … a one-off, and a big heart as well.

'When I came into the side after Alfie Conn, it was brilliant to play in front of him. He was a quiet lad off the park but a lion on it, in the most respectable way. He was a great tackler but not an unfair one.

'There were so many great players during that era at Tynecastle. We had 30 to 40,000 fans going along each week and they were used to success. Davie was a driving force in that no matter how well the team was doing, he would always be pushing us on for more.

'He was a big loss when he went down south but Hearts' loss was Tottenham's gain and he had a wonderful career down there as well. He was a fantastic character.'

Alex Young, who died aged 80 on 27 February 2017, said, 'He was a superb player who feared nothing. It was a privilege to play alongside him. He could run all day, his ability to tackle was immense and he never went out to hurt anybody – he always tried to play the ball. He could pass the ball well to feet too.

'It was a serious business on the park for Dave but he was a good lad who enjoyed a laugh off it.

'I actually played against him a few times in England after I signed for Everton and he was a tough, tough opponent. It's fair to say I would rather have him on my side rather than against me.'

Young, who played with Mackay's future Spurs team-mate John White at Musselburgh juveniles, added in the *Liverpool Echo* in 1961, 'Dave's a pal of mine ... I remember one occasion when our friendship nearly ended. Dave trains as hard as he plays and during a Scotland training session he tackled me so hard that I crashed heavily to the ground. When I recovered myself and started to get up, this was Dave, always the humorist, smiling all over his face, thinking what a joke it was to see me covered in mud. My thoughts at that moment are unprintable. Nevertheless, Dave is a great character.'

John Cumming, who died aged 78 on 6 December 2008, said to the media, 'Dave was a lad who liked to attack. He was an attacker. When he went I just balanced it. He was a hard player and he liked to go forward and he was an extra man with your five forwards.'

Mackay repaid the compliments, especially the ones from Cumming, while praising his Hearts manager Tommy Walker.

He said, 'Willie Bauld, Alfie Conn and Jimmy Wardhaugh: what players. For me, though, John Cumming was the top man. He was a wing-half, like me, and what a brave player. I remember he had a clash of heads with Willie Fernie [at the 1956 Scottish Cup Final]. It didn't put him off and he came back on the pitch after getting the blood cleaned up. I remember saying to him that I would do all the headers in midfield. Did he listen? He may have had a serious head wound but he still kept heading the ball ... the fact he carried on playing that day showed what his attitude was like. He was a real lionheart.

'He [Walker] was a strong man. He kept us under control, well certainly the younger players like myself. I'm not sure about the older players. He was a great tactician as well. He would give us instructions as to the way he wanted us to play. He never ranted or raved though; he was always calm.'

Mackay's opponents while he wore maroon had their tales to tell. They included Alex Ferguson, who was a mere stripling of a forward turning out for his first club, Queen's Park, when he came up against Mackay's Hearts. His story had shades of the one told earlier by Alex Young.

Ferguson, speaking at Mackay's funeral and quoted in *The Scotsman*, said, 'My own memories [of the deceased] start in 1956 as a 14-year-old lad at the cup final at Hampden Park. I was at the Rangers end, of course. Hearts won 3-1 [versus Celtic].

'Two years later I was playing for Queen's Park reserves v Hearts reserves at Tynecastle. The great Mackay was coming back from a broken toe. And I was playing directly opposite him, this skinny little lad from Glasgow coming over to Edinburgh, another country – and don't take that personally, please. He tackled me. Christ! Sorry chaplain [Hearts' Andy Prime], wherever you are. Our generation did not lie down. You had to get up. So I got up with that spirit of vengeance that only a young lad from Glasgow can have. I got up. And I looked at that barrel chest. I looked into his eyes and he says, "Are you all right, son?"

'I really should have said to him, "Dave, is your toe all right?" It is a good memory for me to have. The only time I played against Dave Mackay so I will never forget it.

'He was awesome and I knew I was privileged just to be on the same pitch as him. His aura and presence pervaded my whole intention of excelling – and the radiance about him debilitated me on the night. Going in to tackle with Dave was like running full-on into a brick wall. We crumbled to a 5-0 thrashing.'

Scottish international centre-half Ian Ure, who was to face Mackay on moving south to Arsenal and Manchester United from Dundee, saw our subject play for Hearts.

He said, 'I only saw him once when he was with Hearts and was immediately impressed by him. I was at Tynecastle this day carrying the Dundee players' hamper. Just there for the experience. It was one of his last appearances for Hearts. I didn't know too much about him as I was just an up-and-coming player. But I'd heard about him.

'The game should never have been played. The pitch was brick-hard, icy. There had been three days of frost – heavy, heavy deep frost and

155

there was snow on the ground. It was a farce. When the players came out at the start Dave Mackay was wearing sand shoes. An ordinary par of plimsolls. I noticed that right away.

'Everyone else was skidding about like mad. He could keep his feet. He wasn't the quickest but helped Hearts win, running about – going side to side – with his chest stuck out. Davie just played anywhere in midfield in those days.

'I'm glad someone has asked me about him. He should not be forgotten. I cannot speak highly enough of the man.

'His Hearts side was a good side. I'd read about them and go and see them occasionally. I actually played against all three of the Terrible Trio and John Cumming as a boy for Dundee reserves. They were coming to the end of their careers. Willie wasn't a big guy but was a good header of the ball. John was as hard as steel, had a great left foot and was a nice fellow.' Whatever Mackay went on to do, it was a case of 'once a Heart, always a Heart'.

That was according to Jack Harkness, the former Hearts and Scotland goalkeeper turned writer.

Harkness quoted Mackay and attempted to illustrate his compatriot's relationship with the Jambos when he wrote, 'A player may be transferred. He might even play for two or three other clubs before hanging up his boots but when you meet him it is WE from the very start. "I hope WE win." "Do you think WE will do it this time? WE never had a better chance."'

PART THREE:
TOTTENHAM HOTSPUR

13

'How would you like to live in London?'

BILL NICHOLSON was confirmed as Tottenham Hotspur manager in succession to the ailing Jimmy Anderson on the day he took charge of the team for the first time.

It was Saturday, 11 October 1958, and the former player who had become a coach saw his team celebrate an extraordinary 10-4 win against Everton at White Hart Lane.

But Nicholson knew he had to build up the team. It was a deceptively big win in a season which had started badly and was to threaten relegation more than the title for the Lilywhites. The team that day contained just three of the players who were to become part of the Double-winning side three years later, in Danny Blanchflower, Bobby Smith and Peter Baker, (although Cliff Jones, Terry Dyson, Maurice Norman and Ron Henry were already on the playing staff but either unavailable or out of favour).

And he wrote down the name of Dave Mackay when he first sat down to consider key players to bring in, having first spotted the midfielder's potential playing for Scotland against his England in an under-23 international draw at Ibrox in February 1957.

Nicholson said, 'I saw enough of Mackay to convince me he was a player I would want to have in my side. At the time I was assistant manager and coach at Tottenham and Jimmy Anderson was still the manager. When I took over as manager, Mackay was a name I put down on my list of possible signings.'

Spurs had blown hot and cold since right-half Nicholson helped Arthur Rowe's push and run team lift back-to-back titles in 1950 and 1951.

159

His side went close to a third successive crown but had to settle for the runners-up spot, four points behind Manchester United.

Rowe tried to extend the life of the team steeped in the style he had first picked up coaching in Hungary but probably for too long, perhaps out of loyalty for their achievements.

Ill health saw Rowe step down in July 1955 – eight months after signing Danny Blanchflower from Aston Villa – to be replaced by loyal Jimmy Anderson.

Anderson did not quite date back to when schoolboys stood under a lamppost to form the club in 1882 and he missed the 1901 FA Cup win.

But he had served Spurs in a variety of roles since 1908, thus being part of the club's first promotion the following year in its first league season, the second as champions in 1920, a 1921 FA Cup win, promotion in 1933 and those successive championships under Rowe.

He inherited push and run veterans Ted Ditchburn, Charlie Withers, Sonny Walters and Eddie Baily, plus Alfie Stokes, who were all reaching their First Division sell-by date, and the team struggled in the league in his first season, although they enjoyed a run to the FA Cup semi-finals.

Anderson also had on the staff right-back Peter Baker and left-back Ron Henry, who were destined to become members of the near-immortal 1961 side.

But they were for the future. Anderson knew he had an overdue rebuild to undertake to cope with the present. He signed amateur left-winger Terry Dyson as a professional and captured centre-forward Bobby Smith from Chelsea, centre-half Maurice Norman from Norwich City and, for a British record £35,000, winger Cliff Jones from Swansea, from whom he also purchased a second flanker, 1962 FA Cup winner Terry Medwin.

Add in Blanchflower, the Double-winning captain, and much of the groundwork for the side rated the best in the club's history had been done before Nicholson took the helm, although, as coach, the Yorkshireman provided a football education which proved vital in gelling the existing disparate talents into a cohesive, magical whole for the opening season of the 1960s.

Anderson mixed and matched, calling on Rowe's vets with something left in the tank, such as centre-forward Len Duquemin and centre-half Harry Clarke, trying Smith at inside-left and Norman at full-back alongside them. He was able to pick Jones, who had recovered the form which had tempted Spurs to part with so much cash for him after the Welshman had come back from a leg break following an inauspicious start to his Spurs career. He even found a place for Tommy Harmer, a player who generally did not fit into the quick, short-passing style Rowe encouraged due to his propensity for holding on to possession and displaying consummate ball-playing skills.

Inside-forward Harmer and right-half Blanchflower provided a crucial and intelligent axis for the strike force which helped Spurs finish second and third in the league in the second and third of Anderson's three full seasons in the hotseat.

But Blanchflower and Harmer, generally, went off the boil as did the team at the start of the following season. And the former eventually lost his place after a 4-1 home defeat against neighbouring West Ham United on Boxing Day, leaving Harmer struggling to function effectively without him.

Long forgotten was the stunning 10-4 win against Everton in which, incidentally, Harmer had played a part in most of the goals and saved one for himself in a virtuoso display. The problem for Nicholson, as far as Blanchflower was concerned, centred on the Northern Ireland skipper's pre-occupation with pushing forward when the defence might need a hand, with left-half Jim Iley also prone to exclusive 'forward-thinking'.

Spurs, it seemed, had become reliant on the dominance and imagin-ation of Blanchflower and Harmer together to keep the attack potent.

These were abilities that Mackay would provide down the line. And the Scot would also solve the problem of a quality wing-half capable of attacking and defending to partner Blanchflower after Danny Boy's restoration to the side less than a month before Dave's arrival. The incumbent number six, Iley, wrote Julian Holland in *The Double*, 'Lacked the flair to direct attack, still less to create an attack out of nothing.' These were more abilities possessed by Mackay.

Anderson, largely, and Rowe had provided a strong base for the next great Spurs team, but its key components, bar Blanchflower, were not in place. Nicholson viewed Mackay as the first of them.

Nicholson had become friendly with Tommy Walker and sounded out the Hearts boss about the availability of the player. He was given a firm 'no'.

So he was forced to look to where Anderson had signed winger Cliff Jones in February 1958. Swansea were open to offers for Mel Charles, brother of the legendary John.

Nicholson confessed he was 'not excited' about the Welsh centre-half, who could also play at centre-forward. He was more than happy with Maurice Norman and Bobby Smith in those positions. Disappointed Charles did not disclose a wish to play in any other positions when they met for talks in the principality.

The boss was 'relieved' when Charles rung as arranged to thank him for his interest but to tell him that he had chosen to join Arsenal. Charles's rejection of Spurs was a blessing in disguise, perhaps the most blessed, for it pushed Nicholson into having another go at capturing Mackay.

The season's transfer deadline – midnight on Monday, 16 March 1959 – was closing in and the Spurs boss wanted to get the deal done so Mackay was available for the remainder of the campaign.

It was reported that he wired Jock Richardson, the former Spurs player and his old club's Scottish scout, on Monday, 9 March, asking him to 'sound out' Walker about the 'possible transfer of Mackay'.

Richardson wasted no time and went to meet Walker the same evening at Tynecastle where Hearts defeated St Mirren 4-0 without the services of a sidelined Mackay. The question was posed and Walker replied, 'Not a chance. The supporters would pull the roof off the stand at the thought.'

The persistent Richardson apparently got wind of a reserve match to be played between the Jambos and hosts Saints at Love Street the following evening, and attended – clearly not having taken 'no' for an answer – and got another negative response from Walker. But the difference this time, one newspaper stated, was that he asked, 'What were you thinking of offering anyhow?' Richardson had replied, 'Nothing. I'll leave the financial side to you and Billy Nicholson.'

Canny Scot Richardson, detecting a possible chink of light in the negotiations, wrote his news to Spurs, suggesting the club make a 'concrete offer'.

The Hearts board met on Tuesday, 12 March, and its hand-written minutes, signed by chairman Nicol Kilgour, revealed that they would be 'unanimously' open to a deal at £30,000.

In his autobiography, Nicholson revealed he rung Walker on Saturday, 14 March and said to him, 'Our deadline is Monday, Tommy. Can you let me have him?'

He quoted Walker replying, 'I don't want to lose him.'

Nicholson said, 'Look, I am sure we can agree on a transfer fee. Can I ring tomorrow morning?'

Walker, as per Nicholson's tome, 'agreed' and was 'more interested in doing business' when the Spurs boss called him.

Nicholson disclosed he asked Walker to find out from Mackay whether he would be interested, 'otherwise I'd be wasting my time' travelling up.

Unaware of such happenings, Mackay enjoyed a 'small flutter' on the greyhounds at Powderhall Stadium in Edinburgh on the Saturday evening and, the following day, a roast meal and football chat when he, Isobel and their children David Junior and Derek visited his parents at Glendevon Park.

Isobel picked up the story. She said, 'When we arrived at David's parents', his mum said to him, "Mr Tommy Walker's been on the phone for you. What have you been doing?" He said, "I've not been doing anything." So he got on the phone. They wanted to see him at Tynecastle. David went away and came back. And his mum says, "Well, what's he want to see you about?" He says, "Oh nothing much, just about training." So on the way home, David said, "Isobel, how would you like to live in London?" I said, "Whaaat! What are you talking about?" He said, "Do you know what Mr Walker wanted to see me about? He wants me to sign to play for Tottenham Hotspur." I said again, "Whaaat?" I couldn't take it all in. He repeated it and asked me if I would like to go and I said, "Well if that's what you want to do, yes. I'm fine with that."'

Mackay revealed that Walker had told him he had an 'urgent matter' he wanted to discuss with him before later telling his star when they met, 'I am not asking you to go, because we think highly of you, as you know, but you must consider the matter. Mr Nicholson is coming up to Edinburgh tomorrow … you'll have an opportunity to meet him.'

The whole family was reeling. Mackay himself felt 'rejected'. Mackay, in his autobiography, admitted he was 'shell-shocked' and 'baffled' because 'Hearts were my life'. He searched for reasons why. He and the team were doing okay, and surely, bumper gates and lack of transfer spending allayed any fears Hearts needed the money.

But he insisted Isobel helped convince him to see Nicholson as Hearts seemed to want to sell him anyway. She added in the autobiography, 'David, you talk to Mr Nicholson tomorrow. See how you feel then. The fact is that if Mr Walker and the club are of a mind to sell you, they will. If it means we have to move to London, then we will. We have to go where your work is. That's all there is to it.'

Mackay had a restless night's sleep but 'could not escape the conclusion that he [Walker] wanted to sell me. There was no obligation to present any transfer interest to the players then and now. If he didn't he would have rejected Bill Nicholson's approach.'

Mackay came to terms with the situation and was convinced that Walker knew best, having no doubts his manager had put the 'best interests of the club first'. He briefly pondered whether Hearts were cashing in while they could, given his injury problems, but dismissed it convinced the honourable Walker, a practising Christian, would not knowingly sell another club a 'pup'. Yet he conceded there might have been pressure from the board or, perhaps, a willingness from Nicholson to accept any foot troubles Mackay might have had.

Nicholson took the night train from London and 'arrived in Tommy Walker's office early next morning' on Monday, 16 March.

The Spurs manager wrote in his autobiography, 'I offered £32,000 and soon Walker was telephoning his directors for permission to go through with the deal.'

Mackay arrived at 10am and Walker introduced Nicholson to Hearts' star asset then left them alone.

Nicholson laid his cards on the table. He told Mackay, 'I think you could play an important part in my plans for Tottenham Hotspur.' He would not promise glittering prizes but that 'we will always play exciting, entertaining and rewarding football'. He said Spurs had money for more signings and would provide a house and – what Mackay considered 'more than generous' – moving expenses, also inferring the maximum wage limit of £20 would soon be smashed.

Mackay said, 'I was impressed by Mr Nicholson's understatement, his modesty and his honesty. But I could also see he was a determined man with a dream for his club and I accepted his terms there and then.'

It was revealed Everton heard the 'whisper' that Mackay was for sale and would beat any offer Spurs made.

And Matt Busby, it was believed, would have tried to buy him for Manchester United had he known of Mackay's availability.

Cliff Jones said, 'Matt Busby wanted Dave Mackay. It was after Munich. After losing the likes of Duncan Edwards and Eddie Coleman in it, you could see what a difference Dave Mackay would have made. We [Spurs] were fortunate Bill Nicholson got Mackay.'

Mackay might even have joined Chelsea instead but Blues boss Ted Drake opted for Reading's Sylvan Anderton, according to the Scot's future Spurs team-mate Jimmy Greaves, who was then at Stamford Bridge. Greaves said in his autobiography *Greavsie*, 'Who knows what impact the arrival of Dave Mackay would have had on the fortunes of Chelsea ... such would have been his contribution to the team that I probably would not have been so keen to move on in 1961.'

And Mackay admitted he would have signed for United given the choice at the time as he knew and trusted Busby and the Old Trafford club 'were a better bet', although in hindsight, he was glad he joined Spurs.

But, it was reported, Hearts had no wish to enter an auction and the club minutes for 24 March, again hand-written by Kilgour, claimed there was no other interest.

Mackay was told to keep the arrangement to himself until the paperwork was completed as he left Tynecastle after agreeing the deal, which was completed with an estimated 11 hours to spare before the deadline.

Mackay, who netted his two goals at left-half for Scotland against the Scottish League in an international trial at Ibrox the same evening, said, 'I'd have liked to have said goodbye to my colleagues ... to the fans.

'I would have liked time to consider my options. It was just that 48 hours earlier I had not realised I was a man that needed to consider his options.'

But he was ready to deal with a change, having spoken to Scots playing south of the border, although it was reported he would only have uprooted himself for either Spurs, Manchester United or Arsenal. He said to Rex Kingsley, 'The transfer was a shot from the blue. I'd had six happy years with Hearts ... but I wanted to play in England and when the offer came I couldn't refuse.'

The fans, unsurprisingly, were distraught. Angus Macdonald, on the Hearts Supporters Association executive committee, said to Kingsley, 'There will be widespread disappointment. Dave was part and parcel of Tynecastle. I just couldn't see him leaving Hearts. But good luck to him.'

Paul Cameron, a fan from Edinburgh, 'I'm a faithful Hearts supporter for close to 40 years. Now I've sworn they've had my last half-crown.'

Tommy Walker, the day after the deal, refused to comment on 'the violent reaction to Mackay's departure'.

Dave Mackay packed his bags at the family home in Whitecraig and made his way to Waverley station on Wednesday 18 March, then waited on the platform with friends and well-wishers waiting for the Flying Scotsman to transport him 400 miles to London.

A Waverley porter recognised him, Mackay wrote in his autobiography, shook his hand and said what a 'pleasure' it was to meet him before enquiring where he was going. Mackay told him he was off to London having signed for Spurs. The porter was lost for words and as Mackay pulled down the window in his carriage, he told the local hero, 'Davie Mackay, the Hearts *winnae* be the same *withoot* you.' It echoed what the fans said every time Mackay had missed a game through injury.

It was a similar poignant scene to the one a day or two earlier recalled by Nicholson after securing Mackay.

Nicholson said, 'Tommy [Walker] took me off to lunch at a local hotel and then on to the station to catch the London-bound express. The platform was virtually deserted except for the station master wearing his top hat. He recognised Tommy, who introduced me as the manager of Tottenham Hotspur. The station master inquired, "Oh, and what might you be doing here?" I said, "Hearts have just sold Dave Mackay to us." He was shocked. It was clear Dave Mackay was loved by the footballing public of Edinburgh and it must have hurt them to lose such a good player. That made me feel good.'

Mackay, having conquered the complexities of the London transport system, was given a warm welcome on his White Hart Lane arrival. He met Nicholson, who showed him around. Mackay – who stood 5ft 8in in his stockinged feet – was struck by the size of everything. All he had known at Tynecastle appeared dwarfed. Spurs trainer Cecil Poynton reassured him his foot problem could be sorted. Each player gave him a warm 'hello, good to see you', and some added the word 'again', for

Mackay had played against future Double-winning squad-mates Peter Baker, Danny Blanchflower, Bobby Smith, Terry Dyson, Tony Marchi, Terry Medwin and Mel Hopkins in an Anglo-Scottish tournament match in 1956. Nicholson's push and run colleagues Ted Ditchburn and Harry Clarke were also in the visitors' line-up along with Tommy Harmer and Alf Stokes, while Mackay even got a goal as the Jambos defeated their guests 3-2.

Mackay found crowd favourite Tommy 'The Charmer' Harmer, living up to his nickname. Danny Blanchflower also turned on the charm, praising the new boy to the skies, while dismissing any relegation talk.

Mackay remembered Blanchflower telling him, 'Don't be overawed. You're a great player. One of the best I've played against. I've been telling Bill Nick as much for a while now. You're in good company here, Dave. This is a good side and getting better by the day. Relegation? My foot!'

When he reported to Spurs for training, he was still suffering because of a knock on the right foot he had broken three times at Hearts. It got more painful on the train journey down. And in his first training session at Spurs he was asked to play in a kickabout with the A team (third team) and performed below par.

There had been speculation in the Scottish media about his potential role at Spurs. Would Mackay's attacking instincts be curbed to balance the propensity of Danny Blanchflower to play forward? Would he, indeed, be replacing Blanchflower, who had only recently regained his starting position with Nicholson concerned about the Irishman's lack of consideration for defensive duties?

The questions were soon answered when he debuted against Manchester City at the Lane on Saturday, 21 March 1959.

It was a day which saw British piano player Russell Conway at number one in the charts with 'Side Saddle'. Worldwide, in what was the Baby Boomer generation, an estimated average of 289,242 children were born during it.

One can only guess how many Spurs-supporting mothers soothed by an ivory-tinkling instrumental were tempted to switch from their Dansettes to bedside radios and tune into Mackay's debut.

But 34,493 spectators turned up to witness Mackay, with his sensitive foot protected by strapping put on by trainer Cecil Poynton. Adrenalin replaced pain. He rewarded the vociferous fans who gave their new boy a roaring encouragement with a memorable display.

It was a 'happy relief' from the 'worry' that he had 'crocked himself', and he was able to 'get down to business' as Spurs captain Danny Blanchflower picked up a ball and declared, 'Let's go, fellows – and the best of luck, Dave.'

Mackay came close to scoring and also provided an assist for a Terry Medwin goal in a 3-1 win – with Bobby Smith and Cliff Jones also on target – to ease threats of the drop against relegation rivals.

Any perceived doubts about Mackay, who had replaced Jim Iley at left-half, and number four Blanchflower playing together were swept away that afternoon. They developed an instantaneous and instinctive rapport, with each offering cover when the other surged forward.

As Julian Holland eloquently put it in *The Double*, 'The understanding that developed between these two giants was immediate: Mackay seemed to interpret Blanchflower as though they had played together as boys or, in a previous life, on some wild Celtic field. Mackay's earthy sensibilities provided the perfect foil to Blanchflower's other-worldly inspirations.

The Scot was quick to keep watch on defence whenever Blanchflower was caught in the involved pursuance of an attack. For the first time since he came to Tottenham, Blanchflower was able to direct his whole concentration on attack without having to throw a constant regretful backward look at defence ... and when Mackay, also a great one for the upfield sortie, was drawn out of position, Blanchflower, recognising a great player, was constantly covering for him.'

The partnership seemingly made in heaven also 'rejuvenated Harmer' and Jones 'began to show that it was not for nothing that he had once been thought of as the most promising winger in the four countries'.

It was Blanchflower's second home match back as first-choice right-half and captain after a stunning return in both roles in a 6-0 lashing of Leicester City on 7 March.

* * *

The timing of Mackay's arrival was perfect. Spurs were on the cusp of great, glorious things. He and Blanchflower fitted hand in glove, while Jones was back to his best. Blanchflower's performance against Leicester, which equalled one he put on to defeat Duncan Edwards's Manchester United at Old Trafford in 1957, more than hinted at that.

Mackay said, 'Everything went right for me. It seemed as if there was a guardian angel around anxious to make sure that Mackay did well. When I jumped into the air the ball seem to make contact with my forehead. Even when I twice wildly kicked clear the ball flew across the field to Terry Medwin, our right-winger, and it appeared to be the perfect pass. In reality the ball ran for me in that match more than I have ever known it run for any other footballer. Even mistakes – and they were many – seemed to react in my favour. It was, to say the least, a fantastic experience.

'I did not let them [the supporters] down and played a good game. The pace of the game was significantly faster than that to which I was accustomed. I realised that I would have to train much harder and more often.

'Tommy Docherty among other friends had warned me ... This possibly can be traced to the fact Scotland has so many part-time professionals, and full-time training undoubtedly does give a player's game a vital edge.'

The development of Nicholson's Double-winning team was clearly still a work in progress. But the half-back line which went on to achieve the success was established from day one with Danny Blanchflower and Maurice Norman alongside Mackay; shades of what the Scot had experienced at Hearts with Freddie Glidden and John Cumming. And Cliff Jones had returned successfully from his broken leg, while Bobby Smith was en route to 32 league goals. Also in situ that day was Peter Baker, while Ron Henry and Terry Dyson were on Spurs' books.

Jones is convinced that Mackay's immediate impact was the moment the Glory Glory team sparked into life.

Jones said, 'Bill Nicholson had just taken over as manager and was developing the team when he went up to Hearts and bought Dave Mackay. And straightaway we took off! It was Mackay. His desire and commitment. He galvanised all those around him. It applied to everything in his life. He had to be the best, he had to win. Wherever he went he just changed his teams into winners.

'Also, whenever people talk about Mackay they talk about how hard and tough he was – which he was – but also he was a versatile, highly skilled player. Sometimes that gets forgotten a little bit. He was also the best team player. He had it all.

'Bill Nicholson used to say to us, "Train the way you play." If you are going to train with method you'll play that way. If you are sloppy in training you will also play that way. Bill made sure we trained accordingly and Mackay was there up the front all the time. Pre-season training, we'd have the cross-country to build up the stamina and the leg work. Mackay was always up there. He practised his ball skills. He had everything, Mackay. Volley with his left foot then right foot, against the wall. He made it look easy but you tried it and found it wasn't.

'Hearts had just won the Scottish League and Scottish League Cup – to add to other trophies with him – when Bill went up and got him and we took off straightaway.'

Terry Dyson, the left-winger of the Spurs Double team who became a close pal of the Scot, was delighted, having already played against Mackay.

He said, 'It was brilliant Bill signed him. I'd already played against him two seasons earlier in that Anglo-Scottish floodlit tournament, of course. We had to play against Hearts, Hibs and Partick Thistle. Dave caught my eye in the games we played against Hearts. He was a good player. Class. We had a good team with Danny but Dave made a lot of difference to us. We turned it right round. The reason for it was Dave. We had a good team but when he came in he made it.

'He fitted in off the field immediately too. I remember when he came down for his first game, against Manchester City, we got introduced to him and were just chatting away with him. He was just brilliant.'

14

'Transformed everything'

BILL NICHOLSON lavished praise on the instant impact made by Mackay at the Lane.

Commentator John Motson colourfully announced it thus, 'From north of the border, to the peal of thunder came Dave Mackay.'

And Nicholson was not about to quibble. He said, 'Mackay when he first came here transformed EVERYTHING. It was remarkable. I can't explain it. Because everything was so important. Everything was dynamic. And there were squabbles galore over goals whether they were goals or weren't goals even in five-a-side matches!

'I will always remember the first day he arrived at our training ground … the other players were shaken by his commitment and drive. They looked at each other as if to say, "What's happening here?" At the time we had a collection of seasoned professionals, most of them internationals, and Mackay was able to stir them all up. He brought a new surge into every aspect of club life, particularly in training. Suddenly our training routines became just as important as the matches. If he had served in a war he would be the first man into action. He would have won the Victoria Cross.

'Mackay would have been my first choice as captain, except that we already had a great one in Danny Blanchflower … he inspired and stimulated the team … he seemed to provide an extra spark and give added momentum. I knew we needed to make a new signing as we entered the 1960s. Mackay probably did more than anyone to forge a team capable of winning the Double.'

Mackay said, 'Whether I'm playing football, golf or tiddlywinks, I *have* to win. I used to be the smallest player on the pitch and to win the ball I had to tackle twice as hard as anybody else and I never got out of the habit.

'My two brothers also played for Hearts, and the three of us had a reputation for being ultra competitive.'

A thigh problem – caused by a boil – caused Mackay to miss five of the remaining eight fixtures, but he did enough to ensure Spurs would survive in the top flight. They were virtually safe after a 1-1 draw at Aston Villa in Mackay's second appearance with five games left. Mackay completed his quartet of Spurs appearances that season in the final two matches, a 5-0 drubbing of high-flying West Bromwich Albion and a 2-2 draw at Tom Finney's Preston North End.

But it seemed Mackay and Co. were looking long-term before safety was assured. Julian Holland wrote in *The Double*, 'All who watched them in those last matches of the 1958/59 season could not fail to see that Spurs were soon due for great deeds.'

Mackay experienced a disappointing Wembley debut for Scotland's full international team on 11 April 1959. Replaced by Bobby Evans as skipper under Andy Beattie, who was returning for his second spell in charge, Mackay was part of a 1-0 defeat against the Auld Enemy.

It was an occasion which gave him the opportunity to tweak his domestic arrangements in London while sorting a family home with Isobel.

He had been staying in a hotel in Russell Square but was encouraged by Tommy Docherty to lodge at his international team-mate's home in Cockfosters, north London.

Mackay wrote in his autobiography that the Doc said to him, 'We can't have you living in a bloody hotel. You're moving in with my wife [Agnes] and me and I won't hear of anything else.'

He added, 'They were very kind to a new boy in town and looked after me well. Tommy was obsessed with football, even more than me, and little else was discussed in that household ... who said he only started doing after-dinner speeches when his career in football ended?

'On Sundays, his day off, he'd be up early and off to a charity match. He regularly refereed for the Showbiz XI and he'd drag me along to run the line.'

Mackay also lined up for Scotland in a 3-2 friendly win over a West Germany side including 1966 World Cup finalists Uwe Seeler and Karl-Heinz Schnellinger in front of 103,000 at Hampden on 6 May.

A team-mate that day was John White, from Musselburgh, close to Mackay's wife Isobel's village of Whitecraig. White netted in the first minute of what was his full international debut.

Mackay said, 'He [White] played a great intuitive game … I made a mental note to tell Bill Nicholson about him, as Bill had more than once asked me about any up-and-coming talent in Scotland that I could recommend.'

Mackay had linked up with a player who would soon become another key competent to developing Spurs' greatest team.

The 'new boy' got to know his team-mates closely on a summer trip to Russia. He said, 'I will always believe we laid the foundation of the team and genuine friendship which has since played a notable part in the success of Tottenham Hotspur Football Club.'

He shared a room with Cliff Jones. Mackay said, 'Once again [referring to his experience in South Africa with Hearts] I found a close-season tour of marked value in getting to know my colleagues. Off as well as on the field I got to know my team-mates as men, and for reasons I can never understand – except that we got on – I shared a room with Cliff Jones. Cliff is so Welsh, and I'm so Scottish, I guess we cannot understand each other, which may account for the fact we never argue.'

Mackay played in all the games – a 1-0 win over Torpedo Moscow in front of 50,000, a 2-1 victory over Dynamo Kiev before 60,000 and a 3-1 reverse against a CCCP Select with a 100,000 crowd.

He said, 'The Russian trip, as a football education, was not a marked success … as footballers the Russians had little to commend them. They were tough, rugged and always fair, but the football made no impression upon us.'

But the touring party – which squeezed in visits to the Moscow State Circus, Lenin's tomb and Red Square – picked up fitness tips away from the football field at the Bolshoi Ballet.

Terry Dyson said, 'Bill Nick said he was impressed with the level of fitness of the dancers. Rudolf Nureyev was among them. Bill said he could use bits of what he picked up to use with us in training.'

Jones said, 'The Bolshoi Ballet was amazing. The dancers really were so fit. Bill found out it was down to weight training and employed a weight trainer [Bill Watson] and other teams wondered why we were so much fitter.

'He was an innovator. Now weight training is all part of football training but it is all down to Bill.

Isobel was 'anxious' to find a Mackay family home in London, making a few visits from Edinburgh to view several houses. Spurs had told the couple they could rent a property worth up to around £4,000.

The last trip began with Isobel meeting Dave off the plane on his return from Russia. She said, 'I was waiting. I'd not been anywhere much outside Scotland and could see these photographers. I went over and asked them, "Are you waiting for the Tottenham Hotspur players?" One of them said, "Not blinking likely, we're waiting for the Russian tennis players." They must have been coming to play at Wimbledon or something like that.

'I'd never met the Spurs players and was watching them come off the escalator. David hadn't appeared. But I recognised (assistant secretary) Alan Leather, who had been showing us around houses, and asked him, "Where's my husband?" Alan said, "He's been caught at customs." He'd bought extra cigarettes for our dads.

'I was privileged because I was allowed on the coach to take them back to Tottenham. They knew I was down to look at houses in the Southgate area.'

And the mission was a success because they found one at 26 Whitehouse Way in Southgate shortly after Mackay's return from Russia. The previous occupants were entertainer Terry Hall and his family.

Isobel said, 'Terry Hall was known as a ventriloquist with a puppet called Lenny the Lion. I remember going to the bin and finding a mask of Lenny the Lion. The children were amused.

'Was it a struggle acclimatising to the move? Yes. That was hard. Stranger in a new city? I was. There were no supermarkets. Near Whitehouse Way there was a little shopping centre. It made me feel like home because it was called Hampden Square! It had a little Co-op, bakers. I used to go in and have to repeat everything. I finished up pointing at everything – ordinary things; butter, milk, cheese. In the bakers when I first went in I asked for rolls. "Rolls?" they asked. I was delighted Sainsbury's opened a big supermarket in Southgate. It was like heaven.

'Tommy Docherty and his wife Agnes couldn't have been more helpful. I didn't drive. They used to come and pick me and the children up and take them to their house for many years. We were great friends. Agnes introduced me to Oxford Street and used to take me shopping there.

'I remember one Saturday. It was the start of the season and David was away with Spurs. My mum had been down but had to go back home. There was me in the house that morning with young David and Derek. A knock came at the door and I opened it and it was this lady and she said, "Hello, I'm Betty Blanchflower." It was Danny's wife. She asked whether I'd come round to her home at 46 Morton Way close by for a cup of tea in the afternoon. I replied, "That's nice of you but I've got two wee boys." She left it up to me. I looked at our boys diving about but I took courage and walked to Betty's with them. She didn't mind at all, was so nice and we became friends.

'Terry Dyson and David became great pals and Terry was always round. One day at Southgate, we hadn't been there long and didn't even know the neighbours, Terry came round in a new car to pick David up to go to a boxing evening. David was upstairs putting on his bow tie while I sat speaking to Terry. I just heard David go "whoaa" as he came down the stairs and ran out the house. David Junior and Derek had got into Terry's car and I don't know which one took the handbrake off but the car went across the road somehow into a parked car opposite. And Terry went mad! There was £12 damage and David paid it. It was funny later but not at the time.

'At the memorial to David, Terry came across to us and said to David Junior and Derek with a smile, "Which one of you was it that crashed my car?" I still keep in touch with Terry and Kay Dyson, Cliff and Joan Jones, Terry and Joyce Medwin, Maurice and Jacqueline Norman, Peter's widow Linda and, of course, before she died not long ago, Sandra White [John White's widow].'

Dyson said, 'Dave apologised for it at the time. But it was all right, it was only his kids.'

Bill Nicholson had promised Mackay that he had the funds to plunder the transfer market. He was, unsurprisingly, as good as his word. The manager's next major signing – and the next piece of the Double-winning jigsaw – was Dundee goalkeeper Bill Brown for £16,500 in June 1959. Ted Ditchburn had departed after 20 years' service two months earlier and Ron Reynolds lost the top of a finger in a freak accident, leaving Nicholson needing to strengthen the position with just John Hollowbread as a fit senior stopper.

Brown was a Scotland team-mate of Mackay's for the internationals against France in the World Cup and, under the half-back's captaincy, in the Home Championship versus Wales and Northern Ireland.

Mackay was to play a direct part in the next key component of Nicholson's Glory Glory team being put in place: John Anderson White.

He played with White – and Brown – to help Scotland ease to a 4-0 Home International Championship win against a Danny Blanchflower-captained Northern Ireland at Windsor Park, Belfast, on 3 October 1959. He netted one of the quartet of goals and put in an eye-catching display.

Nicholson had already acted on encouraging reports to see White in Scottish League action for Falkirk and concluded he was 'excited at the prospect of landing him'.

He added, 'White was a tremendous footballer and I knew he would make us a better team.'

Falkirk were thought to be short of cash and had received offers from Leicester City, at £13,000, and Chelsea for White's services.

Nicholson, seeking justification for capturing White, sought the opinion of Mackay, Brown and Blanchflower in the White Hart Lane car park on their return from Belfast.

Blanchflower described White as 'first-class' and said, 'If you can get him, catch the next plane up there.'

But there was a nagging doubt at the back of his mind that the player lacked stamina and was too frail – drawing a parallel with Harmer.

This is where Mackay stepped in to remove the remaining obstacles to signing White. Mackay, agreeing, like Brown did, with Blanchflower's assessment, told his manager, 'He's a cross-country runner.'

And, after checking that out with the army unit where White was completing his National Service, Nicholson offered £20,000 and the next morning the deal was done.

Mackay had got himself a slightly built team-mate with intuition, intelligence and mobility. In contrast to Tommy Harmer, White was always on the move with the help of the stamina he had built up from his cross-country running and sought to give and receive swift balls.

White's signing completed the three-strong fulcrum of goal creators – with Mackay and Blanchflower – which was to be fundamental to ripping up the record books.

Cliff Jones said, 'We really took off when Bill, after making the greatest signing he ever made with Mackay, got John White. You couldn't have got a better midfield than Blanchflower, White and Mackay.'

Mackay strengthened his link-up with new recruits Brown and White to underline his winning mentality to erstwhile club-mate Cliff Jones. They lined up for Scotland with Jones playing for Wales at Hampden on 4 November 1959. And any club allegiance Mackay had with Spurs' Welsh winger was forgotten in the 1-1 draw.

Jones said, 'It didn't matter. You'd get *mullered*. When Dave was at Tottenham he was Tottenham through and through but when he played for Scotland he was Scotland through and through regardless of who he was playing against.'

The fabled Double-winning XI was completed by the signing of Chelsea striker Les Allen in exchange for the talented but mercurial Johnny Brooks to sharpen up Spurs' attack in December 1959.

White had initially replaced central forward David Dunmore but it was felt, in the words of Julian Holland, there was 'too much cerebration, not enough shooting … Harmer and White were duplicating work at inside-forward: the line needed one of them.'

Mackay and his Spurs, even before key signing White and the Christmas present of Allen, along with summer capture Brown, were fast-realising the potential of the side Nicholson was putting together from the start of the 1959/60 season.

They were top of the league after six games and a barnstorming display and first goal from Mackay helped ensure a 5-1 victory against Manchester United at Old Trafford in a magnificent seventh. Mackay, who netted his first home goal as Spurs repeated the United scoreline against Preston seven days later, was lauded as the galvaniser-in-chief.

Holland wrote, 'His firm singleness of purpose complemented the fanciful artistry of Blanchflower. It was soon apparent that in these two … Spurs possessed the finest pair of wing-halves seen together for many a long year.'

Harmer thrived with the greater freedom the pair gave him. Jones, darting here and there in positive fashion, and Medwin on the wings were buzzing. Bobby Smith and Dave Dunmore were grateful beneficiaries at the point of the attack.

Spurs got even better on soft, churned-up surfaces, delivering the potential of a changing-of-the-guard 5-1 victory over champions Wolves. Pretty football got results and they had gone 12 unbeaten.

It was unlucky 13 as Mackay and Co. were pipped 2-1 at Sheffield Wednesday, with the debuting White, who netted the visitors' consolation goal, and Harmer and their slim builds comparable to Davids facing the Goliaths of Wednesday.

The following month another lesson was dealt out by a defensive Bolton, who included Ray Parry, whom Mackay had faced in that schoolboy international at Wembley.

But Spurs replanted their flag at the summit as they defeated Newcastle on Allen's debut on 19 December. And they held on until April – with Mackay becoming the only player to represent both the Football League and Scottish League when he helped the former pip their opponents 1-0 at Highbury a month earlier, alongside Cliff Jones and future Spurs team-mate Jimmy Greaves – until the wheels came off at the denouement.

The moment came with defeat against an ordinary Manchester City when a win would have all but sealed the title. Jones had a goal disallowed with the referee blowing the half-time whistle between his saved penalty by Bert Trautmann and the Welshman's seizing and netting on the rebound. City scored a second-half winner.

To show that the attack was proving its worth, Mackay's Spurs crushed lower-division Crewe Alexandra 13-2 in a fourth-round FA Cup replay, breaking their record scoreline after being surprisingly held to a draw at Gresty Road, although our subject said, 'He [Bill Nicholson] said to me, "Dave, I don't expect to see you going in on tackles like that, risking injury to yourself and others, and getting booked and sent off." Anyone would have thought we were ten goals behind, not ten goals up.'

But any thoughts of a Double were swiftly ended by Blackburn in the next round.

Mackay's former club Hearts might have been able to complete the double of League Cup and Scottish League that season. Yet overall, his new employers were rolling inexorably towards eventual glory themselves. Any cracks would, generally, be more than papered over – they would be firmly concreted.

The Scot and his team-mates were fortunate they had a manager who would supply the sand and cement in Nicholson.

Mackay said, 'You get a few great managers in eras, every ten years somebody else comes up. Bill Shankly, Matt Busby, Alf Ramsey. Bill Nick was as good as any of them. Once he said something, he meant it. That's the way you've got to do it.'

Cliff Jones said, 'Bill ran the club from the boot room to the boardroom. He was involved with every aspect of the football club. Managers now just involve themselves in the team but he was involved in everything. He would notice if a door needed painting somewhere. Something had to be altered. Every part. Loved it. Tottenham through and through.

'He was a good bloke, but you didn't mess with him otherwise you'd be in trouble.'

15

'The main man'

DAVE MACKAY was at the heart of the greatest season in Tottenham Hotspur's near-140-year history. It was perhaps the greatest of any English club. His side were lauded as the Team of the Century, even the greatest club side of all time in some circles, for the way they turned on the style and became the first to wrest England's Double of the Football League title and FA Cup in the 20th century in the same season.

The 1960/61 campaign is etched into the hearts and souls of Spurs followers who witnessed it, or had heard about it from those who witnessed it and got it passed down the generations to those who were trying to celebrate its 60th anniversary in the face of limitations put on it and most other activities by the coronavirus pandemic in 2020/21. And, no doubt, it will remain there, also in the hearts and souls of all true lovers of the beautiful game, regardless of tribal affiliations.

Its base philosophy was Arthur Rowe's push and run with triangles of players swiftly and fluidly combining towards goal with quick and short one-twos. But not all balls were short. The pace was not always fast; sometimes it was pedestrian before bursting into life and thrusting into their opponents' innermost sanctum in blinding, mesmerising patterns. And there was room in Nicholson's framework for individual expression as his side contained a host of talented ball-players. There was also room for those who specialised in finding the back of the net while offering a variety of options for the side's creators by allowing flexibility of movement and positioning. But everything was done for the benefit of the team. Individual aspirations were consumed in the quest.

Mackay and his side combined panache, poetry, power and pragmatism in mind and body in an irresistible blend that entertained, a prerequisite for Nicholson, and got results. Crucially they all got on. Bill Nicholson said in his autobiography, 'We were a team in every sense of the word, and a happy team with it.' There was no hint either of a weak link, a soft underbelly and 'curate's egg' line-ups; perceptions which have been expressed in the term 'Spursy' in the modern day.

Nicholson summed up the way Spurs claimed the Double, saying, 'I tried to keep our football as simple as possible. We had good players but didn't want them to indulge themselves too much as individuals. We've got to be effective, not exhibition players. I used to tell them, "You've got to involve other players like the 1950 side." You are always preaching involvement but the situations come on the field and the player has to do it for himself. The good player will always know what it is best to do. In the 1960 side we had the skill to play the ball first time, like the Rowe side did, but also the skill to play the longer game.'

Tottenham – with their new £1bn stadium, state-of-the-art training ground and six-figure weekly player pay packets – possess a high profile today due to what Mackay's team achieved and the way they did it. Every Spurs side since, fairly or unfairly, is compared to the one considered as near-perfect as you can get. They set the tallest of orders, the ultimate high standard. Just ask all surviving successors in the dressing and board rooms and managers' offices.

Mackay was one of the four pillars on which the side was built. There was Danny Blanchflower, with his flair, intelligence, attacking intent and sheer romance. John White had developed from an individual declaring he wasn't good enough to one defining perpetual motion with the ability of finding space undetected by opponents and linking play; receiving the moniker of The Ghost from Mackay. And Cliff Jones was on the periphery of the other three waiting to receive possession and cut through opponents like butter at speed with the ball glued to his feet, or bravely either spring his 5ft 7in into a leap or dive to head goalwards when the opportunity arose.

It was, in Jones's eyes, Mackay who was the most important of the pillars.

Terry Dyson shared that view, 'We didn't get beaten very often that season. Danny Blanchflower and John White were also key players but absolutely Dave was our best player. Every game was the same. He wanted to play and win. He encouraged us. A big inspiration. We wanted to win every game and we did most times. Obviously we didn't win them all and he was as gutted as any of us. But he gave everything. You could never say to him, "You could have given a bit more."'

Mackay was the complete package. He exuded confidence, motivation, and energy, which clearly spread to all his team-mates that Double season. A once brittle defence was now strong. An attack had an increased number of bullets. And a midfield ruled by him, Blanchflower and White was dominant and inventive. His versatility enabled him to swiftly protect those at the back, cover for Blanchflower and inspire the forwards. He intimidated opponents, even before kick-off when he threw a ball high in the air and trapped it dead as the players came out. It was as if he was inviting opponents to have a touch of it, implying if they did not it would be too late for a feel of the spherical object. His sublime technical skills of ball control and passing were at least equal to his other strengths in the most memorable season of his – and all his team-mates' – career. His physical attributes, compared to those possessed by Duncan Edwards, with whom he played during his army days, received attention.

Holland wrote in *The Double*, 'A finely made statue will try to express the human form in terms of stone; whoever made Dave Mackay is trying to express stone in terms of flesh and bone. His thighs are like the granite buttresses of some secure Norman church; his chest is so square and unyielding that it seems he has a second backbone down the front … at times he seems to not know his own strength.'

Mackay, as he did at Hearts, faced hints that he was a 'dirty' player but his record of never being sent off proved he remained hard but fair, winning the vast majority of committed tackles.

His self-belief was absolute, knowing he had the abilities to overpower opponents and he displayed a demeanour of pure enjoyment of being involved in a sport he loved. He was constantly looking for possession in whatever area of the field, second only to Blanchflower in being on the ball.

Mackay displayed a phenomenal work rate with seemingly endless reserves of stamina – and a long throw akin to a set-piece kick which was so admired by Craig Brown when the future Scotland World Cup manager was still a kid, and Keith Burkinshaw, the Spurs manager who guided Spurs to the FA Cup in 1981 and 1982 and the UEFA Cup in 1984.

Burkinshaw said, 'That Double side could obviously play superb football but they could also mix it up. It wasn't all fluid passing and movement, although that is what they were rightly acknowledged and praised for. They would instantly go direct if the opportunity presented itself and were devastating in that simplicity. Indeed, nothing was ignored in that regard.

'You can't go more direct than Dave Mackay's long throws. His upper body power in that respect was legendary as he looked to pick out Bobby Smith at the near post and Dave was always quick and able to go for it when the chance arose.

'And why not? If you have a centre-forward of Smith's strength and aerial ability then it could be a clinical route to goal. But it only worked because of Mackay's speed of thought and the muscle to get that ball into the danger zone in the blink of an eye.'

Mackay proved himself the complete player in this most complete of seasons.

Before reporting back for pre-season training in preparation for the 1960/61 campaign, Mackay kept himself match fit.

Nicholson had denied Mackay, with White and Brown, the opportunity of playing for Scotland against England at Hampden Park before almost 130,000 on 9 April 1960. Mackay was not happy and said, 'As there were three of us we felt it was a bit unfair on Scotland.'

The manager wanted his players to perform in a crucial club match against Everton, in which the unhappy Scottish trio were reported to have underperformed. Mackay said, 'We were in a huff and probably not in the best frame of mind.'

Mackay was able to join his country's touring party in the summer, with Scotland defeated 3-2 at home to Poland before 4-1 and 4-2 reverses against Austria in Vienna and Turkey in Ankara and a 3-3 draw against Hungary in Budapest.

He was joined by Brown for the four matches, with John White lining up with them against the Austrians and Turks. The internationals reacquainted Mackay with John Cumming and another former Hearts team-mate in Alex Young who netted against Austria and Turkey. His pal Denis Law figured against the Poles and Austrians.

It was a tour which had fun and controversy. There was reason for the Scots to chill out after what Mackay considered a deserved loss. It was a tense atmosphere in Ankara; a match that went on despite 'serious political problems', in an 'electric atmosphere, with a flute band, the beat of the drums and the chant of the crowd' on a 'poor' pitch that was reportedly played on four times each weekend.

At a reception hosted by the Turkish FA, it is understood Mackay was offered £10 by squad-mate Denis Law to walk the length of the table they shared in bare feet. Mackay completed the task for the agreed amount and told his hosts it was a Scottish custom. Law said in his autobiography, 'In those days we always had a banquet after international matches, and matters could sometimes get a bit out of hand. Dave Mackay was the leader of the pack, and I know there were a few shenanigans going on at the top table.'

Mackay also revealed he was part of a 'loud and rowdy' gathering of a few players who had had 'a few to drink' and admitted to bumping into and destroying a marble-topped table back in the room he was sharing with Law. The pair, it seemed, were given a dressing-down by the hotel and the next day back home it was reported how Mackay, Law and other players had been 'wrecking their hotel rooms'.

He insisted in his autobiography that 'it did not happen' and that a reporter had made 'the familiar tabloid mountain out of a molehill'.

There were also newspaper claims he had ignored his manager Andy Beattie's instructions to man-mark his inside-forward, although Mackay said they were 'utterly untrue' and that he had 'played badly'.

In the Hungarian capital there was a 'flare-up' and talk of a players' strike over pay, which Mackay felt made the squad 'appear to be money-grabbing fellows without pride in our country'.

They believed they were to take part in a 'private trial game' before the international, but found out they were performing before a 2,500 paying crowd. It mirrored a warm-up game they had played ahead of the World Cup for which they received a fee. Skipper Bobby Evans, representing Mackay and the other players, enquired as to whether they would get one this time. The answer was no and that was the end of it from the players' viewpoint.

Mackay said, 'Never was there a suggestion that the Scottish players would "strike". Neither, come to that, did the Scottish FA officials wave a big stick at us. There was nothing for either side to cover up. It was just a question of us all asking for a little money on the side and the Scottish FA, as they received nothing from the Hungarians, saying, "Sorry boys, but there is no cash available."'

Back at Tottenham, Mackay might have been developing into the foil for Blanchflower but his skipper set the bar at a height that teams had failed to clear since Aston Villa in 1897 at the start of pre-season in preparation for the 1960/61 campaign.

The romantic Irishman, no doubt encouraged at how close Manchester United in 1957 and Wolves three years later were to achieving what had been considered the impossible, revealed in his autobiography that he said to Spurs chairman Fred Bearman, 'We'll win the Double for you this year – the league and cup.'

And moreover, Blanchflower wanted to do it in style, as he inferred while uttering the quote which has became synonymous with Spurs and part of which was displayed at White Hart Lane and as the Lilywhites of today perform at the Tottenham Hotspur Stadium. Blanchflower's immortal words were, 'The great fallacy is that the game is first and last about winning. It's nothing of the kind. The game is about glory. It is about doing things in style, with a flourish, about going out and beating the other lot, not waiting for them to die of boredom.'

Nicholson, a methodical individual who was a romantic himself despite having a workmanlike playing style, was also optimistic if more measured. He said in *And The Spurs Go Marching On*, 'It felt in 1960 I had a side well prepared to do something. You cannot put it into words; it's a feeling you get. And I had a strong feeling around that time.'

In his autobiography he added, 'I knew we had a good squad of players and felt we could have a successful season. But luck plays such a large part in football. We could be drawn away in the third round of the FA Cup on a wet and windy day in early January and find ourselves out of the competition at the first hurdle.'

There was, though, no actual Double talk on the first day of four weeks of pre-season at the club's Cheshunt training ground, revealed Terry Dyson.

He said, 'There was no talk of the Double – from either Danny, Bill or anyone else there.'

Mackay revealed he heard nothing about Double expectations before the start of the season. But he felt 'our progress' could be 'traced back' to one morning in pre-season, when Bill Nicholson spoke to his players as they relaxed on the grass in front of him before training started.

Mackay quoted Nicholson in *Soccer My Spur* as telling them, 'I naturally feel disappointed we didn't win the league championship last season after such a fine run, but the defence did extremely well. We gave away fewer goals than anyone else. Now I hope the forwards will get more goals and it is up to us all to see that they do.'

And Mackay felt his manager's words hit home. He said looking back after the season in 1961, 'I believe, above all else, that the basis of any success the Spurs may have had can be traced to the ability of each individual player to sink his individuality and skill into the structure of the team without losing any of his own effectiveness.

'It is of paramount importance that everyone fully understands what is to my mind the cornerstone of the policy of the Tottenham Hotspur team.

'This, coupled with using common sense all the time, and adapting ourselves to all conditions ... to keep the ball flowing as much as possible in the middle of the field instead of relying solely on getting the ball to our wingers ... we realise that for the most part taller and heavier defenders are going to win the fight for the ball in the air.

'It was also a case of our forwards keeping on the move all the time. With our chaps running in so many directions, the man in possession found himself in the happy position of being able to pass to almost any part of the field, while the opposing defenders were never able to relax.'

Mackay and the rest of the players put in full days of hard work throughout the month of pre-season. There were country runs, although Nicholson described them more as a fast walk, building up stamina while limiting muscle strain. A lot was done with the ball and through drills such as throwing the centre-half forward at corners, encouraging the support of a player in possession, plus developing fluid attacks with the forwards drifting into spots which caught the opposition out.

Mackay impressed Nicholson with one particular drill, a free-kick routine of chipping the ball over the wall for the man standing on the end of it to run round and pick up. The manager said in his autobiography, 'We have players like Blanchflower, who could chip the ball accurately enough for others like Mackay and Jones to run on to and shoot. With the ball running away from over their shoulder and the probability that the goalkeeper would be running at them, it took a brave man to undertake the second half of the plan. But there were none braver than Mackay and Jones.'

Nicholson's ideas eschewed preconceptions of what would happen in the heat of league and cup battle, ensuring the preparation was merely a framework.

He said, 'Football is a simple game and the simple beliefs and tactics are those which bring the greatest rewards. One of the factors in its success in 1960/61 was that I had a sensible bunch of players who liked each other and wanted to play. There was no odd man out, no maverick in the camp. They were wholehearted enthusiasts like Dave Mackay ... nice people who wanted their colleagues to be as successful as they were. We were a team in every sense of the word, and a happy team with it. There were plenty of laughs and jokes in training ... but there was also a lot of planning and forethought. We worked hard that summer.'

Mackay remembered Nicholson telling him and the rest of the team in the dressing room prior to the season-opener against Everton on 20 August 1960, 'I was disappointed we did not win the championship last year. We were good enough, but it was not to be. I think if we simply carry on where we left off, we will this season. Good luck, gentlemen, and enjoy yourselves.'

'Enjoy' was the operative word for the wing-half's team as they kicked off a record 11 league victories on the bounce with a 2-0 win on a dry and fine day in front of more than 50,000 at White Hart Lane.

Mackay impressed against opponents who included Bobby Collins, injured when Hearts defeated his Celtic in the 1956 Scottish Cup Final, in the playmaker role. Perhaps Everton would have fared better if Mackay's former Jambos team-mate Alex Young, then on the Goodison Park playing staff, had been in their line-up.

Goals by Les Allen and Bobby Smith ensured the two points, but it was Mackay and Danny Blanchflower who took team-mate Terry Dyson's eye.

Dyson said, 'Some said we weren't at our best, that the side were running in like a new car. But we must have played well. Dave and Danny were superb at half-back, Dave in attack and defence and Danny going forward.

'We had a private belief it could be our year to emulate the 1951 side but no one among our group was getting carried away.'

Spurs were unbeatable, powered by the half-back line with Mackay 'a dynamic force of nature' according to *The Double*, a 'template' for the 'all-purpose midfielder'. The player himself saw his role in more prosaic terms, telling *Charles Buchan's Football Monthly*, 'The main job of a wing-half is to get the ball.'

He did a whole lot more as Spurs, who were the best-supported team in the country the previous season, improved their popularity still further with attendances averaging 50,000, attracting 2.5 million overall as they combined an ability to entertain while winning.

Mackay said, 'I was lucky to play for a Hearts team that put the emphasis on skill and then joined a Tottenham side that played pure football, because that was the way manager Bill Nicholson wanted it. Anybody thumping the ball without thought got a right mouthful.

'We enjoyed ourselves. The football was beautiful and delighted purists of the game like Bill Nicholson, Danny Blanchflower and myself. We all believed strongly that if people spent their hard-earned money coming to watch a football match they deserved to be – and should be – entertained.'

The fans flocked home and away to see the team of the moment as it racked up its record 11 victories on the bounce, while banging in 36 goals and conceding just 11.

Through the season, Mackay was convinced the training was a major factor in developing the players, especially the gym sessions.

He said, 'One of the most important parts of our training is the regular five-a-side matches we stage ... and four days a week we put in a 40-minute session ... demands that a man must keep on the move all the time. There is no slacking. It is the finest game I know for building up stamina, quick reactions, and all-round physical fitness. At Tottenham the rules are the same as in a league game and no quarter is asked or given.

'It wasn't big and there was no way out ... I took no prisoners and fights would break out. I'd love to get one of my colleagues in a corner and not allow him out. Sometimes this would lead to an elbow in the guts, with tempers fraying, but once it was over, it was finished. Nobody bore grudges.'

The games were played on a hard, outdoor surface before the gym was built. Ron Henry, a laid-back individual, was on a run during one and Mackay slid in low to tackle and suffered a burn up his leg. Henry said to Mackay in *The Perfectionist*, 'Are you f*****g mad?' But Peter Shreeves, who was to become manager, said in the same book, 'It's all right playing silky stuff on a Friday morning but next day you are going to take on tough characters who are going to kick you a bit … I think it hardened up the players and that was borne out by the results.'

16

Esprit de corps

ANOTHER FACTOR in Spurs' upwardly mobile movement towards glory came during time off as the team spirit was developing at a rapid rate away from the field. Mackay might have been one of the team's stars but there were no cliques. All of the players shared the bath in the dressing room post-match and, not much later, a place at the bar at the likes of the Bell and Hare on Tottenham High Road sipping a couple of halves of lager and chatting with the fans. It's a stark contrast to many of today's players who have no contact with the community after a game, more content to drive off from the ground in their 4x4 to their gated homes.

Players also proved they would not have gone far on TV's *Strictly Come Dancing* by attending The Royal, a dance hall on Tottenham High Road. They might also have turned up for a gig at the music venue Noreik on the district's main thoroughfare, where the Rolling Stones played and the Beatles popped in. They would pop along to Walthamstow dogs a couple of nights a week, something Mackay, with Terry Dyson and Bobby Smith, in particular enjoyed.

Mackay and others such as Maurice Norman, Bill Brown, Dyson and Smith would lunch together each weekday after training and go golfing.

Terry Dyson said, 'The camaraderie among the players was developing at a tremendous rate. It was brilliant … the so-called big stars like Dave Mackay, Danny Blanchflower and John White mixed in. We were one unit.

'We looked after ourselves but also enjoyed each other's company socially. Dave and I and others used to enjoy going to the Bell and Hare pub close to the ground after matches to chat to supporters about the game or whatever. The players certainly mixed with the supporters then.'

Mackay also attended dog nights in his downtime to aid the social bonding of the players. Dyson said, 'I'd pick up Dave to go to the dogs and meet Bob [Smith] there. Dave wasn't a gambler. Maybe ten bob (50p) or a pound. It was the company he and we enjoyed. Greyhound racing was popular then. I'd join Dave and others enjoyed a round of golf after training and lunch.

'We were a nice group of players but not so nice that we wouldn't have a go at each other if something was wrong. With Dave about we were never likely to be too nice. He wanted to be a winner, as we know. And made sure we did as much as we could to make sure we were. And winning certainly helped bring us even closer together.'

Cliff Jones said, 'We'd definitely go in the Bell and Hare or the Corner Pin pub in the Tottenham High Road after a game, and have a drink with and chat to supporters. You don't seem to be able to get near the players these days. Then some of the lads would go their different ways. Mackay, Dyson and Smith would go to the dogs at Hackney Wick or Walthamstow. Percy Chandler was the guv'nor at Walthamstow. They were always doing their money there. Bobby Smith liked a bet. It was all part of it. We were a special team of special players and Mackay was one of them.'

Isobel Mackay, part of a friendly group of players' partners, illustrated how players and fans mixed.

She said, 'At one match, I remember David and Cliff Jones were talking to a Spurs supporter friend from Welwyn Garden City, John Hempstead. He got David to referee games he was involved in on a Sunday and Cliff used to go along to be a linesman. And we'd all go to the pub afterwards and have a right sing-song. David and Cliff did this for a fair few Sundays. David and I made a lot of friends, because the players mixed with supporters. All the players did.'

Mackay and his team-mates carried on having fun on the field too. Manchester City were the only team to take a point off Mackay's men in the opening 16 matches. Even then, one report insisted that for the first half against City, 'magnificent Spurs scaled the very peaks of soccer perfection' in front of close to 60,000 fans.

It was surmised that the admirers of the Spurs way in this season of seasons had been infiltrated by rubber-neckers who just wanted to see the team trip up. This negative group got their wish when Spurs suffered their first and only league defeat before the end of the year. It came against rivals Sheffield Wednesday at Hillsborough, a not-for-the-faint-hearted 2-1 reverse on 12 November 1960. Mackay and Co. went into 1961 having dropped a mere four points, winning 22 and drawing two of 25 fixtures, while scoring 81 goals and letting in just 18.

Mackay was a model of all-round consistency and inspiration, displaying flair, steel, energy and leadership in a 'wonder' team, with pundits becoming louder and louder in their claims – which began on day one – that Spurs would win the title with their imaginative, joyous, clinical, confidence-filled football.

He cajoled, tackled hard and fairly without mercy, protected Blanchflower when the Irishman attacked, marauded forward, made goals and found the net himself.

He scored in a 6-2 home trouncing of Aston Villa which created a Football League record of ten wins in a row, which Spurs immediately broke in the next match without Mackay (who missed only two of the 25 fixtures played by 31 December), a 4-0 win at Wolverhampton Wanderers, Stan Cullis's long-ball team which had finished first, first and second in the preceding seasons.

Mackay was also on the mark in a 4-0 thumping of Nottingham Forest at the City Ground, and in a thrilling 4-4 Lane draw with reigning champions Burnley dubbed 'The Match of the Century' by Bernard Joy the former Arsenal player turned reporter, as Spurs were forced to relinquish a 4-0 lead. He was also on target in a 3-1 double-completing victory over Everton at Goodison Park. His 35-yard rocket earned the headline, 'Mackay brings Spurs joy'.

Mackay was also part of a victory over north London rivals Arsenal at Highbury which produced their seventh successive win from the start of the season, breaking the record set by Preston North End's Invincibles who claimed the first Double in the league's first season, 1888/89. He also helped guide Spurs to a win-double over near-neighbours West Ham United to maintain local pride.

Mackay helped Spurs produce their most 'telling' display against 'the most cherished and respected of post-war sides', Manchester United, dismissed 4-1 at White Hart Lane. Mackay, Blanchflower and White were considered 'faultless' in their 'accuracy', 'inspired' in their 'invention'.

Julian Holland wrote in *The Double*, 'They slowed the game and accelerated it at will. They painted intricate close designs on the canvas of White Hart Lane and linked them with authoritative and devastating sweeps of the brush. For the first half-hour their play was flawless.'

In short, overall, Mackay underlined he was doing rather more than just 'getting the ball' in a period which, I believe, established him as the first and greatest all-round midfielder in the eyes of those who witnessed his performances.

That it helped earn Spurs the accolade of being so above their rivals that it would take the likes of Alfredo Di Stéfano's Real Madrid, en route to five successive European Cups, to give them a game.

And Mackay was picked out for special praise. Phil Soar wrote in *And When The Spurs Go Marching On*, 'Mackay, who seemed to play with a skirl of bagpipes in his game, was the ideal blend of flinty, foraging pirateer opposite his skipper.'

Spurs entered the new year a staggering ten points ahead – when it was two for a win – with bookies no longer taking bets on them for the title. They had produced winning football that was nectar from the gods for anyone with an interest in the game. The defence was rock-solid and the attack scored for fun with the assistance of its triple axis of Mackay, Blanchflower and White.

Mackay, individually, was voted fifth in the BBC Sports Personality of the Year award, and he was tipped for the Football Writers' Association's Footballer of the Year honour, eventually won for the second time by his captain Danny Blanchflower.

Mackay said, 'My profile had risen rapidly … my reputation as a hard man in the game was growing, although this was something I did not nurture. I naturally preferred it when journalists focused on my ball control, passing, long throws, goalscoring. But I did accept and was proud, that my main attributes were my tackling, commitment and, hopefully, leadership … whatever the style, the crowds and the public seemed to like it.'

In the meantime, Mackay and his team-mates had a little light relief in the midst of their Double-winning season. He missed a 5-3 home friendly reverse against the British Army – with Spurs fielding a mix of first-team and reserve players – in October. But he netted twice in an emphatic 5-2 non-competitive win over Dinamo Tbilisi a month later with Nicholson fielding the team which has gone down in the club's folklore, apart from Terry Medwin in Cliff Jones's number seven shirt.

Spurs kicked off 1961 by squeezing past Second Division Charlton in their FA Cup campaign-opener. But Mackay's side lost their first league game of 1961, on 16 January against Manchester United. Mackay and Blanchflower were largely strait-jacketed by Nobby Stiles and Mark Pearson. The injury-hit visitors, with Cliff Jones, Peter Baker and Terry Medwin out, succumbed to their second reverse of the season, 2-0 in front of nearly 66,000 at Old Trafford.

Spirits were restored five days later when Spurs rediscovered the form that had deserted them in Manchester. Pleasingly, from the tribal-minded members of their support, it came as a result of a second win of the season over Arsenal, this time with a 4-2 scoreline. Mackay helped produce a magical moment by starting a slow move deep, before upping the pace by sprinting forward to collect a long Peter Baker ball and feeding Jones, who blasted home.

After Crewe were disposed of in the next round of the cup, it was looking good for the Double on 1 February 1961 as they sat 12 points clear of Sheffield Wednesday at the top and were three steps away from the FA Cup Final, with no injuries. Fallibility had not exposed itself too much.

But the lead started to be cut when Leicester City inflicted a first home defeat of the season on Spurs. And the evening after being outfoxed 3-2 by the Foxes reflected the growing celebrity inside the camp. Mackay told some of those close to him to tune in to *This Is Your Life* which was being broadcast live, a popular television show which 'ambushed' household names to feature on it, having organised significant people who knew the figure to secretly congregate in the studio, some of whom were to tell affectionate tales of their relationship with the star.

Host Eamonn Andrews went to enact the entrapment of one Danny Blanchflower outside the studio, having lured him there under false pretences, as Mackay and other team-mates mingled with relatives and other friends inside. Andrews said to his prey, 'Danny Blanchflower ...' But before he could complete the sentence 'this is your life', the Spurs captain was on his toes, not wanting any part of it.

Mackay said, 'I felt a bit of an idiot because I had told some friends and family of my own to tune in to the TV for a surprise that evening.

I told them as I tapped the side of my nose that I was not in a position to reveal any more. Their confusion was only increased when they sat through an episode of *This Is Your Life* featuring a dear old man who had fostered scores of children!

'Much was made of Danny's reaction and many media commentators applauded what they saw as his stand against the creeping intrusion of television into people's private lives. Personally, I felt Danny would have enjoyed such a tribute and that his reasons had more to do with his private life than his principles. He and Betty were having marital problems at the time and my guess is Danny would not entertain the hypocrisy that the programme might entail.'

Inconsistent results saw the advantage Spurs held over their nearest rivals reduced to just three points with the know-it-alls pointing out how they had blown up at roughly the same stage in the previous season.

Aston Villa were beaten but after disposing of the Midlands giants in the FA Cup, they tensed up in a 1-1 home league draw with Wolves, defeated Manchester City at the Lane and, after beating Sunderland in the cup, they lost to lowly Cardiff and Newcastle United while in between making the final by beating Burnley.

Mackay had appeared a little drained given the effort he had put in, while John White was considered to have had 'a couple of lean months' and an injury to Cliff Jones for parts of December and January did not help the cause.

Julian Holland wrote in *The Double*, 'Mackay had done himself some damage. By mid-March he was lacking his customary fire. His coals no longer burned, his flames no longer danced and leaped.'

Mackay was sidelined for three matches, in which Spurs picked up five points. His return in place of more-than-able deputy Tony Marchi saw him help guide the team to 3-2 wins at Chelsea and Birmingham which left the title a point away.

But just two days before the next league game, which would be against lone rivals Sheffield Wednesday, Mackay lined up for Scotland against England at Wembley. And he, along with all his team-mates and supporters, suffered as Walter Winterbottom's side won 9-3.

Club-mate Bobby Smith notched a double, Jimmy Greaves claimed a hat-trick and his schoolboy nemesis Johnny Haynes was also on target for a rampant home side.

Mackay pulled one back after the interval with the hosts already 3-0 up, but England were without pity.

He later rated that team as the best Auld Enemy XI he had ever known, even better than Sir Alf Ramsey's World Cup winners.

Mackay took that loss badly. He said, 'In footballing terms, it was the worst day of my life. We played crap … I felt such shame for letting my country down so dramatically and I did not know how I could face anyone. After the game Denis Law and I decided we needed to take solace in alcohol and sneaked into the West End for drinks at Malcolm Allison's 142 Club. Alcohol began to dull the senses until we turned and looked over our shoulders to see half the England team, all smiles and bathed in the glow of victory, walking in the door. For opposite reasons, the game ranks as one of the most famous in English and Scottish soccer history.

'That still hurts to this day. It was a freak result and is the only game people seem to remember me playing at Wembley.'

Mackay said in *FourFourTwo* in April 2009, 'Play? I didn't play – I was there but I didn't play! We were terrible. Everything went wrong but it was the keeper who got the blame. He emigrated to Australia – he had to! Denis Law saw him a few years ago and he asked, "Is it safe to come home now?" "NO!" Ha ha! Frank Haffey was his name – "What's the time?" "Nine past Haffey!" Ha ha ha! He had a bad game, but so did everybody else. Your defenders haven't done very well if you face nine shots on goal.'

Scotland team-mate Denis Law joked when asked about that game. He said, 'You just had to bring that up, yeh?! It was without doubt definitely [one of] the worst days of my career. The worst result.'

Isobel remembered the day. She said, 'I was visiting our son David Junior – who had bad asthma – at Great Ormond Street in London that day. I got on the tube at Russell Square and saw these billboards up stating "England 9 Scotland 3". I thought, "Was that a rugby match?!" I couldn't believe it. I confirmed the score when I got home and thought, "Oh my God, I won't be seeing David tonight!" David, Jim Baxter and whoever had gone to this nightclub and so had all those England players. It was devastating for him. When I saw him I just kept quiet and didn't get in his way!'

Scotland's worst defeat since 1954 saw them finish third as England claimed the title. Mackay's international side, which also included John White and old Hearts buddy Alex Young, had lost their opener 2-0 to a Wales team who included goalscorer Cliff Jones and Terry Medwin at Ninian Park in Cardiff on 22 October 1960 before, with Law and Young alongside the wing-half, defeating Danny Blanchflower's Northern Ireland at Hampden on 9 November.

The First Division championship was sealed by Spurs under the White Hart Lane floodlights on Monday, 17 April 1961. A crowd of 62,000 had crammed into the stadium, almost all to witness a coronation. Appropriately it was against Sheffield Wednesday, their only remaining rivals, who were on a 19-match unbeaten league run.

Tottenham only needed a draw for the crown; Wednesday had to win to keep their hopes alive. One reporter insisted Mackay was below his best and distracted in a 'personal duel' with the combative fellow Scot Bobby Craig in frenetic opening 30 minutes, while Blanchflower and White struggled.

Perhaps, in Mackay's case, it was partly because his involvement in such a resounding defeat for his country against the Auld Enemy two days earlier was so fresh in his mind.

If Spurs' Big Three were below par, it would have left the forwards devoid of the usual high level of support, although Cliff Jones did his best with a long run or two. The mean machine which was Wednesday's defence made it more difficult for Tottenham to attempt their free-flowing football.

Mackay was booked in the blood-and-thunder encounter that wiped any grin off the face of referee Tommy 'Smiler' Dawes of Norwich. Wednesday's Peter Johnson also ended up in the official's notebook.

The visitors took the lead through defender Don Megson but the game turned on its head in the last two minutes of the first half as 5ft 4in Terry Dyson jumped tall to win a heading duel with Megson and Bobby Smith seized on the ball to blast the leveller. Then, just 60 seconds later, Les Allen hit the title clincher.

Blanchflower slowed the tempo after the interval but the atmosphere remained intense. Clive Toye wrote in the *Daily Express*, 'It was a heart-lifting, blood-pounding period of fear for Spurs' hysterical fans.' But Mackay and his muddied team-mates survived until Dawes blew the final whistle and ecstatic home fans invaded the pitch.

The victorious players took their bows from the directors' box after the Scot shared a quiet moment with Blanchflower in the dressing room, tears welling up in his skipper's eyes. Mackay would now get an English league title medal to go with the one he earned in Scotland.

He said, 'When the whistle blew, I remember just stopping on the spot and drinking in the jubilation.'

Julian Holland said in *The Double*, 'It was a magnificent night, one on which the whole of English football might rejoice. In the span of this single season, Spurs had raised the standard of the game immeasurably throughout the land. And it was fitting and worthy that they should be England's next representative in the European Cup … The "Double" was half achieved. There remained only the cup.'

Terry Dyson said, 'Dave was a warrior. But even in the heat of battle he had managed to retain a sense of humour. He made out as if he was going to blast the ball past Bill Brown at one point. Another moment, I've read, he had time to crack a joke to Ken Jones, Cliffy Jones's cousin who was a reporter for the *Daily Mirror* and was sitting on the touchline as there was no room in the press box for him.

'Ken said in the *Double* book, "The ball went out of play where I was sitting for a throw-in to Spurs. I put my foot on it as Mackay came across to take the throw. Just before he took the throw he said to me, 'You can have 6-1 Smithy won't get his head to this.' It was amazing that in the midst of such an important game he would think of chatting to me on the touchline."'

Les Allen, who was the second top scorer in the Double season with 27 goals overall, behind Smith's 33, said, 'Scoring the winning goal to settle the title was a good one. But there were so many good ones. There isn't one that overtakes another one. It was a reliable side. We always gave 100 per cent when we played.

'The whole staff were involved in the success. I did my part, as did Bobby. I got 23 league goals and he got 28. But Bobby and I had to get those goals with the kind of players we had around us. Good players like Mackay, Blanchflower, White and Jones. What a team! Everybody fitted around our key players like Mackay. We were all in the right positions. You've got to give Bill Nicholson credit for that. He knew what he wanted.'

The remaining three games were an anti-climax as Spurs completed the second half of the season with ten fewer points and 21 fewer goals than in the first. They missed out on the opportunity of more than surpassing Arsenal's First Division record points haul of 66 with two losses either side of a victory, the second of which against Bobby Robson's West Bromwich Albion saw Mackay and his team-mates collect the championship silverware. Other 'compensations' were that the team fired in 115 goals and conceded only 55 while winning 31 of 42. Nicholson was disappointed in the way the end of the season played out but Mackay confessed that part of the reason was down to players being concerned about picking up an injury prior to the FA Cup Final.

The final was against Leicester City on Saturday, 6 May 1961. It was the moment that Mackay's history-makers were dubbed The Team of the Century.

Terry Dyson said, 'People talk about [Roger] Bannister breaking the four-minute mile and [Edmund] Hillary being the first to climb Everest because they were "firsts". Our achievement and Yuri Gagarin's achievement [becoming the first human being in space] were massive happenings in 1961. They caught the public imagination.'

Cliff Jones said, 'The fact we were first is the thing that counts. You can't take that away from us. We scored goals, could defend and play attractively. The gates were closed everywhere we played. That says it all.

'We bounced off Dave, Danny and John White. We had strength down the middle with Bill Brown, Maurice Norman and Bobby Smith. You couldn't have got much better than that and two good full-backs. We had a Welsh winger in me! He was all right! We also had 11 captains out there – but Dave was the biggest inspiration.'

Les Allen said, 'It was my favourite period in football. I agree you weren't going to get better than that. Dave and all of us players got on. There was a good atmosphere between all of us. Through the whole club, really. There were a lot of good players waiting to try and take our places but we kept the same team for most of the season. You get people who are getting old like me who always remember the team. And they remember things I don't, which is nice.'

Tony Marchi, Mackay's understudy at number six, was rated the best reserve in the league. He said, 'Standing in for Dave was and wasn't a problem because I played in other positions besides left-half. It was hard to become a regular as we had a top-notch team. They entertained everybody, grounds were always full, we played good football and won trophies. What more do you want? Was it the best ever club side? Looking back I would say that's true. Spurs had a side for five or six years which was excellent. It was great to be part of it.'

For Mackay, the Double meant he could 'feel modestly satisfied in knowing I have now won all the major honours in [club] football'.

But he emphasised the club spirit and reserve strength were key as Spurs completed the feat using just 17 players all season.

Mackay said, 'Our skilled players gave their all to the team. We are all good friends and have a tremendous reserve strength.'

17

The Double completed

IT WASN'T the smoothest of rides to the FA Cup Final but the voices claiming Mackay's side were contenders for the Double grew louder as each obstacle was cleared, especially as the club had a history of triumph in the competition when the year ended in one having previously won it in 1901 and 1921.

They squeaked and squelched through 3-2 against Charlton on a boggy surface in their opening match, their first of 1961. Their Second Division opponents refused to be overawed by a team who had won 46 of the 50 points so far available in the top tier. Even though they were not pulling up trees at their own level they unsettled their glamorous hosts.

Mackay had a personal interest in the next round with Terry Tighe, his best pal at school, in the line-up for visiting opponents Crewe Alexandra.

Tighe's Crewe, from the town famous for its railway junction, were derailed for a second successive season at the same stage by Mackay and his Lilywhites, although it was 5-1 rather than 13-2 this time.

Mackay said, 'It was a surprise to me that lining up for Crewe that night was Terry Tighe. We had come a long way from the playing fields of Saughton school ... in footballing terms, my best days were still to come and Terry had played his. Such is the rollercoaster life of a professional footballer, where luck can count for so much. As lads, there was nothing to choose between Terry and me. I have no doubt he could have been a top defender in the English First Division too.'

Mackay was outstanding alongside Blanchflower as Spurs overcame hosts Aston Villa 2-0 before 69,000 in the last 16, seven days after softening up their opponents in the league. And that was in spite of the fact Villa Park had been a 'bogey' ground for the Lilywhites in the competition; losing semi-finals in B6 6HE in 1948, 1953 and 1956.

But Sunderland proved a trickier proposition at a bulging Roker Park in the quarter-finals in front of over 60,000. The ear-splitting Roker Roar intimidated the illustrious visitors and the pitch invasion by their fans after Willie McPheat levelled a Cliff Jones opener provided pandemonium. Mackay reported that a home fan had cheekily asked Bill Brown for his autograph. Spurs, though, were no 'soft southerners', as they held their nerve and defended with steely determination as the volume was turned up to a *This Is Spinal Tap* 11.

Mackay was on the mark again as Spurs, perhaps stung by perceived effrontery to their aristocratic dominance of English football four days earlier, crushed the Wearsiders 5-0 in front of 64,797, a second highest Lane gate of the season, just 235 less than against Chelsea in the league.

It was back to Villa Park and a meeting with Burnley to decide who would go through to the final, which many felt would have made the best decider given the four teams left in the competition; the remaining sides being Leicester City and Sheffield United. Spurs were also aided by Harry Potts's reigning champions from Turf Moor having suffered a European Cup exit against Hamburg three days earlier. Goals by Bobby Smith (two) and Cliff Jones ensured that Mackay would be able to have a crack at completing his own cup double, having lifted the Scottish equivalent against Celtic five years earlier.

Spurs had to wait for four days before discovering who would be their final opponents as Leicester and Sheffield United were unable to produce a goal in two attempts to see who would be joining the Lilywhites at Wembley. But it was third time lucky for the Foxes as Jimmy Walsh and Ken Leek netted to cut the Blades down 2-0.

Spurs were hot favourites but also mindful that the Double had still not been done in the 20th century. Whether Leicester's comments in the wake of their league win at White Hart Lane earlier in the season, when they proclaimed Spurs would not win either competition, increased or decreased any self-doubt emanating down the Lane was moot. Leicester's league campaign, meanwhile, had petered out and was a consideration.

Mackay was looking forward to pushing his part in Scotland's 9-3 humiliation against England to the back of his mind at the same venue.

The week leading up to the showpiece final saw promotion build. Mackay and his team-mates were fitted for matching outfits and also received new pairs of Puma boots.

Mackay was pictured on his hands and knees under a ladder. The media thought it would make a good shot if all the Spurs team – in their kit – gathered around and on the steps at White Hart Lane. Mackay was all smiles despite having John White astride him, Cliff Jones sitting above them on a step, Bill Brown leaning towards the trio and the rest 'stepping up' and hanging on.

Team-mate Terry Dyson said, 'It was a bit precarious. Fortunately nobody fell off and hurt himself! Can you imagine if that had happened?'

The players were booked into Hendon Hall, just five miles from Wembley, the day before the final. Nicholson now wanted them to escape the attention the role of cup finalists can bring.

The players mostly enjoyed a lunch of steak and chips, a few tried the hotel's putting green, and others chilled in their rooms. After an hour they got on the team coach for Wembley to get a feel of the place and the surface in the company of journalists collecting their morning-of-the-match final previews. They returned to the hall for tea to be informed they were going to have a night out courtesy of Bill Nicholson. They all hopped on the coach in the early evening to head for London's West End to watch the recently released film *The Guns of Navarone* at the Leicester Square Odeon. It was a way for Nicholson to distract and relax his players and help improve chances of a decent night's sleep and avoid lying awake in the small hours thinking about the game.

Ironically a scene from the war epic could have instilled negative thoughts in his team as to whether the 'impossible' Double could be completed the following day. Gregory Peck, playing Captain Keith Mallory, and David Niven's Corporal Miller were talking after coming through a hairy adventure. Niven said, 'To tell you the truth, I didn't think we would do that.' Peck replied, 'To tell you the truth, neither did I.'

Fortunately the scene didn't keep them up, with Mackay reporting that he and his room-mate Bill Brown were 'happily tired' on the return trip and got up in the morning 'at our leisure' after breakfast in bed and playing records in their room. The pair joined others – some of whom had walked the grounds – in the communal television room watching *Grandstand* featuring a preview of the match they would be playing in.

It seemed a relaxed morning for most, but it was a tense one for Bobby Smith who, reported pal Dyson, sneaked out early doors to his doctor for a pain-killing injection to mask a twisted knee sustained against West Brom (it followed one on the previous day so he could try and convince Nicholson of his fitness in the final training session before the decider). He had kept the issue secret for fear of missing the big day.

Mackay also had his own physical concern, which was kept hush-hush until after the final. He had carried a shin problem through the final four league games after taking a knock without, reportedly, wearing pads in his previous Wembley appearance; literally adding injury to the insult of Scotland's nine-goal annihilation by England. Rest and treatment by trainer Cecil Poynton ensured he would be available for his swift return to the national arena.

The Spurs party set off in the coach with a police escort after lunch for the short journey on the north London ring road, with crowds cheering all the way. Mackay was up for the challenge ahead. 'I simply could not get on the field quick enough to play my part,' he said in *The Double*.

On arrival, Mackay and the rest went into the dressing room – with good luck telegrams piled on its table – and were each given concise individual advice by Nicholson of the player they needed to keep an eye on. Mackay said in *The Double*, 'It is the smaller and vital parts of an opponent's make-up that Nicholson is so good at detecting.' Mackay also sensed his team-mates were quieter than usual. He said, 'Usually, I think we were a rather noisy crowd … on this occasion no one said very much. Inwardly, I suspected we all felt we'd let everyone down if Spurs did not win and so achieve the Double which had become an obsession for us all.'

The team displayed their new suits to those gathered early in the stadium as they studied the weather conditions and bounce of the ball on the pitch. With rain anticipated after a fine dry morning, they opted for leather rather than rubber studs.

Mackay stuffed thick pads over sponge pads down his socks to protect his shins, Blanchflower was worried about an injured ankle and Smith was now devoid of concern over his dodgy knee, as the team changed before emerging and lining up with the Leicester players in the tunnel. Then, led by their respective managers, they walked out of it on to the pitch to the cacophony of noise made by 100,000 spectators, who had been entertained pre-match by live music including a performance of the cup final staple 'Abide With Me'. There was the formality of being introduced to royalty in the shape of the Duchess of Kent, standing in for Queen Elizabeth II. It was a long way from street football in Glendevon Park.

Mackay said, 'All the players lucky enough to have played in an FA Cup Final will tell you that there is nothing like that moment when you leave the tunnel and emerge out on to the sun-kissed, lush turf. The noise is deafening and the singing, swaying, brightly-coloured crowd a sight to behold. You really don't want it to end.

'I ran up and down and jumped on the spot like a boxer waiting for the fight to start. I clapped my hands together and shouted encouragement to the other lads. In 90 minutes, we could have made history. It's hard to stay calm when you're looking it in the face.'

Destiny was at hand for Mackay and his team-mates. Spurs were favourites and were cheered, Maurice Norman in particular, that the Foxes had replaced ace striker Ken Leek with the talented but inexperienced Hugh McIlmoyle. And when City defender Len Chalmers was injured in a tackle with Les Allen in the opening exchanges – with no substitutes allowed – it looked as though a Spurs victory was being written in the stars.

But we were dealing with reality, not probability theories.

Mackay was prominent pushing forward with the prevalent wind and rain behind him and his team in the opening minutes and helped lay on an opportunity for John White. He calmly controlled a headed clearance from a long throw he had made and skipped by Frank McLintock to produce a deep cross from a tight position in the left-hand corner. White had joked the previous day while treading the turf with Cliff Jones he would score if presented with the ball in a similar position. But the inside-right missed the target.

Mackay withdrew along with Blanchflower as McIlmoyle, Howard Riley and Jimmy Walsh began to cause Spurs problems even though Leicester had been effectively reduced to ten men. Chalmers – the latest to be affected by the injury jinx at the FA Cup Final since the war – was only able to provide nuisance value on the wing with McLintock slotting into his team-mate's right-back slot.

Astute interceptions and a series of pinpoint crunching tackles saw Mackay help to stem the threat of spirited opponents, who knew, even as underdogs, would be unpopular winners with most outside Leicester due to Spurs tickling the fancy of the football romantic in their most famous season.

Cliff Jones found the net from a Terry Dyson cross just before the interval but referee Jack Kelly gave offside.

Blanchflower, with his gift for changing the pace of a game, waved his magic wand as a sluggish Spurs became more enlivened despite the worsening rain. But there remained no breakthrough until 66 minutes when Dyson, after Allen and White had combined, passed for Smith to turn his defender and blast Spurs into the lead and give them the freedom to at last fully express themselves.

It was the 33rd and last goal of the season for top scorer Smith – who held second place behind Jimmy Greaves in Spurs' total goals scored charts with 208 for six decades until Harry Kane became the third member of the 200 Club and passed him in 2020/21.

Smith returned the compliment for Dyson to head the second nine minutes later and Spurs were home and dry in the wet and displaying the kind of mesmerising football that had captured the hearts of the nation throughout most of the season.

Mackay, who characteristically hopped on his right foot before gliding long balls with his left throughout, illustrated his own artistry and versatility in a late cameo which reflected the ball skills he possessed with both feet, aerial prowess, body strength and confidence.

Leicester goalkeeper Gordon Banks punted a long, high ball. Mackay, 5ft 8in, outjumped his opposing inside-forward, City captain Jimmy Walsh, to head the ball to Ron Henry who returned it to Mackay, to feed White first time. His fellow Scotland international immediately returned the ball. Mackay controlled it with his right foot and, as Keyworth charged toward him, switched feet on a clockwise turn to put himself between the number eight and the ball, kneeling down on his right knee before completing the circumference with his left foot. Walsh came again and Mackay, again with his back to his hapless opponent, feinted to go to his right again before going anti-clockwise and moving clear. And, with entertaining, showboating flurries, he performed a couple of step-overs.

Walsh, who was unselected for the Celtic side beaten by Mackay's Hearts in the 1956 Scottish Cup Final, had caught his fellow Scot to concede a free kick in the midst of all this trickery, but the Scot had shown the innate skills he possessed extended far beyond the brawn for which he had become, fairly or unfairly, known.

Mackay was described as a 'stale, tired footballer, uninspired in his distribution of the ball in attack and missing his tackle all too often in defence', by Julian Holland in *The Double*.

That seems a harsh assessment and to this writer largely inaccurate. Okay, Mackay had had a long, hard season and a dropping-off towards its conclusion would only be natural, and maybe he was not at his peak against Leicester, like, understandably, other colleagues. But he was always a winner, no matter what his physical and mental state. Preferably, like Nicholson and Blanchflower, he liked to win gloriously, with a swagger, with style, but he recognised that sometimes, if needs must, pragmatism outweighs performance in order to get the required result. And his solid defensive work, including a few accurate sliding tackles at the back and in midfield, helped shut down Leicester.

He said, 'Personally, I decided that I would be taking no chances in moving forward and that and that I would stay deep in our half and focus purely on defending. We had a one-man advantage. We had five brilliant forwards. They didn't need me or Danny. We'd help ensure that the door remained firmly closed. Bobby, Cliff, Les, Terry and John would have to do their stuff … they did.'

Nicholson was disappointed rather than elated as Kelly blew the whistle and Spurs had taken their place in football's hall of fame.

It might not have been a vintage Spurs performance until the latter stages, but the fact they conserved energy on a stamina-sapping pitch – with centre-half Maurice Norman staying put rather than venturing forward at set pieces – proved a wise approach as Leicester inevitably tired.

Mackay said, 'I remember back in the changing rooms with the champagne flowing and Bill Nicholson came among us and said something along the lines of it being a great achievement, but he was disappointed we didn't play the lovely football we know we could. That took the wind out of my sails. Here was a man whose rise in football was nothing short of meteoric. A man, who in just 30 months, fashioned a struggling First Division side into a team to take the first Double since Queen Victoria died, was expressing disappointment. He had created the so-called Team of the Century yet he was nagged by the fact that on the day we finally scaled the mountain, we did not play at the pinnacle of our abilities and thrill the watching millions. That's a perfectionist for you.'

Mackay and his team-mates climbed the 39 steps up to the Royal Box to reacquaint themselves with the Duchess and receive their medals before turning to greet the acclaim offered by their supporters as Blanchflower held the FA Cup aloft. There was the customary duty of all sides in the position the Lilywhites had found themselves: a lap of honour.

The celebrations extended into the evening at a dinner-dance at the Savoy Hotel in central London with Isobel and other players' wives and girlfriends joining their menfolk. There was a sense of club history as Ted Ditchburn, Eddie Baily, Les Bennett and others joined their old push and run team-mate Bill Nicholson in raising a glass to their successors in the new decade. Four members of the 1921 FA Cup team were also present.

Ernest Marples, the government's Minister of Transport, and esteemed cricket writer John Arlott made complimentary speeches. Singer/comedian Harry Secombe and all-round entertainer Roy Castle performed, while singer Shirley Bassey, who had lost her voice, handed out copies of the single 'Tip Top Tottenham Hotspur' made by celebrity fans in honour of the team collectively called the Totnamites. The players joined in a sing-song with club assistant secretary Alan Leather accompanying on a piano.

Mackay, with Terry Dyson, John White and Bobby Smith, moved on to another hotel up the road where well-off supporters were staging their own celebrations.

The players did make it to an open-topped bus parade along a packed, joyous Tottenham High Road the following day. Dyson picked up Mackay in his Ford. As they got close to the High Road, Dyson reported there was nobody about.

He said, 'I turned to Dave and said to him, "This could be embarrassing." Then we got to Edmonton Town Hall from where the parade was due to start. The size of the crowd was incredible.'

They rubbed shoulders with the dignitaries inside the hall before boarding the bus, which made its way to Tottenham Town Hall as the sun shone on their parade with the crowds now gathered.

Mackay and Dyson adjourned after a civic reception, along with Cliff Jones and John White, to the Bell and Hare. Dyson's mum was staying at the pub – while his dad returned to run the family hostelry back in Yorkshire – and the players continued the party.

Dyson said, 'Dave was clearly in the mood as he found a bowler hat from somewhere and put it on. I think he was trying to copy chairman Fred Bearman's choice of headgear.'

And forever more Mackay and each of the XI will remain in the history books. It trips off the tongue of all lovers of the beautiful game: Bill Brown, Peter Baker, Ron Henry, Danny Blanchflower, Maurice Norman, Dave Mackay, Cliff Jones, John White, Bobby Smith, Les Allen, Terry Dyson. As also should the six performing reserves: Tony Marchi, Terry Medwin, Johnny Hollowbread, Frank Saul, John Smith and Ken Barton.

They remain the greatest team the club has ever produced, and arguably the greatest any club side has produced for that one season. Two and a half million people watched them. The good and the great praised them and a former Balgreen primary pupil was at the heart of it.

Dave Mackay named it the greatest side he ever played in. He said in 1970's interview in *The Sun* with Jimmy Greaves, alongside writer Norman Giller, when asked which one was, 'Well obviously the Tottenham team that won the Double in '61, but the Hearts side with which we won the Scottish championship ran them close. I skippered the team that banged in a British record 132 league goals that season.'

* * *

Frank McLintock, a fellow Scot who was to become a friend of Mackay and knew Isobel, was in the Leicester line-up as Spurs completed the Double, and went on to emulate that achievement himself as captain of Arsenal, Spurs' north London rivals, ten years later.

When I mentioned the 1961 FA Cup Final, McLintock said in mock indignation, 'F*****g hell, I remember that. Len Chalmers got injured early and I moved from midfield to the back four. In the old days you couldn't have substitutes. You just had to go in another position and probably damage your leg even more than it was before instead of being taken off and getting treatment.

'Len went out on the wing, knackered. The big surprise to most of us was the Wembley pitch looked fantastic but it was very heavy on your legs. I'd never really played on pitches like that before.

'They [Spurs] were a bit ordinary and it took two goals late on more or less against ten men. But that can happen. We had to get the defence sorted out and you look for an "away" pass to sneak a goal somewhere. Eventually you are almost certainly going to suffer.

'Looking back you've got to say "well done" to Spurs because they had a really terrific side.'

I asked McLintock how the Spurs team and his Arsenal Double side compared. He said, 'It is difficult to tell. Tottenham had a fantastic side then. Seven outstanding players and other players who were very competent although not as brilliant as the other ones. A top, top side.'

Was it a bigger feat than the one achieved by the Gunners outfit? 'I don't know. To go and win the Double in those days with no [1961] or a little amount [1971] of subs was fantastic really.

'Spurs deserved the Double. They were up there for the whole season. They played great football and had some great players; Dave Mackay, Danny Blanchflower, Cliffy Jones was a brilliant player as well. John White was terrific. Bobby Smith was a tough player, a great goalscorer. They just seemed to have a lot of top players in all different positions.'

And was Mackay the lynchpin, inspiration, heartbeat? McLintock said, 'I think so, but that doesn't mean to say that Danny Blanchflower wasn't as compelling as well. Danny was an outstanding player and gave them that extra bit of class.

'Dave had a bit of everything. He was a terrific tackler – f*****g frightening – and could also pass the ball brilliantly well. He was an all-round player. Mackay and Blanchflower were a great combination.'

McLintock also revealed that Mackay tried to get him to Tottenham. He said, 'I didn't know Dave particularly when Spurs did the Double. I knew OF him, because he was a fantastic player. But I got to know him. And later on he was trying to get me to Spurs. Danny was getting past his best. I did actually consider it but nothing happened. I don't know if it was Bill Nicholson. Certainly the trainer was a lot to do with it, I believe. I heard he didn't fancy me as a player. So it all went past and I joined Arsenal. Alan Mullery went to Tottenham six months later.'

18

Glade all over

VALERIE MACKAY was born in January 1960, a first daughter and third child for Dave and Isobel to follow David Junior and Derek. And like her brothers she entered the world at Elsie Inglis hospital in Edinburgh, as did her sister Julie four years later with their father wanting to ensure his children were born in Scotland and thus able to play football for the country if the need arose.

Her dad wanted to be there for her birth but missed out. Derek Mackay said, 'Spurs were playing at Crewe in the FA Cup just before. Dad asked Bill Nicholson if he could go up to Scotland for Val's birth. Bill told him to go up after the game. It was assumed, I suppose, that Spurs would win. But it was a draw and Dad had to stay down for the replay on the Saturday, the famous one in which Spurs hammered Crewe 13-2. Val was born on the Sunday. But Dad definitely made the other three births!'

Valerie's birth underlined for Isobel the problems with the size of the family home in Whitehouse Way, Southgate. She felt it was too small for five people but that her husband 'wasn't too bothered'.

Isobel said, 'The kitchen was so small at Southgate. It had a sink, a larder, a table for two which you could pull out for the four of us before Valerie. Before I came down, David had got a cooker. It was like a battleship that almost filled the kitchen anyway. I'd left a bigger kitchen in Scotland.'

Something had to give eventually – and it did. Isobel said, 'I asked David, "Could you not say [to Spurs] we need a bigger place?" He said, "No. If you want you can phone the club. I'm quite happy." So I phoned

Tottenham up this day. It was Barbara Wallace, Bill Nicholson's secretary. She said, "Oh, hello Mrs Mackay. What can I do for you?" I said, "Well I've been asking David, wondering whether we could get a bigger house?" She said, "Leave it with me. I'll get someone to speak to you." So anyway it was Bill Nicholson! He said, "Oh Mrs Mackay, what can I do for you?" I said, "It's about the house." He said, "Could they extend it?" I said, "No, I'm not happy here."

'He said, "Well houses are not my department but leave it with me." I was looking for the go-ahead to look for another house and he said we could do that. Anyway, an estate agent came round and I asked him whether he could start house-hunting. He said, "What kind?" I said, "I don't care as long as it has got a big kitchen." He said, "I've got the very house. You can look at it very soon."

'David's mum and dad were down on holiday and we arranged to go and see it. It was a bungalow at 6 The Glade, Enfield. It had a brand new kitchen. The living room was like a ballroom. I said to David, "If we get this house I'll never argue with you again". The houses Tottenham got for you to rent at the time were worth around £4,000. This one was £7,250.' Isobel said in *The Perfectionist*, "'Bill said they would keep the same rent [as Southgate].' Perhaps Spurs recognised it was worth keeping Dave and his family happy. Indeed they were. Isobel said, 'We had a house party and found we had nice neighbours. We were all happy there.'

Mackay's star had risen as high as was seemingly possible in the football heavens. At least domestically. But a double Double in back-to-back seasons would elevate it still higher. This was something Bill Nicholson was to publicly covet, along with the European Cup to seal a history-busting Treble. And, of course, his side's successes of 1960/61 ensured Mackay a return to the premier continental club tournament, with the wing-half having good reason to believe his experiences with Hearts could be more than merely improved upon. Surely Spurs were good for getting beyond the first round?

Mackay's priority seemed to be on Spurs proving their credentials continent-wide. He said, 'We awaited the new season with keen excitement. We believed that the best was yet to come and that we could be the first British club to win the European Cup. That was our main aim. We'd won everything we could domestically so it was natural that we wanted to make history and prove we were the best not just in Britain but in Europe as well. We felt our style of play had more in common with European sides than most English clubs.'

As a member of the Team of the Century, Mackay would forever carry the epithet 'Double-winner' with pride. It is still remembered as a benchmark and considered worthy of celebration today, and, according to Holland's *The Double*, it produced 'the first superstars of the modern age', 'laid the foundations for the modern game' and 'played a large part in helping to define how the game's evolved'.

Terry Dyson said, 'Our side was viewed in most quarters as being as close to a perfect version of that ideal as possible. We tried our best to satisfy the perfectionist in our manager – and got as close as any was likely to in my opinion.'

It was also a team that coped with the increased pressure of being favourites to the extent that each match was like a cup final. Pressure was relieved by victories and emotions expressed in exuberant goal celebrations – criticised in more strait-jacketed circles – by a group who had become friends as much as colleagues.

The bandwagon was certainly rolling off as well as on the field. Full-blown football commerce was largely two decades away, but roots were sprouting in N17 as a result of Spurs winning the Double. Mackay got a book deal with Stanley Paul for *Soccer My Spur*. Others, such as Danny Blanchflower, appeared in advertisements. There was also sponsorship to be had.

Spurs had presented the Football Association with a dilemma by completing the Double. What could the governing body do about the annual Charity Shield match between the champions and FA Cup winners which prefaced each season? The 1961/62 season was the first time they faced such a dilemma since the game was put on the fixture list in 1908.

The powers that be put together an FA XI made up of a strong England team, minus the Spurs players, and managed by national boss Walter Winterbottom, to take on the Team of the Century at White Hart Lane on 12 August. A full-strength Tottenham team won 3-2. Johnny Haynes, Mackay's bête noire as a schoolboy, put the representative side ahead before the hosts charged back through goals by Les Allen (two) and Bobby Smith, then West Ham's Johnny Byrne scored a consolation for the illustrious visitors. It was another trophy for the trophy collector from Edinburgh.

Spurs were able to field their famous and already immortal XI as they opened their league season by the seaside seven days later. But Mackay, after helping the Lilywhites beat Stanley Matthews's Blackpool 2-1 at Bloomfield Road, was sidelined for the next three matches, a win and loss against West Ham and a Lane victory over Arsenal in which his pal Terry Dyson created history.

Mackay was delighted as a near-60,000 witnessed Dyson secure the only hat-trick by a Spurs player against Arsenal at the time of writing. Interestingly, Mel Charles, who chose Arsenal instead of Spurs, triggering Bill Nicholson's swoop for Mackay, was in the beaten Gunners line-up.

Everything was going swimmingly in the league as Spurs remained unbeaten at the Lane until late November when Leicester City gained a small revenge for their FA Cup Final defeat by overturning the hosts 2-1 with Mackay in the middle of another three-game absence.

Mackay and Co. might not have been the master blasters of the league season before – winning just six instead of each one of their opening 11 fixtures – but had put themselves in the hunt for back-to-back titles.

By then they had successfully begun their first campaign in the European Cup with the game-changing arrival of Jimmy Greaves and the FA Cup run still to come.

Mackay's initial attempts to add to his European Cup experiences did not go down too well with the locals in a Polish mining town, it was reported.

Spurs' opening match was behind the then Iron Curtain against Górnik Zabrze in Katowice.

It was a steep learning curve for Spurs on and off the pitch. Nicholson described the mining town as 'very depressed' and the best hotel 'terrible' on a reconnaissance visit. Danny Blanchflower witnessed prisoners digging up cobblestone roads with guards carrying machine guns, while women cut grass in the park close to the stadium with scissors.

On the field, Spurs found themselves 4-0 down as Mackay became the target of vehement verbal abuse from 70,000 incensed home supporters, many shaking their fists and threatening retribution following one challenge by the Scot which was deemed to have provoked a 'terrifying situation'. Cliff Jones and Terry Dyson pulled back goals after the hosts were reduced to ten men when Jan Kowalski was injured after a challenge by Mackay. Spurs were booed and whistled off at the end of what was the first leg of a preliminary tie; viewed as adopting an over-physical approach. It appeared the only sign of gratitude emanating from disgruntled hosts was a lump of coal shaped into a railway truck.

Mackay said, 'I think we believed passing through the round would be a formality, but we were rudely awakened by the passion of the crowd and raw determination of the Poles.'

Seven days later, it went from the ridiculous to the sublime as Mackay shone, along with his team-mates, in the first of the fabled Glory Glory Nights. Supporters dressing as angels – in response to the 'no angels' description of their side by the Poles' coach in the opening leg – seemed to inspire the first known home performance of the tune which became synonymous with such Lane occasions, 'Glory Glory Hallelujah', based on the 'Battle Hymn of the Republic' penned by American writer and political activist Julia Ward at the beginning of her country's Civil War to the tune of 'John Brown's Body'.

Mackay dubbed the 8-1 drubbing of Górnik 'one of the best games I have ever played in'.

He added, 'We were irresistible … [and] played the sort of game that Bill would have liked us to play against Leicester City in the cup final. It was an exhibition of the Double side at its best.'

A perfect hat-trick from Cliff Jones, one each with his left and right foot and another with his head, a double from Bobby Smith and one apiece from Danny Blanchflower, Terry Dyson and John White boosted an ecstatic packed house, which include your author's late father Maurice. The 'wall-of-sound' atmosphere was electric as Spurs, wearing all white, swarmed over their opponents.

Mackay was out for the first leg in the next round away to Dutch champions Feyenoord but his replacement Tony Marchi helped secure a 3-1 win in a stadium in which they would become the first British winners of a European club competition. Frank Saul, 18, scored two and Terry Dyson one with a performance manager Bill Nicholson described as 'muddled'.

Mackay returned for the second leg on 15 November. Spurs put on a conservative performance in stark contrast to the home display against Gornik and the match ended 1-1, enough for them to ease through.

But the night was most memorable for Mackay as he sustained a hairline fracture to the side of his skull – and then returned to the action after treatment before collapsing back in the dressing room at the end.

He clashed heads with Dutch defender Kraay and both ended face down and motionless. Kraay carried on but Mackay was stretchered off.

It was reported initially that he was 'severely concussed and that two doctors were debating whether to send him to hospital'.

Mackay regained consciousness in the dressing room and asked, 'What am I doing here?' He was 'permitted to go back' on to the field.

Cliff Jones said, 'I saw it. He clashed heads and went down. I can remember running over to him. He's lying there, and when Mackay stays on the ground, there's something wrong. [Trainer] Cecil Poynton came between each of us and rolled him over to try and give him some smelling salts. And there was blood pouring out of his ear. I thought "Jesus Christ". You didn't have to be a scientist to know there's something wrong there. He got taken off and I thought, "That's it, we're not going to see Mackay again." And all of a sudden there's a big roar and Mackay's standing on the touchline and comes back on to the pitch. I thought, "I don't believe this," and then we got into the dressing room and he's collapsed and rushed to hospital. He had a fractured skull. That was Mackay. Just an incredible man.'

* * *

Two days after the game, the seemingly indestructible Mackay said to the *Daily Mirror*, 'I don't feel too bad. My head is a bit sore.' Isobel, who was not at the game, said, 'I've heard a few stories about all this. There's Cliff's one when he saw the blood coming out of David's ear and obviously he got taken off, then he came back to play. There were no substitutes and David didn't want to let them down, I suppose. Then the story goes from Ron Henry – God bless him, he's no longer with us – that David came up to him and said, "My vision is not good", and David collapsed in the dressing room with a fractured skull after the game finished. These were things I just didn't realise at the time.'

* * *

Mackay felt Spurs' hopes of a triple trophy haul for the season were enhanced when Jimmy Greaves signed for £99,999 from AC Milan in December 1961.

He already had first-hand experience of what it was like to face the Dagenham goal machine, who was also captured in a cloak-and-dagger swoop.

Greaves had scored on his league debut as a teenager at the Lane when he was with his first club, Chelsea, for whom he netted 132 goals in 169 games before the lure of Italian lire took him to Milan.

Mackay said, 'I became more convinced we could do it when Bill Nicholson swooped for Jimmy Greaves … I had played against Jimmy when he was at Chelsea and when he had played for England, and he never had a bad game. At that time, Jimmy was the best player in the country and if Bill had said to me that he had £100,000 to spend and asked who he should buy, I would have said Jimmy, no doubt.'

Greaves was destined to become the top scorer in the five leading European leagues with 357 goals – a figure only surpassed by Cristiano Ronaldo in 2017 – in only 516 appearances in top-flight domestic football. Some 266 of his goals came for Spurs.

He immediately showed why Mackay had so much faith in the player who would one day name the Scot as Spurs' best ever player.

After limbering up with a goal double for the reserves against Plymouth Argyle at Home Park, Greaves bagged a hat-trick on his first-team debut.

Mackay also played a major role in the 5-2 win over mid-table Blackpool, who included Greaves's England team-mate Jimmy Armfield.

He had scored in the previous match, a 3-1 home win over Birmingham City, playing in the number ten shirt, but reverted back to his more familiar number six in place of Tony Marchi with Greaves taking the inside-left top against the Tangerines.

Greaves converted a long throw from the Scot for his first Tottenham goal and headed his second via a pinpoint cross by the former Glendevon Park street player in front of nearly 43,000 eschewing the joys of Christmas shopping on Saturday, 16 December 1961. It was love at first sight for the players and supporters in N17 for a striker who went on to become a record-breaker for the club. Les Allen, whose goal had clinched the title in the April, had done nothing wrong and in fact lined up with Greaves that wintry afternoon, but Bill Nicholson had added a player who he believed appeared to do what seemed almost impossible and improve the Double team. And Allen, who notched a second successive goal double against Blackpool, was the one who largely made way for him.

Mackay said in his autobiography Greaves was 'immediately starting a love affair with Tottenham fans that survives to this day'. He was 'like a man possessed' as he netted 30 goals by the end of the season.

Mackay's eyes were getting wider and wider at the prospect of ripping the history books up again, maybe for good. There was the possibility of a double Double and, indeed, the treble, including the continent's premier club knockout, 27 years before Manchester United became the first team to reach that pinnacle.

He said, 'The treble was beginning to look like a serious possibility. Our league form had not been as explosive as the previous season, but we were up there and no other club was running away with it as we had done, and the FA Cup campaign was yet to start.'

19

In his element

THE EUROPEAN Cup campaign reflected Dave Mackay's optimism as it resumed behind the Iron Curtain on Valentine's Day in 1962. Spurs headed to the picturesque Czechoslovakian capital Prague, the City of 100 Spires, covered in snow as it was at the time. A romantic image on a romantic day, but Mackay's side swapped much of their romantic style for a more pragmatic approach. Bill Nicholson had clearly taken to heart the Katowice nightmare, in which Mackay had enraged the home following, and the defensive display ensured they only had a 1-0 deficit to overturn in the second leg against a strong Czech outfit back at the Lane.

Mackay shone in an attacking role as the number ten as Spurs sealed a semi-final slot by defeating Dukla Prague 4-1 on a snow-bound White Hart Lane pitch described as an 'ice rink' 12 days later.

It was a case of the iceman cometh as Mackay netted twice, as did Bobby Smith, to complete a 4-2 aggregate triumph on another Glory Glory Night. His first showed his ball skills, bringing down a pass from John White with his left foot and firing home with his right. The second was a blast from a Smith back-header. His 'sheer physical fury' was also a factor in Super Spurs – playing controlled football at pace without ice skates – mastering the Arctic-like conditions as they did. 'Glory Glory Hallelujah' rang out in a white-hot atmosphere created by over 55,000 spectators.

It was considered that observers from Real Madrid, Benfica and Standard Liege – who had already made the last four – now knew the size of the task which faced any of them if they were pitched against Spurs in the draw taking place in Paris the following day.

Mackay's boys were matched up with Benfica, the reigning holders, who had defeated Barcelona in the final the previous year. Bullish Spurs believed they would get through and expected to play and beat an ageing Real Madrid in the final.

Cliff Jones said, 'Real were a great side. Di Stéfano wasn't bad. Puskás was all right too. Gento wasn't a bad winger although I was better looking! But I don't think they had a Mackay.'

They felt Madrid, who had won the competition for its first five years from 1955–60, had peaked and were on the downward slide.

They also had Jimmy Greaves available in the competition for the first time as they took on the Portuguese champions for a place in the decider.

The first leg on 21 March 1962 proved a test of their mettle in front of an intimidating atmosphere at Benfica's Stadium of Light. Spurs were shaken at the intensity of the crowd. Bar 500 travelling fans, the remaining 85,500 'terrifying' home supporters 'snarled, roared, screamed and whistled in an endless Niagara of noise'. The 'fast, skilled and needlessly ruthless football' of the hosts put Spurs on the back foot.

Observers felt the combination of Greaves at outside-right, Danny Blanchflower at number ten and Tony Marchi at four struggled.

But Mackay appeared to don his William Wallace persona and 'roused' the visitors, although upsetting the locals with his 'brusque' handling of star Benfica forward Eusébio. He also laid on an opportunity for Cliff Jones which the winger was unable to take.

Not a lot went right for Spurs as Greaves and Smith had goals disallowed for offside – with neutral experts doubting the decisions – and the hosts took a 3-1 lead into the second leg.

Terry Dyson said, 'We got done there. The referee slaughtered us over there.'

But Mackay remained unfazed after he and his side had to run the gauntlet of a 'gloating, howling' crowd which invaded the pitch at the finish. Ever defiant, he proclaimed in the *Daily Express*, 'We shall do them at Tottenham, just wait and see.' His prediction came true to a point.

The biggest home match in Spurs' history took place on a dry, becalmed evening on Thursday, 5 April 1962. It was not a night for faint hearts. Mackay was in his element and was later described by Benfica superstar Eusébio as the 'best all-round player in the world'.

Your author could see the floodlit theatre that was the Lane illuminating the night sky and dominating its surroundings like an alien spacecraft that had landed in London N17 from his back yard a few streets away, and hear the close-to-deafening wall of sound of the home fans singing 'Glory Glory Hallelujah' which must have rocked the foundations of each of the stadium's four stands, especially the noise made by those in the three-tiered eastern structure backing on to Worcester Avenue. I was wishing it had not been a school night and therefore was having to settle for seeing the action on television and devouring the following morning's newspapers.

The importance of the second leg against the Eagles from Lisbon to the London club has only been either equalled and superseded elsewhere by the first leg, the 1963 European Cup Winners' Cup Final and the 2019 Champions League Final and semi-finals.

Mackay and his team-mates, kitted out in all white, rose to the occasion in terms of battering Eusébio's side like a heavyweight champion using his opponent as a punchbag, it was reported. If Benfica had been a boxer under such a siege they would have been fortunate to have been wearing scarlet shirts to disguise the bloody noses. The opponents were, observers informed us, out on their feet as the final whistle blew. Just a minute or two earlier Mackay had come within the width of the crossbar of forcing an extra game in Brussels to decide the tie. It followed Cliff Jones and Greaves each going close. They also had another Greaves goal chalked off controversially for offside; an effort the 'scorer', not known for criticism, felt should have been given.

Spurs secured a 2-1 victory on the night with Bobby Smith and Danny Blanchflower scoring after an early Jose Aguas goal for the visitors gave the hosts a bigger mountain to climb than the one they faced prior to kick-off. The 64,448 witnesses – with thousands locked out – ensured a total of 508,087 had watched Tottenham's eight ties with 238,717 in the four at the Lane. But the European dream was over, at least for one season.

Ian Wooldridge wrote in the *Daily Mail*, 'Benfica, champions of Portugal, survived 90 minutes of football hell that would have destroyed almost any other team on Earth … for 65 minutes they withdrew into their own red fortress round their own penalty area and withstood the greatest pounding Spurs have ever mounted … [it was] the most exciting finale I have ever seen in a football match.'

David Miller described the night in the *Daily Express* as 'the most electrifying 90 minutes of European football I have ever seen on an English ground'.

Mackay said, 'If Jimmy's goal had stood, I'm sure we would have prevailed … The match was shown live on television and the British public agreed it was one of the finest they had ever witnessed; for us it was bitterly disappointing. We'd fallen at the penultimate hurdle and hadn't deserved to. I was flattered, though, when I read in the papers afterwards that Eusébio had said I was the best all-round player in the world.'

And outstanding Benfica midfielder Mario Coluna said in the *Express*, 'Mackay is an extraordinary player. The half-back line is one of the best I ever played against in the world. Tottenham fought very well.'

Bill Nicholson said, 'I lost count of the near misses but the one I'll always remember is when Dave Mackay hit the crossbar.

'My men played too quickly. They were too hurried. Their enthusiasm ran away with them … if we had kept our heads the result might have been different.'

Experienced Benfica manager Béla Guttmann, who eschewed a warm-up for his players so they would not be intimidated by the crowd, said, 'It was the hardest game of my life. I thought Spurs would equalise in the last ten minutes.'

The Eagles' star goalkeeper Costa Pereira added, 'This was the hardest game we have ever played. Tottenham are one of the best teams in Europe.'

In 1961/62, the promoted Tractor Boys of Ipswich Town stunned the English top flight with the tactic of deep-lying wingers, especially Jimmy Leadbetter, to supply the twin spearhead of Ray Crawford and Ted Phillips, taking advantage of the fact their First Division rivals were unfamiliar with having Alf Ramsey's team as opposition.

And Mackay's Tottenham joined the stunned when they were defeated 3-2 at Portman Road on 21 October 1961.

It was a similar story again in the return fixture – with Tony Marchi in for the sidelined Mackay – under the White Hart Lane floodlights on Tuesday, 14 March 1962, seven days before the team took on Benfica in the Portuguese capital.

Nicholson had pipped Ramsey to the Spurs post, so perhaps these defeats were, in the gentlemanly way which characterised the demeanour of the future England World Cup-winning boss, Suffolk punches in the solar plexus for him from the future knight of the realm.

But Nicholson insisted he had a plan to deal with Town's tactics and said it was Mackay who felt there was no need to change the way Spurs played to suit their opponents' approach.

Nicholson said, 'At a team meeting before our first match against Ipswich I suggested that our midfield players should mark Stephenson [the other winger] and Leadbetter, leaving the full-backs free to move inside to help take care of Crawford and Phillips. Blanchflower agreed with me, but Mackay didn't. He said we had just won three matches playing the way we wanted to play. "Why play just to suit them?" he said. "We're good enough to beat them playing our normal style." It was one of the few times I bowed to the players' wishes. We lost 3-2 and when the return match was played … we went down … playing the same way. If we had picked up two of those four points, we would have won the championship because our goal average was superior to that of Ipswich.

'I was keen that we should change marking tactics, and have our wing-halves mark their wingers instead of their full-backs doing the job. This was because they had wily Jimmy Leadbetter pulling the strings back from deep and I believed that if our half-backs could do a smother job it would enable us to raid forward while, we hoped, Blanchflower and Mackay throttled them before they could set up anything.

'But there was a disagreement about playing it that way and I conceded the point because I did not want them to play a tactical plan they were unhappy about … They beat us home and away … If we had beaten them 3-1 at White Hart Lane we would have done the Double again; it is just as simple as that. It was all a question of tactics.'

Ipswich's Ray Crawford scored home and away against Spurs for the eventual if unlikely champions. He said of the White Hart Lane encounter, 'If they had beaten us that night they would have gone on and won the league. They were the finest team. Elegant. They'd have made good champions, but we did all right.'

It appeared that Spurs had enough time to rescue the situation yet they dropped five points in their remaining six league games.

Even then they made a fist of it by winning their final three away matches, the last of which was revenge for a 2-1 home reverse over Leicester at Filbert Street.

But it was too little too late as they finished a point behind runners-up Burnley and four adrift of Ramsey's title winners.

Nicholson was able to prove to his players the wisdom of adapting their roles to undo Ipswich in the FA Charity Shield match at the start of the following season. Portman Road was bathed in sunshine as Mackay's Spurs had fun under the celestial body, dismantling the hosts 5-1.

Nicholson said in *And The Spurs Go Marching On*, 'There was no nonsense. This time I put my foot down and told them very firmly that we would play this one my way, which we did.'

A lesson learned, but it came too late for Spurs to repeat the back-to-back feat Nicholson enjoyed as a player for Arthur Rowe's push and run team.

Spurs managed to lift the 1962 FA Cup in style to earn the right to face the champions in the Charity Shield and help soothe any feelings of anti-climax in a season Mackay dreamed might deliver the treble.

It was a momentous year for popular culture with Brian Epstein becoming manager of the Beatles, the Rolling Stones forming, Bob Dylan producing his first album and Hollywood film star Marilyn Monroe passing away. In political circles, the Cuban missile crisis – involving leaders John F. Kennedy, Nikita Khrushchev and Fidel Castro, with their respective countries, the USA, Soviet Union and the Caribbean island of Cuba at the centre of the issue – threatened the escalation of the Cold War and world peace.

Mackay's Spurs took their place on the back benches of 1962's history by being part of only the second FA Cup Final to be filmed in colour. And it was a better spectacle than the first, their Double-clincher the year before.

Mackay was an ever-present throughout a tricky run to the Wembley decider, with the ties taking place in the shadow of Spurs' European exploits. Away draws in each of their rounds leading to the last eight did not make for a smooth path.

But Mackay helped his side clamber over the obstacles; overcoming First Division rivals Birmingham City 4-2 in a replay after a 3-3 deadlock at St Andrew's and easing to a 5-1 win at lower-league Plymouth Argyle,

Dave, Frank and Tommy Mackay

Mackay's mum
Catherine and dad
Thomas outside 18
Glendevon Park

Dave Mackay as
a toddler

Dave Mackay's birthplace

Dave (back, left) with brothers Tommy and (in
front) Ronnie and Frank

Schoolboy Mackay (front, fourth from right)

Mackay (back, far left) and brother Tommy (front, far left) with Scottish schools' trophy winners Saughton

Schoolboy Mackay (front, third left) with Scotland

Mackay (back, third left) with Slateford Athletic

Mackay (back, far right) with Scotland Juniors

Mackay (middle, fourth right), with Newtongrange Star

Mackay on national service

Mackay (front, middle) with Army trophy winners

Mackay looks on for Hearts. Picture by Morris Allan who passed on 23 February 2015

Hearts' Dave Mackay (second right) in 1956 Scottish Cup Final win against Celtic

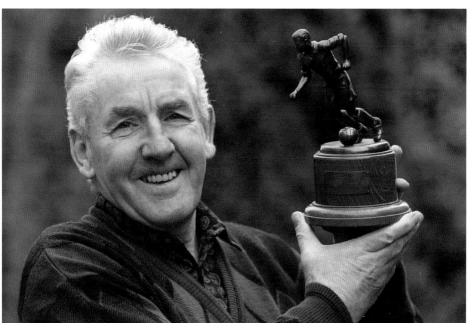

Dave Mackay with the 1958 Scottish Footballer of the Year trophy he won with Hearts

Pals Pilmar Smith, Peter Williamson and Davie Williamson, plus dad Thomas, see Mackay (centre) off to Spurs at Waverley Station, Edinburgh

Unadulterated joy from best pals Dave Mackay and Terry Dyson celebrating a goal by the former against Crewe Alexandra at White Hart Lane en route to the FA Cup and the Double in 1960/61

Spurs' historic Double winners of 1960/61 with their trophies. Back row, left to right: Bill Brown, Peter Baker, Ron Henry, Danny Blanchflower, Maurice Norman, Dave Mackay. Front row: Cliff Jones, John White, Bobby Smith, Les Allen, Terry Dyson

Spurs' 1962 FA Cup winners: Back row, left to right: Peter Baker, Maurice Norman, Bill Brown, Ron Henry, Dave Mackay. Front: Terry Medwin, John White, Danny Blanchflower, Bobby Smith, Jimmy Greaves, Cliff Jones

Dave Mackay and the rest of Spurs' 1963 European Cup Winners' Cup winners and the trophy. Back row, left to right: John Smith, Terry Medwin, Ron Henry, Peter Baker, Bill Brown, Maurice Norman, Bobby Smith, Mel Hopkins, Dave Mackay. Front row: Les Allen, Cliff Jones, John White, Danny Blanchflower, Tony Marchi, Jimmy Greaves, Terry Dyson, Frank Saul

Dave Mackay, second left in the front row, with the Scotland squad prior to defeating England at Wembley in April 1963. Back row, left to right: Billy McNeill, Denis Law, Ian Ure, Ian St John, Bill Brown, John White, Jim Baxter, Eric Caldow, Unknown, Unknown, manager Ian McColl. Front: Willie Henderson, Dave Mackay, Alex Hamilton, Davie Wilson

Dave Mackay nurses the left leg broken at Old Trafford the previous December as he watches Spurs lose to Chelsea at White Hart Lane in February 1964, with children Valerie, on the lap of family friend, the late Lenny Kenny, Derek and David Junior, who are either side of their dad

Dave Mackay suffers a broken leg for the second time, comforted by referee Peter Songhurst. It is in a Spurs reserve match against Shrewsbury Town in September 1964

Dave Mackay grabs Billy Bremner of Leeds United at White Hart Lane in August 1966. An iconic image which Mackay 'hated' as he believed it portrayed him as a bully

Captain Dave Mackay leads out Spurs (in white) behind manager Bill Nicholson for the 1967 FA Cup Final alongside Chelsea captain Ron Harris who follows his boss Tommy Docherty, a friend, 'landlord' and World Cup team-mate of our subject

Mackay on parade as he shows the 1967 FA Cup to thousands packing Tottenham High Road

Mackay signs autographs while at Spurs

Mackay with a picture of his Spurs boss Bill Nicholson

Dave Mackay signs on watched (left to right) by Derby County chairman Sam Longson, director Mr Rudd, secretary Stuart Webb and manager Brian Clough

Mackay with Roy McFarland and Alan Hinton during his last game playing for Derby County, a 2-0 win over West Bromwich Albion on 1 May 1971

Dave Mackay shared the Football Writers' Association Footballer of the Year award with Tony Book in 1969. Mackay (front row, first left) joins fellow Football Writers' Footballer of the Year winners to celebrate the 50th award to Gianfranco Zola (front row, third from right). Back row: Pat Jennings, Bill Slater, Steve Nicol, Ian Callaghan, Frank McLintock, Tony Book, Emlyn Hughes, Frans Thijssen, Clive Allen. Front: Dave Mackay, Bobby Charlton, Sir Stanley Matthews, Gianfranco Zola, Gary Lineker and Bobby Collins

In 1971 Mackay was appointed
player-manager of Swindon Town
but left after just one season to take
charge of Nottingham Forest. He
remained at the City Ground until
October 1973, when he returned to
Derby as manager following Clough's
resignation

Neil Martin,
Mackay's
player, assistant
and pal

Isabel Mackay in front of the painting by Brian West of Derby captain Dave Mackay holding the 1969 Second Division trophy and being congratulated by Brian Clough and Peter Taylor

Manager Dave Mackay, assistant Des Anderson and their 1975 title-winning Derby squad with trophy. Back row, from left: Des Anderson (assistant manager/coach), Ron Webster, Peter Daniel, Colin Todd, Colin Boulton, Graham Moseley, Archie Gemmill, Steve Powell, Rod Thomas, Henry Newton, Kevin Hector, Gordon Guthrie (physiotherapist). Front row, from left: Francis Lee, Charlie George, Bruce Rioch, Roy McFarland, Dave Mackay (manager), Jeff Bourne, David Nish, Roger Davies, Alan Hinton

Mackay with friend and lifelong Derby fan Frank Chorlerton and League trophy and FA Charity Shield at the Baseball Ground in 1975

Derby manager Dave Mackay is on the visiting bench against Chelsea at Stamford Bridge, with young Rob White, son of John, close by (far left). From Rob White Collection

Training in the Middle East

Mackay's dad Thomas and coach and pal Joe Kinnear in Dubai

Mackay with family and friends outside the entrance to Zamalek's stadium. Mackay is holding grandson Daniel, sister-in-law Maureen is at the back and wife Isobel is standing next to him. The other figure is a Zamalek fan

Mackay opening The Poplars sports ground in Burton Joyce

Dave Mackay with daughter Julie and Scotland team-mate and pal Denis Law at our subject's ruby wedding celebrations at the Swan Hotel in Nottingham

Denis Law holding a 'tenner' (£10) while bantering with Dave Mackay (right) and Des Anderson during the ruby wedding celebrations for our subject at the Swan Hotel in Nottingham. Perhaps Law was about to 'get the next round in'

Mackay in replica Hearts shirt

Dave and Isobel Mackay with Pat Jennings (second from right) and Wayne Rooney

Dave and Isobel Mackay at black-tie event

Isobel and Dave Mackay with (left to right) Julie and Valerie

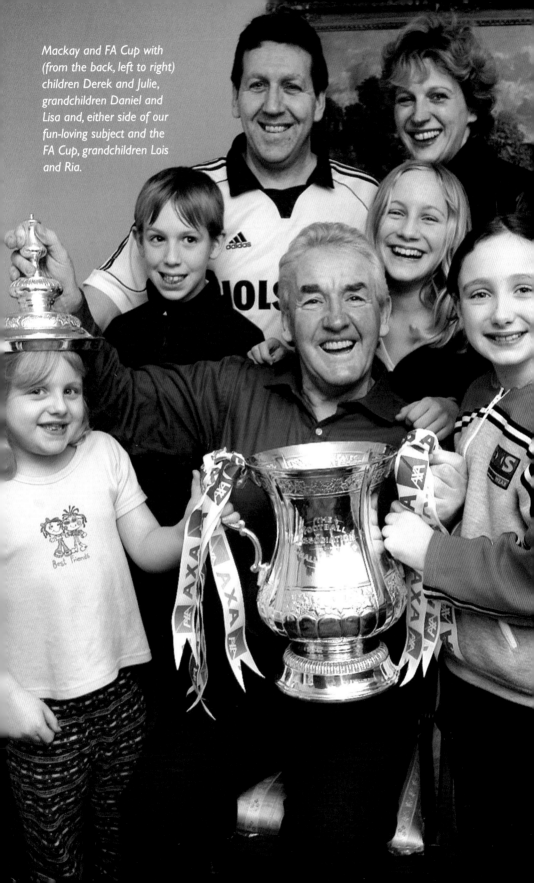

Mackay and FA Cup with (from the back, left to right) children Derek and Julie, grandchildren Daniel and Lisa and, either side of our fun-loving subject and the FA Cup, grandchildren Lois and Ria.

with Greaves scoring another Home Park double. Top-flight West Bromwich Albion were defeated 4-2 at The Hawthorns in between the Dukla Prague matches.

The FA Cup was a big crowd-puller and the biggest domestic White Hart Lane crowd of the season saw Mackay and Co. overcome Aston Villa 2-0 in the sixth round in front of 64,000, a figure even higher than the best home league attendance (63,440) when a consolation goal from the wing-half saw Spurs pipped 2-1 by Arsenal on 23 December.

It set up a semi-final date with Matt Busby's Manchester United at Hillsborough on 31 March, although Spurs' warm-up was far from ideal. They suffered the body blows of the crucial home league reverse against Ipswich four days after beating Villa, and the loss to Benfica in Lisbon was ten days before the Sheffield date.

A season which Mackay believed could add three major prizes to the Tottenham trophy cabinet seemed to be at a turning point with the odds of continental and domestic league successes stacked against them.

But with an inspirational player like Mackay no one in the Spurs camp was letting their heads drop and United, with Bobby Charlton, were defeated 3-1 before 65,000.

Mackay and the Lilywhite troops had to wait nine days to discover who would be their opponents with title rivals Burnley held by struggling Fulham over at Villa Park the same afternoon as Spurs were seeing off United. Harry Potts's Lancastrians, who had taken the title just two years earlier, emerged 2-1 victors over Bedford Jezzard's Londoners from the replay at Filbert Street.

It was a dream final – the Team of the Century versus the 1960 First Division champions. The Clarets were littered with stars of the day, including Danny Blanchflower's Northern Ireland team-mates Jimmy McIlroy and Alex Elder, prolific striker Ray Pointer, England winger John Connelly, Scottish stopper Adam Blacklaw and Footballer of the Year and cerebral skipper Jimmy Adamson.

And, as they finished ahead of Spurs in the title race, they were rated slight favourites even though they had not won the trophy since 1914.

But victory would see Spurs re-write a little more football history as only the fourth club to win back-to-back FA Cups, following on from The Wanderers, Blackburn Rovers and Newcastle United.

Mackay was among nine of the Double-winning side who lined up against Burnley on Saturday, 5 May 1962; Terry Medwin replacing Terry Dyson, and Jimmy Greaves coming in for Les Allen.

The wing-half revealed how the team were refusing to cry over spilt milk. Self-confidence, a personal quality he always possessed, was a collective quality of the Spurs team. He said, 'We were not a team to mope and, although there was great regret that we had not been able to achieve the treble or European glory, we soon put it behind us.'

The belief the team had in their own abilities was reflected by a 'trick' Mackay and Blanchflower worked up – and the captain wanted – to act out on the big day.

Mackay said, 'Danny and I spent hours in training together discussing tactics, practising moves and improving ball control. One of the things we worked on was a little trick we had up our sleeve. Danny was our penalty taker and we devised a move whereby instead of striking his penalty kick at the goalkeeper, he would feign a shot but instead just tap the ball forward a foot or two. Once the goalkeeper had dived, I would step forward and place the ball on the other side of the goalmouth from where he had landed. It was pure theatre and showing off, but we wanted to do it and decided to unveil the move on the biggest stage.'

Mackay was asked by Blanchflower, 'Are you up for it Dave? If we get a penalty at Wembley?'

The Scot said, 'Danny was mad like that. Bill Nicholson would not have approved … but Danny wanted to be part of one of the most famous goals in history.'

The final build-up was similar to the previous year, although Queen Elizabeth II, dressed in the colours of Spurs' north London rivals, replaced the Duchess of Kent as the royal in attendance. The Spurs supporters rattled their rattles and waved their blue and white balloons as they joined in the pre-match community singing, singing 'Pack Up Your Troubles'. Spurs certainly had a chance to pack up theirs after two-thirds of the treble had slipped through their fingers.

Jimmy Greaves put Spurs ahead after three minutes, having predicted he would inside five. Jimmy Robson levelled just after the interval before Bobby Smith put Spurs back in front from a John White ball. And late on came the moment Mackay and Blanchflower had prepared for when Tommy Cummings handled a Terry Medwin shot on the line.

Skipper Blanchflower grabbed the ball and looked around for his partner with whom to perform the party piece. He had a 'manic grin on his face'. Mackay, for once, confessed he 'simply lost my bottle'. The pair were concerned that if they 'fluffed it' by 'wanting to show off' it might allow Burnley to come back into it and lose Spurs the European Cup Winners' Cup spot their team had a firm grip on. Had Mackay agreed to participate, the glory experienced in the continental competition the following season might have never happened. Unperturbed, Blanchflower converted the spot-kick.

Mackay and Spurs had their silverware and could search for more on home and foreign fields in 1962/63 – after the celebrations featuring few speeches, a limbo dancing act and a slow waltz for Bill Nicholson and his wife Grace, always known as Darkie on account of her hair colour.

Overall, during the final, Mackay displayed most of the tools in his armoury to help the Lilywhites overcome Burnley. He exuded confidence in his hitched-up shorts and muddied white shirt as fine rain began to fall. His ball skills remained finely developed as he showed how comfortable he was with either foot. It could be a simple side-footed pass forward with his left to either Cliff Jones, Danny Blanchflower or John White. Or a curled one down the line with the outside of his right. One time he found Bobby Smith and when the ball went astray he retrieved it with a shuddering challenge. He remained composed throughout. He was the king of cool when he gained possession of a forward Burnley ball in a corner to the left of Bill Brown's goal. He appeared possibly trapped as he was hassled by Ray Pointer at his back. Mackay simply feinted to the left to throw Pointer and moved to his right. With three deft touches of his left foot, he worked his way round the floundering Clarets number nine, to escape and supply, unhurriedly, a short ball to Blanchflower to get Spurs on the attack.

He nipped any threat in the bud using his innate positional sense to intercept. A through ball from Jimmy McIlroy would have put Pointer in on goal but Mackay's awareness cut it out. He dealt with a series of crosses into the box, denying the likes of winger Gordon Harris. He performed his ability to put in a crunching tackle in the form of a block or a slide; Pointer again being frustrated on the edge of the Spurs area as the wing-half went to ground to win the ball. Even a whack on the shin in a one-to-one challenge with Burnley right-back John Angus did not dent his effectiveness. He also found time to attack and Smith headed his deep left-wing cross just wide. His long throws caused consternation in the Lancastrians' camp, while he had a couple of shots blocked. Then there was the sheer spirit and will to win. Spurs were 3-1 up, the 90 minutes were up and referee Jim Finney was about to blow the whistle as Mackay raced to the touchline as if his life depended on it to block tackle Harris. TV commentator Kenneth Wolstenholme observed, 'He never gives up.'

Mackay, perhaps, had underlined Eusébio's view of him as the best all-round midfielder player in the world.

He was the picture of delight as he held his left arm aloft and jumped up with both knees towards his chest while attempting to twirl a long ribbon of bunting around his wrist before disappearing down the tunnel after the lap of honour.

Mackay said, 'It was unthinkable that the best side in the land would finish the season empty-handed. We were not even slightly intimidated by the occasion. The 1962 FA Cup Final was the performance that Bill wanted the Leicester final the previous year to have been.'

20

'My dad was always for the club, never himself.'

DAVE MACKAY was still at his peak as he helped his Spurs glory team create its last re-write of football history.

Mackay was a monumental figure as he guided them into the final of the 1963 European Cup Winners' Cup – and he was up for completing the job.

It was in a memorable year which also featured the Profumo Affair, involving a government minister and model Christine Keeler, the Great Train Robbery and Beatlemania.

But what Mackay and his pals were attempting to achieve was at least the equal of any of that to members of the British public who also loved their football.

No team from Britain had secured a major trophy in a major continental club competition. Mackay had expected that his Double winners would achieve the milestone in the European Cup the year before. Yet despite their disappointment against Benfica, he was bullish about Spurs' chances in the competition for the domestic cup holders.

It ended in bittersweet tears on the sidelines, however, as he was out injured with his team defeating Atlético Madrid 5-1 in the final at the De Kuip Stadium in Rotterdam on Wednesday, 15 May 1963.

He said, 'Jimmy Greaves says in his autobiography that he came over to me whilst the cup was being paraded around the ground during the post-match celebrations and that he tried to comfort me, as I was not feeling part of it. He remarks it was the only time he saw me cry. Cry I did, but I was feeling a cocktail of emotions that evening and the occasion had shaken and stirred them. Delirium at our success and disappointment at having not been part of the climax … it remains one of the regrets of my career.'

A groin strain had forced him to decide to pull out – for the sake of the team. Bill Nicholson revealed in *The Perfectionist* he would leave it to players to judge their fitness for themselves because 'the man who is keen to carry on is going to make a more positive contribution to the team effort than one who is reluctant to play'.

But it was a 'heart-breaking' day-of-the-match resolution for Mackay on this occasion. Mackay admitted in his autobiography to considering lying and declaring himself available 'but I knew that I was being selfish beyond the limit'. He said if he played he would have been a 'passenger', particularly with no substitutes allowed in those days.

He added in another publication, 'I knew in my heart of hearts that I had no real chance of playing in that final and it was a huge disappointment. I was weighing it up in my mind, but I knew if I'd chosen to play and we'd lost, it would have been my fault.

'Certainly that is how I saw it. So I had no choice but to say no. If I'd have said I was fit, I'm sure Bill would have played me.

'Of course I was delighted that the team won and won easily, and they didn't appear to miss me as they won 5-1. I still got a medal, but it was heartbreaking to watch rather than play.'

Derek Mackay said, 'It was only a twinge but he was so worried because he wasn't 100 per cent and didn't want to risk not being at top fitness and let the team down. So he left himself out.

'He couldn't believe how the match unfolded, I think. He was looking at Atlético and I think he would have thought, "Oh, they are not that good. I could have played." My dad was always for the club, never himself.'

Wife Isobel added, 'My party arrived at the ground and David was there with his Spurs top on. When he said he wasn't playing I was so disappointed. I was never so disappointed in my life. He must have felt gutted. He must have decided it was too risky. Blooming heck, he could have walked and played, it was such an easy game.'

Terry Dyson, a two-goal hero on the day, said, 'It was a massive, massive blow. We were absolutely gutted. Dave was our talisman. He had been brilliant in the matches leading up to it. Dave's swashbuckling performances were the big reason we'd reached the final. But he didn't want to play because he didn't want to let the side down. As he was my mate I knew how shocking it was for him to miss out.'

It was a second personal blow in the same week for Mackay, who'd had a storming season but was pipped for the Football Writers' Association Footballer of the Year trophy by legendary 48-year-old winger Stanley Matthews.

Dyson said, 'Dave should have won it this year although it seems the FWA wanted to recognise Matthews for a second time before he retired.'

Mackay's absence, it seems, dampened down Nicholson's belief that his outfit in all white would don their charger of the same colour and emerge triumphant.

Jimmy Greaves, as quoted by journalist David Miller, said, 'Bill Nick's confidence seemed to have gone because Dave Mackay was injured and couldn't play. He always thought Dave was his key player.'

Certainly Miller described Nicholson's pre-match team talk as 'funereal'. And the fact that there had also been question marks over the fitness of the remaining two members of the team's hub, Danny Blanchflower and John White – who eventually declared their fitness – could not have lifted his mood. Dyson said, 'Bill praised our opponents to the skies before Danny reminded us all how good we were.'

Tony Marchi took Mackay's place at number six and played a blinder with Mackay's close pal Terry Dyson having the match of his life, with Greaves also getting a double and John White one.

Mackay's deputy spent his days relaxing watching television and doing crosswords which 'helps keep your brain active' when we spoke as autumn gave way to winter in 2020.

Aged 87 and living in quiet retirement by the sea in Maldon, Essex, there was nothing wrong with his recall of the biggest day of his professional life.

And he revealed how he and Mackay talked about his injury at training on the morning of the match.

Marchi, born into a paternal Italian family close to the Lane in Edmonton, said, 'Dave had done a lot to get us to the final but was injured. We were in training in the morning and he couldn't run because of the injury and he spoke to me about it. I should imagine he was gutted but he was injured so what could he do about it?

'It turned out good for me, yes. But I'd played in most of the rounds as well and so I feel I deserved a place. It was wonderful to be part of it all.'

Marchi insisted Mackay certainly wasn't a party-pooper as Spurs celebrated in a bar next to their hotel. He said, 'Was Dave quiet afterwards? No, no. He wasn't that sort of fellow. He was okay. He was pleased.

'The atmosphere was excellent. Everybody was patting me on the back. We had a dinner and a dance in the evening, a big celebration with the cup on the table. What more do you want?

'Have I still got my medal from that night? No. I sold it. I got into a few money problems so I had to sell my stuff. Mind you, what could I do with it? I've got two boys. They can't cut it in half, can they? There you go. Most of my stuff went that way.'

Marchi, who played with Bill Nicholson at Spurs, was rated the best number 12 in English football, the ultimate super-sub for a super team.

And as his most regular position was at number six, he generally had Mackay in front of him and a regular spot in the first team.

Mackay said, 'I was so happy for Tony Marchi. Tony was a great player who had the personal misfortune of playing for a club at a time when they had one of the finest teams in all football history. At any other First Division side, he'd have been a regular ... being part of that historic European victory must have been some compensation for him.'

Mackay, though, did play an indirect part in the final. He proved an inspiration to his mate Dyson on an unforgettable night as Spurs romped home to secure a record that will never be beaten as the first British winners of a major European trophy.

Man-of-the-match Dyson revealed he invoked his inner Mackay. He said, 'We were 2-0 at half-time but Atlético pulled one back through a Collar penalty as they slaughtered us for the first 20 minutes after the restart. Shots were raining in. Rivilla joined in the onslaught from right-back. He belted in a goalbound shot. As the ball left his boot, I thought, "What would Dave do here? He'd put body and soul into somehow getting in the way. And perhaps injure himself doing so." It inspired me, so I launched myself at the ball knowing I would get hurt because of the power of the shot. And bloody hell, it did as it hit me right across the shins. I went down like a sack of potatoes but I'd saved a goal. It was just the lift we needed. Who knows what would have happened if Rivilla's shot and gone in and made it 2-2?'

A few minutes later Dyson scored his first goal to make it 3-1. Spurs then clicked through the gears to finish off the Spaniards, and it was Dyson who completed the nap hand with a wonder goal five minutes from time.

Mackay was there to congratulate his erstwhile team-mates, but he reserved a special hug for his mate Dyson.

Dyson said, 'Afterwards in the dressing room Dave, although he must have been devastated as he didn't actually play, couldn't have been more pleased for us. He wore his heart on his sleeve in private as well as on the field and gave me a massive hug with tears in his eyes. We enjoyed our embrace. It was one of many touching moments. We knew we were experiencing something that didn't happen every day; something wonderful in our lives, something we would always remember.'

Mackay's wife Isobel then came over to congratulate the two-goal hero in the stadium restaurant as the players and their wives and girlfriends munched sandwiches and sipped drinks post-match.

Bobby Smith, it seems, was delighted Spurs had proved a club director wrong. The board member had said to him before the game that Spurs would lose because Mackay was absent. Smith was quoted as saying at a public Q&A in Cheshunt in 2007, 'Afterwards, I went up to the director and said, "We showed you!"'

Marchi had performed earlier in the competition but it was Mackay whose star shone brightest in the lead-up to Rotterdam.

Mackay revelled in the opening salvo of the fight to add a unique piece of silverware to the trophy cabinet.

They were drawn against Rangers from his home country in what was dubbed the Battle of Britain. The first leg was held under the lights at a heaving White Hart Lane on the night of Halloween in 1962.

Close to 60,000 witnessed Mackay helping to take the game to his compatriots, who included Edinburgh-born Ralph Brand and international team-mate Jim Baxter.

Desmond Hackett wrote in the *Daily Express*, 'Bold Dave Mackay, the man who had thrown down the gauntlet at the feet of the invading Scots, was the first to strike.

'Mackay almost had the Scots sounding off a lament when he went into a goal bid that ignored any thought that he might break his leg in the attempt.

'Mackay made himself a one-man raiding party, a lone chieftain seeking to leave behind him a line of wrecked enemies.'

Fellow Scot John White headed two, Les Allen and Maurice Norman netted one each and Bobby Shearer put through his own goal for Mackay's hosts to win 5-2 in a full-blooded and skilled encounter which possessed 'a moving spirit of nobility and pride' between Scotland and its traditional Auld Enemy and created a 'whirlpool of savage noise'. Perhaps domestic pride superseded continental glory for 90 minutes.

Mackay said to the *Express*, 'It was hard but never rough and I was delighted with the way Rangers chose to play aggressive football.'

The Big Freeze – which became a major feature in football and the rest of the UK for the 1962/63 season – was about to get going. And it was six weeks before Mackay returned to his homeland to complete the overall victory. Commentators north of the border predicted their would-be heroes would overcome as the Lilywhites shrivelled. But Mackay was confident and declared, 'I don't think Rangers are good enough to give us a three-goal start.'

Mackay laid on the first goal of the second leg for Jimmy Greaves after just eight minutes, a moment which all but silenced the previously expectant majority of the 80,000 packed into Ibrox. Going by Mackay's logic, a four-goal advantage was beyond the hosts and the crowd appeared to accept that, although they were aroused enough to boo the Scot for a foul on Willie Henderson as the hosts sought to cancel out Greaves's goal.

Bobby Smith, who had been recalled after losing his place up top, bagged two in a 3-2 win which ensured Spurs' passage through, 8-4 on aggregate. Rangers made a fist of it in an 'electric atmosphere' and twice fought back to level through Brand and Davie Wilson.

But Mackay and Spurs lost his half-back partner Danny Blanchflower with the cartilage problem which was to threaten his final spot and, at 37, his future career and sidelined him for a total of 22 games. It was sustained when the Irishman was 'sandwiched' by a pair of Rangers players. And the matches the Tottenham captain missed included the four that ensured their date with Atlético Madrid.

The Big Freeze caused such fixture disruption in the UK and Europe that the second round of the competition was delayed until Tuesday, 6 March.

There was another trip behind the Iron Curtain to a country whose national team had been beaten in the previous year's World Cup Final – to Czechoslovakia, and specifically Slovan Bratislava.

The sun shone as Mackay and Co. ran on to the pitch muddied by the warming weather at the national stadium, and Spurs struggled. Thankfully for them, Mackay, in perpetual-motion mode, and Tony Marchi tirelessly put out fires. And, aided by fine goalkeeping from fellow countryman Bill Brown, the visitors were able to limit the hosts to just a 2-0 victory.

It was a rugged encounter and the second leg nine days later was similar. But most importantly for Spurs it also displayed the attacking skills of Mackay, who stormed forward at regular intervals and put the hosts ahead. The Mackay–Marchi wing-half partnership mainly caught the manager's eye as Spurs swept to a 6-0 win to repeated choruses of 'Glory Glory Hallelujah' from over 60,000 on the terraces and in the stands on another Glory Glory Night.

Bill Nicholson said to the *Daily Express*, 'This was a victory for power. Slovan are a good footballing side, but our wing-halves … powered up the field like they used to last season and not very often this year. They won us the match.'

Mackay was rated the hero as Spurs edged hosts OFK Belgrade 2-1 in the first leg of the semi-final in a clash described as 'brutal'.

The capital of Yugoslavia, as it was then, is understood to have been 'battled over' in 115 wars, razed 44 times, bombed five times and under siege on countless occasions.

And, although a football match cannot compare with such things, the meeting on Wednesday, 24 April 1963 was played out in a 'volatile atmosphere' with Spurs needing their own Braveheart in Mackay to survive and come through it.

There was a series of flashpoints. Bobby Smith was hacked down by Dragoljub Marić who found himself flat out seconds later with the Spurs striker the prime suspect, and Tottenham took the lead through John White from the free kick.

Mackay was at the second flashpoint, adjudged to have handled in his own penalty area and the hosts equalised from the spot-kick.

Dyson said, 'The ref said Dave handled even though the ball deflected off his boot. The award seemed harsh.'

The third flashpoint saw Jimmy Greaves become the first Spurs player sent off since trainer and former full-back Cecil Poynton in 1928. The striker had taken a swing at Srboljub Krivokuca and missed after his opponent had done likewise.

Dyson said, 'The bloke thought Jimmy had clattered him when in fact it was Bobby Smith. They were right so-and-sos. One of their geezers spat in my face. But by then I'd got the winning goal.'

Mackay was moved to number ten in place of suspended Greaves for the return leg as Blanchflower came back into the side for the first time since Ibrox. And the Scot showed a Greaves-like eye for goal to put Spurs ahead. He also showed his versatility and swashbuckling spirit to ensure all but one attack from the visitors – who gave it a go – came to nothing.

It was a relatively peaceful evening in comparison to the events at the Red Army Stadium eight days earlier as Cliff Jones and Bobby Smith added to Mackay's effort to secure a 3-1 win and a final place, to the delight of the near 60,000 under the Lane lights.

The FA Cup, in contrast to the continental competition, proved a damp squib for Mackay's Spurs. The Big Freeze had decimated the football calendar at home as it did abroad. But Spurs managed to stage their opening round against Burnley on 16 January 1963, a midweek work afternoon with 33,000 fans, some perhaps throwing 'sickies', present. The Lane pitch was covered in snow with the white lines and circles providing the only glimpses of the grass surface, and a bright orange ball was used. But Spurs lost 3-0 and any dreams of an historic third successive FA Cup triumph melted in the snow, while easing fixture congestion and leaving the hosts to concentrate on Europe and the First Division.

After Bill Nicholson had proved his point about how to deal with Ipswich's deep-lying wingers with their 5-1 win in the FA Charity Shield match to prelude the 1962/63 season, Spurs – with Mackay at the fore – won five of their first six fixtures as they went on to prove the nap hand at Portman Road would not be the only big-scoring victory that term. Spurs were in the mood for hitting the back of the net. Jimmy Greaves led the way by breaking the club scoring record for a season with 37 and overall the team cracked 111, just four short of their record haul when lifting the Double. They scored in all of their first 19 games, with eventual champions Everton halting the run by forcing a goalless draw. They averaged five goals a game on one seven-match autumn run which included a 9-2 annihilation of Nottingham Forest, six against Manchester United, five versus Leyton Orient and four in a draw with Arsenal.

Spurs had a second 4-4 draw at the Lane, against Ron Greenwood's promising West Ham United, who included Bobby Moore. It was memorable for Mackay as he cracked the only hat-trick of his Spurs career – and second overall – in the thriller.

They even encouraged title talk after defeating Liverpool 7-2 – with Greaves netting four – after losing 5-2 at Anfield three days earlier in an Easter double-header.

Mackay so impressed against Bill Shankly's Reds at the Lane that Desmond Hackett reported in the *Daily Express*, 'This was Mackay's day. He wore his black suit of mud with the defiance of an Indian brave in all the majesty of his warpaint. Once, when he was struck down in a bone-bruising tackle and lay writhing, the packed arena hushed. The fans knew that the indestructible Mackay must be sorely hurt. He rose limping. But as he moved into a chest-jutting gallop the roar of relief went up like a thundered prayer.'

But the fixture disruption and leaky defence, which conceded 62 goals, weakened their challenge. And the season – which only had the relief of a brief break to play Egyptian side Zamalek and see the pyramids in Cairo – tailed off with Mackay missing four of the final five league games, in which they picked up a meagre three points. They finished runners-up but it was the second season in a row in which hopes of the championship were scuppered by a disappointing run-in.

Mackay said, 'We trounced Nottingham Forest ... and it could easily have been 18. Forest had been a goal up. The previous week one of the Sunday writers had reacted to our defeat at Sheffield United by saying we were an ageing side past our best. That had rankled. In the league we were unbeaten between December and March and during that period put together a six-match winning streak. Our form was ... too patchy to win it [the title].'

In the meantime, Mackay returned to the international arena to gain the sweetest of revenges for a Scot. He had been hurt after being part of Scotland's 9-3 loss to England in 1961 and, along with other members of his humiliated side, he had been sidelined. Perhaps it was because he and they were a reminder of the nightmare in the eyes of the selectors. But it seemed the wounds had healed sufficiently for Mackay to be recalled for the Home Championship showdown against the Auld Enemy at Wembley on 6 April 1963.

Mackay lined up with Spurs team-mates John White and Bill Brown and pal Denis Law against strong opponents who included Spurs mates Jimmy Greaves, Bobby Smith and Maurice Norman, plus Bobby Moore. And his team took the game 2-1 thanks to a couple by Mackay's wing-half partner Jim Baxter in front of over 98,000. Scotland had sealed the title.

He regained the Scotland captain's armband for a so-called friendly against Austria at Hampden on 8 May, seven days before Spurs' European Cup Winners' Cup triumph. It was a match which was to 'stick in the mind' of the Glendevon Park graduate because of the 'uncharacteristically filthy play' by the visitors. Austria had Horst Nemec sent off for spitting and Erich Hof dismissed for a 'diabolical' waist-high foul before ref Jim Finney abandoned the game 11 minutes from time with the hosts leading 4-1. Finney, who had taken charge of the 1962 FA Cup Final, said, 'I stopped the game because there was no saying how it was going to end. It was getting completely out of hand. Somebody might have been seriously injured.'

Mackay said, 'I always thought of the Austrians as a gentle, non-violent race. The referee Jim Finney did not see to moderate the Austrians' behaviour.'

Mackay also skippered his country to a 4-3 defeat against Norway in a calmer friendly encounter in Bergen close to the Arctic Circle on 4 June 1963, while Spurs toured in a warmer South Africa.

21

Broken legs, broken hearts

DAVE MACKAY detected an 'end of an era' feel about the historic Rotterdam triumph after heartily joining the post-final shindig at Scheveningen by dancing to 'Please Please Me' by the Beatles and Cliff Richard's recording of 'Summer Holiday' with his 'emotional state' having 'stabilised'.

He said, 'When I went to bed I lay awake with a nagging sadness; a sadness one feels at times of extreme happiness, a sadness that emanates from knowing that things may not be this good again. In my heart I knew the victory marked the beginning of the end of the Double side.'

The reflective tone adopted by Mackay in the wake of the European Cup Winners' Cup win proved insightful. Spurs' Double team had peaked, placed its flag on top of the mountain and begun its descent, hastened by the unexpected, the predictable and the tragic. Mackay's first leg break, the retirement of Danny Blanchflower and the death of John White all came within one of the blackest periods in the club's history, which began in December 1963 and ended in July 1964. The triple trauma threatened a career, propelled another into an alternate one full-time and left a young wife widowed.

And a lesser consideration was that those seven months cost the team its three-player hub, the engine room that provided the energy, heart and brain for what was cited the greatest English club side of the 20th century.

The Mackay–Blanchflower–White axis was, I would argue, even more important to the functioning of our subject's Spurs team than the likes of 21st-century Virgil van Dijk and Kevin De Bruyne and their coalitions to Liverpool and Manchester City.

Mackay began the seven months of hell for Spurs when he broke his leg for the first time. There was no inkling of too much awry at the start of the 1963/64 season for either player or club. Although the Scot missed three of the early games and his side lost to Stanley Matthews's promoted Stoke City and crashed to a freak 7-2 reverse at Blackburn Rovers, Spurs won eight of their first ten fixtures, soon thumping Birmingham City 6-1 to go top. A switch from a 2-3-5 formation to 4-2-4 with Blanchflower playing as a second centre-half by the side of Maurice Norman and John White playing a deeper role in midfield appeared to be working well. And Mackay's troops were still among the front runners for the title as they moved towards the start of their defence of the European Cup Winners' Cup.

In between, Mackay skippered his country to victories over Norway, scoring twice in a Hampden friendly, and Wales in the Home Championship, aided by club-mates Bill Brown and John White and soon-to-be-Spur Alan Gilzean. He also led Scotland in a 2-1 defeat against Northern Ireland in Belfast with the same trio in support.

Mackay was rated the heartbeat of the club and international teams by his team-mates, fans and neutral observers but the pulse stopped in the eighth minute of the second leg of their opening European Cup Winners' Cup tie against Manchester United at Old Trafford on Tuesday, 10 December 1963.

Mackay, ever influential, had scored the opener – with Terry Dyson adding the second – as they defeated Matt Busby's side 2-0 in the first leg on another White 'Hot' Lane night seven days earlier. It was a bounce-back win after Mackay and Spurs had suffered a 4-1 Old Trafford league defeat in the league a month earlier; an occasion which was to prove Blanchflower's last first-team appearance before his retirement was announced in June 1964.

But the Theatre of Dreams was re-christened the Theatre of Nightmares for Mackay and Spurs on the fateful night that ended ten-man Tottenham's Cup Winners' Cup defence – with United winning 4-1 and going through 4-3 on aggregate – and threatened the Scot's playing future.

Tottenham were on the attack after David Herd had halved United's overall deficit. The ball bounced up around the edge of their penalty area and Mackay and Cantwell ran towards it. Mackay's eyes were firmly on the ball, which looked as if it might be high enough to head. But it only rose to stomach/chest height so Mackay stopped and lifted his left leg to try and get in a shot as Cantwell closed in.

With his focus on the spherical object, Mackay was sent reeling back as Cantwell ran, sprung and collided into him while raising his right foot. Mackay's body twisted in the air. It seemed the studs of Cantwell's boot had connected with Mackay's leg and Iron Man fell on his front, putting both hands down on the grass before rolling to his left once and, on his second spin, stopping almost face down once more. Cantwell had had Bill Foulkes and Pat Crerand in support and the former carried the loose ball away as Cliff Jones jogged to a halt. Foulkes was playing on with the stricken Mackay outside his eyeline, no doubt. Jones had a clear view of his prostrate, motionless team-mate whose left foot had been twisted 90 degrees.

Depleted Spurs put up a spirited rearguard action but Herd got a second and, after Jimmy Greaves had halved the deficit, Bobby Charlton struck a double to compound the visitors' misery of losing their most influential player in the days before substitutes were allowed. Nicholson said in his autobiography, 'Such was Mackay's influence on the side at the time that I was convinced we would not have lost had he not been injured.'

Mackay said to the *Daily Express*, 'It was just one of those things. Two of us went for the ball. I got there first and the thing just happened. I knew my leg was broken. I heard it break.'

He added in his 2004 autobiography, 'I made no fuss at the time and even went along with the party line that it was a 50-50 ball.

'Commentators like to call these clashes 50-50 tackles – especially if someone has been hurt. I got to the ball and Cantwell got to my shin. I heard the crack and, if what people tell me to this day is true, so did half the crowd.

'I did not feel any immediate pain, but felt immediate panic when I looked down at my foot … I really believed that if [trainer] Cecil Poynton rolled down my sock and undid my bootlaces, we would find that my leg was detached.'

Mackay said in the *Observer*, 'It [the leg] didn't get broken, it got smashed. When I go to Old Trafford each year people still say to me, "I was there and heard the crack."'

He absolved Cantwell of deliberately aiming to cause the injury when he added, 'No one intends to break your leg.'

He said in *Bill Nicholson: Football's Perfectionist*, 'I don't think Cantwell was anywhere near the ball. He may not have set out to break a bone but that was the end result. I had a reputation as a hard player but I was never a dirty player and wouldn't have been able to live with myself if the situation had been reversed.'

Mackay denied a suggestion he tried to play on by saying, 'I couldn't carry on – my toe was touching my knee; I couldn't believe it. Tib and fib broken.'

Jones said, 'It was a bad one. They lifted his leg and it was bent. It was a compound fracture. The bone had come through the skin. I thought, "Jesus Christ! He'll never come back from it." But he did. Incredible.

'Mackay ALWAYS went for the ball. In some ways that is why he got injured because other players would turn their shoulders and go over the top a little bit. That's how he got done a couple of times with his tackles. Sometimes he might take the man as well but he always played the ball first. And that's a fair tackle.'

United manager Matt Busby said to the *Express*, 'We are terribly sorry about Dave Mackay. It was a tragedy for Spurs. In fact it was a tragedy that both clubs couldn't have met full strength in what has been a great European Cup Winners' Cup tie.'

Mackay was stretchered off leaning on an elbow, typically trying to play down the physical hurt he must have felt. Suspended United ace Denis Law rushed down from the stands to comfort his pal in the dressing room until the ambulance arrived to take him to hospital.

And he declined an anaesthetic according to Arsenal player turned journalist Bernard Joy, when the leg was set at a Manchester hospital after the consultant, a United fan, had turned on his transistor radio to catch the game going into extra time. Mackay's medical expert informed him it was 'a bad break in two places' that could end his career.

Mackay said, 'I knew this only too well. Terry Medwin [a fellow Spurs player] had been forced to retire after his leg break.'

He was allowed to return to the team hotel where he hosted visitors in his bedroom, including Cantwell, international pal Law, and team-mates including close pal Terry Dyson, Jimmy Greaves and Bill Brown.

Mackay said in *Bill Nicholson: Football's Perfectionist* about Cantwell's visit to show remorse, 'I was in no state to vent any anger.'

Cantwell, who passed aged 73 in 2005, was clearly an admirer of Mackay. He said in the *Manchester Evening News* at the time, 'Outstanding of the Spurs ten fighting men was the smallest of them all – wee Terry Dyson, who stands only 5ft 4in. He dropped back to an extra centre-half position where he displayed the heart of a lion. He looked like a pocket Dave Mackay – and you cannot hand out bigger praise than that.'

Law said, 'I remember that particular night, being with him and going to see him afterwards. One of the worst injuries you can get as a player. Personally, you just felt at the time, "Well, that's the end of your career" if you broke your leg. But he came back. That was the type of guy he was. Such a strong guy.'

Joy, working for the *London Evening Standard*, was another to join the stream. He said, 'Mackay's bedside reading is a James Bond thriller, *Thunderball*, an apt title for the 007 of soccer.'

Mackay told him, 'The specialist says it is a clean break and had set well. I broke bones in the right foot three times when with Hearts and so I am used to making a comeback.'

He travelled back from Manchester Piccadilly to London St Pancras with the team the following morning. His injured leg was stretched out on to the opposite seat while he was playing cards with mates Terry Dyson and Bobby Smith who, on arrival back to the English capital, got him in a wheelchair to transport him to a black cab and home.

But once indoors with his family, Mackay started to faint due to 'indescribable' pain. His wife Isobel understood he was to go into hospital next day but she put her foot down and told the club that it was not good enough when they mentioned the existing arrangement. Instead, an ambulance was fixed up to take him to the Prince of Wales hospital in Tottenham High Road where they reset the leg at the start of a six-week stay.

Isobel said, 'It is a story that could never happen these day. I think David gave me the first phone call from Manchester to say he had broken his leg. He remembered when he was getting his leg put in plaster that the boy seemed more interested in listening to the match on the radio. Noel Cantwell thought it was an accident when he came to see David.

'The next day he came home in a taxi from the train station. Terry [Dyson] and Bobby [Smith] I think were with him. We had two steps down to the lounge and David came in there. He was going to the Prince of Wales hospital the next day, apparently. Later on he needed to go to the toilet but had to climb the stairs to get there. He was in so much agony he couldn't climb them. So I thought, "I can't manage." I phoned up Spurs and spoke, I think to the trainer Cecil Poynton – don't think it was Mr Nicholson – and explained David's in so much agony I don't know what to do. He said, "No, no he's going in tomorrow." I said, "Look, he needs to go now."

'Can you imagine that nowadays? Harry Kane breaks his leg and has to go on a train and in a taxi. Even then I didn't think it was that good for someone who had broken a leg.

'I remember our friends Tommy and Agnes Docherty came round to see us later on. Tommy said, "Right, you are coming out with us." We went to see the film, the comedy *It's a Mad, Mad, Mad, Mad World* and had a meal afterwards. That was nice of them.'

The leg was in plaster for 16 weeks and, when it was removed so Mackay could begin exercises, his left limb was four inches thinner than the right.

Isobel said, 'Cecil Poynton came round and brought an exercise bike which we had in the lounge. David used to get on that. He worked extremely hard to get back playing.'

Nicholson said, 'He sat for hours every day lifting a 15lb weight on his foot to strengthen it. No one has ever worked harder to get back to fitness.'

Mackay watched Spurs from the sidelines for the rest of the 1963/64 season in between his regime to get fit enough to return to action. The Lilywhites made a fist of a title challenge and went top with a Greaves hat-trick in a 4-1 revenge win over Blackburn on 11 January, before ending up fourth, while falling to Chelsea in a replay at the first hurdle in the FA Cup. John White had impressed in his deeper, more demanding midfield role and Nicholson told him in June he would be building his new team around him, with wing-half Alan Mullery, winger Jimmy Robertson, full-back Cyril Knowles and goalkeeper Pat Jennings having been brought in from March. Forward Alan Gilzean would arrive in December and full-back Joe Kinnear in February 1965.

The Double heroes had started to depart with Bobby Smith joining Brighton in May and Blanchflower confirming the end of his playing career a month later.

Nicholson decided to build his second great team while most of his first one remained on the staff. The manager wanted to avoid history repeating itself, with his own push and run team growing old together rather than being part of a transition alongside new blood.

Coupled with a wage rise, White was buoyant when he went home to Musselburgh in the summer. One day at the start of July 1964, he and his wife Sandra went to the nearby village of Whitecraig. It was to pop in on Isobel, who was staying with her parents having returned north of the border for the birth of fourth child, Julie.

Isobel said, 'John looked ever so well and he had a beer with my dad and he said, "I'm so looking forward to the new season. Bill Nicholson says he's going to build a team around me. Imagine building a team round me?!"'

But it was, tragically, not to be with White struck down and killed by a bolt of lightning while sheltering under a tree at Crews Hill Golf Club in north London on 21 July.

Mackay said, 'I still well up when I think of it. He had asked Cliffy Jones and me to play golf with him but we turned him down because there was a lot of rain around. He went out on his own and got hit by lightning. It was a tragedy that affected everybody at the club, particularly his best mate Jonesie and me. I had been responsible for him joining Spurs, because I'd played with him for Scotland and told Bill Nick that he had to sign him. He was a magnificent footballer, a real players' player who always put the team first.'

Mackay was in Edmonton having a meal followed by a natter with Spurs trialist David Williamson. A call came through from Jimmy Burton, a friend and Spurs fan, who imparted the news.

Mackay said, 'I walked out of the restaurant in a trance and sat down in my car. I switched on the radio to hear the news, but a record was playing. It was "It's Over" by Roy Orbison. I rested my forehead on the steering wheel and cried my eyes out.'

Isobel said, 'I don't think I could speak to David for days. He wasn't answering his phone. He was in Enfield. I was in Scotland. Oh it was bad, bad. Really bad.

'Julie was born on 14 July and I got home on the 21st and I wasn't long in the house and somebody came to the door and my mum answered and she came back and said, "Someone at the door wants to speak to you." I said, "Well bring him in." She said, "He won't come in." So I went to the door and said, "Do you want to speak to me?" He said, "I just want to know how well did you know John White." I said, "What do you mean how well DID I know him? I know him very well. What's wrong?" He said, "I can't say anything. Could you tell me where his mother lives?" I said yes and came in and thought, "I need to phone David." He wasn't answering his phone. And I didn't know what to do so I waited, and waited. And the news came on at six o'clock. And there was the news. John White had been killed. I thought, "Oh my God, oh no. It's not true." It was a terrible tragedy. Honestly. To think I had seen him two or three weeks or so before and he was so happy. Unbelievable.

'My family showed me something recently. It was a photograph of David with the Spurs chairman Fred Wale presenting him with a medal on the cover of a programme. The headline is "Dave Mackay receives his medal". Spurs had got a European Cup Winners' Cup one done especially for him. In the background it shows Bill Nicholson and players Danny Blanchflower, Cliff Jones, Bill Brown, Alan Mullery, and John White. Such a happy John White. It is May 1964. Two months later John was gone.'

At the funeral service and cremation in Enfield, Mackay remembered White the prankster, such as how White and his close friend Cliff Jones rode into a hall where a Spurs party had gathered on a 'borrowed ice-cream vendor's bike shouting "ices, ices"'. Perhaps it was the competition he had with White and Jones to flip a half-crown coin 'from foot to the forehead, catch it on their foot and flip it up again so that it landed in their pocket'. He spoke of his friend's delight at winning the Double, about his wife and children, and how Isobel had told him about that 'pop in' visit during the summer.

He said, 'It was a dignified and touching day as Britain said goodbye to an excellent footballer and, more importantly, a lovely, lovely young man.'

Pat Jennings remembered the occasion vividly. He said, 'Attending John's funeral was my first day at the club. My first meeting with the players. They and John had been through so much together. They were massive mates. It put a dampener on the whole pre-season.'

Terry Dyson revealed how players and staff had an 'eerie' three minutes of silence on the pitch on the morning he reported back for pre-season training. He said, 'We were all crying, especially Dave Mackay.'

Tony Marchi, the last Spur to see White alive, said in the *Biography of Tottenham Hotspur*, 'I finished (hitting practice balls at Crews Hill) around lunchtime and went into the locker room and there was John. I said, "Hello, John. Who are you playing with?" And he said, "I'm going to play a round with some friends." We sat having a chat.'

Then that other 'unthinkable' occurred on his football comeback that fateful sunny afternoon of Saturday, 12 September 1964 when Mackay stepped out for Spurs' reserves against Shrewsbury Town.

The odds of a successful comeback had to be longer the second time around. Nicholson underlined the point when he said in *Glory Glory*, 'Apparently the bones had joined together too solidly the first time [in reference to the injury sustained the previous December], affecting his blood circulation.'

And Jimmy Greaves added in his autobiography, 'The extra weight put a burden on his left leg, effectively making it susceptible to a fracture.'

But this individual had fought back from the first, a double break, and from foot fractures sustained with Heart of Midlothian. And, even more remarkably, he had come back from the fractured skull sustained against Feyenoord at the Lane in Spurs' run to the semi-finals of the European Cup in 1961/62. He put it all in and imposed upon himself a strict diet to avoid gaining any extra weight caused by enforced inactivity. The lesson was learned after a cautionary word from Nicholson after his manager had driven to see him straight after returning to White Hart Lane from West Ham with the first team, concerned his fallen talisman had paid the biggest of prices trying to help Spurs reserves attempt to tame the Shrews.

On seeing him, Nicholson said, ' "Well, Dave," I said "You've done it again". He smiled. I continued, "There are lessons to be learned from the first time, aren't there?" I was referring to the fact that he allowed his weight to increase (by a reported two stone) while inactive, making it difficult to regain fitness when he resumed training. This time he was careful not to eat or drink so much. I never knew anyone so determined to get back on a football field. It was being suggested that he might never play again and that spurred him on. The two breaks left him with a slightly misshapen leg, but it did not worry him or restrict his movement.'

It was clear that Mackay would leave no stone unturned in order to return. At White Hart Lane, he was to be seen putting in the hard yards, running up and down the terraces to build up strength in his leg.

Alan Mullery said to the club, 'I remember him running up and down terraces to get fit after breaking his leg the second time and that energy to get back and play football. He put his body through it to get back playing again and that's what he did.'

He only took time off to support worthy causes such as raising money for the John White Fund, and acting as a referee as the London Maccabi Association hosted a Tottenham All Stars XI of the 1950s on Sunday, 27 September 1964. Mackay, with your author and his father Maurice present, officiated as best he could after donning the Spurs away shirt – dark blue with white facings – as members of Bill Nicholson's push and run team, including Ted Ditchburn, Harry Clarke and Ron Burgess, performed.

After all, it was Mackay who, among others, recommended Nicholson to sign tragic compatriot White.

Mackay's mood was unaffected by the recovery process at home. Isobel said, 'David was his same old self around the house. He liked a laugh. He had a six-inch, one-to-two-inches thick piece of wood at the back of his plaster. I don't know if that was to keep his leg from moving about and heal quicker – or stop him going out, because he couldn't get his trousers on until our lovely German au pair Annelise – who has sadly passed away – came to the rescue and altered the inside leg.'

Derek Mackay remembered how his dad maintained his sense of humour through the fractures. He said, 'Dad used to go and watch the games with his broken leg in plaster. After one we were sitting in the kitchen at Enfield with his friend who was a Spurs fan and a great character. And Dad has convinced me – as he's sat there with this massive plaster on – that he'd played that day. I had a vision of him playing in his Spurs kit with the plaster.

'Mum's got a big scrapbook with these banner headlines from newspapers declaring "Mackay finished". They really thought he was. But once the plaster was off he built his legs back up on the fitness bike Spurs had brought to our home. He worked so hard. Amazing.'

Two days before Christmas in 1964, Mackay resumed training. Nicholson said in the *Coventry Evening Telegraph*, 'Dave feels pretty fit and his leg feels stronger than it did at the same stage after the first break. It is still too early to say when he will play in a match again.'

There was still a long way to go but Mackay had been given his first major green light. He still had to be patient and missed the entire 1964/65 season so as to make sure he was fully ready for the trials and tribulations of first-team football at the top.

In his absence, Spurs slipped from being kings of Europe and First Division title contenders. They ended their league campaign sixth, 16 points off champions Manchester United, and only beat lowly Torquay after a replay in an FA Cup run which fizzled out at the second hurdle, against Chelsea.

But he put 100 per cent effort into his second comeback, reflecting each and every performance on the field.

Pat Jennings saw it first hand behind the scenes. Jennings, then a teenager, said, 'I can remember one day when he re-started training, somebody was crossing balls from the byline in line with the edge of the 18-yard box. And Dave was on the penalty spot and just volleying them in. I thought, "Cor, this is Dave Mackay, like." I hadn't seen him play, only on the telly but now here he was.'

22

The second coming

THE SECOND coming of Dave Mackay as a first-team footballer after recovering from having his left leg broken again came on Saturday, 25 August 1965.

And it was no false dawn. He emerged from the players' tunnel at White Hart Lane for the first time since disappearing down it on a stretcher 11 months earlier, making a first appearance in the first team for 19 months. It gave him a 'wonderful' feeling and he added, 'The crowd made such a fuss of me.'

All his efforts paid off. He put it simply when he said to Jimmy Greaves in the 1970s, 'I was determined to play again.'

Leicester City, the team his Spurs had defeated in the FA Cup Final to seal the Double four years earlier, provided the opposition.

There were just two other members of the Glory Boys of 1960/61 alongside Mackay – Bill Brown and Maurice Norman. Stopper Brown was on borrowed time with up-and-coming Pat Jennings having shared the role with him since the Irishman arrived from Ron Burgess's Watford, and Norman's spell at the Lane was reaching the end. He had been switched back to full-back from centre-half to accommodate Laurie Brown, signed from Arsenal the previous February, but suffered a career-ending broken leg in a friendly win – with Mackay on target – against a Hungarian Select XI three months hence.

The survivors from Tottenham's greatest side were becoming thin on the ground, with just the sidelined Cliff Jones and Ron Henry still on the books in addition to those who faced the Foxes.

Terry Dyson had moved to Fulham, Peter Baker to Durban City and Les Allen to QPR in March, May and July. Bobby Smith had switched to Brighton in May the previous year, a month before Danny Blanchflower's retirement. Plus there was the tragic passing of John White in the July. Mackay's understanding with the new players was to be tested.

Of the full team that day, Mackay had yet to play with Cyril Knowles, Alan Mullery, Laurie Brown, youth product Derek Possee, Alan Gilzean and Jimmy Robertson.

But Mackay more than merely eased back as he, typically, fired up his team-mates old and new as the Foxes were outfoxed 4-2 – with Jimmy Greaves, Knowles, Possee and Robertson on target – to the delight and relief of Nicholson et al at Spurs and right-minded football lovers in and out of the game.

He had been missed. Certainly, Spurs hadn't been the same in his absence. They only won once on the road – against Nottingham Forest – while finishing sixth the previous season.

Mackay earned glowing reports and played down the plaudits, but said, 'I played a good game but doubt if I was man of the match … that game ranks among the most special for me in my entire career.'

The opening fixture of the 1965/66 season provided the green light for a silverware-winning comeback for 'Miracle Man' Mackay – always a fighter, always a winner – bringing a happy ending to the most traumatic tale of his playing career.

Astutely and appropriately, Nicholson appointed Mackay, his most natural leader, as club captain after the Leicester win. Mackay said, 'Bill Nicholson boosted my confidence no end by congratulating me warmly and telling me he was making me club captain.'

It continued to lift Mackay, who hit a couple of goals as Spurs won four of their opening six fixtures in an unbeaten start. He also underlined that his fitness was not to be doubted.

The Super Skipper was a fixture for the rest of the season, missing just the one league game – and that wasn't until February. He was assisted by the swift development of the striking partnership between Greaves and Gilzean. Greaves – who had been scoring for fun since his Lane arrival – netted what George Best called the best executed goal he had ever seen in a 5-1 win over his Manchester United at White Hart Lane in October, and it was Mackay who set Greaves on his way for it.

Mind you, the G-Men were temporarily put on hold when Greaves was sidelined by hepatitis for 12 games soon after he blew Best's mind. Even so, he still managed 15 in his 29 league appearances.

Mackay was more than happy. He said, 'I felt in control of my own destiny for the first time in quite a while. My instinct to win was undiminished and I wanted to partner Bill Nick, as Danny had done, in the quest for perfection and entertainment … I felt Bill had purchased wisely and we would soon be challenging for the championship once more.'

The fire was clearly still in his belly as he helped his transitional outfit, playing attractively and with a little more steel, to finish eighth, quadrupling the away wins total from the previous season to four. It was a reasonable effort given the new-look side's level of development, and his eye for goal got him a double as Spurs kicked off their FA Cup campaign with a 4-0 home win against Middlesbrough – although the Lilywhites' hopes ended when he returned at Preston after missing an epic 4-3 Lane victory over old rivals Burnley.

The Spurs team were clearly still a work in progress and, after he had given Joe Kinnear his first-team debut in a 4-1 home loss to West Ham United, Nicholson bought in Terry Venables from a Chelsea side managed by Mackay's old 'landlord' Tommy Docherty in May; the unrealistic hope in some circles was that he could replace the late John White.

Mackay and the latest new boy, it was reported, had a bumpy start to their relationship soon after Venables reported for training. The pair were on opposite sides in an indoor practice match. Mackay 'boxed off' Venables with the intention of preventing him from passing the ball. Venables claimed in *The Biography of Tottenham Hotspur*, 'As I tried to go past him, Dave hit me right in the balls with his fist.' When Mackay repeated the action, Venables lashed out and 'punched him in the face' and 'things remained a little strained between us for a couple of days'.

Mackay said, 'Terry thought I was over the top one day and caught me with a cuff over my eye … and it cut me a little … I returned a couple of blows to areas of the body that did not bruise so easily and we became the best of friends.

'We had skirmishes in the gym, with six-a-side. You always had battles there – not fights, but nearly. I want to win the game, win the ball and be in there challenging. And some players get upset and fight back. But I don't remember hurting anyone.'

There's no room for sentiment in football, as they say, and Mackay would not have expected to be shown any by his club – despite Nicholson's affection for what he brought to the side – or his country.

He had clawed his way back for Spurs and on 2 October 1965 the Iron Man came back for Scotland as national team manager Jock Stein called him up for his 22nd and final cap.

Mackay, with Spurs team-mates Bill Brown and two-goal Alan Gilzean, plus pal Denis Law, was in the team pipped 3-2 by a Northern Ireland side containing his club goalkeeper Pat Jennings and the young, incomparable George Best, in a Home International Championship match in Belfast. He said, 'It was to be my final cap and we lost … but I thank Jock for sealing my comeback.'

Law has reckoned Mackay as one of Scotland's all-time greatest players. Law, also rated in that exclusive club by many himself, said, 'Without a doubt. It was just the type of player he was. He battled so hard for the whole 90 minutes. I was very fortunate to play alongside him.

'I heard Sir Alex Ferguson say that Mackay would be his first choice as captain if he named his favourite Scotland XI. I would be the same. He was a born leader.'

Law also felt that Mackay's international career being limited to 22 caps was because he played in England. He added, 'It was a bit like they didn't like these guys playing in England. They preferred to have players playing in Scotland. That's how I felt. Dave didn't get the number of caps a lot of players who played in Scotland did. I really do think that was the reason why the Anglo-Scots didn't get the caps they should have.'

According to the *Sunday Post* in the wake of Mackay's passing in 2015, Ferguson had begun a selection debate about the best ever Scotland team while Aberdeen manager three decades earlier, declaring, 'Well, first in is Dave Mackay, brackets, captain.'

The iconic former Scotland and Manchester United manager added in the foreword to Mackay's autobiography, 'He was the best Scottish player in an era of excellent players yet he only won 22 caps. This was due to an in-built prejudice against so-called Anglo-Scots on behalf of the Scottish selectors. It is ridiculous that Dave and Denis Law paid the penalty for any poor performance on Scotland's part on a regular basis. Mackay could and should have captained Scotland for 15 years.'

The *Sunday Post* underlined his thoughts by asking and concluding, 'The best all-round Scottish player of all time? Sir Alex Ferguson certainly thinks so.'

Ian Ure, a Scotland team-mate, got to know Mackay the man rather than the tough-guy perception. He said, 'I only met him briefly, most times at international get-togethers, because we played together. He was a very quiet guy and didn't say a lot. But he wasn't shy. He didn't come across as brash, outgoing or anything like that. A kind of stolid individual, I feel.'

In the summer, Mackay attended the World Cup Final with his pal Ninian Cassidy, where he cheered on Ramsey's England to victory over West Germany, after a Spurs tour to Bermuda and the United States in which his side twice faced and failed to defeat Celtic.

And he maintained his trophy-winning habit, albeit in a minor competition – although it was a giant piece of silverware – by helping his club win the Costa del Sol tournament in Spain, sealing it with a 2-1 win against a Mallorcan team called Benfica.

In the meantime, Nicholson beat Manchester United to the record £95,000 signing of centre-half Mike England in August with Norman still trying to rescue his career and Laurie Brown disappointing. It completed the rebuild; Bill Nick's second great Spurs team was ready.

Mackay appeared to sense Norman would, unlike himself, not be coming back from the leg he had broken as he sat soaking in the bath at the Lane with Cliff Jones and the defender. He noticed Norman's foot 'pointed outward at a worrying angle'. It reminded him of the state of his foot following the collision with Noel Cantwell which resulted in his first experience of a similar injury and reflected, 'There but for the grace of God went I.'

Also, he felt Norman, when back in training, limped as he ran. He was right and Norman never played competitive football again, missing out on a third World Cup finals and a third FA Cup Final before retiring in June 1967.

Mackay was saddened for the 'big lovable man and an integral part of the Double-winning side'. But he was delighted with the player who proved a successful long-term successor. Mackay said, 'As usual it [the signing of Mike England] was a shrewd transfer by Bill as Mike quickly established himself as the best centre-half in the Football League.'

Five days after glory on the Iberian peninsula, Mackay and debutant England lined up for Tottenham against Leeds United with White Hart Lane bathed in late summer sunshine, rivalling the temperatures in Mallorca, as the 1966/67 league season kicked off.

It was an exciting time for the domestic game with the home country champions of the world. Each team had its share of superstars. West Ham had World Cup-winning trio Bobby Moore, Martin Peters and Geoff Hurst for starters. George Best, Denis Law and Bobby Charlton were at Manchester United; Liverpool had Ian St John and World Cup winner Roger Hunt; Arsenal possessed George Graham and Frank McLintock; Everton's dream midfield trio was Alan Ball, Howard Kendall and Colin Harvey.

Spurs could boast Mackay, Jimmy Greaves and Cliff Jones. And they all lined up against their Yorkshire visitors this day, along with England.

It was clear against Leeds that England was a dominant and reliable force, destined to help settle Pat Jennings, now the regular number one but still only just turned 21, develop into one of the best goalkeepers in world football.

Goals from Alan Mullery, Jimmy Greaves and Alan Gilzean ensured a 3-1 victory over Don Revie's famous side which had finished runners-up for the previous two seasons. Leeds included the likes of Johnny Giles, Bobby Collins and Billy Bremner. Jack Charlton, fresh from helping England lift the World Cup, was absent through injury but Paul Madeley was a solid replacement. Terry Cooper also played.

The match is, though, best remembered for an incident involving Mackay and Bremner captured in arguably the most famous football picture of all time, by legendary snapper Monte Fresco. It hung on the wall of Sir Alex Ferguson's Old Trafford office when Mackay's friend and fellow Scot was Manchester United manager. Mackay regularly had it thrust under his nose to autograph and he refused to have it on the cover of his autobiography despite the pleas of his publisher. He grew to 'hate' it as it depicted him as a bully.

Your author, along with the rest of the 43,844 present, saw diminutive Bremner kick Mackay's left leg, the one that had been broken twice before. Mackay was reckoned 'indestructible' and the fact he had come back from both injuries hardened that image. But a third comeback? Would he still prove indestructible? Mackay believed Bremner's action risked another leg break, one that might have proved third time unlucky and ended one of the great footballing careers.

Fortunately for the Iron Man it didn't, but he was left incensed. He grabbed Bremner by his shirt collar and pulled and twisted it, threatening to lift his worried-looking fellow Scot off the ground. His face was contorted, his jaw and chest jutted, his teeth gnashed. Mackay admitted in *The Legend of Billy Bremner* by Bernard Bale that he had fouled his Leeds adversary, but it was clear he had not expected such a retaliation.

Referee Norman Burtenshaw rushed over, blowing his whistle as he ran. Spurs midfielder Terry Venables and Johnny Giles of Leeds looked on. The official gave both players a stern talking-to and awarded Leeds a free kick.

Burtenshaw said in his autobiography, 'The test of a hard man is whether he can take it as well as give it out. Dave Mackay, the toughest player of my time could take it.'

Mackay said, 'The photograph of myself and Billy Bremner has become one of the most familiar images of football from that era. I have been asked to sign it many more times than any other image from my entire career and I have grown to dislike it. There I am, like Desperate Dan on steroids, manhandling a smaller and terrified-looking Bremner. It smacks of the bully. They say every picture tells a story and so does this image, but it is not a real one.

'Bremner was my pal, but when he pulled on his Leeds shirt he seemed to become a different man and for some reason he kicked me on my newly healed bad leg. He could easily have broken my leg for a third time. I was enraged. For a couple of seconds I lost my rag and was temporarily capable of breaking his neck in return. I grabbed him by the front of his shirt and lifted him from the ground. Our faces almost touched as his legs dangled in the air. The moment passed, but not before photographer Monte Fresco had captured it.

'What many people don't know is that we went to the nearest bar after the game and had a good drink together.'

So what did he say to Bremner at the flashpoint? Mackay was quoted in 2007, saying, 'I just grabbed him and called him a dirty little bastard. That's all in the past now.'

Isobel said, 'I was there and thought David would get sent off. It looked like he was going to boot Bremner out of the ground. Oh my goodness, I can't believe the number of times he signed that photo for people. David went to Billy Bremner's funeral [in 1997]. He wasn't meant to. It was on the spur of the moment, I think. They were friendly in a way. He was Leeds and David was Tottenham, but they used to have a drink and that.'

* * *

Mike England was right next to the incident. He recalled, 'It was like "wow". Bremner went over the top. As tough as you are the one thing you didn't used to do as a player was get your studs and go over the top of the ball. Billy Bremner did and Dave just lifted him off the floor. They played together for Scotland, but he didn't care about that, he just knew that Bremner had done something that he shouldn't have done and he certainly let him know.'

Jimmy Greaves said in his autobiography, 'Billy had been a naughty boy that day. He had gone over the top on me for a start. When he executed a similar tackle on Dave, Dave took exception to it … if an opponent went outside the rules, either written or unwritten, Dave would take exception. On such occasions as the one with Billy Bremner, Dave would, quite literally, take the matter in hand. He was a lawmaker rather than a lawbreaker.'

Bremner said in *The Legend of Billy Bremner*, 'Dave Mackay thought I was going to have a go and he grabbed hold of me first. I was actually innocent. I had made my point and that was the end of it, but I think he believed that I was going to give him and everyone else a good kicking. We had a laugh about it later and, to be honest, I love that photograph because it shows me with one of my all-time heroes.'

Mackay was proud of the fact he was not sent off throughout his career, and always sought to avoid any reinforcement of 'a perception of me in some quarters that I was a dirty player or, worse still, a bully'. He pointed to the fact that Nicholson, and his Hearts boss Tommy Walker, would not have tolerated him in their side if he had been 'dirty and cynical'.

He felt that 'myths take hold'. He was miffed that the Scottish FA chose the picture when he was inducted into its Hall of Fame, and 'hurt' when labelled as one of *Soccer's Hard Men* in a video film, as were Billy Bremner, Jack Charlton, Norman Hunter, Graeme Souness, Bryan Robson, Peter Storey, Nobby Stiles, Steve McMahon, Tommy Smith, Ron Harris and Vinnie Jones.

23

Fairytales can come true

BILL NICHOLSON'S new team was packed with class and steel and an ability to entertain the bottom line; all qualities the Double side possessed. The manager had combined the best of the old in the shape of Dave Mackay, Cliff Jones and Jimmy Greaves as representative of the glory days, with individuals such as Pat Jennings, Joe Kinnear, Cyril Knowles, Alan Mullery and Mike England who were destined to carry the torch on into the 1970s.

But it was Mackay who was the most irreplaceable component. He was the one player who galvanised the team with his leadership, lion-hearted competitive streak and unyielding confidence in himself, just as he did with the side of the early 1960s. This led to Spurs going close to a second Double again.

He admitted he was never quite as good as before. How could he be after the broken legs, and when approaching the age of 33 going into the 1966/67 season, despite being a player once described as worth three others in a Ralph Finn book?

Spurs had a quality side in the Spurs tradition with class oozing from goalkeeper Jennings and full-backs Knowles and Kinnear at the back to the G-Men up front, with the likes of Alan Mullery in between. More importantly, Mackay was close to being back to his imperial best and providing the X-factor which turns quality sides into winners. He remained as essential and irreplaceable as ever. Julie Welch wrote in *The Biography of Tottenham Hotspur*, 'Some had his skill. No one had his attitude, his furious competitiveness, his aura of self belief.'

His enthusiasm and love of the game were infectious. Observers reckoned the bone-shuddering strength of his tackling was as powerful as it ever was and his passing even better. It was believed he had lost a little speed, but made up for it by way he paced his own game. Those who wrote him off were at a loss for words. The Miracle Man was living up to his nickname and more, as the 'inspiration and driving force' of the team.

Jennings, for one, was impressed. He said, 'He could do everything. Pass, head, score goals, tackle, show skill. Wherever he needed to be he was there. He had an unbelievable knack. You'd think, "Right, there's only one pass on. A left foot." But all of a sudden he would change and put a right-foot pass away across the other side of the pitch as opponents swayed across that side of the pitch waiting for that left-footed pass. The times he did that ... and scored goals. Few people would pass him on a one-to-one as well. You could go past him but not you AND the ball.

'He was such an intelligent footballer and led by example. [There were] always one or two in the team that weren't the bravest and didn't like the tackles. If you played in Mackay's team you had to put your foot in – or else. I'm only going on when I played with him. What must he have been like in the early 1960s.'

Mackay's mentality was reflected in the positive change in attitude of the team in 1966/67.

He felt, for instance, there had been a negative outlook when it came to away games. The team had improved on a mere one victory away, at Nottingham Forest, when he was out for the whole 1964/65 season with four in his return campaign.

But that wasn't good enough for Mackay and 1966/67 saw them record nine triumphs on the road, more than any other team in the top flight, while scoring 23 away points, more than Denis Law's Manchester United, the champions, and runners-up Forest.

He said in *The Tottenham Hotspur Football Book* by Dennis Signy in 1967, 'The side were going away convinced they were going to be beaten. Now we travel to away games sure we are going to win.

'We had a series of free-for-all discussions. Everyone had a say. It was much better than cliques forming and groups of defenders skulking away after a match and blaming defeat on the forwards, and vice-versa. The talks were great. They cleared the air for us.

'It would have been no good at all if players sulked over things that were said. Some had a go at me for not marking people or doing something else they reckoned was wrong. We all had our say.'

Mackay and Co. won four of their opening six league games, and after an erratic spell they finished off the campaign going 16 fixtures without a reverse. Half of them were with clean sheets as defenders were assisted more by forwards, and they ended up with 56 points, their highest since 1961 and in third spot, missing out on second on goal average. Greaves was banging in the goals, Mike England and Terry Venables had settled, Pat Jennings went from good to great and Frank Saul was emerging largely at number 11 in place of Cliff Jones who was sidelined more often with injury due to the buffeting the brave Welshman took. And confidence flowed. Mackay, amid Bill Nicholson's second great team, might have helped it complete a second Double to make up for going so close in 1961/62 if the first half of the campaign had been as good as the second. Their Captain Courageous led them to the 1967 FA Cup to complete a fairytale comeback that could have proved more unbelievable than *Peter Pan*, *Cinderella* and *Beauty and the Beast* combined.

The oldest and most lauded domestic knockout competition in the world would demonstrate the increased resolve Mackay had helped instil on the road, namely in two tricky away ties at Millwall and Birmingham City and another against title rivals Nottingham Forest at neutral Hillsborough.

The Lions prided themselves on giving visitors an unwelcome welcome at The Den, exemplified by the eerie, rising monotone of their supporters; an attitude which developed into a 'nobody likes us but we don't care' siege mentality in the 1970s when their supporters became synonymous with hooliganism. Cold Blow Lane had sent shivers through 59 teams in a row in an unbeaten home run for the south London club, which came to an end a week before the tie with defeat to Plymouth Argyle.

Even so, the Second Division hosts provided a hostile welcome with that lingering, intimidating montone wafting from the home collective all over the ground as your youthful author sought the reassurance of his dad that we would return to the family home in one piece. Mackay had only previously visited The Den to watch pal and Lions player Des Anderson, who was to become his right-hand man for a large portion of his managerial career. And he helped inspire his team, limited in displaying their artistic skills by the muddy, cloying conditions, to a performance which displayed their heart for a battle and came away with a goalless draw in a full-blooded encounter in front of 41,000.

Mackay was struck on the 'come on, dare you, go and win' atmosphere and how 'fighting on the terraces first caught my eye'. He and his team found Millwall would not go quietly with Spurs squeezing through 1-0 in the midweek replay under the Lane lights thanks to a lone Alan Gilzean goal, with Mackay again a rock-like presence alongside half-back partners Mike England and Alan Mullery.

The next round saw more Second Division opposition and Mackay confirmed that Spurs 'comfortably disposed' of Portsmouth 3-1 at the Lane in a personal display which emphasised the fierce warrior of pre-double leg break was fast re-emerging to command his troops; the G-Men shared the goals.

Mackay's Lilywhites then drew another side from the second tier, again at the Lane, and the match-up against Bristol City almost cost him his proud record of never receiving marching orders in his entire career.

He and City's combative Johnny Quigley were reported to have locked horns like two Scottish red deer stags early on. And the tension exploded after Spurs were awarded a free kick close to the touchline. Mackay disclosed that Quigley threw the ball in his face as the Tottenham skipper sought to collect it and take the set piece. He reacted with a punch to his rival's solar plexus. It was reported the referee 'hurried across, pushed the players apart, and pointed for Mackay to follow the line of his finger towards an exit from the game', and that players of both sides 'engulfed' the official and that the two combatants 'made a great show of shaking hands for all the world to see'. Both sides 'appeared to be trying to make the referee either enforce or nullify his apparent decision' and 'even using hindsight, one cannot be sure what the referee intended'. He 'waved play to proceed' after talking to both players involved.

Mackay, who had played against Quigley in the 1962 9-2 cutting down of Forest, said, 'I was once sent off but refused to go … the ref had blown for a foul to Tottenham and Quigley had picked up the ball. I ran over to take the ball from him for the kick but for some reason he decided to throw the ball smack on my nose. It hurt and my instinctive reaction was to whack him. Common sense said not. Instinct prevailed. He doubled up and toppled over … when I looked round the referee was running towards me. His arm was outstretched. I pleaded and tried to tell him what had happened but he was having none of it.

'I turned to Quigley, but he had made an amazing recovery and had sprinted into the box. I galloped after him and dragged him back to the bemused referee. "Now tell him what you did." Fair play to the man, he told the truth. I thought that, if I was going, then I'd take this rascal with me but it was even better than that – the ref ticked us both off and didn't even take our names ... there were no hard feelings between Johnny and me, and I later met up with him when [Mackay was in the Middle East] he was coaching in Kuwait and helped him get a position in Saudi Arabia.'

Mackay was able to take a firm grip on the game as Quigley's performance evaporated. But the tie was far from straightforward for the hosts. After Greaves put Spurs in front on ten minutes, City missed a sitter through Bush and also wasted a twice-taken penalty for handball against England, the first saved by Pat Jennings from Tony Ford and the second shot wide by Chris Crowe. Greaves was able to show how it was done from the spot and Spurs won 2-0.

Mackay abandoned his customary forward promptings to ensure that Spurs kept a clean sheet as his side drew 0-0 against Birmingham City, yet another Second Division side, in the quarter-final at St Andrew's. It was reported that the assistance he gave to the defence included a 'backhander' to full-back Cyril Knowles as he was concerned the full-back was about to retaliate to home 'niggling' tactics.

It was said in Ralph Finn's *London's Cup Final*, 'The referee could not very well send off the Spurs skipper for striking his own man, could he?' Apparently not. And Mackay was part of a magical performance recalling the Double year as the representatives of England's second city were sent home having been 'walloped' 6-0 on a wet surface. Greaves and Venables each scored twice with Alan Gilzean and Frank Saul making up the six of the best.

Mackay helped Spurs prove they were capable of defeating top-flight opposition when they faced title rivals Forest at Hillsborough in the last four. And Mackay was central to the 2-1 victory, pushing forward in buccaneering style, providing the familiar crunch in his tackles and covering all over the pitch. It was another inspirational performance as Greaves and Saul bagged Spurs' goals in the 2-1 win.

Mackay also took satisfaction from stuffing a pre-match boast by Forest coach Tommy Cavanagh back down his throat. Cavanagh had opined, 'We'll crush Spurs like grapes.' Mackay said, 'Some grapes.'

Jennings said, 'Can you imagine making a statement like that with Dave Mackay! Dave played so well. There was a cross into our box and Mike England went to mark their big centre-forward Frank Wignall but Dave said, "Leave him to me" so Mike went round the back to pick up someone else and Dave collided with Wignall who struggled after. There's a picture of Frank showing he had a bad arm!'

Chelsea overcame Leeds in the other semi-final to ensure Mackay would lead his side out against a team managed by his old landlord Tommy Docherty on Saturday, 20 May 1967. It was the opportunity to become an integral part of football, let alone Tottenham, folklore as the Miracle Man who returned to football heaven from an injury hell.

He was centre stage for the first all-London FA Cup Final, the first to allow substitutes and last to be televised in monochrome. It was the established aristocrats of N17 who had built a tradition on playing the beautiful game beautifully against the new kids on the block in their first Wembley final; Hush Puppy-wearers partial to a night out at Walthamstow dogs versus long-haired, trendy individuals who hung out in the über cool King's Road, the epicentre of Swinging London culture. And, of course, the Mackay comeback tale. There was plenty for the media to build up.

The Summer of Love was around the corner with the advent of psychedelia brightening up fashion, music and art. But the weather gods produced a dull day – although it was far from a dull match – before a 100,000 crowd. And the sun even broke out in the first half after rain had wetted the surface before taking a back seat.

And an internal row over player bonuses and tickets within Stamford Bridge evidently helped with Tottenham's psychological advantage, judging by the body language of the two teams as they took the field.

The Blues looked blue, the normally bubbly Docherty stern-faced, with Ron Harris seemingly distracted as he gazed to his left and Tony Hateley, a big-money replacement for the injured Peter Osgood, apparently unfocused as he played up to a camera operator videoing the moments. They seemed agitated.

Mackay led the more relaxed and focused-looking, strong Spurs team out behind a beaming Bill Nicholson, cupping a full-sized ball before bouncing and juggling it and tossing it from hand to hand, having emerged from the tunnel to tread on the vaunted pitch, before spotting a face in the stands and pointing with a smile breaking out on his craggy visage. There appeared a unity and spirit among those in white, and even a sense of fun with Jimmy Greaves having revealed a prank played on Eddie Baily, phoning up Bill Nick's assistant saying, 'Mr Baily, your brother Bill has phoned to say he won't be home [inspired by the popular song 'Won't You Come Home Bill Bailey'].' There was another on team-mates Cyril Knowles and Frank Saul when shampoo was unbeknown to them squeezed on their heads after they had already rinsed off what they had applied.

Mackay introduced the Duke of Kent to his team as both opponents lined up opposite each other under the iconic twin towers of the world-famous stadium. Then Mackay and Co. discarded their white tracksuit tops, with dark blue edging. It was down to business. He had no need to indulge in any mind games, such was his belief that Tottenham would win.

Terry Venables said in *The Biography of Tottenham Hotspur*, 'What stands out was the absolute confidence of Dave Mackay; there was no question in his mind about the result … he kept saying we would slaughter them, there was not a chance that we would lose. Nor was he saying it just to give the rest of us confidence, he was genuinely convinced we would win. As usual, he was right.'

Mackay played a more subdued role than usual, concentrating on defence and leaving the swashbuckling forward runs he was known for making to opposite wing-half Alan Mullery.

The surprise tactic, with Mullery having been re-educated from holding back by Bill Nicholson, was not the only one. At full-back, left-sided Cyril Knowles was known for his marauding runs down the flank, while right-back Joe Kinnear held back. Again roles were reversed as Kinnear put in a player-of-the-match display.

And the impressive Alan Gilzean mastered the opposition in the air and on the ground as he took advantage of a shock tactic employed by Docherty, who decided on a flat back four rather than operating the sweeper system which had stymied the Scotland international in Spurs' equal worst defeat of the season. The absence of Chelsea talisman Osgood with a broken leg also appeared to help Spurs' cause.

Spurs impressed against a young side who put in the blood, sweat and tears with their hard-running, counter-punching style but were unable to match the class and cohesion of Mackay's team.

Mackay helped put Spurs in front just before the interval. His free kick sent Mullery away and the England international thundered a drive which cannoned off the shin of Harris. As the ball dropped on the edge of the penalty area, Jimmy Robertson volleyed home.

Observers felt the crowd was subdued, but your author maintained it was more a case of being absorbed.

And as Mackay congratulated fellow Scot Robertson, the volume was switched up and 'Glory Glory Hallelujah' – a version recorded at the Beatles' Abbey Road studios by a full-voiced Mackay and his players as the club's cup final song in the build-up to the big day – spread around those of a Lilywhite persuasion. The dominance now had a tangible result.

Spurs looked graceful and rhythmical and doubled their advantage – with Mackay again at the beginning of its creation.

He slung a long throw-in towards the Chelsea goal, which was partially cleared, and Robertson headed the ball down for Saul, left on the sidelines for the two previous domestic finals of the 1960s, to swivel and score. Again Mackay joined in the celebrations, but this time hanging on to the edge of the group and leaping in the air with both legs tucked underneath him.

Bobby Tambling halved the Chelsea deficit late on but there was never a danger that Mackay's men would fold.

Bolton referee Ken Dagnall blew his whistle and Mackay went round patting each member of the side on the back while politely shaking the hands of vanquished foes.

Then he led the team up to the Royal Box to receive their medals, and as captain he collected the FA Cup from the Duke of Kent. Mackay deserved every moment. He had twice made the journey – in 1961 and 1962 – but completing it for a third time tasted the sweetest.

As he left the platform to start his descent, Mackay gave himself a moment. He hugged the trophy and gave it a kiss. No one could begrudge him after what he had been through with injury. It seemed love was in the air – or rather undiluted delight – when Alan Mullery planted a smacker on the side of his captain's face as they began the lap of honour.

Mackay said in the *Sunday Express* at the time, 'Every sportsman has his supreme moment. I had mine … when the Duke of Kent presented me with the FA Cup … the greatest prize English soccer has to offer.

'They say I'm a tough guy but my eyes began to cloud over and the multitude of blues and whites worn by the fans just mingled together as I moved up the steps to the Royal Box; a memorable moment, one I will never forget.

'Even I must admit that I had long lingering doubts about ever feeling the sun and rain on my back on this great day after twice breaking my leg.

'Chelsea manager Tommy Docherty helped make my great day. He said we were a fine young side. As a 32-year-old, I hasten to agree.

'I think we gained a worthy victory. It made me proud that it was gained under my leadership. Whatever success I have had as a captain in recent years is in no small part due to playing under Danny Blanchflower. Danny and I may be as different as chalk and cheese when it comes to temperament, but I'm a far better player for having played under his wing.

'I may be the veteran of the team but that lush Wembley turf never gave me the slightest worry, although a couple of my much younger colleagues evidently felt it pulling at their leg muscles.

'I never had any real doubts about victory … I am firmly convinced the side can develop even further … Tottenham can be a far greater team.'

Mackay added in *The Tottenham Hotspur Football Book* by Dennis Signy, 'People ask me what style Tottenham play. I don't know. I do know that I am a believer in off-the-cuff, common-sense football. Off-the-cuff play will beat any pattern.'

Jimmy Robertson said, 'Dave's comeback to lift the cup was a great story. He made the point he'd never lost in a cup final at Wembley which was reassuring at the time. It was a dream for me to score and win my first trophy.

'I remember something that always sticks in my mind because afterwards there was a banquet at the Savoy Hotel. Dave had enjoyed quite a few drinks. And he was, I wouldn't say legless but he wasn't far from it. He wasn't capable so I organised a room for him to stay overnight.'

Centre-half Mike England said, 'Break your leg twice, make a comeback and win the FA Cup at Wembley is like a *Boy's Own* story.

Dave played the anchor part and released Alan Mullery and others to go forward. Bill Nicholson used to encourage us, myself as a centre-half included, to do that if we had space in front of us. I loved that.

'Every footballer's dream from when they are a little boy is to play at Wembley in the cup final. It was something very special. You feel so proud. A sense of achievement.'

Pat Jennings, who made a crucial save from Charlie Cooke in the final, said, 'It was wonderful for Dave after what he'd been through. It was fantastic for all of us as a lot of us had not been in a cup-winning team before. It was a glamour competition in those days. We finished up om the same points and goals as Forest in the league but they had a better goal average. That season was the nearest our team ever got to doing the Double. It was seriously talented.'

Derek Mackay, Dave's second son, said, 'It was such a great story with Dad coming back from a broken leg twice. My sister Val sent me a little video recently that I'd never seen as dad was preparing to go up to get the cup and it was the famous commentator Kenneth Wolstenholme, who goes, "Here he is. Dave Mackay! We all thought he was finished; there he is going up to collect the FA Cup."

'I was nine and I've got great memories of being on the open-top bus parading down the High Road to the Town Hall to be greeted by the mayor the following day. I've never seen – even up to now – that many people on the streets. All the way. There must have been at least 100,000, definitely. As far as the eye can see. In the buildings, hanging off the buildings. I'll never forget it. It was all amazing.'

Valerie Mackay said, 'We were all so proud of dad. And, coincidently, Derek's junior school won their cup that year too! He'd have been too modest to tell you!'

24

'A born leader'

THE DAVE Mackay-led Tottenham seemed destined to build on their third FA Cup victory in just seven years, a triumph which extended an unbeaten run to 24 games playing with skill and steel. There was a blend of wise old heads like Mackay and skilled younger players who had picked up invaluable experience and confidence during the 1966/67 season.

Perhaps Bill Nick's second great team at Tottenham might even emulate the feats of the one which joined the immortals by sealing the Double?

It looked okay at the start of the following season. Spurs secured a decent 3-3 friendly draw with full-strength Celtic, who were fresh from becoming the first British club to win the European Cup in May. Mackay's side – unchanged from Wembley – impressed before 91,708 at Hampden Park on 5 August 1967, with Jimmy Greaves (two) and Alan Gilzean on target against the Lisbon Lions. The match-up was to commemorate the centenary of Queen's Park, the first club in Scotland and based at the national stadium.

And it was the same score as Spurs held champions Manchester United 3-3 in the FA Charity Shield match at Old Trafford where Mackay claimed a part in an extraordinary goal by stopper Pat Jennings.

Jennings said, 'It was a free kick just outside our box. Mackay was running up to take it. I said, "Give it to me, Dave, I'll knock it up." He did that. I was trying to pick Gilly [Alan Gilzean] up with the kick. It bounced over Gilly and their goalkeeper Alex Stepney. I'd never seen it happen and wondered if the referee would give it [the goal]. He did and Mackay claimed the assist because he knocked the ball back to me!'

Mackay was happy enough as his Spurs picked two wins, including a 5-1 demolition of West Ham United, and a draw in their opening three league fixtures. But in the hammering of the Hammers he suffered a trapped nerve behind his left knee and it sidelined him for 11 games. Spurs' results became erratic in his absence, most notably in a 4-0 reverse against Arsenal at Highbury after back-to-back wins against Wolverhampton Wanderers and Sheffield Wednesday.

His return for a 1-1 draw against Bill Shankly's Liverpool at Anfield on the eve of Bonfire Night sparked a run of two victories on the bounce, against Southampton and, more sweetly, Chelsea. But the side returned to its inconsistent ways as title hopes faded away and Spurs ended the season in seventh.

Any hopes that Mackay and Co. could enhance their justified reputation as knockout cup kings were soon stifled. Their defence of the FA Cup began in style with victory over Manchester United, who were to lift the European Cup later in the season. But after easing into the fifth round via lower-league Preston North End they came unstuck against Liverpool who themselves were dismissed after two replays by eventual winners West Bromwich Albion.

In Mackay's absence, Spurs made a meal of edging through against Hajduk Split in what was still Yugoslavia as they began their third European Cup Winners' Cup campaign.

They came away with a 2-0 advantage in the first leg on 20 September 1967 with a solid performance in the face of exploding rockets and screaming sirens emanating from the home support. And after taking an early lead in the second leg, they had to settle for a 4-3 home win as they edged through.

Mackay returned for the second round and another hostile environment as his side were pipped 1-0 by hosts Olympique Lyonnais amid violent scenes on 29 November. Alan Mullery was sent off for retaliation as he was kicked in the mouth and laid out by host striker André Guy, an incident which sparked a brawl. And more violence ensued at the interval with Alan Gilzean and Bill Nicholson caught up in a clash with Guy. The occasion was described in the media as a 'riot' with Nicholson blasting the match as 'a disgrace'.

Mackay led Spurs to victory in the second leg, but the 4-3 scoreline saw the visitors go through on goal difference.

It was the Scot's last hurrah in the competition as he chased a winners' medal after missing out on one five years earlier and all in all it was a frustrating season for Mackay.

He hinted at regret that he had not pulled the curtain down on his illustrious career after skippering Spurs to the 1967 FA Cup.

Mackay said, 'I could not have wished for a better climax to my career at Tottenham. There's no topping this, I thought. I should have retired from playing there and then. It would have been the perfect end to a comeback from the football graveyard.'

And he pulled no punches when it came to analysing his own performances during the anti-climactic 1967/68 season.

He said, 'We lacked consistency … I, for one, was conscious that my contribution was not as high as it once was. This made me unhappy and frustrated … before the final knockings I decided to retire. I went to Bill Nick saying I didn't think I could do the job any more.'

Ironically, the decision was made two days after a 3-1 loss against soon-to-be-crowned champions Manchester City at White Hart Lane, the opponents and venue for his Spurs debut.

He said, 'As I traipsed off the pitch, I knew I was no longer good enough to play in the top flight. Age and two broken legs had made me sluggish. If I had been manager I would have dropped me and put me out to grass.'

Mackay played his 318th and final competitive match for the Lilywhites against Wolverhampton Wanderers, whom his Spurs had replaced as the dominant force in the country, at Molineux on 11 May. The result was anathema to a winner such as Mackay with Spurs beaten 2-1.

After nine years, three FA Cup wins, a league triumph and a run to the European Cup Winners' Cup Final, the Spurs career of the player rated by colleagues and fans – and many others – as either the most important, influential, best or greatest in the club's history was over.

Bill Nicholson, Mackay's only Spurs manager, said, 'There were many outstanding players at Tottenham during my years as manager, and when I was asked which one I considered my best signing I always declined to answer. There were so many, including Jimmy Greaves, Pat Jennings,

Cliff Jones, John White, Mike England, Alan Mullery, Alan Gilzean, Cyril Knowles, Martin Chivers, Martin Peters and Dave Mackay.

'I suppose most people would assume my choice would be Greaves because he was the best striker of his era and the game is about scoring goals. Greaves had a far superior goal record than any of his foremost contemporaries, including Denis Law, George Best and Bobby Charlton. It is very hard to choose between half a dozen of my players, but I think I must select Dave Mackay as my best-ever signing. Not only did Mackay make such an enormous contribution on the field but his dynamic character was also a major influence in training, and everywhere he went and in everything he did. The effect on the other players was remarkable.

'He was a truly great player with far more skill than he was ever given credit for. He had a delicate touch, two good feet and was such an intelligent reader of the game that it came as no surprise to me that Brian Clough converted him into a sweeper at Derby. In midfield for Tottenham, Mackay was a mighty player, powerful in the tackle and very fair.'

Cliff Jones, besides Spurs team-mates, played with Duncan Edwards, John Charles and Stanley Matthews and against Pelé, George Best and Eusébio, as well as taking part in the World Cup finals.

Jones, who spoke at Mackay's funeral in Edinburgh – where he also carried the coffin – and at the memorial in Enfield, said, 'Dave was the best and most influential player I've played with and one of the best I have EVER seen. He had it all. All the top players you can think of, he ranks with them all. Even Duncan Edwards. Can you imagine a team with Duncan Edwards AND Dave Mackay? My God! It would be unstoppable. And then Bobby Charlton and Jimmy Greaves up front. Wow!

'Spurs were the team to see in the early 1960s and most of it was down to Mackay. Absolutely, the top, top man. A good team player, a leader, an out and out winner.

'He changed teams and proved it. Everywhere he went teams won. His whole [sporting] life was about he had to be the best. He had to win, whatever it was. We played golf at Spurs and he used to batter us!

'He was also a terrific family man; four children, married to his wife for years and years. A humble, ordinary guy. Fun to be with – so sociable. A great lad. He lived life to the full but turned it on when he went on the field. A great character.

'Anybody who played with Mackay would rate him. I count myself fortunate to have played with the likes of Dave Mackay.'

Terry Dyson said, 'Every game was the same for Dave. We wanted to win and we did most times. We didn't get beaten often, especially when we won the Double. And he wanted to play. The way he played, it encouraged other people. We had a good team but when he came in it made it a great one. We'd been struggling but he turned it right around with Danny, who was the perfect captain.

'He helped me personally. He helped the rest of the team. He inspired us. We didn't have a bad team but Dave was our best player. Dave was tough and could take a knock. He would get whacked but shake it off. When he got into tackles, it made you try and copy him. The rest of the team would think, "He can do it, so we can do it!" He was the core of the team with John White and Danny Blanchflower. Bill Nicholson and Dave always got on all right. There was no reason for them not to get on because Dave gave his all in every match.

'We used to go in the gym after training and have a game of one-touch. We used to play in there for ages, me and Dave. I hardly ever beat him. Another example of how much he was a winner came in a snooker session I was part of. He was playing someone for half a crown [25p]. This fellow hit a ball that went all round the bloody table and luckily, for him, went in. Dave snapped his cue.

'As people have said, he had a lot more ball skill than people thought. He did these exercises where he would volley the ball against the wall about 100 times. One after another. There was that coin juggling thing he did where he throw one up and he'd catch it on his foot, flick it up again and into his pocket. He was, as I've said, fun to be with socially. If we played away, travelled up on the Friday and were bored, there were a few of us who would try and play keepy-up with an orange, including Dave, John White and myself. I kept one up for about four. Dave would keep going until the orange was completely squashed up. I know Fergie [Sir Alex Ferguson] loved him.'

Pat Jennings, the other former Spurs team-mate to carry Mackay's coffin at the funeral, said, 'There's a lot to write about Dave Mackay. They'll never be another Mackay. A born leader.

'He was not just a great player who could do everything – and was very difficult to pass in the tackle – but led by example. His influence rubbed off on us players. He got the best out of everybody around him.

'He had brilliant ball skills. When he went out he used to kick it up in the air and control it on the way down. It was his way of showing people that not only could he tackle, but he had the skill to go with it.

'He used to show his ball skills in training too. When he did you just had to stand back and admire them.

'I never got to see the great John White but I believe that Dave Mackay was responsible for helping get him to the club.

'Mackay was a one-off. Like Bill Nicholson said he was his best signing ever. And look at the players we've had through the years like Greavsie, Mike England, Gilly. Mackay was just special.

'He was a lovely bloke. I remember I never had a car when I first joined Spurs. He had a Jaguar and would loan it to you. That's how generous he was.

'Dave was a micky taker, always saying, "Put your caps on the table." And when I said I had a few and did he joked that if you kept the ball up twice you'd get an Irish cap!'

Jimmy Greaves, via his agent Terry Baker, said, 'Dave was a lion of a man. In my opinion the best player ever to play for Spurs. He had everything. Timing, strength, vision, leadership and ability. There have been few better British players in the history of the English game. He was a great friend to us all.'

Greaves pointed out in his autobiography how Mackay's 'infectious enthusiasm' rubbed off on his team-mates, adding, 'Dave was world-class … He tore into opponents and he tore them apart. Playing against Dave must have been like walking through a lion's cage wearing a three-piece suit made of sirloin. Dave was a mighty player, ferocious in the tackle but always fair.

'Not only did he make an enormous contribution on the field, his dynamic character was also a major influence in training, in the dressing room and everywhere he went and in everything he did. Leadership in action, not position, and Dave was a man of action. Dave adhered to a strict code of conduct. He put everything behind every tackle, but always played the ball and expected similar treatment himself.

'The fact Dave Mackay courageously fought back from a twice-broken left leg was the mark of the man.'

Greaves was grateful to the Scot for making his first Tottenham goal on his debut against Blackpool at White Hart Lane on 16 December 1961.

He said in his autobiography, 'Dave Mackay was a long-throw specialist who could hurl the ball into an opponents' box from fully 40 yards. Dave's ability to achieve such distance … made him unique in football at the time. It was as good as a dead-ball kick.

'Against Blackpool I managed to lose my marker Dave Durie and that gave me a yard of space to get on the end of Dave's throw-in. I think that goal did a lot to endear me to the Tottenham supporters.'

Terry Venables told Will Mott, the former ITV News sports reporter, 'I think he [Mackay] was the best midfield player, all-round player I'd ever seen or played alongside. I'm really privileged to have played with him.'

Venables emphasised Mackay's positive dressing room influence on top of his 'toughness' and 'ability' as he added, 'He'd make your life worth living just being in his company. That closeness made Spurs.'

Mike England said, 'Dave was a born leader. Everyone looked up to Dave Mackay. He was the captain, and everyone knew he was the captain because of the way he just led everyone along.

'He was just great with me being a young centre-back at Tottenham. I learned so much off of him. He played just in front of me, the anchorman in midfield, and I had Phil Beal next to me.

'Dave was part of a crafty old move from Bill Nicholson. Bill introduced me to Dave and other top players before I'd signed, as if he was saying, "Wouldn't it be great to play with these players?" He must have told them I was coming down and signing as they were saying "nice to have you with us".

'People used to say, "Dave Mackay, he's a tough sod." What many didn't realise was how skilful he was. He was incredibly skilful. Sometimes that fact gets overlooked because of the way he played and led with that toughness and will to win. He could do anything with a ball.

'I would rate Dave very highly among everyone I've played with. There's not many Dave Mackays. He was the all-round package, who could do a bit of everything. That earned him respect.

'He certainly didn't like to lose at anything. He would always do his best to make sure he didn't. That used to come across at half-time. Bill Nicholson would come to address us and say what he had to say. Dave, just before we went back out again, would have a go everyone and say a few words. He always did that. He was the captain and took on that responsibility.'

Wales captain England insisted Mackay was his best skipper. He said, 'Oh yes, without any doubt. He was a proper captain. It takes a special kind of player to be a captain. Especially when we played. He had the leadership qualities and total respect of all the other players, which a captain has to have. Everyone took notice of Dave Mackay. I was pleased in some ways I had those qualities myself having learned so much off him.'

Les Allen said, 'Dave was so on top of everything. He got everybody going and was so good at everything. Whatever angle the ball came to him he dealt with it easily. He knew what he was going to do before he had the ball. If any of us were not up to scratch he'd soon put you right.'

Maurice Norman said to the club, 'He was everything to our team, Dave. A wonderful player, one of the greatest I've ever played with. He was a tough nut to crack. So strong, it was unbelievable. I'll always remember our tussles with Leeds United and the likes of Billy Bremner, Norman Hunter and Jackie Charlton. He would say to Billy Bremner, "If you come over that halfway line, that's your lot!"'

Bobby Smith said at the Cheshunt Q&A alongside Mackay in 2007, 'Dave was worth two men. You were guaranteed that he would give 100 [per cent].'

Jimmy Robertson said, 'If I was to pick my best team, he would be the first pick. He would have been the first for any of his managers as his determination was infectious. A big personality and never held back in a match or the gym or on the golf course! We used to play golf every Monday if we didn't have a midweek game but you'd never win with him. It was just not possible. If you were winning you'd be out there until he won. He'd have lots of ways of winning – criticising your swing or inventing a rule!

'He'd give you a b*******g when necessary but when he made mistakes he'd be the first one to hold his hands up. He knew his strengths as a footballer, but wasn't arrogant or big-headed. He was humble.

'He changed position after his broken legs, more defensive rather than marauding forward and he became effective at it. No question he was Bill Nicholson's best signing.

'When I went to Tottenham there were three other Scotsmen there, Dave, Bill Brown and John White, and they looked after me. They'd put me on the right road.

'Off the park, Dave was great company. He enjoyed a drink and was just one of the boys. He was totally different to what people might imagine him to be having seen him play. He was a thoughtful person, great company.'

Spurs reserve John Sainty, who played in the Combination game in which Mackay suffered a broken leg for the second time, said, 'He was my hero. The best player I've seen in my life. He could do anything as a player. If he hadn't had 50 tackles in a game he would not have thought he'd been in a game. In the gym in training, it was a pleasure to play with players like him because Dave was so good. He was an exceptional player.

'He wasn't the big "I am". He would help anybody he could. If he saw someone taking the mick out of you, he'd tell them to mind their own business.

'If I could have been anything like him I'd have been happy. I respected him so much, as I've said, I went to his funeral in Scotland on my own. I wouldn't have missed that.'

Defender Phil Beal, who played more than 400 first-team games, benefited from the support of Mackay when making his Spurs debut against Aston Villa on 16 September 1963.

Beal, who helped Spurs win the League Cup twice and the UEFA Cup in the 1970s, said, 'No one could have been more encouraging than Dave. He protected me like nobody else because I was a youngster coming into the team. If he thought someone had done something to me, he'd stick up for me. He'd say "leave it to me".

'When I was a kid, a youth team player, we used to train in the afternoon after the first team in the morning. We did ball skills and Dave used to join in like he was one of us.

'We used to finish with a five-a-side and Dave took no prisoners. Just because you are a 15-year-old doesn't mean to say that you hold back in a tackle. Dave went in as though it was the cup final. He used to encourage us. The fact he would come back to join in showed that just because he was in the first team that he should not rest on his laurels. It opened my eyes as to the work and dedication you need to become a professional footballer.

'When I was in the first team and he was captain, Dave feared nobody, was confident and never lacked concentration. If you made an elementary mistake he would let you know. Some players do that now [make a mistake] and it is just accepted. That wouldn't happen with Dave. He wouldn't stand for it. It wouldn't be acceptable to him, even if you were a great goalscorer like Martin Chivers was for Tottenham. But there again he would be the first one to turn around and praise you and give you a pat on the back if you've done something good.

'He played further back than in his early days when we played together, but he was adaptable. I would always say he was one of the best defenders I've seen in my career. I never saw him have a bad game. I'm grateful I had that time playing with him.'

Steve Perryman, Spurs' all-time record appearance maker and 1981 and 1982 FA Cup-winning captain, who attended Mackay's funeral, cites working with the Scot as 'being in the presence of greatness'.

Perryman said, 'I got involved with the club as a 15-year-old, training there once or twice a week, and progressed into being an apprentice professional. You were aware of Dave's influence around the place. Sitting on the touchline [during matches], you were so aware by the way he carried himself, he had everybody at his command. The ref, the opponents, the crowd were all under his spell. At training you were in the presence of greatness.

'What a man. In later years, Dave was responsible for helping me to make my Spurs debut. When Spurs went up to the Baseball Ground to face Dave's team for the first time and they beat us 5-0, I was 13th man. Bill Nick was not happy. And little Willie Carlin scored a header for them from a corner when he was about five foot nothing. So Bill made changes for the next week. I was one of the changes.

'Dave was an influence on me as Spurs captain. You couldn't copy Dave Mackay, but there were certain attributes which are the same – putting your opinion out there for people to follow. You don't follow someone who hasn't got an opinion. Therefore you get this aura. That's great power if it is in the right hands and I like to think that in me and particularly Dave Mackay it was.

'I remember as an apprentice, the trainers and coaches – with their white coats on – at Tottenham talking when I was cleaning the players' boots. One asked, "Is Dave Mackay the best Spurs player you've ever seen?" A couple of them at least would name Ron Burgess. There were common denominators. Both were wing-halves and captain types. But if Ron Burgess was a better player that Dave Mackay, he must have been some player.'

Alan Gilzean waxed lyrical about Mackay, who became a good friend, clearly taking on board a request from Bobby Wishart, our subject's childhood team-mate and adult opponent when Hearts faced Aberdeen, to 'look after this guy [Gilzean] because he can play a bit'.

Gilzean was quoted about his fellow Scot's influence at the Lane and more in *The King of White Hart Lane* and *The King of Dens Park* by your author, which took the remarks from *The Spurs Show* podcast and *Tottenham Hotspur*.

Gilzean said, 'He [Mackay] was the heart of the club – a fantastic leader – a guy you'd want in the trenches with you. Every game he played in, he wanted to win. We were playing golf once in San Francisco, Jimmy Robertson, Mackay and myself, a knockout tournament between the three of us. I was out of it. Coming down the 17th, Robbo and Mackay were level. There came a downpour. Heavy, heavy rain. Puddles started appearing on the course. So Mackay got on the green with his second shot. Jimmy Robertson's second shot stuck in a puddle short of the green. So he says to Davie, "Water hazard! I can move the ball." Mackay says, "You don't move that ball. That puddle was there before you played your second shot. Get on with it." He would never give anything – in practice matches, on the ball court. It was never a knockabout with him.'

He added to Spurs, 'What was Davie like as a captain? He was the driving force behind the whole club, Mackay. He was one of those who would play with positivity, there were no grey areas with Davie.'

John Duncan followed the Mackay route from Scotland to White Hart Lane in the 1970s, hailing from Alan Gilzean's east coast club Dundee. He said, 'All the Spurs players, when you are discussing football, say Dave Mackay was the greatest player they've ever seen. There was not much doubt or argument about it. They all did.'

Denis Law played regularly for Manchester United against Mackay's Tottenham. Law said, 'When I played for United against him with Spurs it was always a tough, tough game. You knew he would be getting straight into it. Even if he was your best pal! Someone you looked up to. He was, as others have said, a winner – at everything. Tiddlywinks, football, whatever.

'We had a beer together after games. It was a different world to now. He was a terrific guy. Was he fun or serious? Both. He was serious when he should have been and you could have a laugh when he should too.

'It was a lovely time for football when Dave Mackay played for Scotland and went on to Spurs. They both had terrific teams and that was due to Dave Mackay.'

Ian Ure also faced Mackay during his Scottish international team-mate's time at Tottenham while playing for Arsenal and Manchester United. He said, 'I played against him loads of times. Most of the time we got a "doing" and got beat, because Spurs were a good side then.

'He was the best player I ever played with and against. If I was to pick a team of all-time players I've played with and against he'd be number one. And he was in his prime at Spurs.

'He was a perfect footballer, who had everything. A "dig", ability, a great left foot, a great passer of the ball and a leader. He galvanised and led from the front. No one who wasn't pulling their weight would get away with anything. He wouldn't bark, shout or bawl. He just had command in a quiet way.

'He could tackle like a lion. He was also a beautiful player who could caress the ball, chip it with backspin and the next minute he would be sorting some big, huge giant out. A great all-rounder.

'He was a wonderful captain for Spurs after Danny. It speaks for itself that he came back from the two broken legs to do so well with the teams he came back to. You can only write good things about Dave Mackay.

'Dave's famous team that won the Double in the early 1960s was possibly the greatest club side I've ever seen. They played like the great Spanish team Real Madrid and Barcelona as well. They passed the ball around. Find the ball and if a man's not covered, give it to him. Then be available to get the ball back. A simple game. You had all kinds of great players in that team – Bill Nicholson knew how to pick them – but Mackay was their best player by far. Danny Blanchflower got all the praises but he wasn't nearly as influential as Mackay was. He was the heartbeat of the team.'

Frank McLintock faced up to Mackay for Leicester and then Arsenal in north London derbies. Mackay's Scottish team-mate said, 'Dave

Mackay was a fantastic player for Tottenham Hotspur but so was Jimmy Greaves, Cliff Jones and John White. But if you look for their top players, Dave has got to be there all the time.

'He was Spurs and I was Arsenal and during our games against each other we'd fight like cat and dog, but afterwards we'd go for a drink together and never think anything of it. We were mates.

'I think he used to come down to a pub I had. A lot of players did. Footballers are footballers and they get to know each other.

'I know Isobel very well. A lovely person. I phone her up now and again. My wife died and she wrote me a lovely letter. An amazing woman. She was a big influence on Dave.'

Derek Mackay recalled one of a multitude of reasons for his dad's popularity off the field during his last season at Spurs.

Derek said, 'He was the same in his private life as he was in his profession. So unselfish. We went to this little sports shop in Southgate one day. He tried these boots on. The young lad there recognised Dad and was loving it. Dad has gone for these two pairs of Adidas. And Dad's going to me, "You try this pair on?" So I got a pair. Dad said to the kid, "The boots, charge them to Tottenham Hotspur." And the guy said, "What about your son's boots?" Dad said, "No, no. I'm paying for them." He said, "Dave, I can make it out to Tottenham." He said, "No, it's not right. I'm paying for my lad's boots."

'But can you imagine that now? They get hundreds of thousands now for wearing boots. And my dad, with all the things he'd won, is getting two pairs himself – and paying for mine!'

PART FOUR:
DERBY COUNTY

25

Brian Clough

WHAT NOW for Dave Mackay? His plan to retire as a player would end one of the game's great careers.

Mackay, it seemed, was ready to carry that intention through by revealing he harboured hopes of 'moving upstairs' to assist Bill Nicholson, but with Eddie Baily already in the role he did not want to upset the apple cart at the top of the club's managerial hierarchy.

On the face of it, his aim was true. The guy was close to 34 when 34-year-old outfield players didn't get the medical and scientific support his modern-day equivalent receives.

Would his old Scotland manager Matt Busby be interested in dissuading him from hanging up his boots a decade under the bridge having produced the champions of Europe at Manchester United? Unlikely.

Maybe a top-flight team below Spurs might be interested in practising the art of persuasion? Possibly.

Mackay revealed that Nicholson was 'shocked' at his decision to quit as a player. His manager felt he still had a couple of years left in the tank. But was Nicholson's view irrelevant if his favourite signing thought it was empty?

It looked like we would find an answer to the imponderables when Nicholson called Mackay into his office during the close-season in 1968 and informed him that Hearts wanted him to return to Tynecastle. And it wasn't just anybody from the club who had made the approach. It was his Jambos mentor John Harvey, once his trainer and now the Edinburgh club's manager in place of Tommy Walker at Mackay's spiritual home. Mackay understood from Nicholson that Harvey wanted him as a player-manager and to actually be a replacement in the hot-seat. He flew to Edinburgh for talks and was met by former Hearts team-mate Jimmy Wardhaugh.

Mackay was keen to go back, but not as a player. He said, 'The desire for a homecoming was strong but I did not want to play football at Tynecastle again … to meddle with history. I could imagine middle-aged men standing on the terraces saying to their sons, "See that fat guy out there huffing and puffing? He used to be Davie Mackay."'

It seemed everything was close to being signed, sealed and delivered for the nostalgic return to his old stomping ground when a bolt from the blue struck, smashing any homecoming for a would-be Tynecastle prodigal son into a zillion pieces. It came in the shape of Brian Clough.

Clough was a former England international striker who had had his playing career cut short by injury but was now on the low rung of the management ladder with ambitions to climb to the top as swiftly as possible.

A Yorkshireman like Nicholson, Clough had just led Derby County to 18th in the Second Division after his first campaign in charge at the Baseball Ground. It followed a two-year managerial baptism at Hartlepool United in which he led the re-election regulars to eighth in the Fourth Division.

It wasn't a sparkling CV but what Clough lacked in experience and achievement as a boss he made up for in front and, a shared characteristic Mackay possessed in spades, self-confidence. He also had a shrewd advisor on which players to buy in assistant Peter Taylor, who had been with him since he began attempting to be a hot shot in a hot-seat.

And it was Taylor who recommended to Clough that he should sign Mackay to give the promising youngsters being collected together at the Baseball Ground – such as Roy McFarland, John O'Hare, John Robson and Kevin Hector – a leader. Clough was overawed by Mackay's stellar reputation, viewing him as 'famous' and a 'very big name'. He felt he had one chance – no chance. He said to his number two, 'Get Mackay? You must be bloody joking.'

Mackay had played against Clough in an under-23 international in which the Englishman sported a black eye, and knew about his curtailed playing career and going into management, but would have known little else.

Taylor persuaded his partner to give it go. Clough rang the Mackay family home in Enfield while its paternal head was in Edinburgh talking over the move to Hearts.

Isobel said, 'It was quite funny. David was talking to John Harvey over this weekend. John was a nice man. I knew his wife Bunty. Hearts wanted him back. They were going to give us a house – worth considerably more than the Derby offer – in the posh part of Edinburgh. In the meantime, I got a phone call. There was this man. He wanted to speak to David. I told him, "Oh, he's not here at the minute, he's up in Scotland." He said, "Have you got a contact number?" I asked, "Who are you?" He said, "I can't tell you." I said, "No, I'm not giving you a contact number." He phoned a couple of times and I said, "No. I'm sorry." So I didn't give him any number for David.

'David came back, I think it was on the Sunday. I said, "Well how did things go?" He said, "Well, maybe we'll go back to Scotland but I'm thinking it over for a few days." I said, "There's somebody been phoning for you. I don't know who he is. He's phoned two or three times. He wanted to speak to you."'

A 'day or two later', Clough, four months younger than Mackay, drove down to White Hart Lane, confessing he was 'as nervous as hell' and that 'arriving … from the Baseball Ground was like turning up at Buckingham Palace having just left a Wimpy Bar'.

Clough said in his autobiography he was 'in awe of Bill Nick; one of the great managers, whose team had not only won major trophies but had done it with a style and flair and honesty that I hoped my team might emulate. I felt like an imposter – a beginner in his field, about to try and take away one of the most influential and famous players. But I was brash and cocky … dismissed my uncertainty long enough to blurt out [to Bill Nicholson], "I've come to talk to Dave Mackay."'

Nicholson told him Mackay was off to Hearts the following day before, according to Clough, taking a phone call and leaving the Derby boss to wait in a passageway seat at the ground until the Scot had finished training 'for what seemed like an entire day'.

Mackay confirmed when they did hook up that he was off to his first professional club, but Clough persisted and his prey agreed to meet up with the Derby manager after a bath and change of clothes. Mackay revealed in his autobiography that part of the Clough charm offensive included him saying, 'I'm building a team at Derby County that will be in the First Division in two years and champions within five, and I want you to lead it. Interested?'

Clough claimed Mackay turned down a £10,000 signing-on fee but would accept £15,000 and agreed to £14,000, saying simply and immediately 'done'; the small transfer fee (estimated at £5,000) placed on the player by Bill Nick to help his 'greatest signing' get a decent personal deal had, it seemed, the desired effect.

Isobel said, 'David came home at lunchtime to tell me he was signing for Derby County. I went, "What?!" But whatever David did was all right by me. I'd go along with him anytime. He said to me, "You know the man you wouldn't give the phone number to was Brian Clough." I said, "Who is Brian Clough?" Brian must have thought David could do a good job at Derby, which he did. Eventually, I met Brian and we had some great, great times.

'David then told me how he had to phone Hearts to tell them that he wasn't coming because he felt he wasn't the player he was and they wanted him to play and then be manager or something and didn't want to let anyone down.'

Mackay put pen to paper for Derby County on 24 July 1968 and said, 'Brian Clough's generous salary and three-year contract was a massive vote of confidence in my longevity.'

Clough said in his autobiography, 'I hadn't signed just a player, I'd recruited a kind of institution ... the perfect addition ... the crowning glory.

'I never made a more effective signing in my entire managerial career ... when I look back across all the many and varied signings during my time in management Dave Mackay has to be the best. Not only did he have everything as a player, but he was the ideal skipper; a supreme example to everyone else at the football club.'

Clough also wanted Mackay to switch from covering every blade of grass as a marauding midfielder into a sweeper behind the back three. It appealed.

Mackay said, 'He was evangelical about Derby. His enthusiasm was infectious and his confidence shocking. What he said to me about playing as a sweeper appealed to me. Suddenly, I could see a few more years of playing football opening up. Danny Blanchflower once said footballers are a long time retired and he was dead right. Here I could carry on playing the game I loved into my dotage; Derby supporters didn't know me from Adam and therefore we owed each other nothing. If I failed and crumbled it would not happen under the microscope of Spurs or Hearts. Management could wait.

'Cloughie knew my legs had gone and told me just to use my positional sense and guide young Roy McFarland at the heart of the defence. Brian wanted me for my leadership qualities and I slotted in comfortably, more as a conductor than the old-style competitor. Others did the running for me and I just kept motivating them with the odd tackle and a flourished fist. I think opponents were frightened of my reputation, not realising that I was nothing like the player I'd been at Tottenham. But it all worked very well and I was nicely paid.'

He might have considered his tank was empty when deciding to pack it in after the 3-1 defeat to the soon-to-be-crowned champions Manchester City. He argued about his physical limitations, although observers insisted he still possessed a tackle which respected writer and broadcaster Bryon Butler thought could have earned him 'a living felling trees, demolishing walls or breaking up tanks'. But his nous and attitude remained totally intact.

Julie Welch wrote in *The Biography of Tottenham Hotspur*, 'The man had much more to give. All that will. That fire. That refusal to crack under pressure, that mindset that had transformed Spurs from a pretty but brittle side into a team of immortals was unleashed on an unsung Midlands club built on journeymen.'

A 'journeyman' has been defined as 'a worker, skilled in a given building trade or craft, who has successfully completed an official apprenticeship qualification. Journeymen are considered competent and authorised to work in that field as a fully qualified employee.'

So a few of the players Mackay led that season would come into that unstarry category. Defender Roy McFarland from Tranmere Rovers, Hartlepool graduates John McGovern and Les Green, a midfielder and goalkeeper respectively, and forward Kevin Hector, via Bradford Park Avenue, had served 'apprenticeships' in the lower leagues; John O'Hare was considered surplus at First Division Sunderland, whom he joined to replace stricken striker Clough three years earlier. Former England winger Alan Hinton, whom Mackay faced in that 1967 FA Cup semi-final against Nottingham Forest, had also dropped down a division.

Clough recalled the moment he realised the Mackay Masterplan as the team's 'anchor' would work. He said in his autobiography, 'Perhaps he was still uncertain about the anchor role we had in mind until that moment when he put his foot on the ball, resisting the temptation to whack it any old how, so demonstrating to the rest of the team the value of a calm head and a determination to pass the ball whenever possible. That was the moment we knew Mackay was going to make better players out of those around him – not least McFarland, who developed into a magnificent defender of the highest class. I believe that was the moment when Mackay realised he could do the job we had in mind. From that moment on, we just went out and p****d on everybody.

'We had so much confidence it was coming out of our ears. We felt unbeatable and it all stemmed from Dave. He brought a swagger to the team, to the whole club. He was absolutely bubbling in training ... win, lose or draw it made no difference to his mood. The younger players would look at him in open-mouthed admiration. I've never known a collective spirit stronger than the one we built at Derby at that time ... Mackay gave the team that moral courage, an air of confidence that produced a sense of adventure. Soon we were producing a calibre of football that excited spectators which drew attention to a football club which had spent too long in no man's land.'

Mackay added in *Derby County The Glory Years*, 'It gives a player incentive to move on to a new club. With me the move to Derby was a matter of personal pride. The Derby people were going to say when I arrived, "Mackay? Well, he was a good player." They had only seen me on television. I had to prove to them that I was not finished.

'Like when I joined Spurs from Hearts. I was an international player at the time, but the people in London did not know me. I had to prove myself then too.'

Mackay was appointed captain but did not cast a magic wand for the opening fixtures. There were two reverses and three deadlocks before goals from McFarland and O'Hare sealed his first victory as a Rams player against Oxford United at the Baseball Ground on 31 August 1968.

The signing of experienced Willie Carlin from Sheffield United for £60,000 provided added influence to that exerted by Mackay. And

Carlin began a pivotal midfield partnership with Wales international Alan Durban, signed by Clough's predecessor Tim Ward, who also captured Hector, as Derby gave the representatives of the university city a lesson.

The fact that Rams chairman Sam Longson had backed Clough with the signings of Mackay and Carlin underlined his support for the Clough–Taylor axis, support which the managerial duo had not received from other members of the board after the team had slipped a spot to 18th in the duo's debut season in charge.

And Mackay and Carlin were able to help repay Longson's faith.

Derby, 18th in October, only lost two more league games, won 14 of 18 from the turn of the new year and finished off with a club record nine victories on the bounce – conceding only rarely as they swept to the Second Division title, something the club had not achieved since the outbreak of the First World War. The crown was sealed the day they went into the Lions' Den to beat Millwall 1-0 in their third-to-last fixture on 12 April, having conceded only 31 goals in 40 fixtures.

Mackay had been singled out for praise after Derby had kicked off an 11-match unbeaten run to the end of the campaign by battling to a 3-2 victory over Blackpool at Bloomfield Road on 8 March.

The Guardian wrote, 'What a difference Mackay has made. From a middling, muddling erratic team last season, Derby have been transformed by his experience. He bristles with authority, he shouts, he gets results from his younger colleagues. To see him pace his game, to recognise danger when none is clearly evident, and then, in averting that danger, spring his forwards into animated creativity, is a delight.'

The Rams had won their first major trophy in the initial FA Cup Final after the war in 1946, but had only struck top silverware once since, lifting the Third Division North crown in 1957, before Mackay proved Clough's dream was not a flight of fantasy.

Mackay was colossal, especially with his will to win, on-field management and assistance in ensuring a tight Rams' rearguard. They conceded a mere two goals in that season-finishing nine-match run. But they could also turn it on up front with 16 goals smashed in their opponents' net in the final five games.

It was no wonder 20,000-plus crowds were flocking to the Baseball Ground as Mackay's counter-punchers racked up the points with 16 league wins. They equalled a 13-year-old record of ten away victories, while Hector top-scored in the campaign with 16.

Promotion meant they were back in the top flight after a 16-year absence. And the title trophy was presented to Mackay in front of 32,000 supporters – three times the size for the last fixture two seasons before – rammed into the Baseball Ground for the last game of the season, which saw a final flourish as visiting Bristol City were beaten 5-0.

* * *

Mackay was delighted to have a painting of the presentation on his wall at the family home; he is clutching on to the trophy with one hand as Brian Clough shakes the other with Peter Taylor behind them. He said, 'I love that painting and I loved that moment. Brian West, the artist, used a photograph to paint that picture and, as is often the case, the painting is far more evocative that the original photograph.

'Of all my special days in football, this day ranked as one of the most special because it was so unexpected. A year before, I had sat in Bill Nicholson's office conscious that, although the mind was willing, the body was less so. I could tell he thought this [going to Derby] was not the right move for me. I had gone to the Baseball Ground hoping for no more than keeping Derby out of the Third Division and looking maybe for a cup run or two to provide a high-profile swansong.'

Mackay also cast his shadow over the League Cup, jutting out his chest and leading from the front as Derby made it through to the quarter-finals.

After victories over Chesterfield and Stockport, Derby were pitted against Chelsea. The Scot's new troops dug in to draw at Stamford Bridge, and in the replay before 34,346 at the Baseball Ground on 2 October, the Rams secured a shock 3-1 victory over a First Division outfit who were to finish a spot above Spurs in fifth by the season's end. Mackay even got on the scoresheet. Son Derek said, 'It was a bit of a wonder goal, a goal which was voted one of the best ever at the Baseball Ground by Derby fans at a "do" Dad attended just a handful of years before his passing.'

It cancelled out a strike by Peter Houseman in the 77th minute to spark late efforts from Alan Durban and Kevin Hector. Mackay said, 'It was after that … I realised Brian Clough was not a complete fantasist and that this team I had joined was becoming a bit special.'

His Rams managed to repeat the feat of felling a top-flight outfit after holding them at their place when another 34,000 in DE23 saw their heroes overcome Everton to make the last eight.

But they went out to eventual winners Swindon who edged through to the semis thanks to a single goal in the replay, following a goalless draw.

Mackay, who missed just two matches throughout the season, was at the centre of lavish praise from all quarters, not just in Derby. He was so praised in fact that he was named as joint Footballer of the Year by the Football Writers' Association, alongside Manchester City veteran Tony Book.

Jimmy Greaves asked Mackay for *The Sun* in the 1970s whether sharing the accolade 'spoilt it for you'. Mackay said, 'No, I was just proud to have won even if it was a joint award. Tony Book is a smashing bloke and he had an outstanding season. I would have been choked if I had gone through my career without getting the award because I never had false modesty and knew I deserved it. The fact that you never got it, Jim, is a joke.'

McFarland, greatly praised by Clough in his charm offensive to win Mackay's signature, formed an almost instant rapport with Mackay at the back.

McFarland, the Rams' own player of the season said, 'I was a Liverpool boy who had joined Derby. I first saw Dave playing for Tottenham at Goodison Park. Everton were by far the better team. I'd read what people said about Dave Mackay but this day was tough for him. He wasn't keeping up with the pace and didn't do particularly well.

'If we move on to the start of the next season who do we sign but Dave Mackay. It was a surprise but half the team Brian signed the previous season had stories about how he convinced us to sign after recommendations from Peter Taylor. I'd played for Tranmere on the Friday night and Brian was knocking on my door in the early hours of Saturday morning. I can see even Dave, being experienced and a year older than our manager and knew in his mind what he wanted, being convinced by him, by his commitment and what it was about. That's the power of Clough and Taylor.

'Dave was such an enormous figure for all the young kids like me at Derby County at the time. Frank Wignall, Alan Hinton and Alan Durban were older, even Kevin Hector, but I'd say 50–60 per cent were kids learning their trade. Besides me the other youngsters there included

John O'Hare, John Robson, Ronnie Webster, Jimmy Walker and John McGovern.

'There was one thing that stood out pre-season. At the end of a 400m training run, Dave came in. There was another with a younger group in which we'd push each other along. Brian said to Dave, "Leave this one out." Dave said to him, "No, gaffer, I'll do it even if it takes me two days."

'We knew he was 33, maybe 34 and there he was running round this track. Wherever he finished he finished. Dave would not duck out of anything. A bit of an insight for us into what sort of character this guy was. Such an immense character and what a great, great player. I feel very honoured and very fortunate to have played alongside him in the rebirth in a sense of Derby County.

'I learned my trade when Dave Mackay walked through that door. From the moment that I met him to the moment he left, I was learning from him every single day of my life. It was an education for all of us.

'He had been in football long enough to know when to belt it, kick it out of play, and when to pull it down and play. I tried to follow this and Cloughie pulled me to one side and said, "Roy, just in training you're getting caught occasionally trying to play, pull the ball down all the time." This was because the player alongside me – Dave – was doing those things. He would take a risk. But when I took a risk I wasn't savvy enough to read the situation. But I soon picked up on those little traits he had.

'One of our early games that season, we were playing at home. We had a free kick between the 18-yard box, and the touchline on the left-hand side. All of a sudden our opponents' centre-forward ran to cover the goalkeeper because in those days you could pass it back to the goalkeeper to give yourself a breather. Dave walked over to take the kick and Les Green, our goalkeeper, ran past him. He said, "Dave, leave it. Get up and I'll kick it." He was a decent kicker, Les. And Dave said, "Greenie, get in goal. Do what I tell you. Get in goal and just be ready." He said, "What do you mean?" Dave said, "Just be ready."

'The centre-forward stood probably about three or four yards inside the 18-yard box stopping Dave from playing back to Les. Dave Mackay had a habit of when he was going to kick it with his left foot of standing back from the ball on his right leg and rub his left boot on the sock to clear any muck.

'Everyone expected he was going to kick the ball up to John O'Hare or Kevin Hector and see what happened. As he goes to kick it, he half-turns and chips the ball over the centre-forward towards Les. Greenie is not really ready for it but reacts and picks up the ball. The crowd went wild. That's the type of guy he was. Why take that chance? But he had that ability, that confidence to do that. We cracked up and talked about it and Dave was always, "What do you expect? This is me, this is what I do." And it was. Honestly, it was unbelievable.

'But more importantly on that football field he led the team out of the Second Division to fourth in the First the next season to qualify for Europe.

'He was our manager on the field. I can understand now, little stories that do come out. I mean Greavsie always said he was the best player he played with. I would say exactly the same.

'The funny thing is that we didn't start the season particularly well. Cloughie knew the balance wasn't right and signed Willie Carlin from Sheffield United. He was, like Mackay, a winner. But he would be in your face whereas Dave would talk to you sensibly. So we were learning from Mackay and had this little bastard Carlin.'

But McFarland was convinced that Mackay's signing was the catalyst for the promotion. He said, 'Would we have got it without Dave? Not a prayer! We would have given our best and improved but he carried us. He was such a character off the field and influential in everything that went off. He had so much belief and confidence in himself that it rubbed off on everybody. We felt cock-a-hoop and looked forward to games. We were just loving it – all through this guy in his first season with us. And it was only my second season. We had a hell of a celebration party at the Midland Hotel after we beat Bristol City 5-0 in our last game of the season.

'Our performances against First Division opposition [in the League Cup] were unbelievable. We were confident with our football with Dave.

'Cloughie never confronted Dave. Dave didn't put a foot wrong. We went on early pre-season tours. This might have been after our first promotion. We went to Germany and drove almost through from north to south playing games. One was against the equivalent of a Third Division team. They were lovely people who invited us out after it. Cloughie and Peter said to Dave, "Make sure they are back at midnight because we are leaving early." We had so much fun with our hosts. The atmosphere was lovely and they had just provided a crate of beer so we carried on. Suddenly we said to Dave, "Hey, skip, it's 11.30, don't you think we should be getting back? It will take us a good 15 or 20 minutes to get back to the hotel." And he said, "No, no, we'll just have one more." One more? About five more to finish the bloody crate off.

'We pulled in about one o'clock, about an hour late. Brian was sitting in the corridor with his vest and underpants in the hall. We had to go past either side of him to get to the lift to go to our rooms.

'We're all quiet going in and John Robson just says, "Hi gaffer, all right? You been waiting here long?" Well half of us just burst out laughing. You couldn't help it. And that was not the thing to do. We all got in the lift and to our rooms. Anyway, there was a meeting the following day. He slaughtered all of us young whippersnappers. He said, "You're all a disgrace. I'm very disappointed in all of you. I've trusted you, I gave you time off so you could be in by midnight. None of you were back by then." And he said to John Robson, "You can stay behind. I want a word with you." He was going to fly John Robson back home, although he didn't. We said, "Gaffer, we're wrong."

'But Brian never said a word to Mackay. He NEVER picked Dave out. He was just the captain and was never wrong. To be quite truthful he never was, although on this occasion he mistimed it.

'I think it was on the German tour he showed some fancy dan stuff in training. We found a not very up-market training area but it had goalposts and a net. We finished off a real good, hard physical session with some crossing from Alan Hinton from the right and Jimmy Walker from the left and volleying and heading the ball at Les Green. We'd been doing this for 20 minutes.

'I think it was Brian said, "Come on lads, we've had enough." Dave said, "Just one more." So Alan Hinton pings a ball from the right wing. Dave's running in, and he turns his whole body round. So his back faces Les Green in goal and heads the ball backwards off the back of his head – and it flew into the top corner. Everybody just cracked up. Les didn't have a chance. We'd never ever seen anything like thatl before. A lot of players find it hard when a cross is coming in to judge it, and then head with your forehead. That's the confidence Dave had.'

John McGovern was to follow his former Pools boss Clough to Leeds and, as captain, to Nottingham Forest and back-to-back European Cup wins.

McGovern, also a pallbearer at Mackay's funeral, got into the team after starting the 1968/69 campaign coming up 21 in the reserves.

He said, 'Clough said, "Dave Mackay runs the dressing room." You'd be aghast at a statement like that these days. But Clough and Taylor were good judges of character. And it worked like clockwork because you were looking at a winner through and through in every aspect of the sport in Dave. He was a senior pro along with Willie Carlin.

'Cliff Jones said at his funeral that Tottenham were a good team which became a great one when he joined. The perfect statement when describing someone like Dave Mackay. He wanted to win.

'There was a tremendous quote in the newspapers at the time. Something like, "Dave Mackay is 34 years old, overweight and past his best." But he was the best player at Derby by a mile.

'The so-called wise pundits or newspaper reporters who wrote that obviously didn't understand the guy's character at all. Yes he was a little bit overweight yet in those days nobody really put you on scales and said, "You have to be this weight." But his spirit, attitude and commitment carried him through as it had done throughout his whole career especially after having two broken legs, something players probably wouldn't recover from nowadays. It was a mere hiccup to get over the broken legs. The most positive thinker I think I've ever met in football as a player

'Would we have got promoted without him? We did have a very good side but Dave was someone everyone in the dressing room respected bar none. There are some dressing rooms where players don't get on with one another and show that respect. There was absolutely tons of respect for Dave Mackay. If Dave and Willie said something you'd do it.

'Dave would gee you up in a game if you did something he thought you shouldn't have done. You had a manager who was an absolute expert at doing that. When he's got two experienced pros doing it out there on the field, and especially Dave as the captain, you are giving everything you've got every time you walk over the white lines for the manager, the captain, the club and the supporters.

'Clough would come into the dressing room and have some words to say. A rollicking or a pat on the back. Dave would keep you on your toes as well. He was a shining example of how you should commit yourself on the field of play. And every opponent wanted to beat Dave Mackay because he was that good.

'Was Dave and Clough's relationship a good one? Dave was the captain and Clough the manager. It was the same as myself and Clough at Nottingham Forest. People said, "Did you get close to him [Clough]?" I said, "No." You don't get close to him because he's your boss.

'The manager tells you what he thinks you've been doing out there on the field. And when you've got someone like Dave – as Clough did at Derby – to echo that message to the players out there you can't lose.

'We started the promotion bid simmering, got to the boil and went supersonic towards the end with the confidence that was running through the side.

'The defensive record was a big part of it and Dave was the fulcrum, the heart of the defence, geeing everybody up. I can always remember when we went out for the very last game of the season at the Baseball Ground and Clough said, "If I see any of you showboating, I'll take you off and fine you. Because I want you to play the way you've played all season. That's why we are here where we are at this moment." And Dave went out and was back-heeling them and flipping and flicking them over his shoulder. He back-headed them too. I've never seen anybody ever do that again. And I thought, "What's Cloughie going to do when he goes off?" Do you know what he said? "Brilliant, Dave." Anybody else, he'd have fined them and taken them off.'

Mackay's children recalled when their dad first played for Derby.

Son Derek said, 'I was ten going on 11 and it must be that age where you can keep certain memories. I remember my dad actually being on the pitch and doing certain tackles. When he first signed for Derby it was, "Who are they? Crikey!" It was great. We still lived in Enfield but we used to go up. We mainly used to sit up in the stand at Derby. Me, my mum and brother and sisters. You could also get in the dressing room and get all the autographs. It was amazing. I think it was mainly with mates of Dad's, Tottenham fans who would take us up in the car for certain games.

'Derby were doing well and it was a great atmosphere. It was a tight, enclosed pitch and four high stands at the Baseball Ground. I remember once meeting Brian Clough. We must have been in the players' lounge with all the wives and kids. Cloughie came in. Mum said, "This is

Derek." And he patted me on the head and said, 'All right, a *dahling*?!'
He had an aura about him. Even then. It was like another world to me.
Dad used to say after the game that Cloughie, who was younger than
Dad, used to pop his head around the door of the dressing room and say,
"Where's Dave?" When he spotted him he would add, "Are you all right
for next Saturday?" Dad would go, "Yes." And Cloughie would go. He
wasn't bothered about the rest of them!'

Daughter Valerie said, 'When Dad moved to Derby County we didn't
know about them, really. This was before Dad started playing for them.
Anyway, my brother Derek and I got this picture of the team – something
to do with Esso – and learned all the names of the players off the caption.
Then we went to Derby to see some of the matches. There was a song
being sung that went something like, "We've got the best team in the
land, we've got Dave Mackay," and it went on to mention all the players'
names. We thought it was great because they weren't that well known
but we knew all the names.'

26

'Exceptional player, exceptional human being'

DAVE MACKAY'S manager promised that Derby would not be making up the numbers in the First Division on their return to it after 16 years for the 1969/70 season. Brian Clough's prediction of the title heading to the Baseball Ground within five years laid down the ambition of Mackay's extrovert boss. Mackay had clearly begun to believe that it was not mere rhetoric. That Old Big 'Ead – as Clough was to become christened due to his extrovert image – might not be 'bonkers' after all. Mackay was 'relishing' a return to the big league.

There were no big signings before the season started, an approach viewed by Mackay as an act of faith in the players who had earned Derby a return.

Mackay's men spluttered without losing at the start before four wins on the trot – kicked off by a 2-0 win over West Brom in which Captain Fantastic netted – put them top of the pile in mid-September.

And they underlined their dominance by completing an unbeaten 11-match start by thumping Spurs 5-0 in front of a ground record 41,826 attracted by Mackay facing his former employers. It was a day that left him with mixed feelings. There was no sentiment displayed by him before kick-off. Spurs had lined up with Pat Jennings, Cyril Knowles, Alan Mullery, Mike England, Jimmy Greaves and Alan Gilzean, members of the Tottenham team that had sealed the 1967 FA Cup under Mackay's captaincy.

Mullery wrote in his autobiography, 'As Spurs skipper, I walked up to the centre of the ground to spin the coin. Mackay was the Derby captain and, as I shook hands with him, I said, "Dave, it's really lovely to see you." He snapped back at me, "We're going to stuff you this afternoon. I mean stuff you."

He later told talkSPORT, 'They did! Bill Nicholson was not amused. He ripped us to pieces for letting Mackay play the way he played. The most amazing thing was that after winning the cup in 1967, the following season Dave Mackay was on his way and between then and 1970 we didn't win a cup. Then we won the League Cup in 1971 and the UEFA Cup in 1972, so it took another three years to build a side without Mackay as captain.'

But after Mackay's apparent wish had come true he 'took no pleasure in the discomfort of my old pals'. He felt 'embarrassed' for Bill Nicholson on what was a 'poignant' occasion for him.

The Rams' next home game produced another big win, against a Manchester United side including George Best and Bobby Charlton. The fervent home support and tight pitch created an intimidating atmosphere at the Baseball Ground, with opposing teams almost literally feeling the breath of the fans around the touchline. Mackay's troops reputedly also caught opponents on the hop by going for an increased attacking approach rather than solid defence and counter-punching. The pitch, though, got heavier as autumn gave way to winter and spoiled Derby attempts to employ their more forward-thinking style and they went off the boil.

They had a run of three reverses in four before blowing away the Liverpool of Bill Shankly 4-0. But results were up and down until the February when Mackay scored as they beat Arsenal at the start of a six-match winning run which in turn was part of a 12-game unbeaten sequence to the end of the season. And Mackay missed just three games. He said, 'If it wasn't for that mid-season slump, we could have won it [the title].'

His Derby also showed their teeth with a run to the last eight of the League Cup where they were knocked out by Manchester United 1-0 in a replay, although hopes in the FA Cup were ended by Queens Park Rangers in the fifth round.

Mackay described it as 'an excellent season' and said his side had proved 'they were no flash in anyone's pan'. Moreover, the player himself proved he could still cut it with the big boys.

John McGovern said, 'We went up with Dave and we never looked like relegation material. Not at all.

'I remember beating Spurs 5-0. It was some result. When the final whistle went I ran to the touchline. There was typically six inches of mud at the Baseball Ground. And I shook hands with Jimmy Greaves. He was my idol. I kept a scrapbook of him and Denis Law. I was still keeping them. My hands were covered in mud. I sat in the bath with my right arm up so I never got the mud wiped off my hands. When I got home my mum clouted me behind the ear and said "get that washed".'

Mackay was commuting to Derby. His family home remained in Enfield while he was put up at the Midland Hotel opposite the main train station in the town. He generally went home after a match on a Saturday and returned Tuesday.

Derek, his second son, said, 'We never moved from Enfield when he was a player because he knew he wouldn't be playing forever. We'd move house when he became a manager.'

Mackay said, 'I was soon feeling very at home. Whilst not ideal being separated from Isobel and the children for most of the week, I loved the luxury of the hotel and it felt like home.' He 'knocked about with fellow players Roy McFarland and Jimmy Walker'. Mackay even loaned his Mercedes car a lot to Walker who told him with a smile, 'I was speaking to one of my mates on the phone last night and he said, "Jim, I saw Dave Mackay driving your car yesterday."'

Derek believes Dave 'sometimes got to train at Tottenham a little bit' while at Derby.

Bill Nicholson was still in charge and appeared to harbour regrets of allowing his best signing to leave, given his revelatory exploits in his first season away from the north London club. Derek said, 'I don't think Bill realised he could play dad in another position.'

Roy McFarland joined Mackay as a resident at the hotel from nearby digs. He said, 'We used the hotel before home matches when we'd have a fillet steak – the last thing they'd give you now. We knew the place well – we had our promotion dinner there – and, with Dave having based himself there since joining the club, Brian moved me in.

'I had the pleasure of staying with Dave at the hotel for about two years. He used to commute between Enfield and Derby and, although he got extra days off, never slackened off his fitness levels as he trained in London.

'Dave had a suite overlooking a garden, which was three times the size of my room. You couldn't swing a cat in mine. But I enjoyed it.

'Every night I'd bore Dave sick asking about Jimmy Greaves, Danny Blanchflower and other Tottenham players he'd played with. And about the Double, winning the FA Cup three times.

'He'd say, "Roy, let's have our dinner and enjoy it. And, maybe tomorrow you can ask me a few more questions." I wouldn't let it go. I just pelted him with questions every bloody time we sat down and had dinner. I couldn't get enough knowledge. For me, this guy was full of knowledge.'

Valerie recalled one piece of 'knowledge' her dad passed on to McFarland during their stay at the Midland. She said, 'The hotel restaurant was closing. I believe someone was trying to get autographs and Roy was going "no, no" because he was worried he was going to miss the evening meal. Dad took him to one side and said, "These are the people who pay to see us, Roy. We sign first and eat after."'

Mackay entered the world of endorsement for beer at Derby. Danny Blanchflower had his breakfast cereal Shredded Wheat to promote at Spurs while further afield, World Cup-winning heroes Bobby Moore and Geoff Hurst were the 'faces' of Double Diamond beer, George Best helped sell more Cookstown sausages, and your author's dad Maurice recalled cricketer Denis Compton showing the public the Brylcreem hair gel look. But Mackay, it seems, had been largely untroubled by advertisers wanting him to promote their products at Tottenham, beyond lending his name – and claiming no financial remuneration – to a tie business.

Mackay felt Derby were 'looking after me very well financially', revealing that, according to one director 'off the record', he was the 'highest-paid' player with the club.

But he was able to supplement his wages by promoting Younger's Tartan beer after turning down a hair dye firm which claimed application of its product could hide grey hairs. One slice of extra income, however, had negative repercussions. The club paid him for a regular article he wrote for their matchday programme, which was 'one of the reasons' Derby got investigated for 'financial irregularities' and led to the team being banned from European competition after qualifying for the UEFA Cup by finishing fourth on their return to the First Division.

Mackay said, 'It was never a secret that I was being paid for this, but I think there was some problem about how it was being accounted for in the books. Football managers over the last century have fallen foul of such investigations and, although there certainly has been some fraudulent activity, the bulk is down to ignorance of the rules and regulations.'

The 1970/71 season would be the third and last on Mackay's playing contract with Derby County. And ahead of it he ensured another piece of silverware would be added to his list of trophies with the winning of the Watney Cup, for the leading goalscoring teams from each division of the Football League who were uninvolved in Europe.

As the 'financial irregularities' issue had put paid to a continental campaign, Mackay's men made the most of the opportunity. And the man himself got on the scoresheet as they secured a 4-1 final win in front of 32,000 at the Baseball Ground against Wilf McGuinness.

But Mackay – 36 in the November – 'accepted' that there would be no extension to his three-year playing deal. Brian Clough insisted he would be able to play on, but the realist in the Scot knew he would not be part of Clough's future plans. For a start, Terry Hennessey had been signed for £100,000 from Nottingham Forest early in 1970 – becoming Derby's first six-figure signing – and, according to Mackay, it was 'no secret' he had arrived to take his place, although ultimately it was Colin Todd, signed from Sunderland for a club record £170,000 in the February, who would form a central partnership with McFarland.

Clough was rebuilding apace and Archie Gemmill had arrived from Preston North End in September with Carlin moving on to Leicester City the following month. Clough turned up at Gemmill's home and refused to leave until the player had agreed to the move, a tactic understood to be prompted by the team's erratic start to the season. John McGovern had bagged a couple in a 4-2 win over Wolves which sparked a run of three wins after an opening-day loss against FA Cup holders Chelsea. But three reverses on the bounce triggered Clough's door-stepping.

Yet results remained negative and after Mackay's side lost 2-0 at Arsenal, the Rams were one spot off the relegation zone in 20th.

Clough replaced Les Green with Colin Boulton in goal after a 4-4 home league Boxing Day draw with Manchester United – in which Mackay scored – had dismayed the manager, and Todd arrived in the February.

Yet, despite the chopping and changing and impending departure, Mackay managed his first season as an ever-present in the league side and was named the club's player of the season, with Todd having to settle for a spot largely at full-back. And the skipper guided the reviving Rams to a respectable ninth as Frank McLintock's Arsenal sealed the first half of their Double by claiming the league title.

Mackay was delighted with the newcomers because they benefitted the side, displaying the characteristic he always had of putting the team before himself. He described Gemmill, who debuted for Scotland against Belgium in the February, as a 'human dynamo' and Todd as a 'gifted, fluid defender who played gracefully … a natural successor to Bobby Moore in the England team'.

Mackay also felt that Derby had, with McFarland, the 'classiest defence in the country'. McFarland, who became the first Derby player to receive a full England cap in the Clough era when he played against Malta in February 1971, appreciated Mackay's impact on and off the pitch. He said, 'The only way Brian and Peter would sign players would be if they got better than what we had. So the majority of the team stayed together and did well while Dave played for it and was, with myself and Toddy [Colin Todd], the basis of the one they built that won the First Division championship.

'Dave was an exceptional player, but more importantly an exceptional human being. He was humble and knew his place but if anybody was asked to jump off that roof, swim across that lake, somebody needs to take that penalty, he'd be first in line. "Leave it to me," he'd say. That's the best way I can describe him. He was fearful of nothing.'

McFarland added with a smile, 'The only thing he was fearful of was probably his wife Isobel! I hope Isobel won't mind me telling you the story but Dave took me down to London when we were playing together. Cloughie had given us three or four days off and Dave wanted to see the family so I went down with him. We got down there on a Tuesday night and Dave said to me quietly, "We're going out to the dogs." I said, "Okay, Dave." I went to my room and said hello to Isobel.

'We go to a pub first and meet one or two of Dave's friends and go to the dogs. It may well have been Harringay Stadium and we had a super night out. We went back to the pub, where there was a lock-in with Dave's old pals. We had a few drinks and got home about 1.30am, might have been later.

'I get up in the morning and Isobel is in the kitchen. And I come in and say, "Morning Isobel." She asks, "Well, Roy, what do you want for breakfast, a full English?" I say, "No, not really. I'd like some scrambled egg and a bit of bacon if that's all right? And maybe a tomato?" She said, "Good. Sit down. I'll make you a cup of tea." So she made a cup of tea, put it down and was cooking my breakfast.

'So Dave walks in. It is about ten or 15 minutes after me. He says, "Isobel, can I have a cup of tea please, darling?" She says, "Make it yourself." He says, "What?" She says, "Make it yourself."

'Dave being Dave made the cup of tea. She continued to cook the breakfast in front of me and Dave says, "That looks nice. Can I have a bit of that Isobel, please?" She says, "Make your own."

'I sat there and thought, "Shall I give Dave my breakfast? This is his house, he brought me down here."

'Anyway, she didn't do it for him. She didn't make him a cup of tea. She was absolutely fuming. She says, "If you can't come back home on time when you are coming home to see me you can do everything yourself. You can make your own tea and your own breakfast." He had to take it. And she didn't do it. I thought, "Oh, s**t." I apologised to Dave, saying, "Sorry, I had a lovely breakfast and you didn't." All he had was Corn Flakes. He said, "It's not your fault, it's mine."

'We had plenty of happy times with her as well, though. Dave's family adored him and he adored them. That's the way it should be.

'Isobel was his biggest influence in football and life. She was a bloody strong woman, I tell you!'

Isobel said, laughing, 'I remember the breakfast story. It was while we lived at The Glade in Enfield. David and Roy had gone to the dogs and were quite late coming back and that annoyed me. The following morning Roy and I were up and I asked him if he wanted breakfast. David gets up and says he'd like the same and I told him he could make it himself!

'David and I had a wonderful time at Derby. I went to watch him regularly. Brian [Clough] and myself got on very well. Not long before Brian passed away, he used to come up and say to me, "Your husband kept me in a job and what's more he taught my [son] Nigel how to play football." Every time I met him he used to say that. That was nice for him to say that.

'There was a paper came through the door one time, it was the *Derby Telegraph*, with an article in which Brian said David was the best player he ever signed, which was also nice.'

England international Colin Todd was grateful for his captain's input in helping him bed down in Clough's group. The defender went on to help the team Mackay sparked into life lift the First Division title in the season after the Scot's departure, taking over as partner to Roy McFarland in central defence.

Todd said, 'When Brian signed me it was to replace Dave Mackay, which, eventually, I did do.

'There were about 13 games left of the season and I played a few with him. Dave played alongside Roy McFarland and I was right-back. It was my first association with him. He was a good leader, a good character and well respected. And obviously a very, very good talent.

'Did I have an idea of him as a player in his pomp at Spurs? There were certain players that you looked up to in the top teams like Tottenham, who tried to sign me, Leeds, Man U, West Ham. They all had players you'd recognise and could identify. Dave was one of them. You looked at what he'd gone through, how he battled back against injuries. He couldn't play his marauding game any more, but his head got him through games. He didn't have to run, he could read the game.

'I was about 21 and it could have been daunting replacing somebody like Dave Mackay. You never know how things are going to pan out.

'He had helped to make Derby what they were as a team. Clough would have thought it was the right time to sign him with some youngsters in the team. Roy, who was only about 22, and Dave got on extremely well. Dave was an outstanding player. It worked out extremely well for me in taking over the mantle from Dave. I got on with my job, developing a good partnership with Roy when we won the title in 1972. I did it to the best of my ability and I got recognised as well. I'd been recognised at Sunderland playing for the under-23s but I got my first [full international] cap when I was at Derby.'

John McGovern oozed appreciation for Mackay the captain, footballer and 'life and soul of the party' at Derby. He said, 'You couldn't do anything but have enormous respect for him. If you don't pick up what it is all about to become and stay a good class footballer from having someone like Dave Mackay playing alongside you week in, week out, then there is definitely something wrong with you as a professional footballer. You learn from good examples. Ignore the bad examples. And he was the best example out there on the field of play, about how to commit yourself to winning a game of football.

'I never saw him lose a 50-50 tackle. I've seen the Norman Hunters, Tommy Smiths and [Ron] "Chopper" Harrises tackle but not like Dave. He was unique in every way, in a sense.

'Did the manager and Dave clash because they were strong characters? No. He was a player and Brian was the manager. Brian didn't have to tell Dave Mackay what to do when he went out on a football field.'

* * *

Clough was unequivocal about what Mackay meant to him as a player. Clough, who passed on 20 September 2004, said in a televised interview with commentator and presenter Brian Moore, 'Dave was THE best. Cornerstone is an underestimation of David Mackay's influence at Derby County. He was THE Derby County in the Second Division and the First Division and, eventually, [his influence led to] the First Division Championship and European Cup days.

'David was a competitor at every level. He lost his temper when he lost, and lost his temper with his colleagues. But they were all impressionable young men, as I was, and we were all standing back in awe of David. Not only was he playing and winning championships and matches for us … he didn't know he was doing my job as well. But I soon twigged he was doing my job so I was very grateful.

'Eventually he played sweeper, but he was used to covering every blade of grass on a football pitch … and that was his image. And you couldn't visualise his sitting at the back and using the vast experience and enormous talent he had. But he didn't know he had it [for the sweeper role] until he played there. It's like most of us, it is brought out on certain occasions and Dave Mackay was certainly the best player in the Football League at the time.

'He was better than Bobby Moore, who was playing for England, who I tried to sign afterwards when David had finished or during the same time or wherever. And Bobby Moore ended up with 108 caps.

'The best thing I did was I won the Second Division at Derby and got promotion with Nottingham Forest out of the Second Division.

They were vivid and are still to this day better than the European jobs [two Europe Cup wins with Forest] and the First Division championship [with Derby]. It just depends on what makes you tick, what turns you on and all that type of thing. That was the first sign of success at two clubs. Getting Derby with David Mackay and Nottingham Forest out of the Second Division gave me more pleasure than everything else.'

Mackay revelled in his 'brilliant' time under Clough. He said, 'He picked on everyone else except me. I never had a bad game with Brian. If it was a bad game on a Saturday, there'd be a meeting on the Monday, but I always had Monday off. The other players never gave me problems; I was quite popular with the guys. McFarland, Todd and McGovern were all brilliant players, and Gemmill later.

'I had never come across anyone quite like Brian Clough. Tommy Walker was a deeply religious man who exuded inner and outer peace, and Bill [Nicholson] and Matt [Busby] were real gentlemen of the old school.

'Clough introduced me to a world of four-letter insults ... he was a whirlwind in the dressing room. A man of extremes – hostile one minute, almost loving the next. But his players adored him and that was the key to his success. They were transfixed by his stunning self-belief and loyalty to them, and could see he was changing their lives and their destiny.

'Peter [Taylor] was as important as Brian in the partnership and found the players. Brian's job was to ignite them.'

Mackay was able to end on a winning note with Derby as close to 34,000 fans at the Baseball Ground said goodbye to their Captain Fantastic, and he ended his three-year Derby odyssey by leading the Rams to a 2-0 victory over West Bromwich Albion on 1 May 1971.

Yet Mackay's own future was up in the air and he had 'no immediate plans'.

PART FIVE: MANAGEMENT

27

Becoming a boss

DAVE MACKAY'S future might have been undecided but he was undaunted by the prospect of having to consider 'what next?' as the curtain drew on his playing career at Derby County.

The Rams, thanks to Clough's faith in him, had given it unexpected extra time which had 'given me three seasons of playing entertaining and rewarding football', for which he was grateful.

He had lost his heart for a third time to a football club, saying in his autobiography, 'I loved those clubs [Hearts, Spurs and Derby] in equal measure.'

But he was not bereft enough to lose his footing on terra firma, concluding the 'romances' had been 'wonderful' but were now 'over'. He was confident 'something would turn up'.

And it did. Brian Clough wanted to speak to him in his office and Mackay believed it was to advise him to hang up his boots, or even offer him a testimonial. But instead he was told that Swindon Town of the Second Division had 'come in' for him, offering £30,000 for him as a player and the opportunity to combine the role with that of manager at the County Ground down the line.

Mackay was stunned as the fee was about six times what Derby had paid Spurs, although Bill Nicholson had kept that figure low to help his favourite signing secure a decent fee when signing on. And he was closing in on turning 37. Mackay said, 'I could barely bloody walk, let alone play.'

Mackay had already decided he wanted to give management a bash, so it seemed a natural progression to up sticks for the west country to link up with the 1969 League Cup winners given what was and wasn't on the table.

He had proved his abilities as a leader on the field to his team-mates and managers. And he had picked up 'a great deal' and stored the information supplied by Tommy Walker at Hearts, Bill Nicholson at Spurs, Brian Clough at Derby and Matt Busby with Scotland. He respected them.

Mackay said, 'I've been lucky to play under three of the greatest managers ever in Tommy Walker at Hearts, Bill Nick and then Cloughie. I have learned so much from the three of them. They are completely different personalities but have the same fundamental belief that football is a game of skill. The principles I hold are the same as when I first started out with that wonderful Hearts side.'

Mackay was motivated to make a fist of management and pledged to roll his sleeves up and give it everything he had, reflecting the attitude he always had as a player. He also had his innate self-confidence that he could 'make an impact' as a manager and 'could contribute to steadily improving their situation'.

He signed as a player who believed he would become manager, understanding the current Swindon boss Fred Ford was on board with the long-term arrangement for the new arrival to replace him. Mackay said in his autobiography that he was given 'the impression it was a smooth and agreed succession' and that the directors were 'hoping we could do another Derby'.

Mackay was delighted to be able to get another campaign as a player under his belt, at least, in a lead-up to taking a place in his first managerial hot-seat, and putting out any fires amongst the players unsure whether to treat him as a team-mate or management.

But he immediately discovered, 'Fred might not have been totally in the picture (or the one that was painted to me).' He told the club he would decline replacing Ford until the incumbent's contract, which 'had some time to run', had ended.

Ford guided Swindon to within four points of promotion to the top flight – ending up in fifth – in 1970, and they dropped back to mid-table in his second season. Mackay and Ford tried to make a go of the situation at the start of 1971/72, but the Scot judged there was a difference between his playing experience at the Baseball Ground as compared to the one he found at the County Ground. At Derby, he had more young players willing to do his running as he commanded the team from sweeper.

But at Swindon the team was older and there was a loyalty to the players who had claimed the League Cup and promotion in the same season, who he felt 'were not about to run themselves ragged for poor old me'.

He could not prevent the Robins from a rocky start. Mackay was able to help them to a 2-1 win over Charlton Athletic in his first home league appearance for the club on 21 August, but it was the only one in the opening four games before he was then sidelined for three.

On his return, he helped his team to back-to-back wins against Fulham and Cardiff City. Mackay, wearing the number six shirt, was unable to help sustain the results and by the end of October could only assist in one more victory – against Blackpool – before Ford was dismissed after just four wins in the opening 15 league games.

Mackay believed his manager's position had already been made 'untenable' anyway, feeling Ford had been under 'tremendous pressure' to quit. And he said in his autobiography, 'It was a shambles and typical of the way many managers are treated.'

He 'got on with it' after taking over on 1 November, while carrying on with his on-field activities. Mackay had no wish to rock the boat internally in his first season as a boss. He guided the team into the calm waters of 11th place, just one spot higher than the one achieved by Ford the previous term.

And he managed to play most games by the season's end. His final match of the campaign was as a substitute in a 2-1 win over Portsmouth at Fratton Park on 1 April 1972. It also marked the 573rd and last senior club appearance of his career.

* * *

While he was dipping his toes as a manager, many of the players he helped develop at Derby were lifting the First Division title under Brian Clough. Mackay said, 'I was a little bit jealous … and sad that I couldn't have held on just that little bit longer at the Baseball Ground.'

And Bill Nicholson's Spurs, captained by Alan Mullery, were lifting the UEFA Cup, enabling the club to be the first from Britain to capture two major European trophies. Most of the side were former Mackay team-mates such as Pat Jennings, Alan Gilzean, Joe Kinnear, Cyril Knowles, Phil Beal and Mike England. Mackay said, 'I was so glad … it was a deserved reward for Bill and his ongoing commitment to playing entertaining, flowing football.'

Mackay the manager took stock in the summer of 1972 as he sat back with his family in their Enfield bungalow after staying at Swindon's Blunsdon House Hotel during the season, plotting just how he would step things up and put his own stamp on the playing squad to at least take a step towards the feats of former employees, even if they were incremental.

He said, 'The success of my former clubs brought my position into sharp focus … I was in a footballing backwater struggling to learn a new trade at a club with little money and fans who had no reason yet to bestow any automatic affection or respect on me … it was a lonely position for a man who had been used to being at the centre of planet football over the previous 20 years.'

He flexed his muscles by bringing in Des Anderson, the former Millwall player he knew from their home town, as his assistant. Double-winning Spurs team-mate Les Allen was appointed chief scout.

Mackay felt that defender Rod Thomas, midfielder Peter Noble, and winger Don Rogers, were players capable of performing in the top flight. He was also impressed by the dependability and leadership qualities of the experienced Stan Harland and Frank Burrows.

Mackay believed he could build a freshened-up squad around them by injecting it with youth. But these kind of injections costed money and to buy them in players had to be sold.

Mackay had been shocked that Swindon had not spent some of the cash generated by their League Cup-winning run on significant bolstering of the squad. But now he was considering breaking up that side, which did not make him too popular.

He sold Wembley skipper Stan Harland to Birmingham for £15,000 soon after taking over as boss. Mackay said, 'To me it was good business. Stan was in his early 30s, past his best; to the fans it was a betrayal and a flawed decision. They were right and I was wrong on one count … Stan played some great football for Birmingham and helped power them into the First Division.'

Flogging local folk hero Rogers to Crystal Palace went down like a lead balloon among the support, and Mackay soon swapped the County Ground for the City Ground of Nottingham Forest in November 1972.

He revealed in his autobiography that a Forest director had 'sounded me out' about succeeding Matt Gillies as his Robins left the stadium on the bank of the River Trent with a 2-2 draw on 21 October.

He considered Swindon was a work still in progress but felt that improvement was 'slow', and he would be viewed as unsuccessful if things failed to improve 'significantly'. Worse still, he feared that his managerial career could be finished in its infancy should Swindon drop back to the Third Division. Mackay was not comfortable about failing to complete the task set at Swindon and was convinced he would eventually have overseen 'a steady improvement', but felt hamstrung by lack of funds.

He said, 'I don't know if too many tears were shed over my resignation as Swindon manager; some were glad to see the back of me, especially after I sold Don Rogers to Crystal Palace for £170,000.'

Don Rogers defended Mackay over his sale to Selhurst Park on the Swindonweb website in 2015, 'It was the directors at the time told Mackay to sell me, so it's a chance to put the record straight because he was always criticised for that by Swindon. The directors told him the club needed the money and he was to sell whoever he could get the most for. And Crystal Palace came in for me for £150,000, which at the time was a lot of money. He had no choice, really. Unfortunately, I don't have much experience of playing under him because he arrived just as I was leaving, but I do remember playing against him [with Mackay a Derby player] when we won the League Cup in '69. We beat Derby in a fifth-round replay in extra time.'

Winger David Moss, who played for Mackay at Swindon, said, 'Selling Don probably made him less popular with the fans. But Dave could handle it. He wasn't fazed.

'I think by that time Don – my hero – had been at Swindon a long time, at least ten to 12 years, and, I think, realised it was his last chance to test himself in the First Division. And Crystal Palace's manager was Bert Head who managed a 16-year-old Don at Swindon.

'I had to step in to fill Don's boots, which was daunting. Eventually I was to win over the fans big time but got a lot of criticism when I first went in the team. That I was nowhere near as good as Rogers. I knew I wasn't. I was learning and eventually got to a good level.

'Most of the League Cup-winning team was there when Dave took over, getting older together. They were my heroes and Dave tried to go with it but things move on. It's evolution. A lot of people criticised Dave, that he used Swindon as a stepping stone. I don't agree. His thinking was to be Swindon manager. And then the opportunity to step up and go to Forest probably came earlier than he expected. It happens. Football people move on all the time, especially nowadays.'

Mackay was also criticised for signings such as Republic of Ireland international striker Ray Treacy, who cost a reported club record £35,000 from Charlton Athletic.

Moss said, 'Some of the fans didn't like a lot of the signings he made. People associated him with Tottenham and that London players were coming to the club, which had been unheard of. That didn't go down well but I always stick up for him when people criticise that period because of what he did for me.'

Moss remained grateful to Mackay for helping launch his career as a 19-year-old winger.

He said, 'When he first arrived as a player the reaction was "bloody hell, it's Dave Mackay". He was a famous player. One of the greats, and a top man. I used to take a great interest in his Spurs team. Burnley was my team who were Spurs' rivals and I saw them play each other at White Hart Lane and Spurs beat Burnley in the FA Cup Final. As a young player I looked up to him and thought "this is it, I'm training with Dave Mackay". I was a winger playing in the reserves, trying to make my way and getting nowhere fast.

'When he became manager, quite early, he put me in the first-team squad. He must have seen something in me. That was great. He introduced me slowly and gave me my debut as sub and full debut against Hull and Watford at home, and I made a goal for Peter Noble in each one.

'It was all so great after banging my head against a brick wall. I was in and around the first team for the remainder of the time Dave was there so I owe him a great deal. He started my career.

'As chief scout for the Liverpool academy I was involved in the team effort to get a few who have done well around Jürgen Klopp's first team. I also helped get Raheem Sterling to the club and he was sold for £50m to Man City. But none of this might ever have happened but for Dave Mackay. I could have been released. So I owe him a great deal.

'Dave also did a great thing for me at the end when he was leaving. I was a young lad, recently married with a young baby in a dingy little flat in Swindon. Dave called me one day after training to let me know he was leaving for Forest. I was choked because of what he had done for me.

'I was a nobody, probably. But he had arranged for us – myself, wife Yvonne and daughter Nikki – to move into a club house. When he handed me over the keys he said, "I've managed to organise this." I'd known about the house and that it was empty but been told by the club secretary, "We're saving it in case we sign a first-team player." And I walked out with my tail between my legs.

'Dave Mackay must have known about this and gone to the secretary and said, "David Moss is going in, he'll be a first-team player in the future, get him that house." He didn't have to do it. What a gesture. I've never forgotten that. I was able to buy it for a good price down the road. So Dave Mackay started me on the housing market. I even owe him that!

'Also, as soon I was pushed towards the first team he called me in out of the blue and almost doubled my wages because I was on peanuts. Everything he did for me was positive. He was always encouraging me as a winger to take people on, get in the box and score, but if I lost the ball he wouldn't criticise me. He wouldn't criticise any of us doing that. He was true to his word.

'He was surprisingly quiet as a manager. When he came as a player, even aged about 37 he looked a great footballer. But his management style was quite relaxed and calm, which surprised me. I saw him blow his top after a bad performance with the whole team – you knew he was serious – but rarely picked out individual players. He tried to get the best out of what he had.

'He was reserved but determined and knew what he wanted. His demands were high, but he did encourage players.

'The first team had been the same 13 or 14 players. You couldn't break into that. He came and shook that up. He wanted a younger team with more energy; free-flowing, quick, one-touch, pass and move. He wanted us to attack defenders, get crosses in, and score goals. He played for fantastic teams who did that. Maybe we didn't have the quality throughout the team to do all that he wanted to do.

'One who did have the quality, though, was Rod Thomas, who was in the League Cup Final win over Arsenal. Dave knew he was top-class.

You could see it in training every day. He was a full-back and nobody got the better of him. If wingers tried to jink past him, out would come his long legs. It was no surprise Dave signed him when he became Derby manager and was looking to improve the team.

'Dave led by example on the training pitch. He trained every day with the team, and was a great communicator on the pitch and off the pitch. We were looking for a bit of fun at the end of a session and trying to hit the crossbar from the halfway line. Dave was watching us all miss it or go close about six or seven times and he just jogged on in his own little way and said to one of the lads, "Give me the ball, son." When he got it he put it down, clipped it against the crossbar and just jogged off laughing. He only had his training shoes. Brilliant. We all stood back and applauded. But I don't think he played much after he became manager. I might have played with him in training or a reserve game.

'Dave, at the right time, used to enjoy himself socially. He had no problem with his players doing the same as long as they trained and played properly. At club functions, he was fantastic. He would go and have a chat around the tables.'

Mackay was succeeded at the County Ground by former Spurs team-mate Les Allen, promoted from chief scout. Allen kept Swindon in the second division by the end of the 1972/73 season but, understood to have been given 'little cash to inject into an ailing side', was unable to halt a slide and was sacked in the February of the following year with Robins en route to rock bottom and the drop, despite Danny Williams, the League Cup-winning boss, being reappointed in succession.

Allen said, 'I'd had dealings with Dave after our playing day at Spurs and he got me in. It worked well. He was terrific. He gave you a task to go out and watch any players and he never interfered. He wanted me to go with him but I carried on with Swindon. Dave was pretty straight as a manager, as he was as a player. He did well as one.

'We got on well and he was the first one to put his name forward when I had a testimonial match when with QPR. He said, "Put me down to play. I want to play in that match."'

28

Sowing seeds for Forest growth

ROOKIE MANAGER Dave Mackay believed he had taken charge of a 'big club' in Nottingham Forest. The 1959 FA Cup winners had maintained a top-flight place for 14 years until relegation the previous season under Matt Gillies, the Scot who bossed Leicester against Mackay's Tottenham at Wembley 11 years earlier.

Mackay also knew from personal experience how good Forest could be. When his Spurs faced them in the 1967 FA Cup semi-final, the East Midlands side were favourites. They also finished above the Lilywhites and four points off the title that season.

The club had kept faith in Gillies and went unbeaten in five, winning three on the bounce, at the start of their return season in the Second Division, but had tailed off, provoking the unidentified board member's October conversation with visiting manager Mackay.

Mackay also sensed that Forest were genuine in trying to revive the good times and had the potential in their playing staff to back it. He was taken by the quality of the likes of Martin O'Neill and Duncan McKenzie, with Scotland internationals Tommy Gemmell, a European Cup winner with Celtic, Doug Fraser and Neil Martin also on the playing staff.

Plus Forest had promising youngsters such as Viv Anderson, Tony Woodcock and John Robertson. He sensed also that there would be money to spend on players with decent crowds to boost coffers. He felt, with assistant Des Anderson and coach Colin Murphy, that they were 'on to something big'.

It seemed that Mackay and Forest would be a good fit. He still commanded respect for his powers of inspiration by the more experienced members of the squad who knew him as a player. One, Fraser, it is understood might have risked his manager's displeasure by ignoring Mackay's signal for him to be substituted before indicator boards were introduced during one match. But the full-back revealed the depth of his regard for his compatriot in an interview with *The Scotsman* in 2019. The defender, who had helped West Brom to win the 1968 FA Cup, became a prison guard at a Nottingham jail after retiring from the game. Gangster Reggie Kray was an inmate. When asked whether he feared Kray, Fraser said, 'I wasn't scared of him. Dinnae forget: I played football against Bremner and Mackay – two right tough cookies.'

Mackay knew Rome wasn't built in a day and mapped out his battle plan; getting to know the players with his managerial mindset rather than as an on-pitch opponent was top of his agenda before any implementation of his philosophy on the field.

He said, 'The hardest thing I found when I went to Nottingham was to get to know the players. You cannot do that in a fortnight or three weeks. It takes time … to get to know them, to get your ideas over to them. If you walk in and try to tell them everything you want you won't get anything done. It's just a gradual process of making sure they know what you want from them on the park.

'The place was certainly like a bit of a mortuary when I first went there. Everybody there was down and almost out and the atmosphere was terrible. But, all the same, it was a good challenge for me, because even then I could see it was an excellent club with excellent facilities and it was, more or less, a First Division club which was in the Second Division.'

A winning start underlined the positives of having Mackay at the helm. On the eve of Bonfire Night in 1972, his Forest charges defeated Anderson's old club Millwall 3-2 at the City Ground. On target were compatriots Gemmell and John Robertson, plus Alan Buckley.

But it proved a false dawn. Martin netted against Cardiff City at Ninian Park in the next game but Mackay's side went down to the first of three defeats on the bounce, slipping to 15th. The board hinted that he would have time, barring relegation, to develop and improve the playing squad and the manager sailed into calmer waters as Forest finished 14th with Mackay feeling that the supporters appreciated that the team was on an upward curve.

Mackay said, 'I didn't worry about the results to start with. There are always clubs like this every year, a successful side who has started to slide.'

His side also figured in an extraordinary third-round FA Cup tie against West Bromwich Albion, the 1968 winners en route to relegation from the First Division that season, which went to three replays before Forest were shown the exit door.

The Mackays finally moved from their treasured Enfield bungalow to the village of Burton Joyce, just five miles outside Nottingham, during the summer of 1973.

The plan was to uproot once Mackay had finished playing. There was talk of the brood setting up home in Wiltshire when he was transferred to Swindon Town from Derby County. But now he had started a job purely as a manager, talk was acted upon.

The family found another treasured dwelling in a village they still live in, with the same removal firm that had taken them from Whitecraig to Southgate.

Isobel said, 'A Mr Wade ran it, a lovely man. He moved us to Burton Joyce free of charge. He also passed on furniture from us to our parents. I think he did business in Scotland and would ask us, "Is there anything you wanted taken up?" I often wonder what happened to him.'

Valerie remembered the moving in and how future England international Viv Anderson was among a group of young Forest players who helped lug the furniture and other household essentials off the truck on a morning off from training.

Isobel wanted to reward the helpers with something to eat and drink, but was unfamiliar with the way the cooker worked in her new home, so she popped round the corner to where the previous occupants had moved for instructions.

But she had another problem – there was no frying pan to rustle up some bacon for butties to feed the hungry workers. Valerie said, 'Nana Dixon – my mum's mum – was down from Scotland helping us with the move from Enfield and said, "I've got a frying pan in my suitcase." She had kept one Mum had chucked out in the move from Enfield, because it was "too good to throw away". Obviously it was meant to be!

'The players had arrived in a bus with their kit on as we were waking up and getting dressed. They had been up and down with the furniture and the other stuff when the removal van arrived, and they were able to get their bacon sandwiches, and a load of Kit Kats Mum had got in.

'I'd have been 14 and about five years later when I started going about the town, now and again I'd see Viv and speak to him. He always said "bacon sandwiches", remembering the day.

'I loved our new home but missed Enfield more than I thought I would. We were very happy at The Glade and I enjoyed my school, Merryhills. If I won the lottery I'd buy our old Enfield home. But we have wonderful memories of both places.

'I remember when Dad took me to my new school – swapping Merryhills in Enfield for Carlton le Willows – for the first time and introduced himself to the lady at reception and explained how his daughter was coming to the school. She got muddled and confused as the head teacher's name was Mr Mackay!'

Derek said, 'I thought how great it would be to live near Nottingham. It meant we would be seeing Dad a lot more. He'd be there for tea-time. Regularly.'

Mackay wanted to prove himself at the City Ground and it looked as though he could start to deliver at the start of the 1973/74 season. He said in *Goal* at the time that he felt his team had 'stopped the slide and can go forward again'. He guided Forest into promotion contention by October.

McKenzie thrived and his promising youngsters like O'Neill were growing up fast. Martin and McKenzie were among the goals, as was O'Neill. Mackay also signed little-known 22-year-old Leyton Orient midfielder Ian Bowyer.

Martin was convinced that Mackay helped sow the seeds for the two European Cup successes Forest enjoyed under Brian Clough at the end of the decade. He said, 'It was a hard time when Dave came in as Forest had just been relegated to the Second Division. Dave wanted the team to go forward and play attacking football. We had plenty of attacking players when he came but the back four was not too clever. So he had to concentrate on the defence quite a lot.

'He had a lot of the young players who were just starting to come through, like Martin O'Neill, John Robertson and Tony Woodcock. When Cloughie got there they were well into the first team. Cloughie had the start of a really good side there. By the time Dave left we were quite a good side.

'I had played for Forest against Dave when he was a sweeper at Derby. He used to say to Roy McFarland, "Arrest him, get to him, he must have spring in his heels!" Roy would say, "That's what I'm trying to do!"'

Mackay was settled professionally, and domestically he was 'very happy'. He was developing a side which would eventually be inherited by Clough and burst out of the Second Division to the highest pillar in Europe. The players were playing for him, and he felt the supporters were behind his efforts.

It would take 'earth-shattering' events at Spurs and Derby for him to leave a project which was clearly fulfilling him every which way.

He had harboured hopes of becoming Bill Nicholson's assistant before being swept away to Derby on a tide of Brian Clough's unquenchable enthusiasm and belief. And with Bill Nick becoming more disenchanted by the game with pragmatism outweighing entertainment in approach and hooliganism, there could well have been a call from the Lane to Mackay to succeed the greatest manager in the club's history at any time.

In fact, it seemed more likely than any communication from the Baseball Ground. The Clough revolution was in full swing and the club seemed to be going forever upward. Derby had lifted the First Division title for the first time – plus the Texaco Cup – the season after Mackay had helped them to a solid start in the top flight before switching to Swindon and a managerial career. As Mackay was guiding Forest to 14th position in his first season, Clough led the Rams to the semi-finals of the European Cup, overcoming Eusébio's Benfica before exiting against Juventus in the semi-finals. He also helped Derby stun Spurs 5-3 in the FA Cup at White Hart Lane with Roger Davies completing a late hat-trick en route to the last eight.

McFarland said, 'Brian and Peter knew Derby had the nucleus of a team that could go places when the positive changes had happened with Dave when we knew we were going in the right direction. But we would strengthen bit by bit. Each year a good player would be signed. After Toddy, David Nish [a British record £225,000] came. They weren't afraid to pay top money and felt that would carry us further and bring more success. It did. They were ready and prepared when Dave left.'

But suddenly the foundations of forward motion began to shatter due to a shock of seismic proportions, which rocked football and produced one of the biggest stories emanating from the game during the 1970s, and arguably beyond. Eventually we saw a 'novel' based on the tale which in turn became a film, although both caused their own controversies.

It all erupted on Monday, 15 October 1973, just two days after Mackay's Forest had lost 2-1 to Leyton Orient at Brisbane Road.

And it meant a return to the Baseball Ground rather than White Hart Lane for the Scot.

29

'No other manager could have done it'

DAVE MACKAY was catapulted into the centre of a project that was either 'a marvellous opportunity for a young manager or a poisoned chalice' in October 1973.

Mackay was attending a Forest reserve match at Northampton Town's County Ground after his first team had been derailed by the Orient express. As he stood in the near-deserted Cobblers' boardroom, he saw Sam Longson approaching him. He knew exactly what the Derby chairman he served as a player was going to ask him – to succeed Brian Clough as manager.

Mackay said, 'I liked and admired Brian and likewise the chairman Sam Longson, a down-to-earth millionaire who had been nothing but fair and honest with me. He said I was the only man in the country who could replace Brian Clough as manager and he was right.'

And Mackay picked up the chalice, poisoned or otherwise, with Des Anderson as his assistant. Mackay had watched a football soap opera unfold from a distance; one instigated by Clough entering the Rams' boardroom to tender his and partner Peter Taylor's resignations on Monday, 15 October 1973.

He said, 'Like the rest of the country, I was transfixed.'

The events were interpreted in the 2009 film *The Damned United*, a fictional version of Clough's spells at Derby and subsequently, for 44 ill-fated days, Leeds United, based on the book of the same name by David Peace. Mackay later sued the filmmakers over 'its inaccurate portrayal of the events surrounding Clough's departure from Derby and Mackay's appointment', saying in the *Daily Record*, 'They twisted it.'

It had appeared business as usual at the Baseball Ground at the start of the 1973/74 campaign. Derby lost only one of their opening seven games and, after a blip at Coventry, they slammed Southampton 6-2. Clough had even strengthened his squad by signing £100,000 midfielder Henry Newton from Everton. But the proverbial hit the fan when Clough entered the boardroom and announced the resignation of himself and Taylor. It was just two days after a Kevin Hector goal had sealed a victory over Manchester United at Old Trafford. A display of how much discontent there was below the surface for the incumbent management team.

Clough cited a mix of reasons for the decision. There was the breakdown of his relationship with Longson, which he described as 'a genuine, close friendship, between an old man and a brash young upstart, in whom he saw an opportunity to fulfil his dreams' which lifted 'run of the mill' Derby into the big time. Clough reckoned 'friends he didn't know he had' asked Longson, 'Who runs Derby? – you or that big-headed manager of yours?' Tayor helped undermine it by telling Longson how 'Brian runs this club'. Clough felt he 'had become too big' for Longson, and said, 'He wanted more of the limelight himself.'

Beyond the perceived 'resentment' of Clough's 'high profile' and 'media commitments', Taylor had been miffed by director Jack Kirkland asking him to explain what he did at the club. He had been the individual who talent-spotted players, like Mackay, who had turned the club's fortunes towards the skies. Clough said in his autobiography, 'Jack Kirkland belittled him ... he [Taylor] was adamant – he was off. His pride was more intense than mine. I quit for both of us ... as usual, he stayed at home and left it to me to do it for both of us.'

Clough admitted that Longson had called his bluff, and wrote that the chairman thought 'our resignations would either be rejected immediately or that the board would have a rethink and eventually call us back'. He admitted his regret at the resignations, saying, 'We were fools. We made the wrong decision. Neither of us was compensated one penny. I'd recently signed a four-year contract and it had all been thrown out the window.'

A fuse had been lit and Derby dominated the headlines at the front and back of newspapers. All the first-team squad, bar an absent Henry

Newton, signed a letter 'unanimous in our support' for the re-instatement of the management duo. Players threatened to strike, many with an unbreakable faith in the manager who believed in them when others appeared not to.

The club were investigating Clough over 'irregularities', while the former boss was suing Derby for defamation. The fans – also, seemingly, the town – were up in arms about the loss of their 'Messiah' with banners claiming 'Clough in, directors out' during a protest. The people had spoken and the players shared their view. They held meetings to discuss how they could help bring back Clough, with the man himself attending.

Clough confessed in his autobiography that he 'was behind much of it, attending meetings' that 'brought a state of siege to the Baseball Ground ... Even I underestimated the impact our resignations would have. Bedlam broke loose. I've never known a group so united as the players Taylor and I had assembled.'

The players threatened to 'down tools' for the home match against Leicester City on Saturday, 20 October. Clough claimed he 'had to step in', telling them, 'That's pushing it too bloody far,' and adding, 'Had the players gone through with their threat god knows what would have happened. They might have all been suspended. They could have caused the shutdown of the entire club. Their determination to have us reinstated became a crazy crusade that threatened to get out of hand.' And the players responded as they secured a 2-1 win over the Foxes with McGovern and Hector on target and coach Jimmy Gordon in caretaker charge.

The media had it that Bobby Robson, the Ipswich Town manager, was first asked to replace Clough, yet to Mackay it was clear he would be the only person able to take over and sort out the mess.

Mackay said, 'I was under no illusions. I knew I was only being offered the post because there was no other person who might be able to unite the players, fans and board behind the club in the midst of this mass revolt. I had achieved nothing in management yet and, although the start at Forest was promising and my time at Swindon by no means a failure, I still had it all to prove.

'I did not have to think long about the offer. You either see a glass half full or half empty. I see it as half-full. Derby ... could have been viewed as a marvellous opportunity for a young manager or a poisoned chalice. I was not happy about leaving Forest but I knew Derby County and this job was my destiny.'

Again, Mackay had left a job 'unfinished', and the Forest fans vented their spleen. He said, 'The fans had every right to not be too happy … I saw those feelings close up after my last game in charge. Angry fans had gathered in the car park and made threatening noises.'

He took charge at the Baseball Ground on Tuesday, 23 October 1973 with the spectre of Clough hanging over him. He had hoped 'the whole thing would fizzle out' when the ex-manager and his partner Taylor took charge of Brighton & Hove Albion a few days later – but it didn't.

* * *

Stuart Webb, the Rams' secretary at the time, said to the *Derby Telegraph*, 'When Dave came back to Derby there was a period of several weeks when there was still dissent and some of the players gave him and Anderson the silent treatment. Mackay met the players individually, and by the time those meetings were over they all knew exactly his position, "I'm manager, and you'll be treated on merit like everyone else. Now knuckle down or you are away." However, there was still resentment within the playing staff, and with the fans' frustrations still bubbling away the board began to wonder if they had made the right decision. It was vice-chairman Jack Kirkland who reassured Sam, "Brian has resigned, he has gone. Dave is our manager and we must stick by him."'

A whole month after Mackay had taken the reins, there was an 'open letter', ghost-written by Vince Wilson, from his old manager to him printed in the *Sunday Mirror*. It included this advice, 'Throw my chair out of the office. Throw the sign out of the dressing room which read, "The biggest crime in football is to give the ball away to the opposition".'

But Clough admitted he didn't help matters overall. He said in his autobiography, 'It was ironic that Dave Mackay, my key signing, who launched the great revival of the old club, would be brought in to replace me as manager. He once said that his biggest problem in taking over was that I wouldn't let go. He was absolutely right.'

Mackay had enough on his plate in sorting the discontented playing staff. But, typically, he was up for the challenge. Anyone who knew him would have told you he'd be unfazed through that innate self-confidence retained from his youth and displayed, to quote one example, when he rescued his brother Frank from that knife-wielding stranger close to the family home.

He had already personally dealt with a phone call at home from Derby captain Roy McFarland after agreeing to take on the job. McFarland, whom Mackay had helped develop into an international class defender by playing alongside him, pleaded with him not to return as the players wanted Clough back.

Mackay told him, 'I've accepted the job, Roy. Simple as that. Brian's not coming back and if you don't get me, you'll end up with someone else.'

When he arrived for his first day in the job and parked his car, supporters made their feelings clear when they declared 'f*** off Mackay, you are not welcome here'. And one thumped his windscreen, which caused Mackay to leap out of his car to remonstrate as the fan put on the after-burners to escape. Mackay tried to make light of it by telling the protesting supporters still there, 'Tell him to come for a trial. I think we could do with him on the wing.'

He said in a *Goal* article reprinted in Simon Sharp's *Derby County The Glory Years*, 'Brian Clough is a great manager but there are other great managers too. I know everyone is watching me but I'm not frightened by it. Neither do I blame the players for trying to get Brian back. I have worked with Brian and know what he can mean to the players. If I had been a player here when all this blew up I would have been the first to sign that letter asking for him to be re-instated.'

He met, as per Webb's observations, with the players and repeated what he had told McFarland and Henry Newton, who had also phoned him. And he added that if any did not like it they should ask for a transfer 'because we have a job to be getting on with … no one walked'.

He reckoned the task was 'not that difficult'. Mackay said, 'I'd been offered the job and was determined to take it. The players were upset that Cloughie and Peter Taylor had left and were against the board. They said to me that if I came back there'd be problems. I had a meeting with them and said, "Hey, I'm coming back; if you want to leave, you can leave." They didn't frighten me. If I'd been someone else it might have been different. I've no idea how Brian felt.

'There was a lot of political tension at the time with the miners' strikes. And if I'd still been Derby captain I'd have been disappointed that Brian and Peter had gone too. Those players would have beaten any other manager coming in – but me, I'd not long left the place and knew all the players as individuals, who's the tough guy and who's the weak guy. And they knew I knew. That helped me. My job as manager was to handle the players, and I had to handle the board as well. Of course, the fans treated me differently when I won the League, but they were never really angry at me, just at Brian Clough leaving.'

It was a difficult start. Mackay's first game as boss saw Derby draw 0-0 at West Ham in a First Division fixture, and his side were defeated by QPR on his home debut in the dugout. Reverses at Robson's Ipswich and then Sheffield United completed a hat-trick of league defeats on the bounce, before home deadlocks with Leeds and Arsenal. The Rams had slid from third to 15th while netting a mere two goals in total under Mackay. In the meantime, his outfit were knocked out of the League Cup by Sunderland after two replays, scoring just once.

Calls from Bring Back Clough campaigners, who handed out leaflets and car stickers, grew louder. And even Mackay admitted it was 'the roughest ride of my professional career'. He felt himself one or two games away from the boot.

But his side secured their first victory next time out as goals from Roger Davies and Alan Hinton sealed a 2-0 win against Newcastle United at St James' Park ten days before Christmas. It was a result Mackay felt was obtained against the run of play and when they received a comfortable FA Cup draw against non-league Boston United it indicated to him that perhaps Lady Luck was positioning her smiling gaze Derby's way. Mackay said, 'That was the turning point.'

Spurs were beaten with a couple more Hinton goals and the Mackay bandwagon was rolling, incredibly, back to third place – which earned them a UEFA Cup spot – by the end of the season, with the help of the signings of attacking midfielder Bruce Rioch at £200,000 from Aston Villa, and Rod Thomas, the £80,000 full-back who had played with and under him at Swindon. Mackay said, 'I thought he [Rioch] was among the best players in the game and would prove a snip at £200,000,' with his 'surging runs' and 'goals scored with his powerful power-driver of a shot'. The Bring Back Clough campaign 'began to switch off'.

Roy McFarland, who was Derby's club captain, said, 'When Dave Mackay came in as manager the place was upside down. We didn't want to play football. We were going to get on a plane to Spain and say, "If you are going to play, play the reserves in our place [for the Leicester match]." Luckily, we didn't go the whole hog. We chickened out because of the threat of being under *sine die* [indefinite suspension]. It was a difficult time for the football club and the players. But more importantly, it was a difficult time for Dave Mackay who took the job as manager. Him and Des Anderson were absolutely first-class. They got us back playing football, and to winning the title in 1975.

'It was horrendous. We were having clandestine meetings with Brian and Peter. The players were hoping the board would change their mind and ask Brian to come back. Don't forget it was Brian and Peter who resigned. That's the worst of it. Brian said it was the worst decision he ever made in his life, and that he'd never do it again. But he'd left.

'I think for Dave to walk in knowing what was going on was incredible. Did it surprise me knowing the man? Not at all. He wanted to come back and manage. He knew the majority of us. We'd played with him for three years. But we wanted Brian back. That was the thing.

'We did everything we could to do that. We went too far, there's no doubt. I'll put my hand up first. I was captain, the leader of the team. I'd taken over the captaincy from this great player, Mackay.

'I'm pleased to say that the education I got, we got, from him as a player eventually took us to the first championship. It was a great thing to lead that team, and win the First Division.

'But when Dave Mackay first walked through that door [as manager] he had so many issues to deal with. And he dealt with every single issue and problem. The major thing for him was getting us back playing the way we should be playing, and to give commitment to the football club and the supporters. He got us doing that. He was patient, because we went off the rails more than once trying to get Brian and Peter back. We were wrong.

'In hindsight, we all know what we tried to do, persuade Dave not to take the job. It was crazy. At least, we players came to our senses and said, "You know, this is stupid. We've got to get back playing football. That's what we get paid for." The guy had been very patient. Yes, he's had a go at us once or twice. And Des Anderson had more of a go at me once, told me what he thought of me as a player and as a person and what I should be doing at this particularly worrying time for the football club.

As I said, the penny dropped, and we just realised we've got to move on in life, get to playing football, doing our job.

'Dave and Des gave us enough rope to get away from Brian and Peter, and then dragged it back in. They pulled us back in bit by bit. I don't think any other manager could have done it other than Mackay.

'The one thing about him – despite all that went off through this time – he didn't bear any grudges. To the day he died, we'd meet up for a drink at Derby County functions after we'd both gone off elsewhere. He would grab me and give me a big hug.'

John McGovern said, 'It wasn't an easy time when Dave became manager. I remember Dave coming into the dressing room and putting down a sheet of A4 white paper on the table in the middle of it and saying, "All I want to know is, who wants to play for me at Derby County?" And he walked out. Strangely enough I was the first one who got up and signed the paper. Roy McFarland had a go at me. He said, "What are you signing that for?" I said, "He's the manager of Derby County and I happen to play for them." It was common sense to sign it. Clough had gone and Dave Mackay was the new manager. Why not sign? It wasn't an agreement, just a sheet of paper. I had that much respect for Dave.

'John O'Hare signed it as well. We were the two players who eventually followed Clough to Leeds.

'Brian Clough did phone me up – Roy McFarland would have told him what had happened – and said, "Did you sign that piece of paper?" I said, "Yes, I did. You'd gone and he was the manager. You know how good Dave was as a player so I was quite happy to work for someone at least I knew."

'He didn't say anything. That's the only time he hadn't given me an immediate, scathing reply. There was a movement to get Cloughie re-instated but I'm pretty clear when I look back. Simply that he'd left and Dave was the manager.

'One of the players came up with the idea of going on strike for the next game. He said, "We won't turn up." I said, "You can't do that. You're not going to turn up for a game and the supporters are coming. That's silly. First of all the club will fine you. Then the PFA, if they've got anything about them would say you can't do it. It is against the rules. But you shouldn't out of respect for the club." Thankfully, they didn't go out on strike and make an absolute mockery of football. Football makes enough of a mockery of itself over and over again without needing help from a group of players.'

Colin Todd added, 'Things had gone pear-shaped with Brian leaving when he [Mackay] came in difficult circumstances. But Dave wasn't fazed. He was a good character, very strong mentally. We always thought we'd get Brian back. It came to a point and Dave told us, "Brian's not going to come back and the sooner you forget about trying to make that happen the better it will be for you. If you want to go, go." He'd stamped out the Clough rebellion. None of us left. We backed Dave and it panned out very well. We had a very successful season. His philosophy was to score more goals than the opposition.

'And he made some astute, brilliant signings, Charlie George, Bruce Rioch and Franny Lee to mention just three and we went on to win the championship under him with a very attack-minded team. I won a PFA player award under him.'

Isobel Mackay said, 'It went sour when the management thing came up. When Brian left and one or two players didn't want David, which I found odd. Roy McFarland phoned him up and said, "Don't take the job, Dave. We're hoping to get Brian Clough back." But David told him that he'd already met Sam Longson and that he was the new manager.

'David never spoke to any of the family about it at all. I didn't like it myself. I thought it was all wrong, but he just stuck two fingers up and got on with it. I don't think anybody else could have taken it over having to deal with the players and that. Like David said, when that film *The Damned United* came out it was all wrong. What they did about David, that he didn't want Brian Clough to come back. He said if he'd been a player he'd have been doing the same. But he was away at Swindon.'

30

The real deal

KEY DEFENDER Colin Todd said that Dave Mackay underlined how he 'had won us over' to produce an 'outstanding' season as a championship-clinching Derby County manager in 1974/75.

Mackay might have sparked the revival of the Rams under Brian Clough as a player. But it was a different ball game as a boss, especially with the furore over Clough's departure after leading them to top spot in 1972 and the semi-finals of the European Cup the following season.

Yet Mackay achieved it while completing not just a 'double' but a 'triple' as he joined an exclusive club by guiding Derby to the top-flight title as manager after having won it as a player, having already lifted the Footballer of the Year statuette. Fellow Scot Kenny Dalglish also became a member of the group by repeating the awesome threesome in the late 1970s into the 1980s and got a knighthood for his troubles, while Mackay got the cold shoulder rather than the royal sword on the upper joint, with the Rams sacking him a little over a year after he helped them bring home the most coveted title in the English game.

In between, however, he believed 'for the first time' that he 'did not feel the hand of Clough' on his shoulder as the league trophy made its way back to the Baseball Ground for the second time in three years.

He said, 'I felt vindicated and a sense of enormous personal satisfaction … [I had] great admiration for the players. All of them. They had put the trauma of 18 months earlier behind them.'

Mackay believed he turned Derby into his team rather than the one created by his illustrious predecessor.

The writing was on the wall as he had told his players pre-season, 'Forget the troubles of last season. From now on we'll do things MY way.' His way was a more attacking, adventurous philosophy, imbued with the influence of his managers, although he said, 'I liked the way Clough did some things. There were others that I didn't like.'

It was an attitude underlined when he bought in experienced England international striker Francis Lee from Manchester City for £100,000 to help boost the goal tally and add his nous. After all, Lee had a rich pedigree having won the title, the FA Cup and the European Cup Winners' Cup, besides two FA Charity Shields, with City.

Mackay also brought a calm approach in contrast to Clough, along with a self-assurance and honesty that the players respected and appreciated.

Although Mackay had brought in Lee, midfielder John McGovern and front-runner John O'Hare were tempted away by Clough, who had now swapped Brighton for Leeds United. Clough signed them after surprisingly succeeding Don Revie at Elland Road for 44 infamous days of internal bust-ups – inspiring the book and film *The Damned United* – before he was sacked.

Mackay said, 'Later, when I took over from Brian and he'd gone to Leeds and burnt Don Revie's desk, he came to see me in my office to sign McGovern and John O'Hare and said, "Why haven't you burnt my desk?" Ha ha!'

And Roy McFarland was sidelined, having ruptured an Achilles tendon playing for Joe Mercer's England alongside Derby team-mates Colin Todd and David Nish in a 1-0 win over Northern Ireland at Wembley in May 1974.

* * *

Mackay sensed a 'great opportunity' to come out on top before the 1974/75 campaign began. He pointed out how rivals Liverpool and Leeds, runners-up and champions in 1973/74, were undergoing change. Anfield boss Bill Shankly had stepped aside for Bob Paisley and Revie for Clough. He believed Paisley and Clough would not do as well as their immediate predecessors due to the shake-up, causing 'a terrific upheaval for the players'. He reckoned that his own players, bar any newcomers, 'have adjusted' – in the time Mackay felt he needed – following the trauma prevalent at the Baseball Ground after Clough and Taylor's departures.

He pointed to the third-place finish achieved at the end of it and was 'doubtful if Brian could have finished any higher'. This gave him 'a measure of satisfaction', and he added, 'That showed other people are able to manage Derby County. There were quite a few around who seemed to think that impossible – that Derby was Clough's County.'

And he rammed – if you will excuse the use of the verb in this context – that final point home with Derby's return to the peak of their Everest by the season's close.

Mackay's team lacked what champions need in the early part of the season – consistency. There was only one win to boast in the opening seven fixtures, with Roger Davies and Kevin Hector sealing a 2-0 victory over a decent Sheffield United side. Mackay then suffered a defeat at former club Tottenham, in the last weeks of Bill Nicholson's 16-year White Hart Lane reign, and at Birmingham City. The other games were drawn.

But for Beatles fan Mackay things were 'getting better' up to Christmas and he felt his side 'steamed ahead' after the holiday period.

There were a host of rivals to the crown as Derby made their bid for top spot, such as Liverpool, Ipswich Town, Everton and Stoke City.

But Mackay was delighted with the 'great football' and 'emphatic wins' being produced. A Boxing Day victory over Birmingham set off a four-match winning run, which included Lee netting back-to-back in victories over his former club and Paisley's Reds. Another run, perfectly timed from March into April, saw his Rams win six of seven, beginning with two points against relegation-threatened Spurs and involving two five-goal thumpings of Luton Town – with Roger Davies scoring all five – and Burnley in successive games. A reverse at Stoke during that spell proved their only one in the final 11 fixtures.

The title was sealed four days after the penultimate match against Leicester ended in a goalless draw at Filbert Street. Mackay and his players were attending a supporters' dinner-dance evening at the Bailey's nightclub in Derby, when Peter Daniel picked up the fans' player of the season award. Ipswich, the only team who could deny the Rams the crown, were playing at Lee's former employers, Manchester City, that same evening.

Bobby Robson's Tractor Boys had to win to string out the race until the final day of the season that Saturday when Derby, already on 52 points, were due to sign off the campaign against already-doomed Carlisle United.

Mackay picked at his prawn cocktail, understandably distracted, as BBC Radio Derby commentator Barrie Eccleston sat opposite keeping him updated with the goings-on at Maine Road, via the transistor radio he had jammed against an ear. As the whistle sounded through his speaker, Eccleston declared, 'We're champions.'

Cue party time and Mackay 'accepted a glass of champagne' as he 'hugged' Isobel and then his players. Mackay said, 'It was fantastic. A big roar went up. We won the league having a night out. The celebrations started right away. Help yourselves, I told everybody. I couldn't care less because we've won the league. We were all still drunk when we played on Saturday!'

Team captain Archie Gemmill was presented with the trophy as Derby were only able to complete their season with a goalless draw against the Cumbrians three days later. Perhaps Mackay's hangover theory applied, although that may do a disservice to visitors earning a small consolation for a wretched campaign, to date their only one in the top flight.

Mackay reflected on the achievement. He said, 'Surprised me a little. I expected to be in the top four. I mean, I expect us to win every time we play anyway. And I expect my team to win the league every year. It doesn't happen like that.'

And he was fulsome in his praise of the players who did it. Peter Daniel clearly had proved a more than adequate deputy for McFarland in the eyes of the supporters and the club's management, with Mackay, impressed by his whole rearguard, saying the defender had 'stepped out of the shadows and performed brilliantly'.

Mackay was delighted for all his players, highlighting Colin Todd and goalkeeper Colin Boulton for their solidity, Bruce Rioch for the 'impetus' he provided and top-scoring with 15 goals, 'thoroughbred' Alan Hinton, Davies for his historic five goals against Luton, Hector for sticking to his task and bagging 13, Gemmill, McFarland's deputy as skipper, for 'covering every blade of grass', plus Henry Newton, Ron Webster, passing 500 Rams appearances, Rod Thomas and Steve Powell for, like all the others, being 'brilliant'.

Francis Lee was selected for a special mention. Lee, with a proud chest similar to the one possessed by his manager when a player, might have been considered 'too old' at 30 but had proved a shrewd signing and rewarded Mackay's faith with 14 goals, all but two in the league, and plenty of hustle and bustle. His explosive shooting and dynamism charged up the central strike force and the Baseball Ground faithful took to him.

Mackay said, 'I was especially happy for Franny, who would not have placed a bet on himself ever playing in another championship side.'

When asked how lifting the crown compared to championships with Hearts and Spurs, he said, 'It was fantastic.'

Mackay insisted he remained a Clough supporter after emulating the Yorkshireman's title feat at the Baseball Ground. And when asked what was the best advice he got from Clough he referred to the 'burn your desk' quote, saying his predecessor explained, 'It gets rid of the stench of the old regime.'

Clough in turn appeared to recognise Mackay's feat in the face of the circumstances surrounding his succession. He said, 'Mackay was Mackay, as solid as the player on whom I had pinned my faith, and he saw it through with a great deal of dignity.'

Colin Todd lifted the PFA Player of the Year award for his efforts in helping to secured the championship. He said, 'Dave had had a season where he bedded himself in as manager. He had won us over – which was the important thing. You got some idea how the new season would go when the results came and people started to play with confidence and belief.

'Part of football management is to pick players up and knock them down but he didn't have to that season because it was, in general, an outstanding one.

'Dave embedded into the players about knowing who we were playing against. That was important. In that era we never had dossiers, although we'd have team talks. Dave's approach in the dressing room before and after games was very calm, but he also instilled aggression, which is something he had as a player, to make sure you dominated your opponents individually at first and then collectively.

'Dave's philosophy was to score more goals than the opposition whereas Brian was more about not being negative but keeping a clean sheet.

'Clough was totally unique in management. If you look at his record, it was incredible. If he had stayed at Derby County, I believe he would have achieved the same as what he achieved at Nottingham Forest, where he won two European Cups. Remember we had got to the semi-final with him at the Baseball Ground.

'Cloughie's man-management was outstanding. His motivation good. That's not to say Dave's wasn't. He had a different manner to do things. Probably more open in his talking, a bit more relaxed.'

Roy McFarland came back after his injury for the final four games to help the Rams seal the title. He said, 'With all the troubles he'd had it was brilliant for Dave to manage us to becoming champions. A wonderful character, he got us back to playing football.

'I'd seen every game as a spectator up until I returned from injury. It was great to watch the guys play so good again. Peter Daniels did a tremendous job in my place alongside Toddy. It had been touch and go when I won the title with Derby in 1972 and it was the same again. We were losing games at the wrong time. There was bit of pressure before we won it with a game to go. It was lovely when we learned at the supporters' dinner that we'd won it. We enjoyed the parade with the trophy on the Saturday.

'I'd played catch-up after snapping my Achilles with England and having an operation. I was getting back to fitness by the end of November but then had problems with my other Achilles, and more surgery. It was a partial tear. It was long and hard getting back and I was delighted to be involved in the last four games and celebrate with the trophy. The surgeon did a magnificent job. I've not had a problem with them since.'

Archie Gemmill went on to help Clough win the league title and European Cup at Nottingham Forest, captain Scotland and score one of the most memorable goals of the World Cup finals in 1978, against the Netherlands. He appreciated the platform Mackay and Anderson gave him. Gemmill said, 'Dave and Des deserve every credit they get. They brought in their own players, great players, and played wonderful attacking football. I don't think anybody could complain about the type of football served up.

'It was wonderful captaining Derby to the title. The job was easy because [we had] quality players. Our method is to go for goal all the time. Take it from me, there wasn't a shirker in the outfit.'

Bruce Rioch, Derby's top league scorer that season with 15, said, 'It was exciting. I wondered if a top club would take the risk of signing me. With Villa, I had all four cartilages removed from my knees. Very few players to carry on after four operations. Our manager never seems to change tactics. His orders are to attack home and away.'

The season also produced an impressive two-leg victory over Atlético Madrid in the UEFA Cup after Derby had defeated Servette Geneva in their opening round. They then suffered a surprise exit in the next against Velez Mostar from Yugoslavia after winning the first leg 3-1. Mackay's men made it to the fifth round of the FA Cup before being pipped 1-0 by Leeds, managed by Clough's successor Jimmy Armfield, and suffered a surprise 5-0 League Cup opening-round reverse at Southampton, relegated from the First Division the previous season.

But nothing took the shine off the title glory.

Mackay always had a positive mindset. Negatives such as defeat never infiltrated it, so when he pondered how the 1975/76 season would pan out he thought big. Derby had become a football backwater before he arrived at the Baseball Ground. Sure, Brian Clough and Peter Taylor were in situ, but the pair had not torn up any trees. Mackay's arrival as a player, as Clough acknowledged, lit the fire and put the club's name in lights.

Clough capitalised on it as he led the charge to the league title after his best signing had moved on. Now, as manager, Mackay had emulated his much-vaunted forerunner in the collection of English football's most hard-earned trophy. And he believed he could take the club even further – to European Cup glory.

As a player, he came close with Spurs. Now as boss he felt his Derby could do what Jock Stein did at Celtic in 1967 and Matt Busby had done at Manchester United a year later. Living up to the Lisbon Lions would be a tall order. Following in the footsteps of the Old Trafford giants, who had been helped into the semi-finals by Denis Law before his Scotland international team-mate and pal was sidelined by injury, would also be no mean feat.

Mackay felt the quality of football his side had produced in the second half of the championship-winning season was a match for anyone in Europe, but he felt the playing squad needed bolstering.

There were no talismanic superstars in the Derby dressing room beyond Francis Lee, perhaps. There was certainly no one to match the likes of the Bhoys' Jimmy Johnstone and Bobby Lennox or United's Bobby Charlton and George Best.

Mackay tried to get a superstar in the shape of Peter Osgood before the charismatic striker quit Chelsea for Southampton in March 1974.

He remembered Osgood as a tough opponent from when his Spurs came up against the Blues. The forward was tall and rugged, no shrinking violet, had superb technical ball skills, a light touch, an eye for goal, was a match-winner and possessed a magnetic personality which made him such a fans' favourite that they picketed Stamford Bridge when he was axed after falling out with manager Dave Sexton over his lifestyle. Mackay met Osgood, unconcerned about the player's 'lively' off-field reputation, and was disappointed that he chose the Saints.

But a chance to sign a forward of similar character came along by chance in July 1975 as Mackay relaxed on a family break in Scotland during the close season. He read that Charlie George, a pivotal figure as Arsenal won the Double in 1971, would be able to leave Highbury for £100,000.

Mackay thought it would be a bargain for a proven match-winner. There was a touch of the rebel about George, but he had height, strength, mobility, ability, confidence and a striker's instinct mixed with a willingness to work his socks off.

Our subject got on to assistant Des Anderson to look into it and was shocked to discover the Gunners' died-in-the-wool local hero, brought up in the Arsenal catchment area of Islington and who had stood on Highbury's infamous North Bank terracing, had agreed to join north London rivals Tottenham.

Mackay hung on to the word 'agreed' – that George had not signed. He grabbed a draft contract and drove to London to convince George to join his champions and European Cup contenders. Mackay revealed in his autobiography that George would have signed for Tottenham the day before but Spurs manager Terry Neill wanted him to do it the following day at a press conference. He pulled out the contract as he met George, having been told by the player he would 'love to play for you and Derby'. George signed it there and then.

Mackay said, 'I knew Charlie George would rather not go to Spurs. And if Matt Busby had come in for me, I would have gone there. As soon as I knew anybody was up who I wanted, I phoned them straight away – don't delay!'

George himself revealed on RamsTV that Brian Clough, who had by then taken charge at Nottingham Forest, also wanted him, but, according to Derby's in-house channel, the 'pull of Dave Mackay was too great to turn down'.

He continued, 'It's over 40 years ago now since I joined Derby. It was a funny move really because the move came out of the blue; I had a phone call out from Dave Mackay and he asked me if I would be interested in signing for Derby.

'I met up with him in Carlton Towers in London and we did the deal within 20 minutes. Nottingham Forest were actually in for me as well, but I went with Derby and I have no regrets because I thoroughly enjoyed it.

'Derby had just won the league and I felt it would be a wonderful opportunity for me to come and play with a great team. I played with a freedom I knew I could play with.

'I don't think you truly appreciate the players you are playing against until you play with them. I played against Colin Todd, Roy McFarland, Dave Mackay, Alan Hinton, Bruce Rioch and David Nish, who was a cultured left-back, and Franny Lee was one hell of a player. I thought we could do something with the players we had.'

It proved a key signing. George had discarded his long, lank hairstyle for a perm to reflect the times but not his ability, attitude and charisma. He was just what Mackay needed on the continent and, indeed, for the title defence.

But first there was another trophy to be won with the FA Charity Shield. George, on his debut, helped Derby to a 2-0 victory over Trevor Brooking and Frank Lampard Senior's West Ham United, who had defeated a Fulham side skippered by their former captain Bobby Moore in the FA Cup Final in May.

George was unable to produce a goal as Kevin Hector and the fit-again Roy McFarland scored in front of 59,000 at Wembley on the Rams' first visit since lifting the FA Cup in 1946.

But Mackay's new signing would not have to wait long. He hit the target on his league debut in the season-opener against Sheffield United at Bramall Lane and bagged another at Tottenham before securing instant home hero status by scoring his first goals in front of the Baseball Ground faithful in a 2-1 win over Manchester United on 24 September.

George admitted he had a few nerves when it came to the reaction he would receive from the Derby supporters upon his arrival, having stuck two fingers up to the home fans while still an Arsenal player during a 1972 FA Cup tie. His flying start for Mackay's Derby eased his personal fears. He said, 'I was a bit nervous about joining after giving them the V-sign while I was at Arsenal, but I didn't need to have worried. I got on great with the crowd from the very start, but I remember that they went crazy when I gave them the V-sign!'

Any lingering doubts were washed away on a famous night when he helped Mackay celebrate 'the best game I presided over as a manager'.

It came on Wednesday, 22 October 1975. Derby had overcome Slovan Bratislava in the opening round of the European Cup. It earned them a double date with six-time champions Real Madrid.

The Galacticos of the Bernabéu, including German World Cup-winning duo Günter Netzer and Paul Breitner and European Cup winner Pirri, found their way from their glamorous home in the Spanish capital to the more modest surroundings of the Baseball Ground in the East Midlands and were thumped 4-1 with George bagging a hat-trick in front of 35,000 stunned spectators.

Mackay said, 'Charlie may have had his best ever game [for us]. The players all played a blinder … we were electrifying. We left them with a mountain to climb.'

Frustratingly for the Scot, they managed to scale it. George was able to score in front of a reported 120,000, the biggest crowd to have watched a Derby game, in the second leg. But the hosts completed a 5-1 win on the night to go through 6-5 on aggregate, after extra time which was only forced by a tie-levelling equaliser from the spot with independent observers stating the penalty was awarded despite a 'blatant dive' by a home player. Mackay's Rams were up against it before kick-off with Francis Lee and Bruce Rioch sidelined by injury.

Mackay said, 'I refused to instruct the team to play defensively or adopt any time-wasting tactics … I got some stick but my whole football breeding was to entertain, to play fairly and give one's all. Never did Tommy Walker, Bill Nicholson or Brian Clough tell us to waste time or adopt cynical defensive tactics.'

George said, 'I feel people make a lot of the hat-trick, but two of them were penalties weren't they! I was always that confident when it came to penalties, so I always felt I should score them.

'The other goal that night was a good one, and I actually think the one I scored in Madrid was the best – but it never got a mention because we were beaten 5-1.

'The one from open play at the Baseball Ground was all about timing. I managed to come on to it and find the bottom corner. I could strike a ball well, so it was all about timing and I caught it sweetly.

'It was devastating to lose how we did in the second leg. Personally, I managed to score four goals in two games against Real Madrid and still end up on the losing side. I think that we could have done really well in the competition if we had got through.'

But domestically, Mackay's Derby cranked up for a bid at completing the Double. The Rams had pipped Leeds United 3-2 in a bruising league encounter four days before their continental dreams were ended for the season. It saw Lee and visiting defender Norman Hunter sent off for brawling.

And, following the European exit, back-to-back wins over Arsenal and West Ham put them top. Derby also splashed out a club record £310,000 on Burnley and Wales international winger Leighton James in November. They continued to make a positive mark in the race for another title, with George in sparkling form.

George also led the way as Mackay's outfit galloped towards the later rounds of the FA Cup, dismissing Everton, Liverpool, Southend United and Newcastle to set up a last-four encounter with Manchester United, managed by Tommy Docherty.

But George had suffered a dislocated shoulder in a home league deadlock against Stoke City on 24 March and the wheels came off. The Doc's Red Devils beat the Rams in the semi-finals at Hillsborough and they lost three and drew one of their last four to end up fourth behind champions Liverpool, runners-up QPR and third-placed United with 53 points, the same as when securing the championship a season earlier.

It was no surprise that George collected Derby's player of the year award, and the Londoner was also named Midlands Player of the Season.

He said, 'Without being blasé about it, I really do believe that if I hadn't have got injured, when I dislocated my shoulder and fractured my elbow, we would have gone on to win the Double.

'I missed the FA Cup semi-final and I think the stuffing was knocked out of us, without being cocky or anything. I was flying at that time.'

A positive side-effect of a decent season under Mackay saw his championship-winning skipper Archie Gemmill become the first Derby player to captain Scotland when the midfielder led out his country against Wales at Hampden in the Home International Championship in May 1976. Gemmill helped his country secure a 3-1 victory with Rioch netting one of the hosts' goals against a Wales side featuring Rams winger James.

During the season, Mackay lost inspirationsl wideman Alan Hinton. The former Wolves and Forest ace made three league appearances as a substitute but tragedy struck when his nine-year-old son Matthew died of cancer. The flanker emigrated to the United States of America for a change of lifestyle.

And Mackay's dealings with Hinton displayed the manager's compassion – ensuring his player got paid up until the end of his contract, while allowing the winger the time he needed to deal with the situation.

31

Ken's Roller

THE INSTABILITY of Derby County in 2020/21 – with a relegation battle, managerial changes and constant takeover speculation – was a far cry from the relatively solid position Dave Mackay seemed to be in 44 years earlier.

Mackay had managed the Rams to the First Division championship in April 1975 and put them on course for the league and cup Double the following season until talisman Charlie George fell on a frozen Baseball Ground surface and dislocated his shoulder.

He was upbeat about Derby's prospects in the top flight for the 1976/77 season, even though Francis Lee had retired and Roger Davies had been transferred to FC Bruges. Having George available again from the start was one reason for his optimism. Also, he felt a tighter defence would aid the cause. Derby had finished top scorers with 75 goals while fourth the previous season, but had conceded 58.

Mackay said, 'I don't think there is anything more important to Derby than the ability to maintain a respectable goals against column – if we do we'll be hard to stop. I must do something about the number of goals we gave away last season, but I shall never forsake our attacking policy. One of the bright spots for me last season was the form of Charlie George.'

But he was also aware that the 'whispers' had started up again for him to be replaced by Brian Clough despite a memorable if trophyless season. He said, 'Sadly, failure is relative and there were some people on the board at Derby County who believed it was necessary to win something every year.'

Mackay felt there was pressure on him to find a 'target man' to play alongside George as the season got off to a rocky start. An astonishing 8-2 league win over an eventually relegated Spurs – in which George and Bruce Rioch shared seven goals between them – only came after a winless run of eight league games to kick off the season.

Mackay said, 'We were in the lower half of the division and this supplied welcome ammunition for some people in the club who wanted me out ... I was merely a barrier to their dream of Brian Clough returning being realised.'

A club record victory of 12-0 against Finn Harps – against whom Kevin Hector bagged five and George and Leighton James hit hat-tricks – in the opening round of the UEFA Cup on 15 September 'couldn't paper over the cracks'.

Mackay also felt there was discreet criticism of his management regime – with Des Anderson also in the firing line – and previous season's signing for £310,000 of James who 'not quite lived up to his promise', plus personal barbs relating to the Welsh winger's weight and lifestyle.

He sensed a storm brewing and the thunder began to crash and lightning to flash shortly before a weekly board meeting he was to attend as a matter of course just after Derby were knocked out of the UEFA Cup by AEK Athens in November.

Mackay recalled in his autobiography how he sat in his office preparing for the meeting when a copy of *The Sun* was pressed into his hand by Frank Cholorton, a pal and supporter. Cholorton pointed out an article by John Sadler, who was to ghost-write Clough's autobiography, which revealed how a contact of the journalist had been playing golf with directors of an East Midlands club the day before and been informed its manager 'would be receiving his cards imminently'. It was reported, backing up our subject's belief, that there were dissenting boardroom voices relating to Mackay's approach to management, which was considered 'liberal'.

Stuart Webb said to the *Derby Telegraph*, 'Dave fell victim to some dirty work behind the scenes. There was a lot of talk at Kedleston Golf Club, a home from home for some of the directors.'

Mackay knew board members had been on the fairways and had no doubt the article referred to him. He felt it 'unforgivable ... but typical' the newspaper had been told before himself. The red mist descended and he crashed into the boardroom holding the paper and invited the directors to 'stick your job up your arse'. But, after calming down and appreciating the financial consequences of quitting for his family and Anderson, he returned to declare, 'I don't resign. You have to sack me.'

Sam Longson attempted to placate Mackay back in the manager's office. But Mackay insisted the end of his time with Derby was nigh, especially with the chairman 'no longer as powerful as he once was', perhaps in reference to the growing influence of vice-chairman George Hardy.

Mackay asked for a vote of confidence but the board were not prepared to give it. He and Anderson were dismissed at the morning meeting on Thursday, 25 November 1976. Like Clough and Taylor, the pair had only survived for 18 months after winning the title.

The official minutes of the board meeting at the Baseball Ground that morning – which also included a request from Longson relating to the club's defamation case involving Brian Clough – stated under the heading '7778 MANAGER AND ASSISTANT MANAGER':

'A lengthy and detailed discussion took place in respect of the club's present low position in the Football League and general concern was expressed with regard to moral [sic] with the Club. Following a request for a vote of confidence by the manager, DC Mackay, the Board unanimously agreed that this could not be granted and that the Manager and Assistant Manager be relieved of their duties forthwith.'

The minutes revealed that Mackay received an ex-gracia payment of £5,000, tax-free, a company car valued at £3,500, and a settlement on his contract of £4,300 subject to the usual deductions for tax. Anderson also received £5,000 tax-free, a car valued at £2,000, and a £700 settlement.

Mackay's programme article for the league game against Sunderland two days later was pulled, but it reflected his recognition of facing 'any difficult problems' for the 'first time' since 'overcoming my initial crisis at the Baseball Ground'. His belief was that the 'squad is good enough right now to be standing very much higher in the table than we are', and he underlined his awareness of the 'target man' issue.

He wrote in the feature entitled Dave's Diary, 'Pressure is what football management is all about. And a man who can't take it should not be in the job. But it doesn't mean he enjoys it.

'This is the first time I have had to face any difficult problems since overcoming my initial crisis at the Baseball Ground.

'Panic now would be even worse than doing nothing. And doing just that is what I am being accused of, because the much-needed target man to play alongside Charlie George has not yet arrived.

'There were those who openly disapproved when I brought in Charlie George and Francis Lee and when I brought Bruce Rioch up from the Second Division. What we are going to do is to get a striker who can provide us with what we are missing at the moment … Someone who can crack the ball as well as slot it into space for people like Charlie and Bruce to run on to.

'We have looked long and hard for the man who can do this exact job with the players we already have. Up to now we haven't found him because the players who fit exactly into the job are not available. And those who might do it haven't convinced my staff nor myself yet.

'It's no earthly use paying, say, £150,000 for someone who we are not certain can do the job. That really WOULD turn out to be a crisis!

'Without doubt the team's performances come up to all other expectations. At Goodison last Saturday there was universal agreement amongst the neutral that we dominated the game for long spells and were undoubtedly the better team on everything but goals.

'There were errors. Both goals could be traced to defensive mistakes, but most goals can be traced back to just that.

'At the other end we forced mistakes out of Everton but the ball didn't go into the net. This isn't a catalogue of excuses, just hard facts. We know the need, are acutely aware of it, in fact, and have been since the season started. Injuries, suspension and bad luck like that, which brought Everton's opening goal last Saturday, just have to be accepted as the way the ball runs. They affect results but have to be accepted as part of the game.

'Yet the squad is good enough right now to be standing very much higher in the table than we are. If the breaks start going our way and we start cashing in on it as we ought we can start stringing a few good results together. And that will lift our confidence sky high. That's the priority and then an additional striker of the right type class, and temperament could give us that extra boost right back towards the top.

'Many of this squad will be at their peaks during the next 18 months or so and it would be a tragedy if we didn't get to grips and extract the maximum from their potential.'

Mackay was annoyed by those at Derby he felt were still hankering for the return of the dynamic duo, Brian Clough and Peter Taylor. The quest would be illusory with Clough and Taylor busy lifting Nottingham Forest to third spot and the First Division title the following season before back-to-back European Cups.

He said, 'Some people at Derby believed Brian was just waiting to return to his spiritual home and now was the time to push me out … I was aware these sentiments were only silenced because it was impossible to argue with the club's achievements since Brian left. What did make me angry and upset was that the knives were out at the first run of bad form. We were not seriously threatened with relegation.

'I was beginning to lose interest anyway at that time because I wasn't happy with the board. Sam Longson had been moved aside, and I'd already won the league. One of the board members, George Hardy, a scrap millionaire, wanted Cloughie back. Even before he joined the board that was his ambition. But Brian said there was no way he was coming back. I told George, there's only one way the club will go with you in charge: down. I was right.'

Mackay had implemented what he had learned about management from his previous bosses, Tommy Walker at Hearts, Bill Nicholson at Spurs and his Derby predecessor Brian Clough and, largely, it served him well until the golfers on the Rams' board decided otherwise.

He said, 'Tommy was a perfect gentleman and very religious. Bill was the same, though he could get a little annoyed. Neither would shout. But Brian would. As a manager, I never lost it with anyone. The main thing for me was to be reasonable and above all honest with players. If you'd had a bad game, I'm not going to say you've done well; I'll say you were crap and you need to pick up or else. But you get different types of manager who are successful.'

Gerald Mortimer, who reported on the Rams for the *Derby Telegraph* from 1970 until 2002, said of the sacking of Mackay and Anderson in *Derby County The Complete Record* in 2006, 'It was an astonishing decision because they were at least entitled to be given time. It seemed the worst thing that a manager could do at the Baseball Ground was to win the championship and nothing that has happened since has in any way diminished Mackay's stature and achievements. Third, first and fourth in three seasons: those credentials should have impressed even Derby's board.'

Mackay's dismissal provoked back-page headlines. And, given his finely tuned sense of humour observed by those close to him, he would have seen the funny side of Ronnie Barker, as Norman Stanley Fletcher, reading and holding up a tabloid declaring 'Mackay sacked' as his prison officer of the same name entered his cell in the classic TV comedy *Porridge*.

Perhaps he hadn't lived up to the expectations of the directors – or even the Bring Back Clough campaigners – who had been fed a diet of success since Mackay turned up. Those board members and supporters, maybe, forgot the thin gruel they had been served for their supper before the Scot's arrival. Derby had lifted the 1946 FA Cup and taken the 1957 Third Division North championship, but you had to go back to 1915 for their only other significant triumph, the second-tier title.

Striker George said, 'I didn't think Dave should have been sacked and I respected him so much; he brought me to Derby so I was gutted to see him leave. Once he left, I wasn't the same player, that's for sure. I think we could have turned it around with the players we had.'

Roy McFarland said, 'I'm privileged to have played with Dave and then be managed by him. And know him and be invited to his house. He was unbelievable. It sounds crazy, I suppose, but I just love the guy. Forget the football, he was a great, great guy.'

Colin Todd, who went on to manage Derby and others said, 'We [the players] all had a good relationship with Dave. I know Dave and Des Anderson were proud of me when I won the PFA Player of the Year award. We had some great times at Derby with Dave. He had taken the club forward again to win the championship. We did quite well in the European Cup the season after and qualified for Europe again the following season.

'He could handle the characters like Charlie George, and get the best out of them when those players came in. He believed in himself as a player and he certainly saw himself as a good manager. He had a lot of confidence in himself, and why not when you have a championship win under your belt? He was like a peacock, you know. Pluming, he strutted round, and stuck his chest out.

'When Dave went Colin Murphy came in and then Tommy Docherty. The wheels started to come off then. It is a tragedy that after winning the championship, although the next season wasn't bad, it didn't happen again. And in management if it doesn't happen you've got to take the consequences.

'I must have learned from Dave and Cloughie because I went on to win a championship as a manager with Bolton, succeeding Bruce Rioch, which put us into the Premiership. You don't take everything on board. But you must take something, especially when they have a successful spell as Dave did, and give credit to them.'

John McGovern, who had moved on to Nottingham Forest via Leeds by the time of Mackay's departure from the Baseball Ground, hinted he shared his old boss's frustrations at his employers.

McGovern said, 'Dave did okay as a manager. I've tried the management game myself and tended to take over clubs that were "on fire". Somebody said, "You are a fire fighter." You try and do a job. Then you find the difficulties of management because of the lack of knowledge of the people you are working for regarding how the game is played and what is required out here on the field.'

There is no question that Mackay had the Derby dressing room, given the respect shown by his players. Colin Murphy, who had been appointed reserve team coach by Mackay, was put in temporary charge then became the permanent successor in February 1977 when the club accepted that their bid to lure back Clough and Taylor had failed after Clough himself informed Hardy of his decision for the pair to stay at the City Ground.

Murphy's law ensured a run to the last eight of the FA Cup but no trees were pulled up in the league as the side finished 15th, although defender Ron Webster was able to pass the 62-year-old appearance record of 525 held by legendary striker Steve Bloomer when he played in a 1-1 draw at Sunderland in the April. Derby were knocked out of the League Cup in the fifth round by Bolton after Mackay had guided them to the stage.

Mackay's departure signalled a downturn in Derby's fortunes. Tommy Docherty replaced Murphy in September 1977, selling crowd favourite George to Southampton, before being replaced by Colin Addison, and by the end of the decade Derby were back in the Second Division. There were also developing financial troubles and the club faced winding-up petitions from the Inland Revenue and Customs and Excise in 1983/84 – lifted with the help of media baron Robert Maxwell – while slipping to the Third Division for their centenary season the following term.

Dave Mackay with his dad Thomas and daughters Julie and Valerie

Dave Mackay sitting in an armchair with grandchildren Lisa and Derek

Isobel and Dave Mackay with six grandchildren and a nephew. Left to right: Lisa, Craig (nephew), Daniel, Lucy, Lois, Ria, Gregor

Six grandchildren in front of Scottish flags with trophies won by Mackay. Left to right: Lucy, Lois, Gregor, Ria, Daniel, Lisa

Mackay with brother-in-law Pat Dixon

Grandchildren Lucy and Ria in the Dave Mackay Lounge at Pride Park with poster of our subject in Derby kit

Dave Mackay with trophies

Mackay with dad Thomas and brothers Frank and Tommy

Ninian Cassidy (left) with Dave Mackay

Mackay with grandson Gregor and daughter Valerie and trophy won with Zamalek

Dave Mackay enjoying a reception with brothers Frank and Tommy on a tribute night for our subject at the Marriott Hotel in London in the late 1990s.

Craig Dixon, Mackay's nephew, Joe Kinnear, when Newcastle United manager, Dave Mackay and brother-in-law Tom Dixon at St James' Park

Joe Kinnear and Dave Mackay at St James' Park

Craig Dixon, Ninian Cassidy and Dave Mackay in Newcastle dressing room on visit to St James' Park

Harry Redknapp, when Spurs manager, and Dave Mackay at St James' Park

Isobel Mackay in front of a portrait of her late husband, a depiction of the lap of honour at Wembley after Spurs completed the Double by winning the 1961 FA Cup

Dave Mackay signing autographs outside Pride Park

Dave Mackay with Alfie Conn Junior while attending the Hearts v Spurs Europa League play-off at Tynecastle in August 2011

Dave Mackay gives a thumbs up to Spurs fans at White Hart Lane while at the second leg of Europa League play-off against Hearts in August 2011

*Mackay in the
Dave Mackay
Lounge at Pride
Park*

*Jimmy Greaves (left) hugs old Spurs team-mate Dave Mackay at the Royal Mail Stamp launch
at Wembley in 2013 with Gordon Banks and Bobby Charlton looking on*

Sir Alex Ferguson (left) with Dave and Isobel Mackay. Sir Alex often invited our subject to attend Old Trafford when manager of Manchester United

Derek and David Junior with our subject and copy of commemorative stamp

Mackay shows Graeme Souness one of his awards

Dave Mackay's former team-mates Roy McFarland (Derby), Pat Jennings (Spurs) and Gordon Marshall (Hearts) await the cortege at Dave Mackay's funeral service in Edinburgh in March 2015

Sir Alex Ferguson (left) and Denis Law leave the church after Dave Mackay's funeral service

DAVE MACKAY
NOVEMBER 14, 1934 - MARCH 2, 2015

MEMORIAL SERVICE
THE PARISH CHURCH
OF ST STEPHEN
BUSH HILL PARK
THURSDAY, APRIL 30, 2015

Memorial service programme

Isobel with Dave Mackay statue at Pride Park

The Dave Mackay Clock at Pride Park

Dave Mackay's widow Isobel, daughter Valerie and brothers Tommy and Frank at the Forever In Our Hearts Memorial Garden

The Mackay family, plus former Spurs team-mates of our subject and their wives on the tour of White Hart Lane organised by John Jackson (far right) in 2017. Those pictured include Cliff Jones and Alan Gilzean (third and fourth left back row) and Pat Jennings (back row, third from right), along with Eleanor Jennings (second right back row) and Joanie Jones (far right, front row). It was the family's last visit to the stadium

Joan and Cliff Jones, Isobel Mackay and Alan Gilzean on tour of White Hart Lane in 2017

Isobel Mackay with returned Scotland shirt and (left to right) Julie, Derek, David Junior and Valerie

Mackay's children Valerie and David Junior having fun

David Junior and Derek Mackay with the family's 'lucky' Hearts gnome on the day they watched the Jam Tarts defeat Celtic, on a record run of positive results, 4-0 on television

Dave Mackay enjoying life

The Mackay Clan, Left to right, Julie (front left) Valerie (back left) , David Junior, Derek (standing), son-in-law Denis, Dave and Isobel

Derek Mackay with Lindsay Gascoigne, sister of Paul, one of the legends to succeed his dad in the Spurs midfield, at the Back Page Shop in the Metro Centre in Newcastle

Valerie Mackay at White Hart Lane

Julie Mackay in 2021

Derek Mackay at the Tottenham Hotspur Stadium

In the wake of his sacking, Mackay waited. Hoping, perhaps, that Spurs might put him back on the payroll after their relegation but his old club kept a justified faith in Keith Burkinshaw who eventually brought back the good, if not glory, times with the help of Glenn Hoddle and Argentinian World Cup-winning pair Ossie Ardiles and Ricky Villa.

But Mackay revealed he was far from inundated with job offers, despite his recent achievements as a manager. It was a strange time, the first he had experienced of being out of work since leaving school and becoming an apprentice joiner. It was an opportunity to recharge the batteries and spend quality time with his family. It also brought money worries. Even though viewed as having an iron will and mental strength to match, he, understandably, found the experience of being out of the game and out of work for the first time scary and 'salutary'. What would the future hold?

A telephone call was to signal the end of four months of unemployment. It came from Ken Wheldon, the owner of Walsall. The millionaire haulier wanted Mackay to prove himself a superhero and rescue his club from relegation in the 1977/78 campaign.

Wheldon's Fellows Park outfit had slipped into the danger zone under Doug Fraser. The former Scotland international had helped the Saddlers pull off shock FA Cup wins against Newcastle United and Manchester United in 1975 and achieved respectable finishes of eighth and seventh in his two full seasons in charge.

But his side got into a pickle in the 1976/77 season and on 7 March 1977 he left Fellows Park, quit football and entered the prison service as a warder at a Nottingham jail.

Mackay wanted to hear more and agreed to meet Wheldon. He had understood that Wheldon enjoyed a reputation for being tight with money, but the Walsall supremo disproved the theory with an offer his target felt was a 'mouth-watering sum' if he could keep the Saddlers from sinking into the Fourth Division.

Our subject was up for the challenge and started his latest career chapter on 9 March 1977. He said, 'I was happy to rebuild my managerial career over at Fellows Park.'

The fact he had to get the results to pick up his full payment did not daunt Mackay. He had eight games to complete his SOS mission and collect his reward.

It was completed after just four, a 1-0 home win over Brighton & Hove Albion and goalless away draws against Oxford United and, securing the final point needed, York City, following a defeat at home to Mansfield Town. Mackay was able to guide the side to the comfort of 15th place and he was delighted to discover he had a quality striker in Alan Buckley, who scored four goals in the eight games. He was also helped by inheriting former Leeds United player Mick Bates.

Mackay was happy to commit to another season at the helm. He delved into his past to pick up players from former clubs. Tommy Docherty, in charge at Derby by this time, sold him Henry Newton, Jeff King and Tony Macken, while former Spurs team-mate and FA Cup-scoring hero Jimmy Robertson linked up again with his old captain.

Newton had been a member of Mackay's title-winning Rams team after spells at Nottingham Forest and Everton. The versatile midfielder or defender was a former England under-23 international. Winger King had helped Mackay's Derby complete the 1975/76 season with a six-goal pounding of Ipswich Town. Macken was a right-back who could operate in midfield. Mackay had given him his Football League debut in a 2-0 win over Aston Villa on 27 December 1975 and also played him in the return fixture that season. He had gone on loan to Portsmouth and to Washington Diplomats and Dallas Tornado.

Scotland international Robertson also ended up at Fellows Park via the United States where he was playing for Seattle Sounders after spells at Arsenal, Ipswich Town and Stoke City following his Lane departure.

Mackay was also able to call on Alun Evans, the former Liverpool striker, who had missed the latter part of the previous season.

He was rewarded with a fine season at a club whose expectations were lower than the ones he had had to get used to. Sixth spot, with the help of his new recruits and 24 goals from the ever-present Buckley, was over and above what was anticipated, especially after the struggles of the previous season.

And a run from the first to the fifth round of the FA Cup, which included victory over top-flight Leicester City, had the Black Country outfit's faithful in dreamland.

Mackay's troops faced a star-studded Arsenal, who included Liam Brady, David O'Leary, Frank Stapleton, Malcolm Macdonald and the boss's ex-Spurs team-mate Pat Jennings for a place in the quarter-finals at Highbury on 18 February 1978.

Walsall had something to hang on to from their previous meeting 45 years earlier when they had stunned Herbert Chapman's Gunners 2-0 before 11,150 disbelievers at Fellows Park. That encounter – on 14 January 1933 – came when stars Alex James, David Jack, Cliff Bastin and George Male lined up for the opposition. It was the season that Arsenal won their second of five First Division titles in the decade.

But Mackay's would-be giant-killers came away from north London having lost 4-1 before nearly 44,000, with a Buckley goal their lone consolation.

Mackay said, 'There was quite a lot of publicity before the match because Walsall had knocked the Gunners out of the FA Cup some 40 years earlier in one of the most famous acts of giant-killing ever.

'No such luck this time round. They tore us apart and were 3-0 up at half-time. If it hadn't been for the superb efforts of Mick Kearns in goal, it might have been ten. Our defender Colin Harrison had a great game as did veterans Mick Bates and Alun Evans.'

Robertson was sidelined for the showdown against the club he joined after switching White Hart Lane for Highbury in a swap deal with David Jenkins in October 1968, having suffered a torn cartilage after just 16 league appearances for Walsall.

Robertson said, 'I went to America to play for Seattle Sounders for a second time after my contract was up at Stoke [in 1977]. I'd recovered from a broken leg I'd sustained when I went out there halfway through the previous season. Dave contacted me. I verbally agreed to come to Walsall when I came back from America and I stuck by it. But I couldn't repay him. Unfortunately it wasn't the happiest time for me. I think I was only there about three or four months and tore the cartilage. I only went there because of Dave in the first place.'

Mackay had also recruited his former Nottingham Forest striker Neil Martin as youth team coach. Martin said, 'I stayed with Dave during the week and went home to a place I had in Brighton after the match at the weekend. I had a good time at Walsall working for Dave. He was a smashing guy.'

There was optimism going into the 1978/79 campaign on the back of the previous season's efforts. Mackay said, 'I thought we had a realistic chance of getting out of the Third Division.' But everything changed and Alan Ashman, the former West Bromwich Albion manager, was recruited to lead the Saddlers into the new campaign, while Mackay looked for his passport, along with Martin.

Isobel Mackay said, 'I remember Ken Wheldon arriving at our house in his big Rolls-Royce to get David to go to Walsall. I went there once or twice but David wasn't there long. The Middle East came calling.'

32

The cradle of civilisation

ANOTHER OUT-OF-THE-BLUE phone call led to Dave Mackay leaving his career in the West Midlands for one in the Middle East, from the working-class heart of the Industrial Revolution in the Black Country to the oil-rich Persian Gulf and Kuwait, nearly 4,000 miles away.

When Mackay's phone rang, a ceasefire in the troubled region between Egypt and Israel, overseen by the United Nations, was holding. And a month after his arrival, the Camp David Accords saw Egyptian president Anwar Sadat and Menachem Begin, the Israeli prime minister, sign political agreements that led to a peace treaty which earned the pair a share of the 1978 Nobel Peace Prize.

The UN Yearbook for 1978 added, 'It was emphasised in the report that, despite the prevailing quiet in the Egypt-Israel sector, the situation in the Middle East as a whole continued to be unstable and potentially dangerous and was likely to remain so unless and until a comprehensive settlement covering all aspects of the Middle East problem could be reached.'

Mackay revealed in his 2004 autobiography that he never felt any threat to 'our personal safety' during his working assignments in Kuwait, where he spent the most time across two spells working in the transcontinental region. He wrote, 'The cultural tensions that have become such a worry as I write never seemed to encroach upon us at that time. The English [the concept of a Scotsman was not really recognised] were almost revered and were certainly top of the pecking order of respect amongst expatriates.'

The original call had come from Mousa Raschid, who proved to be a go-between. He was a pal of Mohammed Al-Mulla, chairman of Kuwaiti club Al-Arabi. He wanted Mackay to meet him 'and his friend' at the Park Lane hotel in London's West End to discuss 'a football matter'.

Mackay brought along Des Anderson for support and discovered that Mr Al-Mulla had watched and admired Spurs' Double side while being educated in England and saw meeting 'a hero' as 'the greatest honour'. Al-Mulla wanted to turn his mid-table team into one to challenge for the Kuwaiti league and was convinced Mackay was the man for the job.

The chairman got straight to the point and offered Mackay the opportunity of managing Al-Arabi. Mackay asked for and got a salary of £40,000, the equivalent of five times that amount today, wary of the lack of guaranteed income in his chosen field.

Mackay kept Ken Wheldon up to speed and the Walsall chairman advised him to go for the Middle East deal, but to make sure he got something up front. He did – £12,000.

He wanted Anderson to go with him to Kuwait but his regular assistant had taken over a pub. Neil Martin, his former striker at Nottingham Forest, Walsall youth team coach and friend who was keen to launch a career as a manager, got the job.

And there was plenty to occupy Mackay and Martin as they settled into their new employment. As well as the football, there was the adapting to a new lifestyle and culture. Mackay said, 'I got to grips with the culture very quickly.'

The Mackays enjoyed the great outdoors, with the country's sunshine and beaches, as well as making friends and attending barbecues and dinner parties, plus the lack of traffic jams.

The pace of life was slow, with religion a daily part. The men and women wore light and dark ankle-length, loose-fitting thobes respectively; females also donned yashmaks to hide their faces. Skyscrapers, plush hotels and top-of-the-range motors reflected the wealth. People were friendly, respectful, polite – and blunt.

Mackay revealed in his autobiography how a club official told him he was 'very fat' on his first visit to the Sabah Al-Salem Stadium, Al-Arabi's ground. The comment prompted him to go on a diet that worked so well his youngest daughter Julie asked him when he arrived back home in Burton Joyce, 'Dad, where did your body go?'

The Al-Arabi players were part-timers. The majority were either students or trainees in a trade – as Mackay himself was when with Hearts – or students, with army and police force professionals thrown in. Mackay was surprised at the decent standard some of them had reached.

Al-Mulla helped with any communication issues early doors but Mackay soon found a way to work. He said, 'Most of them [could] speak English or semi-English. They weren't dummies. I could speak a bit of Arabic but didn't have to.'

Mackay went close to leading Al-Arabi – based at Mansuriya, in the country's capital of Kuwait City – to the crown in his first season, but had to settle for second spot when his side could only draw instead of beating Kuwait City, their big rivals.

But it was second time lucky as the Scot managed Al-Mulla's pride and joy to their first league title in ten years the following season. He was in charge for four more league triumphs, two Kuwait Emir Cup successes and the lifting of the biennial Gulf Cup organised by the Arab Gulf Cup Federation for its eight member states in its inaugural season, as well as claiming a treble in a glittering path to glory over his eight years with the club.

Mackay's efforts got the attention of the Emir. He was invited to take tea with the country's ruler by club patron Sheikh Fahd, a member of the Kuwaiti royal family. He said, 'Sheikh Fahd was a lovely man who had a passion for football.'

Mackay sought a fresh challenge and, in 1986 after being linked to the Scotland manager's job, which went to Andy Roxburgh, aged 52 he accepted an offer to boss Dubai side Al-Shabab in the United Arab Emirates.

He took Martin with him and signed up former Tottenham team-mate Joe Kinnear to coach the youth players after Kinnear had started his management career at Sharjah, which borders Dubai to the north.

Mackay found that Al-Shabab's players were a shadow of the ones he worked with at Al-Arabi and, despite the best efforts of the management team, the results failed to materialise. By the end of the season Mackay and Co. were history. The Scot had no grumbles and Al-Shabab had paid him big bucks.

So Mackay and his wife Isobel, after a decade away, returned to Burton Joyce. They had missed the wave of new romantic music, most of Margaret Thatcher's time as British prime minister with the rise of yuppies wearing wide-red trouser braces and the wedding of Prince Charles to Diana, Princess of Wales, plus the warming of the Cold War. There was no panic to boost the family coffers as he had earned a decent salary in the Middle East.

Mackay was content to cast his fate to the wind, but he still considered himself vital and keen to find another job in the game.

Neil Martin said of the decision to go to the Middle East with Mackay, 'Well, money-wise there was no comparison. You couldn't have turned it down. And we really had a great time.

'It was funny. When we arrived at the airport – Dave was pretty heavy then – a big embassy car came up to the plane. The steps were brought and we went straight down the steps into the car. It was unbelievable.

'This was all going on when one of the main men at the club said to Dave, "Mackay? You coach?" Dave said yes. He said, "You are too fat to be a coach."

'They were smashing people but they had their way. Dave just killed himself laughing. But we were playing squash every morning for a couple of hours before an afternoon siesta and it soon got his weight down. Dave was a brilliant squash player. I think I beat him once. Even in training games he had to win. Colin Todd said when he was at Derby in these sort of games it was like a tank hitting you when he came up against Dave.

'There were one or two British coaches already out there and they said, "You'll struggle with the team at Al-Arabi you've got now because it is all just young players coming through." But we only got pipped for the league in the first season on the last game. Then we started to win the trophies regularly,

'How did we turn it around? The players were there. There were no transfers in Kuwait, and you had to be a Kuwaiti to play. So you just had to have whatever you had. We were lucky that all the young players we had were really good and keen to learn. It was an oil-rich country and its prince was one of our team. He wasn't a particularly good player but all the other players respected him with him being the prince. At training he used to turn up in his Rolls-Royce but was just one of the lads.

'Climate was a contrast to home. It was very hot, of course. We trained at nine o'clock at night and couldn't have trained through the day. The games were all at night, played on proper grass. Al-Arabi had a lovely stadium. All the clubs did. You couldn't ask for better facilities.

'I did the training and ran with the players. I was still pretty fit, then. I gave them plenty of physical training. They went through the mill and were sick a few times, but they loved it and were easily the most physical team in the league. We used to run teams into the ground in the last 20 minutes. In fact, when I came home for a year to Walsall, they phoned me up, saying, "We want you to come back." Dave was there on his own and they weren't getting trained as hard. They were all delighted I went back again!

'We also worked on set-pieces. Dave used to get those organised. The lad who was the captain had been there for a few years and was well respected and spoke very good English. He led the line in training. So anything you said, he would translate it back to the other players in Arabic. We didn't have a problem that way.

'The players loved Dave. They thought we were brilliant. Winning the games made all the difference. And they went from being down the bottom of the league to winning the league all the time.

'Nearly all the players in the teams were policemen or in the army or air force. None of them really had any jobs. To play for one of the teams, they were top boys.

'They used to wear white robes called either dishdasha or thobe. Dave and I used to wear just our normal stuff. At training it was just tracksuits and all the rest of it. Money was no problem. You could get any gear you wanted.

'There were two Kuwaiti lads who were involved with Dave and I and the team and they spoke perfect English. Anything we wanted, we just told them and it would get done.

'The boy who said Davie was too fat said to me after a couple of years, "You should be speaking Arabic by now." It was a horrible language for me to pick up although other British coaches did but we said no. It was too easy for us with the captain speaking such good English. Mind you, when I came back from Walsall, Dave had picked up one or two Arabic words.

'Dave and I stayed in the same two-bedroom flat. I did the cooking, which was simple. They had supermarkets out there which did English food. It was brilliant. But we got a decent meal when our wives came out. The hoovering and tidying up was left to me.

'Socially, we went to a lot of parties with other coaches in their houses. The families came out for the holidays and we'd go down the beach, but it was too hot to sunbathe.

'We came across a few British coaches who came out there. Geoff Hurst was one. We met up with him at the Hilton Hotel in the city. He was going to sign a contract for Kuwait City, a big club, and Dave went along with him and helped him get more! We secured one title win in the last game against Geoff's team.

'In our last year, Dave signed for £70,000 and I signed for £55,000. Money wasn't a problem over there.

'During that year, Dave went home for a few weeks and I stayed on. Dave wanted me to take the army team for the physical side of their preparation for a cup competition against Iran, Iraq and Qatar for six weeks. He wasn't involved. Most of our club players were in the army team. They weren't a bad side. Tottenham came in and played them and only just won.

'I met Saddam Hussein before the game against Iraq. That was quite a thing to remember. As nearly all our players were in the army, you were dealing more or less with the same players, and just one or two others of the top teams. They were good quality footballers with the physical now added to their game.

'Dave and I met all the country's top boys. Any team we played, it was back to their mansions. We got invited to the palace in Kuwait when we won the league. Just the men. No women.

'We used to be invited to the big mansion in Kuwait regularly and the men would eat first and the women went to the table afterwards. They did not eat with us, even wives. It was the same when we were guests at a London mansion one had. It was funny to start with. Dave used to get Isobel, his wife, going, joking, "We'll see what we leave you."

'Dave's dad Tom came out one time. It was a Friday, which is their Sunday. All the top boys go to the desert with their servants and huge tents are set up.

'We sat around a table, eating rice. Dave's dad looked over at what he thought was semolina with dates on top and said, "I'll think I'll have that pudding." I went to get it for him when one of the boys put his hand over the top. It was covered in flies rather than dates! It put Tom off!

'When Dave got the chance to go to Dubai he told me it was only a job for one. I said, "That's not a problem, I'll stay in Kuwait." They wanted me. Anyway, he got me to go along to the Hilton to meet the people from Dubai and he asked them, "What about Neil?" They didn't have a problem so I went with Dave to Dubai.

'Dubai was more modern and civilised, but wasn't as built up as it is now. Dave and I lived in our own flats and took our wives and children out there. My daughter used to go to an English school without air-conditioning in the middle of the desert. Her face was like a tomato on the bus back home!

'But football-wise it was a disaster. The team hadn't done anything for years. Unlike Al-Arabi it didn't have good youngsters coming through. Not much chance of success. You knew after the first month you weren't going to do anything. And if you don't get success you are out of the door there. It is all about winning. We were there a year and came back.'

Joe Kinnear said of his time in the Middle East, 'The experience was all right. We got a lot of money out of it and the lifestyle wasn't too bad. The standard of football was less than we were used to. We went around the schools and got a youth team out.'

Bonnie Kinnear, Joe's wife, said, 'We were close to Dave and Isobel. We used to meet up, sit round the pool or go to country clubs. I'm sure they enjoyed it as a family. Dave's dad Tom was out there and there is a picture of him with Dave and Joe on New Year's Eve. Dave was a great character. A lovely man.

'He was a good, strong character. The salt of the earth. The most generous person, and would do things for people. A family man, through and through.

'Joe was fine. He's easy-going and mixes easily. People were warm to him. I don't think they'd met anyone like him! Most of them were friendly to us all.

'You saw goalposts everywhere. We had been in Nepal [before the Middle East] and the Gurkha who played for Joe, the country's national coach, would kick lumps out of the opposition yet I don't think there were many promising young footballers [in Dubai].

'I went to the matches as it was okay for wives to attend. Otherwise I did not see any other women – although I see women are allowed to go now – and the wonderful stadiums were hardly filled.

'You were aware of restrictions in the country, especially being female. I had to have my husband's permission to drive. They would stop and ask you if you are married if seen driving. [You had to] be careful how you dressed, no short skirts. But if you behaved and lived your life like you would in any country it was fine.

'It was a semi-dry state. But being expats you were allowed to drink in certain circumstances in hotels but you had to be careful. It was like being at home even though you were away. You couldn't fault the lifestyle. Wonderful restaurants with the best food and wine imaginable. Terrific camel racing in the desert too, and a wonderful golf course. We were well looked after. I also worked in marketing, setting up exhibitions. I thought Dubai was wonderful, one of the best years of our lives. You had the best of everything.

'But the wheels came off with the football. The club had had enough and so had Joe. He wanted to come back to England to work.'

Isobel believes Dave and the family had an 'amazing' experience going out to the Middle East.

She said, 'Going to the Middle East was a big move. Amazing. A bit different, wasn't it? We made lots of Arab friends as well. In Kuwait, David just got on with it. He was the least domesticated man I've ever known. He could do nothing, David! I though, "Oh my God, what's he gonna do?"

'Before he went out there's a story. We went to London to pick up his tickets. My brother and his wife were with us. We stopped at what we thought was the house which had the tickets. They didn't know anything about it. He thinks it is a hoax. But he finds a number and gets the right address. I said to him, "It's not a hoax now, David." We all waited having cups of tea while David spoke to Al-Arabi. He got his tickets and money, and said, "Right, let's go shopping to Harrods."

'We got there and David wanted to buy a music system, record player, with a built-in cabinet. It was £4,000. I said to David, "I'm going to ask for a discount." He said, "Don't you dare." So I went over to the chap and asked, "Is there a discount if we pay cash?" He said, "I'll just go and ask." He came back and said, "How does £400 sound?"

I said, "That'd be lovely." David turned to me and said, "Good girl, good girl."

'We went for a meal then my sister-in-law Anne-Marie and me went shopping, and my brother Pat and David went to a casino. We had an allotted time when we'd meet up. I had bought a coat in this sale, and Anne-Marie had bought something in it too. They [Pat and David] had won at the casino. A few days later David was away to Kuwait.

'The flat he got put into had no air-conditioning. He said, "I'm not staying here." So they put him up in a hotel which suited him. Eventually he got a flat with air-conditioning. You needed air-conditioning, my god. And I don't know how he managed, to tell you the truth. He didn't know how to use a washing machine. He didn't know anything.

'Luckily enough he took Neil Martin. They were neighbours of ours nearby at Foxhill Road in Burton Joyce. Neil was a Forest player when we went there. Des Anderson was to go, but he didn't. So David asked Neil. Well, Neil was the opposite to David. He was very domesticated.

'I used to go out quite a lot. It was a different way of life, culture. They were so good to David. It was unbelievable how they took to him, in particular Mohammed Al-Mulla, the chairman. So nice.

'There was one or two expats there – coaches Brian Doyle, former Arsenal player George Armstrong, George Blues and Johnny Quigley – and we used to meet up at each other's flats.'

Son Derek said, 'The family went out at different times. Us four children were grown up and used to have turns in going out. I went with grandad, dad's dad, mum and family friend George "Pie" Collins. Mum used to go to and fro for longer spells.

'Al-Arabi was a sports club. Besides football, there were volleyball, basketball, swimming and squash teams. They had the Swedish squash champion. He was there to coach. Dad used to love squash and him and this guy played each other for a bet. Whoever lost had to buy the other a meal at this hotel in Kuwait. It was expensive. Probably still is. Dad beat him.'

An article on the Jambos Kickback website, posted the day after Mackay's passing in 2015, explained how Kuwaiti fans felt about our subject's time at Al-Arabi. It read:

'The 1980s was filled with glamour, not just in football but in the whole country overall. Under the new management of Dave Mackay,

Al-Arabi won seven league trophies, two Prince Cups and one Gulf Club Championship. As a Scotsman, many modern-day football analysts look back at the 1980s golden years and compare Dave Mackay to his compatriot Sir Alex Ferguson of Manchester United. Some even call him the "Sir Alex of Kuwait". Indeed, Dave Mackay became known as not only the most successful manager in Al-Arabi's history but also the most successful club manager in Kuwait's entire football history.'

33

Dubai to Doncaster

DUBAI TO Doncaster. That was the next step on the managerial career path for Dave Mackay – and another culture shock.

This time it took him from the oil-rich, luxury tourist hub of the United Arab Emirates' most populous city, which was built on a mangrove swamp from around 7000 BC, to working in a sweet-toothed South Yorkshire market town, part of England's industrial heritage of just over 300,000 folk famed for the production of Murray Mints and Nuttall's Mintoes; its Roman roots dating back merely to the first century AD.

Mackay's 27-month stay with Doncaster Rovers – a mere 40 instead of 4,000 miles from the family home in Burton Joyce – was less sweet and more bitter, or at least less memorable by his standards despite his best efforts.

When your author asked the charming Darren Moore, Rovers' manager in 2020/21 before he moved to Sheffield Wednesday, and a Donny player in the mid-1990s, to speak of what he knew of Mackay's time at the club, the former defender was apologetic as he confessed his box of knowledge on our subject's spell was empty. Moore's approachable Donny defender Joe Wright was the same. The club, post-Mackay, did eventually move on up to the second tier before its residence in the third in the first part of 2021. Yet it seems Mackay was unable to scatter his stardust enough for modern-day incumbents to recall his part in the club's history in an instant due to the negative effect financial limitations placed on progress.

Mackay had been unconcerned about not being offered a 'top-level job' on his return from the Middle East. He said, 'I'd had my fill. But I'd never phoned asking anyone for a job; they phoned me. I liked playing better. Managing was the second best, but I still had a hunger: if we lost I was gutted. If we won I was delighted.'

Besides, Mackay had been in no rush to find employment after a decade 'earning good money' abroad. But he remained vital and keen to work again, although was 'surprised' there was an offer – through Donny – to come back to English football so soon. He took charge at the club in December 1987.

He inherited a difficult task when replacing the sacked Dave Cusack, who had been hampered by squad injuries, illness, transfer ins-and-outs and erratic results. Cusack only had 12 fit players for the 1987/88 opener against Grimsby Town, which Rovers won before four losses on the bounce put them in the relegation zone. After three straight wins, Donny suffered five reverses to plonk them back into the dogfight to avoid the drop.

The club were initially deducted two points under new Football League rules for postponing a fixture with Chester City on 10 October despite having 11 players sidelined with a stomach bug, before they were restored on appeal. Cusack's Rovers had also exited the League Cup in round two against eventual finalists Arsenal.

The town was abuzz that someone with the respected stature of Mackay – with Joe Kinnear as his assistant – had taken the reins. But the magic wand wasn't handy and Mackay was only able to squeeze three more league wins from the rest of the season as Donny slid into the fourth tier. Rovers also fell at the first hurdle in the FA Cup to county compatriots Rotherham United, by then managed by Cusack.

It was all hardly surprising. The club had a solid fan base but, Mackay felt, 'had no money' and was 'finding it difficult to survive'.

Mackay perceived – almost from the off – that the people who ran the club needed him to sell off players to boost coffers to stay afloat.

According to *Donny: The Official History of Doncaster Rovers*, every player was put up for transfer at the end of February 1988, with first-choice goalkeeper Andy Rhodes sold to Oldham Athletic for £55,000 the following month, although Mackay was able to spend £20,000 of that to bring in Les Robinson from Stockport County. And eight players were given free transfers at the end of the season, including player-coach Micky Stead who was a full-back at Tottenham in the mid-1970s.

Another man Mackay flogged was Brian Deane. The striker was transferred to Sheffield United for what the boss reported was £40,000, played for England and scored the first goal in the new Premier League, against Manchester United on 15 August 1992, before costing Leeds United a club-record £2.9m.

Mackay also nurtured young defender Rufus Brevett, who gave Rovers hope for the future by helping the club reach the FA Youth Cup Final during the Scot's first season and was eventually sold to QPR in 1991 for £150,000, a record fee received by the club until 2009/10.

Mackay often selected other members of the youth team in a season in which Donny used 33 players. And his kids' successful run in the FA Youth Cup persuaded the town's council to loan the club £90,000 and guarantee they would be able to start the 1988/89 season.

Rovers chairman Bernie Boldry insisted that the money would go towards tarting up Belle Vue and player recruitment. Mackay brought in four players, including Gerry Daly, the Republic of Ireland international and former Manchester United midfielder, from Stoke City, and former Newcastle junior striker Paul Dobson from Torquay United. There was hope that the mix of youth and experience would enable Mackay's Donny to bounce back to the Third Division at the first attempt.

But it did not go to plan. Mackay kept his team on course for a play-off spot up until the turn of the year, before matters went off the rails. Dobson, Rovers' chief source of goals with an average of one every other game, twice demanded a transfer after being dropped and the manager said anyone who 'wasn't happy' was 'no good' for the club, so Dobson was sold to Scarborough for £40,000. Also, the Inland Revenue presented Donny with a winding-up petition related to an £86,000 tax bill in December, although the club was saved by the directors paying it off with their own money.

It meant none of the players had to be sold. On top of that, Brevett had come back from a long-term injury but results and the league position took a nosedive as Donny lost five and drew two of seven from 28 January to 3 March, averaging under a goal a game. Whether Doncaster could hang on to their league status rather than promotion was concentrating minds at Belle Vue.

Mackay resigned on 17 March – the eve of a home fixture against Colchester United, which ended 3-1 to the hosts – claiming that 'financial pressures' had forced the club to begin considering offers for the top young players, and also that money promised for strengthening the side 'had not been forthcoming'. The board 'reluctantly agreed' to Mackay's request and Joe Kinnear took over three days later.

The club stated they were £500,000 in debt and losing £3,000 every week and were indeed 'set to sell some of their prized youngsters'. Kinnear had to put the finishing touches on the transfer of prospects Paul Raven and Ronnie Robinson to West Brom on his first day in charge. And it was no surprise the team struggled with a weakened team, with Kinnear's outfit winning only one and drawing three of the remaining 11 fixtures, scoring eight. The prospect of going out of the league was only lifted with a point against Tranmere Rovers in the penultimate fixture. It seems Mackay had a point about those 'financial pressures'.

Kinnear lasted until June when Billy Bremner, of the infamous picture with Mackay, returned for his second spell in charge. Ironically, Bremner had succeeded another of Mackay's old Spurs team-mates, Cyril Knowles, for his first. Knowles had taken over from Stan Anderson, who replaced John Quigley – whose confession saved our subject from receiving his only sending-off as a player.

Kinnear said, 'Dave invited me to join him at Doncaster. A bit of a contrast to Dubai! We had one or two decent players, like Gerry Daly. I remember staying on a few months after Dave left before Billy Bremner came back in.'

Kinnear admitted he 'didn't really fancy it' when Mackay first offered him the job as he felt Donny 'sounded in bad nick', but he was 'persuaded'.

He said in *Still Crazy*, 'He [Mackay] said it would get me back on the English circuit … the money was poor, less than half of what I'd been getting in Dubai. And that was all tax-free. I got £22,000 and I think Dave, as manager, was on £35,000.

'It all looked pretty depressing, coming from Dubai, but the people were warm and very friendly. The club was in turmoil, though we didn't know the half of it when we arrived.

'We had to concentrate on scouting the reserve and junior teams of the big northern clubs, and spot the ones with potential, who weren't making it so far. He might fancy coming to us as he wouldn't have to move house. I'd go and see him and promise him first-team exposure. That's how they picked up Brian Deane from Leeds, Rufus Brevett from Derby [Brevett was born in the city but came through Doncaster's youth ranks] and Mark Rankine. Our biggest proper signing for money was Les Robinson. We had the impression that there would be more money available but it didn't seem to be there. Dave began to get disillusioned. He got fed up and resigned.'

Kinnear's wife Bonnie said, 'People said to me, "Did you feel out of place in Dubai?" No. Doncaster? Yes. But they treated us well. Dave and Joe were very sociable people, easy to get on with and we were made welcome. Joe and I bought a lovely little cottage. I don't know of any mishaps or problems. But football's football when you are getting bad results. Dave told Joe, "That's it, I'm leaving." Joe carried on but the wheels came off. I'm a Londoner and was glad to get back there. Joe then got a call from Bobby Gould at Wimbledon and got back into work as his reserve manager.'

Bonnie also revealed her affection for Isobel Mackay. She said, 'She's a strong, wonderful and lovely lady. I'm always thinking about her.'

Isobel said, 'David and I had been good friends with Joe and Bonnie. I remember one time we were living at The Glade in Enfield. David and Joe went to Shenley Lodge Health Farm. This day our door went and it was David and he looked like a ghost and Joe was behind him. I said, "What's happened?" And David said, "Don't panic." I thought he'd had had a heart attack climbing on the ladders or something at this health place. He had just pulled a muscle and Joe had brought him home.

'We went out with Joe and Bonnie once or twice. We exchanged cards. I think Joe and David did a draw for the cup. That was a good few years ago.

'Joe was at a match more recently. I think it was when the players were going out on the pitch at Tottenham. David was unwell then. I saw Joe, and said, "Oh, Joe. Nice to to see you. We'll catch up with you later." But I didn't see him again that day.

'Another time, Joe was staying at a hotel in Nottingham when he was Forest manager [in 2004]. He invited David and me round for a meal. We used to have some laughs with Joe.'

Les Robinson, signed by Mackay for £20,000 from Stockport, believes his Doncaster manager produced a 'decent team' when the club was 'not in a good state'. Mackay's belief in him while they were together at Belle Vue helped spark the defender's 700-game career into life.

Robinson retired as a footballer in 2009 and had switched to working as assistant head of education for children with special needs at Swalcliffe School close to Banbury by 2020/21. He was clearly grateful for the lessons he learned from his old boss, and said, 'Dave signed me on the March deadline day of the 1987/88 season.

'I'd only played eight games at Mansfield and went to Stockport for experience. After three months it was, "you can go back", not "we want to sign you". All I wanted to do was play football. It was never about money. A few people looked at me, but as soon as I met up with Dave in a car park and spoke to him I wanted to come. He did a good job selling Doncaster Rovers to me. I'm glad he saw something, helped me improve and have a decent career.

'He was a total football man. That shone out. He was seen as "the aggressor" as a player but he didn't come across like that as a manager. He was a good man-manager who looked after his team. A genuinely nice guy.

'He'd been a superstar as a player. Anybody in the game would have told you that, but he didn't have to shout about it. We all looked up to him anyway.

'Everybody had that respect. He was the total opposite of a Big-Time Charlie. If anything he underplayed things out of respect for us. He understood it was the Third Division, and that you were not going to get the level he had experienced. He wasn't too big a man for a small job. You could tell he did it for the love of the game.

'Training was always good. He enjoyed joining in, usually the keep-ball at the start of a session. If you missed a day's training he'd come and have a chat with you. He'd reminisce about some of his old days. It was one of the only things about being injured that was any good. You're sitting in the physio's room with a twisted knee and he'd say he had a similar injury and start talking about things past. You heard all these old stories. He was just great to be around.

'We didn't have our own training facilities. We used a couple of schools, and an area I believe was on the old racecourse site. I think we used a car park too, which was run down. The ground was old and had wooden stands. The changing rooms weren't the best. But it was a happy club. We got a good morale going and had great supporters.

'We were eventually relegated in his first season. Relegation is absolutely draining. You know you've done everything you can but you still question if you could have done something more. You feel for the supporters. It makes for a bad summer for the fans and the players. I don't blame Dave for it because he hadn't got his own team by then. He wanted to play good football and got in players he wanted rather than inherited. He signed good players like Gerry Daly, along with Paul Raven, Ronnie Robinson and Rufus Brevett, plus Mark Rankine who went to Wolves. He put together a decent side.

'You'd have thought he might have lost a little touch with the English game after being in the Middle East so long but you've only got to look at the quality of signings – although that makes me sound big-headed! – and the way he assembled his team to see he hadn't. He bought in young ones – me being one of them aged 19 – with a couple of old heads like Gerry who was a midfield general. Gerry's legs weren't what they were but he warmed up by having a bath before a game and he led by example. Dave set it all up well. My dad told me how great he was as a player and that working with him was something to look forward to. See what rubs off by being in his presence! He certainly pushed me on.

'You couldn't do much better as your management team than Dave and Joe. They were like chalk and cheese. Joe was a more flamboyant Cockney-type whereas Dave was quieter. But it was a perfect balance. Anything Dave was lacking, Joe was there for it. Obviously Joe went on to be a great manager in the Premier League which tells you he learned a bit off Dave.'

Robinson left Belle Vue in 1990 for ten years at Oxford, being rewarded with a testimonial against Liverpool in 2018.

He said of the Mackay exit aftermath, 'Joe took over a little bit and then of course Billy Bremner came in – with the attitude he had as a player, "Come on, let's give it one of them" – so I had three managers in a year.'

34

'A strong character'

DAVE MACKAY was convinced that 'all big clubs' could be revived. Birmingham City was one such 'sleeping giant' when an old colleague got in touch with him.

The first time Mackay had met Ken Wheldon was when the scrap metal millionaire rolled up in his Roller at his home in Burton Joyce to persuade him to become manager of Walsall 12 years earlier.

The camel-hair-coated entrepreneur had since swapped the boardroom at Fellows Park for St Andrew's, taking the same role, although by now he was giving it up – selling his controlling interest to the Kumar brothers, who ran a Mancunian 'textile empire' and were promising to plough in cash to aid a Blues revival – but staying on the board.

Wheldon wanted Mackay to help awake the slumbering club. The trouble was that in order for the dream to become reality, the Scot had to overcome a nightmare as Birmingham had just been relegated to the third tier for the first time in their 114-year history. It was a relegation which cost Garry Pendrey his job two years before the end of his contract.

The challenge, of course, did not faze Mackay. You only have to think back to how he dealt with the players' revolt at Derby County and, more recently, the transfer requests of Paul Dobson at Doncaster, to appreciate that.

He said, 'The Blues were a big club with serious committed support, although they did not share the same illustrious history as their neighbours Aston Villa and West Bromwich Albion. The problem was … morale was at an all-time low.

'He [Wheldon] asked me to take over and I did ... Again, I believed that Birmingham could be revived. All big clubs can. Good crowds can help sides win. That is a fact and I have known mediocre teams win time and time again as their supporters literally willed them to do so. Teams that do well, but do not have a core of committed support, never last too long at the top. The fans at St Andrew's are amongst the most passionate in the country and, when I got there, their passion had fermented into anger. They were in the wrong place and knew it and demanded an immediate return to the top echelons. Although I knew I would have to work fast, I relished the challenge.'

Wheldon announced on 25 April 1989 that Mackay, now 54, would take over as manager while also revealing that he himself would be selling his majority shareholding.

He also put on record his gratitude to Pendrey, who had turned down the opportunity to serve as a coach under Mackay, for doing a 'good job'. What Pendrey brought into the club in terms of fees had outweighed what he had spent on players but 'the net result was a poor side', stated Tony Matthews in *Birmingham City: A Complete Record*.

A new manager and new owners brought an air of 'optimism' to the club, despite the relegation. New brooms would sweep clean and allow the club to bring back the good times.

Mackay swiftly got to work by splashing some of the Kumar cash, around £430,000, in signing Dennis Bailey, Phil Sproson, Nigel Gleghorn and Trevor Matthewson. Matthews wondered whether this meant the 'rebirth of the Blues'.

Mackay expended blood, sweat and tears on his new-look team as he tried to revive the second city club, along with his assistant Bobby Ferguson, the former Ipswich boss and ex-Derby player, and coaches Fred Davies and Tony Brown.

But, frustratingly, he struggled to relight the fires. Inconsistency put paid to hopes of promotion and even the play-offs in his first season, 1989/90. Mackay's men were third in September with the help of five wins in their opening seven fixtures, but it was to be their peak for the campaign.

The following month yielded just one victory. It was the same through January and February when his side went 12 games without a win, including a five-goal trouncing at Tranmere Rovers.

Even so, with the help of three victories on the bounce in March, Mackay's Blues managed to keep in the top half and finished seventh, with Bailey proving a success by finishing with 20 goals. Mackay also had to deal with suggestions that Birmingham legend Trevor Francis was being lined up to be team manager with the Scot stepping aside to become general manager before the end of the season. Francis nipped that in the bud by reportedly declaring his preference for continuing to play football in the top flight with Sheffield Wednesday.

Mackay – who, in taking over at St Andrew's, had followed in the footsteps of fellow former Spur Sir Alf Ramsey a decade earlier – brought in Coventry City defender Greg Downs in the summer before the 1990/91 campaign and made him captain. And his only significant pre-season signing helped the Blues off to a flying start as they won their opening four fixtures then extended their unbeaten run to 12. It was Birmingham's best start in 82 years but the fact the run included eight successive draws on the bounce tempered the still impressive feat.

Frustratingly, it was unlucky 13 as the bubble burst when former Blues man Wayne Clarke hit a treble to help hosts Shrewsbury beat Mackay's side 4-1. Birmingham only won twice more in the league until the end of the year and closed 1990 with three defeats in a row.

Mackay was to last only 23 days into the new year. He said, 'I jumped just as I was being pushed.' That moment came four days after an 'embarrassing' 3-0 loss against Cambridge United before only 8,859 at St Andrew's and, claimed *Birmingham City: The Complete Record*, it came after he'd had several 'heated arguments with the owners', and 'terrace protests' against him.

He said, 'In my two seasons at the club, sadly I could not deliver automatic promotion and we finished seventh and 12th. As far as most people were concerned, that was going backwards.'

Mackay was 'peeved' that his exit came after those 12 unbeaten games, but he accepted that so many games in that run were deadlocks 'didn't help' his position.

And he felt he had laid the foundation for promotion the following season under Terry Cooper, shown by his signing Nigel Gleghorn top-scoring with 17 league goals and 22 overall. Mackay also guided City through the preliminary rounds of the 1991 Leyland DAF-sponsored Associate Members' Cup – which eventually morphed into the EFL

Trophy – thanks to victories over former club Walsall and Lincoln City without conceding a goal.

The campaign ended with Mackay's successor Lou Macari and the team he inherited from his fellow Scot experiencing Wembley glory by defeating Tranmere Rovers in the final of the competition, aided by Gleghorn and fellow Mackay capture Trevor Matthewson.

John Frain was a regular under Mackay, a part of the trophy-winning team and a member of Birmingham's promotion outfit in 1991/92. He was in the championship-winning team in 1994/95 which took City back to the second tier, a season after being named the club's player of the year.

The Birmingham-born set-piece specialist said, 'We had a shocking season just prior to Dave coming and were relegated in early April. It was sealed the same day as the Hillsborough disaster [which claimed the lives of 96 fans through overcrowding at the 1989 FA Cup semi-final between Liverpool and Nottingham Forest]. We drew at Barnsley and went down to the third tier for the first time in the club's history.

'Dave took over with the club at its lowest ebb from a playing point of view, having struggled morale-wise for a number of seasons. Also, it was on its knees financially with Ken Wheldon having tried to sell it for a while.

'I think Dave had three or four games of that season in charge, and he used those games to assess who he wanted at the club for the following season. His hands were tied as there was no way the club were going to offload players with one or two years on their contract. The chances of getting fees for those players was very limited. Garry Pendrey had similar issues to the one Dave inherited. It was hoped the Kumar brothers would inject funds. Going into the following season, there were hopes that we could bounce back automatically but looking back that was completely unrealistic.

'It was a young squad. Young boys like myself were on £150–£200 a week. Seniors were on £40–£50,000 a year if they were fortunate. It's a bit different now, of course, because some of the rewards are unbelievable.

'Bobby Ferguson had been assistant manager to Bobby Robson at Ipswich. Bobby was experienced and hands-on. He took control of training and set pieces. Dave was more a motivator. He'd be at training every day to oversee, happy for Bobby to put on the sessions.

'Dave was laid-back considering the reputation he had as a player. We'd heard what a good player he was.

'Dave was a decent man. Straight-talking and wouldn't flan anything. I don't think any players would say that he ever got too close to them. He had different sorts of ways of dealing with the players. Sometimes he'd put arms around the shoulders. Dave was just a nice guy. Hindsight is a fantastic thing, it gives you lots of different perspectives … but it was an impossible job really for whoever was in charge at that time.

'It was disappointing we finished just outside the play-offs in his first season because we'd started the season pretty well. It got the players' and supporters' hopes up that we were going to bounce straight back but it petered out.

'Dave's second season, we never really got going and early in the New Year he left. I don't know if Dave had had enough, or didn't get what he was promised to strengthen by the new owners who came in. But he was limited to free transfers. He tried to bring through young players including myself to form the nucleus of the side. It was difficult for him.

'You've got to understand it wasn't just the playing side of it. It was the behind-the-scenes stuff as well. There was no maintenance of the training ground in Solihull. It was a good facility but it was left to go to rack and ruin. We were begging and borrowing places to go and train. It beggars belief for a club that size. And Dave was having to try not to relay those frustrations to the players.

'It was bizarre the way it panned out when he left. Samesh Kumar, the chairman, called a meeting of the players one afternoon at the ground. We all sat in the changing room and he came in. He wanted to get the players' view on how things were going. I think Dave had announced his resignation to Samesh shortly before it. I don't know why Samesh chose to do that. Perhaps he hoped Bobby Ferguson would stay on and was trying to gauge our opinion about Bobby.

'Dave came down and said, "No, I don't know what he's done that for. I resigned about an hour ago." He thanked us for our efforts and wished us the best of luck. Football being football and footballers being footballers we were wondering who was coming in next. The king is dead, long live the king. It's a brutal industry that way.

'We did have a bit of bounce back towards the end of the season when Lou Macari took over.

'Training was excellent during Dave's time. Dave would take the odd session but he was happy for Bobby Ferguson to take the reins. He could see the sessions under Bobby were first-class, varied. You couldn't fault them.

'Did Dave do any "party pieces" in training? No, he took a back seat until matchday. We'd have a pre-match meal and he'd name the side. Yes, he wanted you to play but, first and foremost, to compete. He tried to drill it into us, saying, "Look who you are up against and win that battle." Sometimes at half-time he left you in no doubt if he wasn't happy, but not "in your face" as you might have expected from his reputation as a player. Self-confident but calm. He was a fair man, and humble. I liked him.

'If he'd have hung on he could have been back at Wembley winning another trophy, but you don't know how it would have panned out. It was an unfortunate time for him to manage. There's been so many false dawns at the club and had been on a downward spiral for a few years from my early years and we got relegated from the old First Division. It took years to arrest. A few managers tried to hold that slide. It was a tough job.'

Frain admitted that the Kumars were 'controversial figures', but said that Mackay kept his frustrations – if he had any – to himself. He said, 'The players didn't get any indication. Towards the end he was getting a bit of stick from supporters. It didn't matter where they were in the table and what situation the club was in, they "expected". Reading between the lines, I don't know if he was given all the assurances at the start of the job or that assurances weren't forthcoming. Perhaps he might have got frustrated at that. Maybe he thought, "I don't really need this?" I don't know.'

Defender Ian Atkins played in every league game bar one in Mackay's first season at St Andrew's before moving to Colchester United. He signed for his hometown club a year before Mackay's arrival, and said, 'Dave and Bobby Ferguson – who knew each other from Kuwait – were both honest good men who knew what they were on about.

'But they had just come into a situation where the club was on a downer. I'd not long joined either, and it was a shock to my system with all the experienced players, like Steve Wigley, sold off. It left us with the likes of myself, Brian Roberts, and Martin Thomas. The rest were good young lads like John Frain and Paul Tait, but they needed to be taught the game. It was a big situation that needed patience.

'Dave was a disciplinarian. A strong character. That's how he was as a player. He had had a good managerial career but was off the scene in the Middle East for a number of years not long before and football changes so quickly. It was also difficult because he was coming into a relegated side who needed to be promoted straightaway with a bunch of kids and may not have had enough staff around him because of the financial situation.

'Garry Pendrey signed me. It was the year they sold a lot of the players off. It was soul-destroying. I came back because I was told we were going into the Promised Land. But it never materialised. It just went from one disaster to another before Dave took over, so he wasn't in a great position. Ken Wheldon – who has since passed away, bless his soul – ran a tight ship. The club was so run down there was no groundsperson to cut the grass at our training ground in pre-season. Finances were low.

'Why did Dave take it on? You wouldn't turn Birmingham down, would you? It is a big club, a big second-city club. I got caught in the same situation as a player.

'I got on well with the Kumars. And Dave had a lot of experience but it was hard to manage the club.

'Dave was new to everybody, especially as there were a lot of young lads who made up three-quarters of the team.

'Money was tight. With relegation the gates dropped to 5,000 in a big stadium. It's not easy for any manager coming in to plug the hole and move it on.

'At least he did that. They didn't drop any further but as we know managers who successfully plug holes never get the opportunity to take things forward.

'Dave was a big name, a great player who had great status in the game. You respect that and respected him as a manager. I also respected him for giving me the captaincy.

'You just have to be strong enough and use your experience to help the young kids along, and transfer over what Dave and Bobby had said. The quality was totally different from the First Division yet you adapt. The kids were brilliant and had good careers but had to learn their trade. With Birmingham there's an expectancy even when the finances weren't there.

'Like Dave, I helped plug a hole so the club could move forward. I came back as player-assistant manager after leaving to manage Colchester

United for a year (1990/91). I was doing everything before Terry Cooper came in as manager and we got promoted.'

The Kumars' business went into receivership due to a 'bank collapse' and their 84 per cent shareholding in City was put up for sale in November 1992, as the club entered administration. Businessman David Sullivan bought it out for £700,000 and put in Karren Brady, 23, as managing director and the Blues escaped relegation that season before going down the following term and bouncing back under Barry Fry, who also secured the Football League Trophy that season. As the Birmingham roller-coaster continued, Dave Mackay was back out in the Middle East.

35

Pioneer's final frontiers

WHAT IS the perception of Egyptian culture? An ancient civilisation dating back as far as 6000 BC to the beginning of writing and thus the earliest recordings of human activity, such as the development of urbanisation, agriculture, government and religion? The building of iconic monuments such as the pyramids, largely to provide tombs for pharaohs, and the Great Sphinx limestone sculpture on the banks of the Nile at Giza? Or the reign of Cleopatra?

Modern-day writing covers the fortunes of sports clubs, teams and individuals via an ever-more-diverse media with clubs such as Zamalek, and players including Mo Salah, the most famous Egyptian footballer of recent times. Salah plied his trade with Zamalek's capital rivals Al Mokawloon before his star rose in Europe. But Zamalek have had their own world star in Mido, who followed a similar path after leaving his home country in 2000, making his name at Ajax, Marseille, Roma, Spurs and West Ham, before returning to his home club and going on to manage it in 2014.

Mido – who I attempted to contact for this authorised biography – was a youth player with Zamalek when Dave Mackay took over as manager of the Egyptian top-flight outfit in September 1991.

Mackay had not pulled up any trees in the English game since returning home from the Middle East, given that he had remained out of work since his departure from Birmingham City at the start of the year.

But his star still burned bright in the Arab-speaking region where he had spent a largely successful decade. What he did at Al-Arabi was fresh in its mind.

And Zamalek still had good reason to think highly of the Scot after he and his Spurs side made a deep impression on the club when they visited for a friendly on 14 November 1962. Mackay helped the visitors to a 7-3 win in front of 60,000.

Mackay understood the match to be the hosts' 'finest moment'. It was often recalled in the media and the Zamalek players involved were considered 'national heroes'. Scoring three times against Spurs' greatest team in the middle of their road to European Cup Winners' Cup glory was no mean feat as Jimmy Greaves and Terry Dyson each bagged two, while Cliff Jones, John White and Terry Medwin completed the magnificent seven.

* * *

Mackay might not have known quite what to expect in Cairo but worries were soon obviated.

He said, 'There were millions more cars on the congested Cairo roads and many of the models were straight out of the 1950s. They zig-zagged around the streets, competing with children, chickens, donkeys, goats and horse-and-carriage cabbies for road space. Unlike Kuwait's air of wealth and modernity, Cairo exuded happy poverty … we fell in love with the place straight away.'

It also helped that Mackay and his family were given a luxury flat in a high-rise block. However, they soon discovered that forces could provide more than mere worrying moments. He was having an afternoon siesta when he heard 'some loud rumbling noises', which he dismissed as being the rough and ready air-conditioning system. Isobel and Julie came into the room insisting they were in the middle of an earthquake. He remained convinced it was the air-con and tried to return to his slumber, but again he was disturbed as his bed moved. He got up and noticed his family were no longer around and peered out the window and saw them waving at him. He returned the wave before realising they were 'screaming' at him and joined them downstairs.

He said, 'They explained that our building, which was 16 storeys high, had leant over and touched the building next to it. That was my first earthquake.'

Work-wise, it all looked promising. Zamalek had quite the history. They had established themselves as a 'major force' by winning a glut of glittering prizes, including the national title six times, 18 Egypt Cups and the CAF Champions League twice. They also temporarily changed their name to Farouk 1 after the Egyptian king had developed a soft spot for the club along the way, and they had never been relegated from its country's top flight. On top of that, Mackay felt the game was 'more developed' than in either Kuwait or the UAE.

Moreover, Mackay found there were 'exceptional young footballers' that he 'managed to motivate and develop a strong team, very quickly', with the assistance of Egyptian superstar and 'national hero' Farouk 'The Prince' Gaffer. The gaffer and Gaffer combination might have left the players wondering who they called 'gaffer', but there was no misunderstanding about what they achieved in harness. Back-to-back titles in 1991/92 and 1992/93 maintained the club's glorious traditions and laid the foundations for a third CAF Champions League success.

To emphasise how rosy everything appeared in the Zamalek garden, Mackay guided his club to victory over bitter rivals Al-Ahly at the first attempt to the delight of the owners and supporters. He compared the depth of this lasting competitive relationship between the clubs to the one in Glasgow between Celtic and Rangers. He felt the fans were 'maniacal in their hatred of each other' and it 'was not safe' to be in the vicinity of either stadium when they played each other. He also made mention of a conversation about a past encounter in which 'the referee was shot'.

Such is the level of importance both clubs put on the fixture, Mackay revealed that counterpart Mike Everitt was sacked by Al-Ahly after the loss to the Scot's Zamalek. Everitt, who had previously managed Al Mokawloon, was replaced by Allan Harris, in the Chelsea team defeated by Mackay's Spurs in the 1967 FA Cup Final.

The rivalry between Zamalek and Al-Ahly was to bite Mackay in the posterior when he discovered exactly what a loss in the Cairo derby match meant to the folk who ran his club.

He told of how one of his defenders received his marching orders in the opening minutes of one particular meeting. He felt holding the opponents to just a 1-0 advantage at the interval was commendable given his side were a player down. Eventually his side's resistance weakened and ended up losing 3-0 against Harris's team.

Mackay expected a flea in the ear from the club directors but believed they would take into consideration the title-grabbing achieved under his watch, and that delaying the meeting the directors had wanted immediately after the game until the morning would enable the board members to develop and attain that perspective. It didn't. He told of how the directors insisted the fact Zamalek had played with ten players against 11 for most of the match was 'not a good enough reason'.

Then came a gesture which seemed to seal his fate. Mackay said, 'I was not about to grovel. I shrugged my shoulders. Maybe that gesture has some rude significance in Egypt that had passed me by. It was at that point they got angry and I lost my job.

'It was a great shame that my time at Zamalek ended with a silly bit of unpleasantness because I had a very happy time at the club and we were good for each other.

'I am told by friends who have visited Egypt for holidays that matches from my reign have finally replaced the Spurs friendly in the affections of the Zamalek fans and that I am held in high esteem by many. That is nice to know.'

Mackay's career in football and life as a working man ended in Qatar at the age of 62. The fourth stop on his Middle East 'tour' provided another pioneering but final job for the Scot.

Mackay told how the country wanted to 'develop their game in line' with Gulf neighbours like Kuwait. The small emirate on the north-east coast of the Arabian Peninsula had already imported British talent to help out, such as former Sunderland defender Len Ashurst and ex-Wales international full-back Graham Williams.

Mackay felt Qatar was 'wealthy and keen to modernise' and he became part of the country's development when he was asked and agreed to manage the nation's youth team in 1993, assisted by fellow Scot George Blues.

Two years later Mackay was in charge of Qatar as it hosted the World Youth Cup for under-20s. The emirate had shocked football when its under-20s finished runner-up to West Germany in the 1981 World Youth Championships in Australia after beating Brazil and England. It also staged the 1988 Asian Cup.

But Qatar took another major move forward in football recognition when it stepped in to replace Nigeria as hosts for the 1995 WYC with the west African country forced to quit due to an outbreak of a meningitis epidemic caused by an ebola virus.

And, with Mackay being in the right place at the right time, Qatar stunned the football world again when holding the more established Russia to a 1-1 draw in the opening game. Mohammed Salem El Enazi, who went on to be a prolific scorer for the senior team and earn a Bayern Munich trial, secured it. He cancelled out an effort from Sergei Semak two second-half minutes earlier in front of an ecstatic 65,000 at the Khalifa Olympic Stadium in the capital Doha. Mackay's men failed to reach the knockout stage following defeats against Syria (1-0) and Brazil (2-0) in front of a total of 100,000 spectators.

Mackay was grateful to his back-up team for the relative success Qatar enjoyed. Besides Blues, his set-up was boosted with the introduction of coach Rene Meulensteen, who he became friends with and would later recommend to Sir Alex Ferguson at Manchester United.

Most of the matches not involving Mackay's side had four-figure attendances, according to Wikipedia.

But 65,000 turned out for the final in which Argentina defeated South American rivals Brazil 2-0 to follow in the footsteps of their 1979 predecessors who were inspired by best-player-of-the-tournament Diego Maradona, who became one of the game's greats and passed away on 25 November, 2020.

Mackay was asked how it was working in the Middle East compared to back home.

He said, 'In the Middle East you had to get results but no one interfered. In this country (England) if you are doing badly the board will get onto you.'

Mackay returned to Burton Joyce at the end of his contract the following year, unsure of his future. What he did not know was that his football career was over.

Son Derek said, 'My dad certainly got around in the Middle East. Remember we all had a family holiday when he was in Cairo. Us children brought our children, who were little then. We saw the pyramids, went on a cruise on the Nile in a big boat and had lovely things to eat. It was amazing. My brother David Junior went out to Dubai. He used to go a lot with our grandad, Dad's dad.

'Dad's lifestyle was fascinating. Dad had this flat right in the middle where ordinary Egyptians lived and worked. It wasn't a holiday place at all. It wasn't far from the pyramids, the Sphinx and a museum.

'Dad used to come back now and again, like at Christmas. That was brilliant. He surprised us two days before one Christmas. We were in the family home in Burton Joyce. Mum had been out there with dad and they just rang the doorbell and walked in. All the family were able to gather in what was a lovely big house and we had a right good time.'

Daughter Valerie said, 'My dad was able to settle anywhere, everywhere! We went out to Kuwait twice and Cairo once. Fabulous memories. That trip on the Nile really was amazing. Dad had thought ahead and planned it all. I'd gone out there with Denis and our son Greg. I recall how people crammed on the buses in Cairo. There were also mad drivers there, although they were mad in Kuwait too.

'The social life was different out in the Middle East, especially Kuwait. I was always sending out different cassettes of all my dad's favourite songs like Chas and Dave, the Beatles, Rolling Stones, Dusty Springfield, Neil Diamond. He loved "Resurrection Shuffle" by Ashton, Gardner and Dyke and "In the Summertime" by Mungo Jerry. He called me "The DJ". Dad loved his music, especially music with a good beat.

'He liked a party. When he was back from Qatar I arranged a surprise ruby wedding party for my mum and dad at the Swan Hotel in Nottingham on 12 December 1995. A few friends came up from London. Denis Law came. There was this lovely book for everybody to put messages in and sign.'

Isobel Mackay said, 'That party was a nice surprise.'

PART SIX: POST-CAREER

36

'What more can a man ask?'

ISOBEL KNEW her husband best and it was her insistence on him having a hospital check-up that led to the discovery that he had cancer, with the 'patient' underlining how she aided his recovery.

Dave said, 'Without her love, care and absolute faith in my recovery, I'm sure I would have struggled both mentally and physically. I called her Dr Mackay because I appreciated the potency of her course of treatment. Never underestimate the love of a good woman.'

Mackay, coming up 62, had felt mentally and physically in good shape when he returned from Qatar in 1996.

He insisted he was 'fit, alert and in possession of all my marbles'.

Al-Arabi wanted him back as their manager. Mackay was 'tempted' even though his 'natural instinct' was not to return to a club where he had achieved glory, as he illustrated when turning down a nostalgic return to Hearts for a dive into the unknown with Derby County.

There was also another offer on the table from Oman, another Gulf country. But he wasn't going anywhere. Mackay had developed a cold sore on his lip which seemed never to heal properly, although in Qatar he had a biopsy which gave him the all-clear.

This was when Isobel became adamant Mackay should get it examined again before any third spell in the Middle East was considered.

A biopsy at City Hospital in Nottingham revealed the cancer. He said, 'I had barely seen the inside of a hospital. Although I was in my 60s, on the inside I remained a teenager and therefore did not expect to experience health problems.

'I was knocked for six, not in a feeling-sorry-for-myself sort of way, but in a what-a-bloody-nuisance type of way … The doctors advised it would be prudent to keep away from the sun and therefore helped us make our minds up [on whether to go back to the Middle East].'

There would be no return to the desert lands which had one of the hottest climates on the globe; a decision also made due to concerns related to the increasing political volatility in the region.

Daughter Valerie said, 'Even though Dad was offered the job to go back, I think my mum said, "No, no, it is too dangerous. You've had cancer with the sun." So they didn't go back.'

Mackay underwent a course of radiation on his cancerous lip and 'it seemed to do the trick'. Although he reserved the biggest praise for the love of his life Isobel, he offered gratitude to his oncologist Mr Chan and the radiologists and nurses who attended him. He said, 'These people [NHS workers], and there are thousands of them up and down Britain, really are the unsung heroes of our country. They don't score goals or make pop records, but their contribution dwarfs anything in the entertainment industry. They are there for all of us when we need them.'

It all signalled the end for Mackay in football and he admitted having trouble getting used to retirement, although he was swift to count his blessings. He said, 'I had a few problems adjusting to relative inactivity, but I had had a good run and there was much to be thankful for. Football, the game I loved and continue to love, had given me a living for nearly half a century. I'd achieved so many things and made my mark. What more can a man ask?

'I have a wonderful family and we have all enjoyed good times and good health. We have grandchildren to keep us occupied.

'I lost my mum and dad on the way, as did Isobel, but few people in their 60s still have parents around. That's being greedy. But it doesn't stop you missing them. Mum went first and I was devastated because I didn't expect it. I still miss her now. I was lucky enough to have quality time with Dad after she died and I was able to take him to the Middle East, where he spent long spells with me. Isobel too had lost her parents by then.'

The Mackays, with their children grown up, moved to a smaller home in Burton Joyce in 1999. Isobel said, 'We downsized to a house similar to the one we had in Whitehouse Way in Southgate. Then we decided we wanted an extension built, and had the kitchen made bigger, a garage and en suite bedroom. It's crazy when you think about it. When we moved we were missing so much space. But the house's position was so convenient for the bus stop and shops.'

Mackay remained in touch with the game locally. His village was filled with 'football people', such as compatriots Neil Martin, Peter Cormack and Tommy Gemmell, plus Don Masson and Masson's Notts County manager Jimmy Sirrel.

Mackay used to enjoy a pint in The Cross Keys with Sirrel, and he and Isobel also invited the Magpies' boss to house parties at Chez Mackay.

Isobel said, 'We used to hold Hogmanay parties which Jimmy would come to with his wife Cathy and Don Masson, the County captain. Neil Martin used to come too. As did Des Anderson, David's assistant manager when they worked together in England, and his wife Lesley. Of course, Dad, Des and Neil had their Forest connections so there were some good-spirited County–Forest discussions!'

Mackay certainly retained his sense of humour in retirement. Valerie said, 'Dad used to have fun back in his Tottenham days with Jimmy Greaves. They used to sit at the bar, say in the Bell and Hare, after a game and bet people to guess who was the tallest out of the two of them. They usually won it because most thought Dad was the taller, but Jimmy was – just.

'Anyone in the family would tell you how funny my dad could be. He maintained that sense of fun when he finished his time in football.'

Derek said, 'Dad enjoyed a laugh. I remember when he was in the company of Roy McFarland cracking one-liners. Roy had asked him whether he deserved a knighthood and he came straight back with, "Knighthood? I'll be lucky to get a night out!"

'In the village, there was a newspaper FA Cup promotion he got involved in. All us kids got our picture taken with the trophy – and then he only went and took it down the pub, The Cross Keys! The guy had gone, "Anyone else you want a picture of it with? Any mates?" Dad said, "Come on, we'll take it down the pub." It was in a lovely big box and they put it on the bar. The locals wondered what was going on and then they took it out – the FA Cup. And all the punters had their picture taken with it.

'There was another time he had some fun with a good friend of his called Cedric. Because of his stature and presence on the field, many times people who met Dad for the first time were surprised at his height, expecting him to be much taller. When dad was retired he enjoyed going to The Cross Keys. This day he was in the pub with Cedric, who said he had a mate who insisted Dad was well over six foot, that Cedric had had a bet with him that he wasn't, and that he could he call for Dad on his way to the pub and bring his mate, who would be delighted to meet him. It meant Cedric would win the bet.

'At the arranged time, the doorbell rang. Dad placed the footstool to the left of the door and stood on it as mum opened the door. Dad was peering down above the door from behind it, his head and shoulders showing. "All right, mate," says Dad. "Pleased to meet you," whereupon Cedric and his pal collapsed in fits of laughter.'

Mackay maintained a daily jogging routine, running five miles. Isobel said, 'David used to go on a run, even when he was in the football. Five miles a day before starting brisk walking. There were a number of people in the village he used to see on the way. They all knew him. The woman in the paper shop used to see him. "It was like clockwork every morning," she'd say. She timed him!

'I can't remember exactly when, he just decided to stop. I didn't know what had come over him at the time. People used to say, "Oh, what's happened to David? We haven't seen him out." I used to say to David, "You're not going?" He'd go, "No, I'll give it a miss." It was strange but I suppose, in hindsight, that's what happens with the illness that developed.'

Derek said, 'He was all right when he did his runs. He hadn't started to get ill. He kept fit and used to go out jogging all the time. Then when he got a little bit older a famous Scottish rugby player called Gavin Hastings used to tell him just walk fast. That it was better for him than jogging. Life went on.'

Valerie added, 'Dad used to run five miles every day. A jog-run. Do a full circle round by the river [Trent]. That's how he met one of his best friends, a chap called Steve, who used to say, "Hi Dave" whenever he saw Dad doing his circuit. They got chatting, Steve started giving Dad cups of tea now and again on his route, and they ended up great friends.

'Steve was a Forest man. When Dad was in the hospital at the end – and we knew it was going to be the end – I had many phone calls with

Steve, talking late into the night. He helped me a lot. He came two or three times to visit Dad. I tense up – not in a bad way – if I'm driving or catch sight of him. I just think of Dad. You just do when you see your dad's friends. Eventually Dad used to do the power walk as he got older.

'He always needed something to do. Perhaps on a Saturday he would go and have a bet on the horses. He didn't like to bet on the horses unless he could watch the races. He never saw the point otherwise.

'He'd also go for a drink in a village pub. It was a good little set-up. Us children had started to have children of our own and he would watch the grandchildren. He'd even walk my daughter to and from primary school. Like his children, his grandchildren all idolised Dad.'

Mackay also kept busy supporting the Burton Joyce community. He opened the £550,000, 12-acre Poplars Sports Ground in the village in May 1998, in his role as president of Burton Joyce Football Club (Seniors).

Parachutist Dave Hickling landed with a 'symbolic key' which he passed on to Mackay in the opening ceremony. The day also featured football, cricket, tug of war, the Sally Ashworth Dancers, the Burton Joyce Line Dancers and 'the music of the 5th Carlton Scout Band'.

Project co-ordinator John Harris said the ground was 'a major project for the village and must be one of the biggest things here since 1925 when the village hall was opened'.

Mackay did venture beyond the rural environs of Burton Joyce in the Gedling district of Nottinghamshire, with visits back to see family and friends in Edinburgh and journeys to watch Derby County. He said in 2004, 'I attend … home games although at the time of writing I'm not sure if that is good for my health.'

Derek said, 'Dad went to Derby a lot, mainly the new Pride Park Stadium. I only went a few times with him as I was working most Saturdays as a shop-fitter. Dad used to go with Des Anderson on most occasions, and also took our son Daniel a few times. Then later there was a local lad called Gareth who would take Dad. A Derby fan, so he loved it!

'Anyway, they would meet up with Des and other ex-Derby players. Roy McFarland, Rod Thomas, Roger Davies, Gerry Daly and John O'Hare were the regulars I seem to remember. It was in the "posh bit" – as I call it – with fans who were in there each game. I always remember one time I took Dad and Des so I couldn't drink as I was driving. Honestly,

I've never laughed so much in my life while sober! The banter they were having with each other just flowed.

'They would carry on in the "posh bit" after the game. When that shut, they would troop down to the Baseball Bar and Grill – named after the old ground – and carry on the festivities there. Also Dad and Des would always pop in to see the manager in his office after the game for a drink, think it was mainly Jim Smith at that time. He actually watched some games from the directors' box next to Brian Clough. There's a lovely newspaper photo of them shaking hands as they took their seats.'

Mackay announced on 31 August 2001 that he would auction off much of his collection of football memorabilia to raise money for his family, including his four children and six grandchildren.

The items included a plaque for managing Derby County to the 1975 championship, and his Scottish and English player of the year awards of 1958 and 1969. League Cup and Scottish Cup winners' medals of 1954 and 1956 were expected to raise £2,000, Mackay's 1961 Spurs Double medals were to be put on sale as a single lot and anticipated to fetch £20,000. His 1963 European Cup Winners' Cup medal would, it was estimated, attract a punter to part with £8,000 (fellow Burton Joyce resident Tommy Gemmell had given an indication of what could be raised when he auctioned his 1967 European Cup winners' medal for £12,000 in 1994).

All of Mackay's mementoes had been in a bank vault since an attempted break-in at the family home 15 years earlier, it was reported.

Mackay said in the *Glasgow Herald*, 'I decided it was time to use them to share something with my family. It was always something that was going to be a difficult thing to do. I know that once they're gone they're gone forever. But they're not really doing anything sitting in a bank vault where nobody can see them – even though there's an obvious sentimental value.

'It would be nice if they ended up back at the clubs where I won them, for the supporters to enjoy. I'm not getting rid of them because I'm penniless. I've got a good pension and can live comfortably.'

He got his wish as far as his 1961 league and FA Cup medals were concerned, his former employers in London N17 intending them to form the 'centrepiece of the club's proposed new museum'.

Spurs press officer John Fennelly said, 'Once we heard that they were for sale we had to have them. There is no better home for them.'

Mackay made journeys to pick up a multitude of awards as well as receiving national recognition for his efforts on a football field.

He was included by the Football League in its 100 Legends list – which wasn't in a ranking order – as part of the celebration of the preceding 99 seasons in the body's 100th campaign in 1998.

Mackay was listed along with former Spurs team-mates Danny Blanchflower, Cliff Jones, Jimmy Greaves, Alan Mullery and Pat Jennings, ex-Hearts colleague Alex Young, Scotland international team-mate Denis Law, and his international schoolboy bête noire Johnny Haynes. They were selected by a panel of journalists which included Bryon Butler.

He was among the first inductees into the English Hall of Fame in 2002 'in recognition of his impact on the English game as both a player and manager'. Again he was joined by Greaves, Law and Haynes, with Blanchflower and Jennings recognised the next year followed by Jones (2013) and Mullery (2015). Also listed in the initial selections were bona fide legends such as George Best, John Charles, Duncan Edwards, Bobby Charlton, Stanley Matthews, Tom Finney and Bobby Moore. Some company.

Mackay achieved the same feat when the initial list of Scottish Hall of Fame inductees was announced in November 2004. He was in an elite club with his friends Law and Sir Alex Ferguson, plus Matt Busby, Bill Shankly, Jock Stein, Kenny Dalglish and Jim Baxter.

In March that year he was an inaugural inductee into the Tottenham Hotspur Hall of Fame at Whites in Paxton Road, along with all his Double-winning team-mates, including the late John White and Danny Blanchflower.

Mackay sat at the top table with Bill Nicholson, also inducted on the night, and surviving team-mates were also in the room, although Canada-based Bill Brown was absent. The Scot spoke in 'glowing' terms about a manager who helped turn him into a member of the club's greatest ever team, describing the Yorkshireman, who passed, with Brown, later in the year, as one of the 'top six managers of all time' .

He was moved as Nicholson died on 23 October 2004. Mackay said to the media on the day, 'I've cried already today. He'd been ill for some time, but when things like this happen it's sad. He did everything for the club. They were fourth from bottom when he took over and within a year and a half we had won the Double. Bill was a marvellous manager, one of the top five in the game over the past 50 years. He always wanted us to play football and sometimes we were winning a game 5-0 and then drew 5-5. He always wanted to go forward. This was the type of manager and man he was. Bill was absolutely straightforward. When he said something, he meant it – he would NEVER go back on his word. He never let us forget we were out there to entertain the public. He was 100 per cent honest, 100 per cent Spurs.'

All of this came three years after the heroes of 1961 celebrated the 40th anniversary of their triumph with a reunion dinner.

There was another inaugural induction for Mackay in 2006 when the Heart of Midlothian Hall of Fame started up.

Mackay teamed up again with former Spurs team-mate Bobby Smith for a Q&A in Cheshunt the following year. He later hooked up with Ninian Cassidy, his long-term friend, and Isobel's brother Tom Dixon in the manager's office after Joe Kinnear's Newcastle had beaten Harry Redknapp's Tottenham on Sunday, 21 December 2008.

Mackay supported Jimmy Greaves when his old Spurs team-mate celebrated his 70th birthday at the O2 Arena in London on 20 February 2010; joined, of course by other Tottenham legends such as Cliff Jones, Pat Jennings, Terry Dyson, Terry Medwin, Martin Chivers and Steve Perryman, plus World Cup heroes Geoff Hurst, Martin Peters and George Cohen. Our subject and the rest joined stand-up Greaves on stage.

Isobel, who was there with other wives Joan Jones and Joyce Medwin, said, 'It was one of the last times I saw dear Bobby and the last time I saw Geoff Hurst. A happy night.'

On 25 March 2010, the *Scottish Daily Record* confirmed how 'football legend' Mackay had secured a legal victory over the makers of *The Damned United*.

It reported, 'The tough-tackling defender has received an apology and an undisclosed sum from the producers of the film, which centres on Brian Clough's ill-fated spell as Leeds United manager in 1974. The movie showed Mackay breaking a players' revolt that was mounted at Derby County in 1973 in an attempt to get Clough reinstated following his resignation in a clash with chairman Sam Longson. Mackay, though, was not at Derby at the time, having left to become player manager of

Swindon Town in 1971. Leeds law firm Ford & Warren confirmed his legal action had been successful.'

After receiving the apology and 'an undisclosed sum' in the first half of 2010 for being misrepresented in the movie, Mackay left the rewards of litigation for adoration in the second half of the year when he returned to White Hart Lane.

37

'Having a right good laugh'

MIKE ROLLO, Tottenham Hotspur's commercial manager, wrote to the Mackays on Monday, 9 August 2010.

The letter confirmed arrangements for Mackay, his wife Isobel and 'two guests' to attend Harry Redknapp-managed Spurs' opening match of the season against Manchester City on the Saturday. The club would put the party up at the Marriott Hotel in Cheshunt the night before. Also enclosed were car park and hospitality room passes, plus an itinerary for matchday.

Rollo outlined in his missive, 'With this season marking the 50th anniversary of our glorious 1960/61 Double we will be escorting you and your team-mates to the players' tunnel just before half-time to re-introduce you all to the White Hart Lane crowd at half-time as we know our supporters will wish to pay tribute to our great team of '61.'

Come matchday, Mackay and other survivors of that team were duly and respectfully introduced on the pitch they had graced during the break of a goalless draw.

Son Derek said, 'The Man City game was the last time I was with him at a game. I remember Joe Hart had a blinder. Tottenham should have won four or five-nil. Dad was getting poorly then. We'd started noticing little things. It was very mild, but he was on form that day. We sat at a table and had a nice meal with Les Allen and his wife Pat and Cliff Jones and his wife Joan. It was so funny. Dad was coming out with all these one-liners, having a right good laugh. He started to deteriorate after that.'

On that summer's day before 35,928 Lane witnesses, stars such as Gareth Bale, Luka Modrić and Peter Crouch, for the hosts, and City's David Silva, Yaya Touré and Carlos Tevez, might have been the main focus of attention for those ignorant of what Mackay and Co. achieved for the Lilywhites.

But to those 'in the know', the presence of the Double winners was rich in significance, a torch to pass on so history would not forget them.

Paul Coyte, Spurs' matchday MC and erstwhile radio presenter, went along the line interviewing all of them, bar Mackay. Coyte was aware that Mackay 'was a bit under the weather' and sought an alternative method of communication.

Coyte said, 'When we did the 50th anniversary, every surviving member apart from Bobby Smith, who had just gone into hospital, was there.

'The idea was that I was just going to go along the line. I'd spoken to a few, Maurice Norman and Cliff Jones. With Dave, I thought, "What am I going to do?" I didn't want to embarrass him and his family. As I got to him I thought, "Right, I'll make something up". I remember saying over the microphone, "I'm going to do something now which nobody ever did on the pitch at White Hart Lane – I'm actually going to get past Dave Mackay." So I made it as a joke – and he looked at me. I'd met him before, knew all the stories about him, but I hadn't seen he was this "hard man". He just seemed this lovely older man, someone the same age as my dad. But – as ridiculous as it sounds – he looked at me with these steely blue eyes and I saw it when he looked me in the eyes. I'll never forget it. I was extremely scared! Then I walked on to the rest of them.

'We had pictures of each player on an old football card – with their clubs stats – and put them all on the screens with some music background as we introduced each of them. Each one came out. We thought it would stir the emotions. But I didn't realise I had tears rolling down my face out of my own eyes! It was amazing. Probably the last time they were there together.'

Mike Rollo said, 'We have had several get-togethers of the Double team. As well as the 50th anniversary there were the 40th celebrations and the Hall of Fame inductions, and before. The players had formed a bond through what they did in 1960/61. It kept them all together. And, naturally, Dave was very much a part of it all.

'I was introduced to Dave in my job but I'd totally admired him from when I started supporting Spurs in 1963 aged 11. He was a great Spurs player, captaining the 1967 FA Cup-winning team. A great player full stop. He helped Derby under Brian Clough beat us.

'In my first year working for Spurs [1984] we'd have get-togethers. Chairman Irving Scholar was an admirer of the Double team and invited them. Dave Mackay struck me as a quiet man, with a dry sense of humour and not full of himself. He used to call me "Handsome" in the early days. I tried to tell him that wasn't the case!

'I'd started the Legends idea – with former players as matchday hosts – in the 1990s and Dave did come down to selected games. He met Ron Burgess, Tommy Harmer, Len Duquemin and Cliff Jones.

'It was like soldiers who had come from a war, they talked about great matches. The guests thought it was unbelievable meeting their childhood heroes. Dave might not have been a regular, but when he did come down from Nottingham it was an event.'

Mackay made what is believed to be his last major public appearances at Tynecastle and the Lane in 2011. Hearts and Spurs had drawn each other in a Europa League play-off over two legs. Mackay was there for both.

Ninian Cassidy, Isobel's cousin and Mackay's close friend, revealed he had been asked by Isobel to chaperone her husband for the first leg on a balmy night at Tynecastle on Thursday, 18 August 2011.

Mackay was introduced to the crowd at half-time but Cassidy recalled how it was touch-and-go that his pal got on to the pitch in time to say 'hello'.

The Jambos' best ever player in many experts' eyes was in the tunnel. He was behind Alfie Conn, the former Spurs maverick and son of Mackay's old Hearts team-mate, who was to take part in an interval draw in front of the 16,279 crowd alongside Mackay. Cassidy was about to lead the pair out when Mackay caught the eye of Joe Jordan, the Spurs assistant manager, ex-Hearts boss and another labelled a 'hard man' during his playing days.

Cassidy said, 'I was sitting with Dave watching the game in the old Gorgie Road End. Terrible seats for someone of his stature – like climbing a mountain to get to our seats. Alex Young, Gordon Marshall and Jimmy Murray, who had played with Dave at Hearts, were there. First half wasn't great from Hearts' point of view, losing 3-0. But Harry Redknapp had a really good team and a lot of good players.

'We had to do the half-time draw with Alfie, so had to leave our seats five minutes before the break to get on to the park via the main entrance and the corridor between the dressing rooms which led up the tunnel on to it. I knew the guy conducting the draw, Scott Wilson, because I'd played football with him. Anyway, we were making our way up the corridor when the away team's dressing room door opened as we passed it and out comes Joe Jordan and Clive Allen, a coach and former Spurs striker. You couldn't have written the script! Joe went, "Dave!" and grabbed him while Clive went, "Dave, mate" and was on top of him. Dave's held up. Scott said to me, "Hurry up, we've got to get the draw done." I told him, "We'll be there in a second, Scott." I'm now lead man in front of Alfie and Dave's behind us, trapped. So I said to Alfie, "Can you tell them to let go because we've got to make this draw?" Alfie walked back two or three steps towards Dave. But stopped and turned round and said to me, "No, if you think I'm going between Joe Jordan and Dave Mackay, you've got another thing coming."

'I had to go back and drag Dave along the corridor. And he and Alfie made the draw. That's my claim to fame when Dave Mackay was at Tynecastle for the last time!

'We went back to our seats behind the goal Hearts were attacking. Hearts got a free kick inside the Spurs box. The wall lined up. Dave is going, "What's happening?" I told him. He said, "Hearts might score?" He loved Spurs but was supporting Hearts. I said, "I don't think so, Dave." We are now standing in an aisle against a barrier. They took the free kick and a guy called Webster had a shot which has come sailing right up into the stand, gone about four feet past Dave who moved his whole body to the left and tried to head it!

'People started laughing and suddenly applauding. I said to Dave, "Did did you try and head it?" He said yes. I said, "You were about four feet off it." He said, "At least I had a f*****g go." How poignant was that? Watching the two teams that he loved and trying to head the ball when he was coming up 77! He was back on the park playing the game. He was there. His mind was there.'

Mackay also met up with Rob White, son of his late Spurs and Scotland midfield partner John, who attended the game with our subject's eldest daughter Valerie. Rob, based in London, said, 'We'd already booked a family holiday with an old college friend of mine and his family near Musselburgh when the game was happening. Another friend, a Spurs fan, was up for the game as well. Val phoned me up, asking where she could get a ticket. Anyway, she got one and said after the game, "Come down and see my dad. He'll be pleased to see you."

'In my brain I'd always thought of Dave as this uncle [referring to being looked after as a child by Mackay when the Scot was in charge at Derby]. Of course I said yes. So we all went downstairs and Dave was in this function room and we went over for a chat. It was brilliant. Dave was a big hero of my Spurs mate, Dan, and I introduced him to Dave. They shook hands and chatted for a bit. Dave seemed absolutely fine, just a bit slow.

'The other mate of mine – from college – was also there and unfortunately a Gooner. So I introduced him to Dave, saying, "This is my mate Ian".' And as they were shaking hands I added, "Unfortunately, he's a Gooner." I'd timed it perfectly. Dave had got a fantastic stare on him. The same one he used on Billy Bremner in THAT picture. He looked at my mate and squeezed my mate's hand harder and harder. My mate was really laughing but also in pain. Dave was 70-odd and my mate was completely crapping himself! It was the last time I met Dave in the flesh. It's a nice memory.'

John Robertson, the former Hearts striker, said, 'I was working in the lounge at Tynecastle that night. Dave was guest of honour. It was funny. He was talking about the height of the Spurs team. He laughed and said, "My goodness, look at the two teams lining up. The smallest player with Spurs is a little winger and he looks bigger than all the Hearts team put together!" He was chatting away that night.

'He was getting on in years and you could understand he wasn't as sharp as when we'd met him previously. But when he and guys like him – which we have learned through memory sessions – talk football they appear to be in a tremendous place. Dave's eyes were bright. He was bubbly, absolutely buzzing. Very much enjoying himself and everybody enjoyed having him. He was the star of the show and deservedly so. He was only man who could conjoin the clubs, and remained revered. All the Spurs and Hearts fans rose as one when they saw him.'

Mackay witnessed star-studded Spurs, the club he loved, overcome the one he still supported 5-0 with goals from Rafael van der Vaart,

Jermain Defoe, Jake Livermore, Gareth Bale and Aaron Lennon. And he travelled down from Burton Joyce to London with Isobel and daughter Valerie for the second leg at White Hart Lane seven days later. It was the occasion of Harry Kane's senior Spurs debut and the player destined to be a striking talisman for club and country made and missed a penalty in the goalless draw. But Mackay took centre stage at half-time when he came on and waved at the White Hart Lane faithful and those who had made the journey from Edinburgh.

Valerie said, 'I went to both Hearts v Spurs games. It was just lovely to hear everybody when Dad went on the pitch at Tynecastle and White Hart Lane. I think he did a little run on to the pitch. The fans loved that.'

Stadium MC Paul Coyte said, 'We felt it would be lovely if he came out. It was a tricky call as we assumed he would not be well enough to get into an interview situation, but he came on and waved at the crowd. He wasn't aware of everything but their big reaction registered. I remember seeing his face and thinking, "Yes, this was the right thing to do."

'I'd interviewed a few players over the years on the pitch. And all the boys to a man pretty much would say he was the greatest Spurs player of all time. It was fitting we were able to do something because it was, I think, the last time he came to White Hart Lane.'

Mike Rollo said, 'I'd organised a VIP trip for about 30-odd Spurs supporters for the first leg. Train, lunch, sightseeing, street acts, the Edinburgh Festival and the game, with Martin Chivers our hosting legend. We had access to the players' entrance with Martin. We met up with Dave and shook his hand. It was a big moment for him being back at Tynecastle.

'We wanted to do something with Dave and the crowd for the second leg back at White Hart Lane. Paul Coyte did a great job of bringing him on. The crowd were cheering when he came on to the pitch. He looked up at the screens showing various pieces of him in action. He enjoyed it, and was very happy. It was lovely for his family and it was a nice way for the crowd to see him in what turned out to be his final time at the club.

'We also walked round the West Stand in particular, Cliff Jones befriended and looked after him with Isobel. He had his photo taken next to a large picture of the 1961 team hanging on the wall.

'Dave was modest when he spoke about the team. He was always modest. His wife Isobel told me, "Talk to him and show him things then all the memories will come back." He did have a recollection factor in his head.

'Isobel protected Dave as he got older. Credit to her that despite his circumstances, she really did look after him. She was the one I always dealt with. I've still got letters from her. A lovely woman.

'One thing the men of the 1961 squad were blessed with was strong women behind them. Joan Jones, Sandra White, who sadly passed away in 2020, Terry Medwin's wife Joyce and, of course, Isobel.'

Isobel recalled a signing Mackay did with England World Cup-winning heroes Geoff Hurst and Gordon Banks and family pal Tommy Docherty at the National Football Museum, then at Deepdale, Preston before its 2012 switch to Manchester.

She said, 'It was a signing with this guy from Preston. We went back to the hotel where we were staying for something to eat and Terry Baker, Jimmy Greaves's agent, came up and said, "Look Dave, when we get back [to the museum] I'd like to get you to do another signing. I've arranged a lift." It was in Geoff Hurst's car. A beautiful car. We get back to the museum and I was speaking to Geoff and Gordon and saying that David had some memory problems. Gordon said his brother was the same. The next thing, the door opens, and this guy says, "You are needed for the signing Terry mentioned." So David did it and Terry gave him a wee bit of money.'

Mackay remained unforgotten at White Hart Lane. Harry Redknapp's first thought after Scott Parker had shone in the 3-1 home league win over Queens Park Rangers on 30 October 2011 was to compare his midfielder to the Scot.

Redknapp said, 'Scott Parker was just amazing. I haven't seen many performances like that. You hesitate to mention him in the same breath as Dave Mackay, who was one of the best players who has ever played at this club, but it was right up there with Dave.'

Son Derek said, 'Harry is always mentioning Dad, which is great. We saw Harry on a TV cookery programme recently called *Saturday Morning With James Martin* and one of the first things Harry said was in reference to Dad.'

Redknapp was asked by British chef Martin about his football background while preparing the former Spurs boss a meal. Redknapp revealed he was invited by a scout to train with Tottenham as a youngster and said, 'It was great spending all day training and being around all the great players of the Double team like Dave Mackay and Cliff Jones. Incredible times.'

38

'Ninian Cassidy, ex-Hearts and Tottenham'

DAVE MACKAY had been a rare visitor to any hospital, beyond the birth of his children and his two broken legs, but he was sufficiently unwell to be admitted to one in Nottingham with a chest infection in June 2012. But the 77-year-old recovered after treatment.

Mackay was well enough the following February to attend the Wembley occasion which revealed that his image along with ten other Football Heroes – all illustrated by artist Andrew Kinsman – was to be issued by the Royal Mail on a set of first-class stamps two months later. The individuals were selected as they were 'supremely gifted, talented players who stood out in their generation and beyond' and had an 'outstanding record on the pitch and represented the home countries'.

The only other Scot picked was his international pal Denis Law. His old Spurs team-mate Jimmy Greaves, who also attended, was among the chosen few. Mackay was yet again in the company of the elite with George Best, John Charles, Bobby Charlton, Bobby Moore, Gordon Banks, Bryan Robson, Kevin Keegan and John Barnes making up the 11 of a group who are each, individually, in the National Football Museum's Hall of Fame.

The stamps were to commemorate the 140th anniversary of the Scottish FA as well as the 150th of the establishment of the rules of Association Football and the Football Association.

Mackay was the subject of a from-the-heart speech by then Royal Mail chairman Sir Donald Brydon.

Sir Donald, knighted in the 2019 New Year's Honours list for 'services to business and charity', also hailed from Edinburgh.

He said to Mackay and all those present at the national stadium that day, 'I remember as a seven-year-old boy we had a garage built at the side of our house and the apprentice joiner who came to put the doors on was none other than Dave Mackay himself. This was 1952/53. For the next three years after every home Hearts game I would wait behind the stand and Dave Mackay, about 40 minutes after the whistle, would come out and take out the programme from the previous week's away game in his pocket. I still have this collection of Hearts programmes complete from those years. That's what heroes should do. They say you should never meet your heroes but I'm thrilled to meet and see him again here today. It is very special for me.'

MC Dan Walker, the BBC TV presenter, did the introduction of the featured players. When it came to Mackay, Walker said, 'When I was growing up in our back garden – it wasn't a particularly large back garden – and my father used to say to me, "You be a tricky winger – and I'll be Dave Mackay," it probably ended up with me in tears holding a shin!

'It is interesting to summarise people's achievements by what others have said about them and the calibre of those others who rate them highly. The great Bill Nicholson said Mr Mackay was his best ever signing. George Best thought him his hardest and greatest opponent. Brian Clough referred to him as "the ideal skipper". Dave Mackay's in the room today, with his daughter Val, wife Isobel, his son-in-law and his nephew. Dave Mackay everybody.'

There was prolonged applause. Valerie said, 'We were so proud. We still get people coming up to me and saying he did this, he did that, and never tire of hearing any stories. But the stamp was the icing on the cake, especially for our kids to see their grandad on one. Great recognition.'

It was to prove one of the last of Mackay's major public appearances as his condition progressively worsened – if not the final one. The family did everything they could and got comfort wherever they could as its patriarch's light faded.

Valerie said, 'We took Dad to the hospital in Derby a couple of times and the doctor said it could be dementia with Lewy bodies [DLB], which is a mixture of Parkinson's and dementia. I believe it probably was that yet it is just down as "dementia". But the Parkinson's was the worst part – the main thing – because it took its toll on somebody who had been so fit.

'Also, Dad had "injuries through sport" acknowledged by the specialist doctor when Mum and me went with Dad to the hospital in Derby. I feel this is very important to include.'

The National Health Service describes DLB as 'one of the most common types of dementia, and says that 'dementia is the name for problems with mental abilities caused by gradual changes and damage in the brain. It's rare in people under-65. It tends to develop slowly and get gradually worse over several years.' Symptoms of DLB include 'problems with understanding, thinking, memory and judgement – this is similar to Alzheimer's disease, although memory may be less affected in people with dementia with Lewy bodies' and 'slow movement, stiff limbs and tremors (uncontrollable shaking)'.

More broadly, the NHS states that Parkinson's disease is 'a condition in which parts of the brain become progressively damaged over many years'. Symptoms listed include 'involuntary shaking of particular parts of the body, slow movement, stiff and inflexible muscles'.

Its overview of dementia is 'a syndrome [a group of related symptoms] associated with an ongoing decline of brain functioning'. Symptoms including 'memory loss, thinking speed, mental sharpness and quickness … mood, movement, difficulty doing daily activities. There are many different causes of dementia, and many different types. People often get confused about the difference between Alzheimer's disease and dementia. Alzheimer's disease is a type of dementia and, together with vascular dementia, makes up the majority of cases.'

John McGovern dropped by the family home in Burton Joyce to take Mackay out before he deteriorated sufficiently to call a halt to the arrangement.

Derek said, 'Dad was still fairly active and John used to take him to the pub where they watched the football on television. It was nice. John did it for a long time until Dad got a bit too ill to go out. Dad started to go in and out of hospital and even then John always went to visit him. These were such great things for John to do.'

Roy McFarland and Henry Newton also visited the Mackay residence. McFarland said, 'Isobel primed us after we'd told her through Val we wanted to see Dave. We knew his condition and Isobel said if we just turned up Dave would ask her, "Why did they come to see me? What's happening? Is there something going on with me?" Typical of Dave wanting to know bloody everything. So we agreed a story with Isobel that we had just popped in on the way home from playing golf.

'It was a very, very tough period. His hands used to shake. It was almost like if he had a drink you were worried about it spilling. Isobel knew exactly what to do. She was an absolute brick for him.'

Jim Walker, like McFarland a former Mackay team-mate at Derby, also visited the hospital. Derek said, 'It was so nice of Jim to come in. He said a few prayers to Dad while he was there. He was part of the Clough squad which won the league in 1972, but missed out on a medal at the time because you had to play a certain number of games. Derby only won the league by one point and it was argued that without Jim scoring the winning goal in a 1-0 win over Crystal Palace [in March 1972] they might have missed out on the title. So he eventually got his medal. Jim also had the story where he used to drive around in Dad's Jaguar and a mate told him he'd seen Dave Mackay "driving around in Jim's car".'

Mackay was under care at home before being admitted full-time to Queen's Medical Centre in Nottingham for the last two weeks of his life.

Valerie helped look after her dad as his illness worsened. She said, 'I phoned and got this physiotherapist called Rob to come round not that many months before Dad died. Mum was questioning why I was asking him to come. The physio had Dad doing exercises of all descriptions. Rob said, "Why has he got a frame?" It was unbelievable. Everything Rob was asking him to do he was doing it. It was like Dad was back in the gym at White Hart Lane. We were all shocked. It was quite emotional for us all.

'Dad didn't have Alzheimer's. He perhaps didn't have memories of the football much, games and stuff like that, but he knew who we were at the end. We all know that. We just did. I'll always be forever grateful for that. We were really lucky, because I know a lot of footballers' families go through hell with the dementia.

'I remember when Mum and I stayed at the hospital, holding my dad's hand and him holding mine. He then gripped it. He knew exactly who we were, making jokes in his usual way.

'We knew Dad wasn't going to live for much longer but I asked if it was possible for him to come home. They said yes. They discussed the possible risk of that and I accepted that he should stay in hospital. We still had Dad with us nine days longer than the hospital expected us to.

'It was so wonderful Roy McFarland and Henry Newton came to see Dad in his last days. I knew Roy cared for my dad but didn't realise how much Henry loved him. Dad was Henry's boss but it was really nice when he was talking to Dad, calling him "Dave" throughout. He held his hand. He said to me, "I came here thinking I'd get really emotional. But your dad's actually given me some strength." To see it that way I thought, wow. It helped me because I felt my dad did have a power. Then, when he went out he stood at the door and he said, "See you, boss." And it was really touching.

'Every time I see Henry – we were both at Des Anderson's funeral [in October 2019] – he talks to me about Dad, saying he was the best. It is nice to hear players managed by my dad say things like that. It is often not the case in football. The boss is different to the players.

'I don't often bring myself to think of certain details. It is too painful about my dad's illness. I blank it out, I suppose. But all we know is Dad was happy every day. Never miserable, never moaned, never complained. I suppose you can't ask for more than that.

'Also, a big blessing during Dad's final years was the bond that developed between my granddaughter Remae as a baby and a toddler and Dad. My dad was amazing with her. We've got the pictures to prove it. That was lovely. He didn't get to meet my daughter Lucy's second daughter, Nariya, whose second name was Davae after dad. My son Gregor's daughter Lilly came along in 2012 and saw Dad a few times. Lilly after the Lilywhites? I didn't think of that connection!'

Derek, who moved on to work in the food hall of a Marks and Spencer store near his Burton Joyce home having been laid off after 21 years as an experienced shop-fitter, said, 'Dad was probably ill for four or five years, really. Progressively. Slowly, slowly it got worse. It was a hard time and really sad. For a long time he used to like watching football on the telly. He had the Sky TV on and all the family gathered around to watch the matches. We'd watch Tottenham and wear Spurs shirts and scarves. We did that right until the end, even when he had lost the power of speech. I remember you'd get [Sky presenter] Jeff Stelling saying, "Here we are at White Hart Lane and it is 1-0 to Spurs." And Dad would put his arm up with a clenched fist, like "yeah, 1-0!"

'Mum always looked after Dad and made sure everything was absolutely perfect for him. It was all for Dad. She'd do any sacrifice to make sure Dad was all right.

'Dad passed away aged 80 but had been ill many years before that. Dad's father Tom lived a relatively active life right up until he died aged 85. It's so sad we lost all those years with Dad.'

Isobel said, 'I remember David's 80th birthday on 14 November 2014. I asked Derek to get the watch he was given when he won the Double with Spurs out of safekeeping. I wanted David to wear it. When he had the watch on the carers we had in for David said, "Look at you!" And then I explained how he won it and they were amazed. And they were all taking photos of him with it on.

'The illness was just something you have to accept and get on with. I was lucky in many ways, David never ever complained. Never once. It was never, "Why me?" He was so good. People used to say to me, "You did a wonderful job." But honestly, Mike, he couldn't have been a better patient. It was hard and difficult at times but he was no trouble.

'It was sad he had to go into hospital. But Valerie and me were allowed to stay for the whole two weeks that he was there. Valerie wasn't happy her dad had to stay in hospital. She wanted me to bring him home but it wouldn't have worked out. She spoke to the consultant but he said, "Well, we could take him home but he could pass away in the ambulance. Or you'd get him back in the hospital. You'd have to go through all this." It was best that he wasn't moved. He was so ill in the hospital and he was allowed to stay there. He had his own room.

'A sad thing was that he had lost his speech and couldn't speak for a while. He had choking fits. We had to get the medics because he had the Parkinson's.

'I remember Valentine's Day in 2015. David gave me a Valentine's card he had got David Junior to buy, and signed it "Dave Mackay". Every card I had from him was signed "Dave Mackay", like his autograph. I've got all the cards he sent me. I don't think I've got one that just says, "David".

'I was still attending mass and went to church on Ash Wednesday four days after that Valentine's Day. I was getting my ashes [drawn on forehead as part of the holy ritual] by Father Joe at the church who said, "I'll come and visit David." I went into the hospital and went to

413

kiss David and he pushed my head back and pointed at the ashes. He'd realised it was Ash Wednesday.

'Later on, Father Joe came in. David had never met him. He says, "Hi, Dave. I don't know if I should be saying this, but I've got a season ticket at Forest." He talked away to David. Another priest, Father Michael, whose sister was a receptionist at Derby County and married to Ted McMinn [a Scottish winger who played for the Rams from 1988 to 1993], also called in to see him. He was a Derby supporter. And a third priest – a Leicester City supporter – came in two or three times to see David. David might not have been able to communicate but it was nice the priests took time to come and see him. That was a big comfort to me. David passed away not long after these visits, remembering us all.

'You knew he was going to pass away but it was still a big shock when it happened. He just kept going. At one time the doctor said, "Do you know if he is waiting to see somebody?" I said, "I don't know." On this Sunday night, my cousin, Ninian, a very close friend of David's, arrived at about 11 o'clock at night. I didn't expect him, but my young brother Tom had been down and been saying when he went back home he'd say to Nin "you've got to go and see David". So on the Sunday night we were in a little room on our own with David. We saw figures through the glass door and Nin came in and said, "Hello, Dave." David put his hand right out to take his hand, you know. He knew … he recognised his voice as well as us.

'Nin's a right happy guy, and he casually said "ex-Hearts and Tottenham Hotspur – never had a game" [repeating the joke the pair shared relating to the fact Cassidy made no appearances for either club]. Nin went away about midnight back to Scotland and then David passed away the next night at eight o'clock.'

Ninian said, 'I wanted to be kept posted and Tom phoned me up and said, "Dave's really, really bad now. Not got long left." I just burst out crying in the phone. It was like losing your dad. I decided I'd visit, and went with a friend called Malcolm. The family didn't know I was going so were surprised to see me when I walked into his room at the hospital about 11 at night. Dave was sleeping.

'I went up to the bed, held out my hand and said to him, "It's me, Dave, Ninian Cassidy, ex-Hearts and Tottenham." He gripped my hand, looked at me and I thought he was saying, "Are you Ninian Cassidy, ex-

Hearts and Tottenham? How many games did you play?" And although I was very upset, it was still a comfort to have seen him and said that to him. They reckon he was holding on for something, that they don't know how he's still living. That's what my cousin said. He told me, "It could be you then, he wanted to say goodbye to you." It was very poignant. A fantastic moment to have seen him and hold that hand and him knowing I was still there. He never forgot his nearest and dearest? Never. Definitely.'

39

Legend

THERE WAS an immediate outpouring of tributes in the media after Mackay's death was announced.

Hearts said, 'Dave lost his long battle with illness at the age of 80 with his family at his bedside in Nottingham. A fearless defender regarded as the club's greatest-ever player, Dave won the league title, Scottish Cup and Scottish League Cup (twice) with Hearts before going on to star for Tottenham Hotspur and Derby County. Our sincerest condolences go to his family at this extremely sad time.'

The club added via the BBC, 'A local hero ... a legend and a man who will be sorely missed and well remembered.'

Supporters movement Foundation of Hearts said, 'The Hearts family has lost a true giant.' And John Robertson, the club's leading league goalscorer whose late father spoke in glowing terms about Mackay, said to the BBC, 'It's a sad day for football. Dave Mackay was an absolute gentleman and a wonderful football player. He was part of the team that was the standard-bearer for everybody at Hearts – to show what could be done. I was lucky enough to meet him on several occasions and he was always the same – a really nice man. He was the complete player. He had energy, he could get about the pitch, he could tackle and he could play when he got the ball. He was a world-class player at the time. He was inducted into the Scottish and English Halls of Fame – that shows you just how good a player he was.'

Spurs said, 'Dave Mackay will certainly always be remembered here as one of our greatest ever players and a man who never failed to inspire those around him. In short, a Spurs legend. We extend our condolences to the Mackay family at this sad time.'

Alan Mullery spoke to Alan Brazil on the former Spurs striker's talkSPORT radio show the morning after Mackay's passing.

He said, 'Dave's influence at Tottenham when I arrived was enormous. Second to none. I've never seen a footballer in all the years I've been involved in it … that had so much influence on teams. If you played anything – might be a three-a-side – he'd want to win. Every time you walked up those stairs at White Hart Lane in those days to come out on to the pitch, he'd set the crowd alight. Unbelievable.

'He was probably the best captain I have ever seen. I've never known anyone like him. He was that good. You talk about greats. This fellow could play in any position. He even went in goal for Scotland for half an hour, and he never let anyone down. His tackling ability was fantastic. I followed him as captain and tried. I never had his ability. I was half the player Mackay was.

'Everything was about winning. When he became a manager he won again. He was just never a loser. If you were losing 4-0 with five minutes left he'd think you'd win 5-4, and he gave that belief to lots of people. If you mention Dave Mackay's name and the football club at Tottenham you just see greatness. A wonderful leader. Whenever he lost, keep out of his way. He wanted to wreck the place. He was that sort of person.

'He was probably the hardest player I've ever seen. The ability he had. The tricks he used to do with coins! He'd be a showman in front of people. I suppose you could say he was a show-off. The greatest show-off I've ever seen.

'A terrific lad. Liked a pint or two but I'll tell you what, when it came down to the matchday and we were playing he'd be there. He'd be leading it.

'The memory of Dave Mackay will never ever be lost on me and thousands and thousands of Tottenham supporters.'

Derby County's president Sam Rush said on Sky, 'Everyone at Derby County is truly saddened at the news that Dave Mackay has passed away. Dave Mackay is a legend at Derby County and his name will forever be etched into the history of the club for the fantastic contribution that he made, both as a player and a manager. Fans still talk of his influence to this day and he will be forever remembered as a true great of our football club. Our condolences and thoughts go to his family and friends at this time.'

Swindon Town said, 'Football fans of a certain age will remember the football legend Dave Mackay, who sadly died this week. As a Scottish international and league championship-winning player with Tottenham and Derby, his name was right up there with players classed as "the very best" of their generation. Mackay also played for Swindon 26 times and managed at the County Ground.'

Walsall said, 'Former Walsall FC manager, Dave Mackay, has passed away at the age of 80. Our thoughts go out to his family at this sad time. RIP.'

Al-Arabi, where Mackay earned the moniker of the Sir Alex Ferguson of Kuwait due to the amount of trophies won according to one affectionate post on social media on a Hearts fans website, also paid tribute.

His son Derek said, 'It was really nice, a lovely big banner. Pictures of it were posted on the internet. Dad did really well there and won loads of things.'

Isobel said, 'The club were so good to David. The chairman Mohammed Al-Mulla was so nice. At the funeral, the details of David's career were on the back page of the service sheet. David was in Kuwait from 1978 to 1986 and that was all missed out. I felt sad about that as he was there all those years and they were so good to him. All the other details were on it, when he was in Dubai, Cairo, Qatar and at home. I wanted to send a service sheet. I felt I couldn't send one to Mohammed's wife Lesley because the Kuwait details were missing. Sadly, Mohammed had passed away by then.'

Doncaster Rovers said, 'The club would like to go on record as sending its condolences to the friends and family of Mr Mackay. The Scot managed Rovers during the late 1980s while the club were at Belle Vue, following his reputable playing career with Heart of Midlothian, Tottenham Hotspur and Derby County.'

The *Birmingham Mail* reported, 'Former Birmingham City boss Dave Mackay has died at the age of 80. The Scottish football legend managed at St Andrew's between 1989–1991. He had previously managed Walsall in 1977/78. The former Hearts, Tottenham Hotspur and Scotland star – described by George Best as the "hardest man I have ever played against" – passed away after battling illness for some time.

'The legendary hard tackler spoke about the state of football in 2009 and how it was harder in his day. He said, "I think there are fewer players of my kind around than there were. Football's changed. In our time it was a tougher game, maybe because of the referees. In the olden days you got away with more hard tackles. As long as they were fair, you were okay. Nowadays a hard tackle can get you a booking, which isn't right if it's not dirty."'

The SFA said, 'The Scottish FA is deeply saddened by the news of Dave Mackay's death. He was a legendary figure with Heart of Midlothian, Tottenham Hotspur and Derby County; an inspirational pillar for the clubs with whom he played with distinction and, of course, his country.'

Former Scotland manager Craig Brown told the BBC, 'He would be in my all-time greatest Scottish team, no doubt about that. He was inspirational in everything he did, a wonderful player. He was an absolutely perfect midfield player and today he would be worth a fortune. You wonder what Dave Mackay would be worth in the modern market. He was in every respect an outstanding exponent. He was hard and respected by his team-mates and opponents alike.'

Tommy Docherty, Mackay's Scottish team-mate, landlord, FA Cup Final rival and friend who passed away on 31 December 2020, said to the BBC, 'He was a tremendous player, world-class. Right side of midfield, left side of midfield, it didn't matter. He was a great tackler and a great passer of a ball. If you wanted to play football, he'd play football; if you wanted to rough it, well, you picked the wrong man. He reminded me of the young Duncan Edwards at Manchester United. Dave Mackay was world-class as a player and as a person. I tried to buy him when I was a coach at Chelsea. I told the manager Ted Drake to buy him from Hearts. He signed for Tottenham. Dave Mackay just wanted to play football; he didn't worry about what he was getting paid. He was great company.'

Former BBC commentator Archie Macpherson said, 'He was a giant of a player. You get players who, when they emerge from the tunnel, immediately they dominate – he was that kind of player. I saw him in the early days at Hearts. He was a ferocious tackler and because of that he gained a reputation of being a hard man. Sometimes people thought he was a dirty player – he was nothing of the kind. He was bold, vociferous, a leader. He dominated so many games. You've probably seen that famous photograph with him and Billy Bremner, holding him up like a wee rabbit that he'd caught in the back garden. If you look at it, it's almost playful. There's a kind of chuckle about it. He was a lovely man. When you see that photo, think of a man who could chuckle as well as hit hard.'

There was a minute's applause for Mackay at White Hart Lane two days after his passing, shortly before a 3-2 Spurs win over Swansea City in the Premier League. It was some compensation for a League Cup Final loss against Chelsea the day before he left us.

Former team-mates such as Alan Mullery, Pat Jennings, Cliff Jones, Phil Beal and Martin Chivers stood shoulder to shoulder with more recent Tottenham glitterati like Darren Anderton, Ossie Ardiles, Micky Hazard, Graham Roberts, Ray Clemence, Paul Miller, Mark Falco and John Pratt as the club paid further tributes to its greatest son.

On the centre circle, Tottenham talisman Harry Kane seemed to be looking along the line to check the rest of his team were joining him and Christian Eriksen to his left in applauding, namely Kyle Walker, Andros Townsend, Eric Dier, Ryan Mason, captain Hugo Lloris, Nabil Bentaleb, Danny Rose, Jan Vertonghen and Nacer Chadli. They all were. So were Swansea's 11 opposite.

Manager Mauricio Pochettino paid tribute in the match programme. He said, 'I would like to end this column paying tribute to Dave Mackay, who passed away on Monday. I have heard great things about him and I know this is a terrible loss for the whole of British football. He achieved a great deal in the game and is a true Spurs legend.'

Derby County also had a minute's applause with 31,522 fans standing up from their seats prior to the Rams taking on Birmingham City, another club Mackay managed, at Pride Park on Saturday, 7 March. A picture of Mackay adorned the cover of the match programme with tributes to the Scot inside it. Victory would have been apt to achieve in memory of the serial winner who helped them to titles on and off the pitch but a 2-0 lead was let slip in injury time for a 2-2 draw.

Hearts made their tributes at their first game at Tynecastle since Mackay's passing on Saturday, 14 March. A half-profile of a youthful Mackay in a Heart shirt dominated the front of the souvenir issue match programme. Around it were the words 'DAVE MACKAY – ALWAYS IN OUR HEARTS #GreatestPlayer'. A roundel of the image covered the centre circle with both teams – each player wearing a black armband – on its perimeter facing each other.

The announcer lifted the microphone to his lips and, with his amplified words ringing around the ground, said, 'As you know the Heart of Midlothian family lost one of its favourite sons this month with the sad passing of Dave Mackay at the age of 80. He was arguably the finest player to wear Maroon, captaining the 1957/58 team to the league championship. He also won two Scottish League Cups and the Scottish Cup during a glittering career at Tynecastle. Dave won 22 caps for Scotland and went on to achieve legendary status at Tottenham Hotspur and Derby County after moving to England. He's sorely missed by everyone. So ladies and gentlemen, Dave Mackay, always in our hearts. Now please recognise his memory with a period of silence.'

The 'period' was, appropriately 54 seconds to reflect the year in the 20th century of the first trophy he won with the Jambos. And as the players broke away to warm up, one, Edinburgh-born winger Sam Nicholson walked back to just outside the centre circle, went down on his haunches and stared at the roundel for a few seconds, perhaps hoping a bit of Mackay inspiration might rub off on the day for the modern-day team en route for promotion as champions. It did as Hearts won 4-0 with Osman Sow, captain Danny Wilson – in the number four shirt so often worn by Mackay – and two-goal Billy King on target against Dumbarton.

The Scottish Football Association staged a minute's applause before Mackay's country pipped Northern Ireland 1-0 in a friendly in front of 30,000 at Hampden Park on 25 March.

Clapping had become an alternative expression of collective grief for the loss of a football legend on similar occasions. It spontaneously broke out to commemorate the passing of George Best in November 2005. The first reported 'outbreak' of the practice was in Mackay's home town before Hibernian defeated Rangers 2-1 at Easter Road.

Mackay would have appreciated his country and first and second clubs following up their celebrations of him by scoring victories as winning meant so much to him. He would also have been as frustrated as Rams manager Steve McClaren with Derby so close to one on their day of commemoration.

40

The Banner Man

DAVE MACKAY'S funeral took place back home in Edinburgh on Tuesday, 24 March 2015.

Sir Alex Ferguson and Denis Law were quietly having a cup of tea together in the Hearts directors' room at Tynecastle on the morning of it.

They were the first guests that Rob White, son of Mackay's Spurs and Scotland late team-mate John, noticed as he entered. And as he looked around the room he was struck by the quality of esteemed folk gathered; perhaps what you would expect of a group paying its respects to a legend's legend.

Rob said, 'Sir Alex and Denis were two people who I'd always wanted to meet. Denis, of course, had links to my dad and what football fan wouldn't want to meet Sir Alex Ferguson? It was incredible the people who were there in that boardroom. Lot of Spurs guys. There were about 30 people. Just the feeling of love and warmth was phenomenal. Dave Mackay was some man, wasn't he?'

Eventually, the room emptied as the guests began to make their way from Mackay's spiritual football home not far from where he was born and brought up in Glendevon Park, north-east across town to Mansfield Traquair church on the edge of Hibs territory to make up the 450 congregated for the funeral service.

The cortege left Tynecastle at 1.15pm and routed down the Gorgie and Dalry roads. It passed the Heart of Midlothian War Memorial at Haymarket just as Mackay and his Maroons team-mates had done on board an open-top bus celebrating trophy victories in the 1950s. Then it travelled along West Maitland Street, Shandwick Place, Princes Street, Leith Street and Broughton Street.

Auld Reekie tried to hold back its tears, biting its collective lip to avoid exposing feelings expressed in the sad eyes of its citizens lining the streets of Scotland's capital city – many sporting Hearts scarves – as the cortege passed by before arriving at the apostolic church in Mansfield Place. Mourners entered and took their seats inside. Widow Isobel, Mackay's children, David Junior, Derek, Valerie and Julie, Ninian Cassidy, and other family were there. Friends and guests included Sir Alex Ferguson, Denis Law, Frank McLintock, and Hearts owner Ann Budge, whose club organised the service. A galaxy of former Spurs stars, many ex-club-mates of the deceased, filed in as a group, immaculately turned out in jackets displaying the Spurs logo and club ties. John Sainty, who played alongside Mackay in the reserve game when the Scot had his leg broken a second time, arrived under his own steam to pay his respects to his 'idol', as did ex-Rangers striker Mark Hateley, the son of Tony, a 1967 FA Cup Final opponent who passed in 2014.

Des Anderson, Mackay's pal and assistant manager, his wife Lesley, their son Des Junior and Des's sister Mary, joined the gathering.

Lesley Anderson, Des's widow, said, 'I met Des in 1962 and Dave and Des must have known each other before they left Edinburgh and came down to London; Dave from Hearts to Tottenham and Des from Hibs to Millwall. Des must have gone to games and seen Dave and they'd remembered each other. Dave and Isobel were there for him when he suddenly lost his first wife. They were brilliant for him as a young guy on his own in the capital. And Dave was best man at our wedding in 1966.

'Des was overjoyed when Dave asked him to join him at Swindon. Of course, they moved on together to Nottingham Forest and had a marvellous time at Derby after a difficult start – Dave showed his inspirational qualities there – and Walsall. They worked well together and trusted each other. Dave was fair, kind and had an inner strength, something he really showed at Derby. Des adored him. He showed total loyalty. It was wonderful. They understood each other professionally and personally. They were fantastic friends before they worked together and always remained that way after football.

'The relationship between the families has been a proper one. They are a lovely family. If you were to see any of them it would be like you only saw each other yesterday, which is what it is like with the old players, especially at Derby. We all enjoyed ourselves when Dave was around. We had such wonderful times, loved the parties and Dave was such fun to be around. We had a fabulous social life with the Mackays. They were a huge part of our lives.

'Des Junior, who walked out at Wembley when Derby played in the 1975 Charity Shield match, and Dave and Isobel's boys got on well. I remember as kids the three of them used to play on the Baseball Ground pitch after a game and Des Junior would ask Dave – he called him Davie Kay! – if he could get the floodlights switched on so they could play, which he did! Des Junior, who has done well for himself and remains the same lovely boy he always was, never forgetting where he came from, flew back from Hong Kong to be at the funeral. Isobel and Val – Derek and Julie had to work – attended Des's funeral at Kensal Green in London in 2019.'

Also present were Neil Martin, his wife Mima and their sons Craig and Neil Junior. Derek said, 'The Andersons and Martins are all very close to us. Like family.'

Others present included two more of Mackay's old Scotland team-mates, Ian St John and Willie Henderson, plus Bertie Auld and John Clark, two of Celtic's Lisbon Lions. The great and good of football were there at a beautiful church.

Meanwhile, a significant trio stood in the shadow of the entrance porch with the outside light reflecting on their sombre faces, shoulder to shoulder, each seemingly lost in their own thoughts.

Gordon Marshall, Pat Jennings and Roy McFarland were former team-mates at the three clubs that highlighted Mackay's playing career: Heart of Midlothian, Tottenham Hotspur and Derby County. McFarland peered out from the shadows into the brightness of daytime as Jennings next to him appeared to stifle a cough and Marshall to the Irishman's left stared into the mid-distance. Each were to be pallbearers at the request of Isobel; partnered respectively by Hearts' leading league goalscorer John Robertson, along with two more former Mackay team-mates, Cliff Jones from Spurs and John McGovern from the Rams, who had also received the same request from Mackay's widow.

No doubt the reason for McFarland's watching brief was to spot when the selected half-dozen would have to begin their duties.

When the cortege arrived, with everyone else ensconced, the pallbearers took their places either side of the coffin; Marshall and Robertson alongside each other at the front, Jones and Jennings second in line and McFarland and McGovern third. They followed a piper who marched slowly up the aisle playing 'Amazing Grace'. If Mackay could have witnessed the scene it might have reminded him of the day he and his Saughton school team-mates had followed that piper out of Tynecastle and back to school after lifting the Scottish Schools trophy; his first glittering prize in a career spent collecting them. Certainly it would have struck a chord with his elder brother Tommy, who played with him that day and was seated next to remaining sibling Frank.

Hearts' chaplain Andy Prime urged those present to join in singing the first hymn, 'Abide With Me', saying it was 'one Dave sang numerous times at Wembley'. Valerie wrote the first eulogy on behalf of herself and her siblings David Junior, Derek and Julie, Mackay's children, which was read by Tommy Mackay, a nephew. It is printed in full in the first appendix section of this book.

Ninian Cassidy spoke and recounted the tales of when he and Mackay had attended that Europa League tie between Hearts and Tottenham in 2011 and lightened the mood by joking then how owner Vladimir Romanov 'was not as gracious as [successor] Ann Budge'.

John Robertson also did a reading as well as acting as pallbearer. He said, 'It was a huge honour to be asked to be a pallbearer and do a Bible reading. The family were appreciative of the respect I gave him by calling him Mr Mackay, in respect of my late dad who would have whacked me round the neck had I not! When I was doing the reading you realise there's all these people, including his family. I didn't want to mess up. I could see my dad sitting at the back saying, "Don't get this wrong!"

'I'd probably have been in a hell of a state being a pallbearer considering the enormity of the occasion but I met Cliff Jones and Pat Jennings before and had a good chat with them and told how things would work. My heart was racing as I picked up the coffin.'

Cliff Jones also spoke. He stirred the emotions when he declared that each time he listens to the 'skirl' of bagpipes performing 'Flower of Scotland', 'I think of Dave Mackay.' He also made reference to how 'proud' Mackay would have been of Hearts having just been promoted back to the top tier of Scottish football, with the manager, Robbie Neilson, and the players who had achieved it looking on. Jones said that Mackay turned a good Tottenham side into a great one.

Sir Alex Ferguson, sitting alongside Law, Ann Budge and Hearts director of football Craig Levein in the front row of the second section of pews, also eulogised his pal.

Sir Alex, with approving nods from the football fraternity spotted by the video camera as he spoke, said, 'They talk of this great courage he had. I think it is unfair. All the papers … everything I've read is about this great courage he had. We know he was the bravest man in the world. We know that. But he was a fantastic footballer. Skilful. Cliff summed it up perfectly. A team that is good can be great by certain introductions. And his personality, his intensity, his desire to win, could make any team. He proved that by going to Derby County and winning the league as a centre-back. He could play anywhere. His record's fantastic. As for his family, it is a privilege to speak here today. I think we have seen the passing of a truly great legend.'

Sir Alex addressed a congregation which included the Spurs contingent made up of Mackay team-mates Alan Mullery, Phil Beal and Mike England, plus Steve Perryman, Clive Allen and John Sainty. Also in the London N17 party were Rob White, press officer John Fennelly and commercial manager Mike Rollo. Frank McLintock, Mackay's friend and Scottish team-mate, was seated close by.

The Old Firm was represented by former Rangers winger Willie Henderson, who helped Mackay's Scotland to that famous win over England at Wembley in 1963, and Celtic European Cup winners Bertie Auld and John Clark. Ian St John also paid his respects.

Hearts had stated on the eve of the event, 'Some of the greats of British football will be in attendance and this is testament to the highest regard in which Dave was held.' The club, having organised the funeral, got that right.

The mourners exited to the strains of Blue Mink's 'The Banner Man', which was appropriate on two fronts. First was the line 'the banner man held the banner high with hallelujah in his eyes', mentioning the 'h'-word synonymous with Mackay's glory years at Spurs. And secondly the cheery, upbeat nature of the 1970s pop hit reflected the side of the Mackay 'joy of life' psyche which had been referred to in the service.

Derek said, 'Dad used to love "The Banner Man", which was a bit of a song for us as well with all the old "glory, glory, glory" in the words.'

Some joined the private service which followed at the Warriston Crematorium. And there was an even jauntier tune playing as the family and friends present left to return to Tynecastle: 'The Sideboard Song', by Spurs fans Chas & Dave.

Derek said, 'It was great when we walked out to "The Sideboard Song", because it brought a smile to everyone's face. That's what Dad would have wanted. Humour can help in those situations, definitely.'

Gordon Marshall, a Hearts team-mate of Mackay's, said, 'Dave got a good turnout for his funeral. He was well thought of and popular. We knew he hadn't been well from Isobel. It was sad to see him go. He loved his football and loved playing for Hearts.'

Mike England, who played with Mackay at Spurs, said, 'It was a nice thing that so many Tottenham players, wearing club ties, were at the funeral to show their respects. Our Spurs party followed the funeral car with so many people lining the streets. It was great the whole city had turned out to pay their respects.'

The day began and ended at the home of Hearts as attendees uttered their tributes to Mackay to Hearts TV.

Alan Mullery compared Mackay to Sir William Wallace, the Scottish freedom warrior, as loosely depicted in the 1995 Academy award-winning film *Braveheart*, a title with a dictionary definition of 'a brave person'.

Mullery said, 'As a leader, I don't think Mel Gibson should have been in that film. I think Dave should have had that part. He wouldn't have stopped at York. He'd have gone down to Parliament in London! You just wanted to do what he wanted you to do. Such an influential and inspirational footballer and captain.'

Pat Jennings said, 'Dave was different class. He could do everything … a born leader who got the best out of whatever player he played with. Wherever you played in Dave's team you played – or else!'

Phil Beal said, 'If you'd done something wrong he'd let you know, but if you did something right he'd praise you. He was one of the best players I've ever seen.'

Steve Perryman said, 'I loved what he stood for. I ended up becoming captain. He was a great influence and someone you always aspired to be like, to try and create the leadership qualities he had and drive your team on to success.'

Sir Alex Ferguson said, 'It's a sad day, of course. We're talking about not necessarily just a great footballer, but a great person. He used to come along to Old Trafford quite a bit. He carried his modesty really well. I think that was his pride. He was a humble person; the greatest personality. Apart from being one of the greatest players Scotland has produced, that tells you why we're all here, from Tottenham, from Manchester United. I think it is a great tribute to him.'

Alan Gilzean said, 'Dave Mackay was an inspirational figure at Tottenham Hotspur. That's where I knew him. Dave would want to be remembered for all the good times he had at Hearts, Tottenham and Derby County.'

Gilzean also recalled when he first saw Mackay play. The Scottish international said to *The Scotsman*, 'I was about 16 or 17, Hearts played St Johnstone in the League Cup. It was the era of Conn, Bauld and Wardhaugh. I was a Hibs supporter rather than a Hearts supporter but I went to watch.

'They beat St Johnstone about 5-0 or something. Even when they were four up, Mackay was still driving them on. It was the same when he was at Tottenham, driving you on. Any shirkers, he let you know. He wouldn't tolerate it.'

Scotsman journalist Alan Pattullo, reporting for the paper Mackay's dad helped print, wrote in the following day's edition, 'Gilzean put Mackay in the same bracket as the Manchester United prodigy Duncan Edwards when asked to rank his former team-mate in the pantheon of greats. Wherever you looked yesterday, distinguished players patiently waited to pay tribute to Mackay. There was a recurring theme – leader of men.'

Daughter Valerie Mackay, 'He touched so many lives? Yes, it's me getting emotional again. We knew Dad was special but I suppose with the funeral and everything brings it home. The reaction to his death, how it was all in the media, and with everybody. The tributes from ex-players, like Roy McFarland. He did an interview for Derby County and was talking about Dad and had to stop because he was getting choked up. Football's not just about getting the results, it is about friendships.

Players bond, especially the younger ones looking up to the older players. It's lovely to hear that Cliff Jones couldn't say enough good things about Dad. Dad had a lot of those friendships in football.'

41

'My best friend'

A MEMORIAL service was organised by Tottenham Hotspur at The Parish Church of St Stephen at Bush Hill Park in Enfield, close to where the Mackay family once lived, on Thursday, 30 April 2015.

The sun shone as many of Mackay's former Spurs team-mates, club officials, family, friends and fans filed in.

Colleagues included Terry Dyson, Cliff Jones, Pat Jennings and Jimmy Robertson. Former Spurs manager Peter Shreeves, Frank McLintock and club ambassador and former defender Ledley King also joined Isobel, fellow family members and friends, plus fans, at the service conducted by Reverend Paul Atherton. Prayers, readings, and a hymn preceded 'reflections and memories of Dave's life and career'.

Jones, as he did in Edinburgh, addressed the congregation, which included your author. He said, 'Dave was known as a hard man but that was only half the story. He had everything that was needed to be a great footballer, was the heart of the team, had an unwavering desire to push the team to win and was undoubtedly part of Spurs' best team.'

Jones recalled being on the receiving end of a Mackay challenge when he turned out for Wales against Scotland at Hampden.

The former winger said, 'I told him, "Steady on Dave, I thought we were friends." And he said, "We are, but today we are not." That showed the spirit within him. He was a wonderful man and true legend of Tottenham Hotspur Football Club.

'Whenever I hear the swirl of bagpipes playing "Flower of Scotland" I think of Dave, a proud Scotsman who never forgot his roots, a great family man who loved life and was a truly great footballer. On behalf of myself, Tottenham Hotspur and all of football, we thank Dave for his football legacy. It was an honour to know him. Until we meet again, dear friend, rest in peace Dave. Diolch-yn-Fawr. Thank you.'

Long-serving Spurs official John Fennelly, the club's head of publications, added his thoughts too. He said, 'Firstly, may I extend the deep condolences of all at Tottenham Hotspur to Isobel and to all the Mackay family. As a lad on the terraces at White Hart Lane, Dave Mackay was a great hero of mine. He was the player we all wanted to be because he shared our passion for the club and always demonstrated a will to win that resonated with supporters. For us he was all about commitment, bravery. A gladiator. He was fierce and determined; leading by example and never taking a step backwards.

'Yet, as I grew older, I fully appreciated just how much more there was to the make-up of this special performer. He was not just an enforcer. He most certainly could play. He possessed all the skills of any player and far more than most.

'He drove forward in possession with a passing range that left shadows for opponents to chase as Dave found space that barely existed for his team-mates to exploit. His control was instant, he was so comfortable and efficient with the ball and his shooting from range was explosive. What couldn't he do?!

'In expressing the club's sorrow to the Mackay family for the loss of a man who seemed an immortal, we also thank them for lending us a man who for a brief time in our long history played such a key role in the most glorious era ever at White Hart Lane.

'There were many key components to Bill Nicholson's Double side. Individuals who came together as a collective to form what was probably the greatest ever unit football this country has seen. At its core was Danny Blanchflower – and Dave Mackay. What a complementary combo. We were indeed blessed.

'There are many great photographs of Dave. Some iconic, some in celebration of a career on both sides of the border that had so many memorable moments. We all have our favourites. Yet for me, it is the pictures from Cheshunt on a warm, sunny day where he is leaping around as the players attend their pre-Wembley photo call. A man happy and at peace. Optimistic and sure.

'In every official posed picture of Dave he is smiling. A true and genuine smile that radiates from the eyes. His team-mates often tell me what fun he was, at work or at play, while it was lovely to hear cherished tales of Dave the family man when we attended his recent funeral in Edinburgh ... he was his own man on the pitch and the very same off it as well. You didn't lead Dave Mackay; you followed. And his team-mates would follow him anywhere. But once the pecking order had been asserted all was fine. And thankfully I only have good memories of him.

'A legendary figure who became part of the lives of all at White Hart Lane. And that endures today. Whenever we invite fans to name their greatest ever Spurs XI, Dave Mackay is there. Probably the first name down. And that's not a generational thing. Youngsters today, no doubt influenced by their elders, are just as aware of his status. He was unique. And they should listen because you can never exaggerate the footballing genius of the great Dave Mackay. A special talent in so many ways.'

Ninian Cassidy read out Valerie's funeral eulogy. Valerie said, 'Mike Rollo [the Spurs commercial manager] asked my mum about reading the eulogy. We really appreciated my mum's cousin Nin doing it. I couldn't have done it.'

The service ended with all of us signing the remembrance book on the way out. I was particularly touched watching his old friend Terry Dyson writing his message as I knew how much Mackay meant to him. Terry said, 'The memorial service was hard. He was a mate. I miss him. A big friend. My best friend. We had some good times together.'

I managed to snatch a brief word with Isobel, whom I'd met at Jimmy Greaves's 70th birthday celebration at the O2 Arena, to offer my condolences before she, other family and close friends travelled to Spurs' training ground for a small post-service gathering nearby.

Among them was Chas Hodges, one half of Mackay's musical favourites Chas & Dave, who had attended the main event.

Derek said, 'It was great having Chas turn up. When we went to the training ground, we were going along the corridors singing Chas & Dave songs along with Chas. Just like we played "The Sideboard Song" after the cremation, it all reflected Dad's sense of humour. He'd have loved it.'

Valerie said, 'Chas was beside my mum as we sung walking along the corridor. Chas said to my mum he would have played at the memorial if someone had asked him. That would have been nice as Chas & Dave were one of my dad's favourites.'

Isobel unveiled a statue of her late husband at Derby County's Pride Park Stadium in September 2015. Other family members present included sons David Junior and Derek, daughters Valerie and Julie and grandchildren Lisa, Daniel, Ria, Gregor, Lois and Lucy, who looked on with the survivors of the 1975 title-winning team. Mackay's brothers Tommy and Frank, and their wives Maureen and Rose, saw the sculpture at a later date.

Mackay's widow was the picture of concentration as she pulled the covering black-and-white-checked sheet aside before kissing the two top fingers of her left hand and pressing them against the lips carved into the face of a full-length sculpture of the love of her life, captured in full Rams kit, holding a ball and appearing to burst out of the wall behind his figure.

She said, 'Does it look like him? It does … he's immortalised. A great honour. I can't thank Derby County enough. He was successful at three clubs, Derby being the smallest one and in six months they've come up with this. It's a tremendous tribute, you've done him proud. I'd like to thank everybody who has gone out of their way to do this.'

John Vicars, Derby County's chief operating officer, said, 'I'm delighted that we have been able to pay tribute to Dave Mackay and, as such, remember his contribution to Derby County in this way.'

Commissioned sculptor Andy Edwards said, 'To play a part in this permanent tribute … is an eternal blessing for me.'

Derek said, 'The sculptor – a Beatles fan – put on hold one he was doing of the group to be displayed in Liverpool as Derby had to have Dad's one reasonably quickly. Dad would have liked that, being a big Beatles fan! Mum's got a miniature replica of the Derby statue on top of the fireplace.'

A bench was inscribed and heart-shaped plaque put on the wall for Mackay at the Forever In Our Hearts Memorial Garden at Tynecastle.

Part of the inscription, revealed in a Hearts website film with the late Scott Hutchison singing 'The Hearts Song' in the background, reads that Mackay was 'a man who never failed to inspire'.

The plaque states, 'All I wanted in my life, nothing else was to play for Hearts which is my dream team. And to play for Scotland. I had no ambition for anything else. Always Hearts.'

The garden is described by the club as a place 'where we remember our fellow Jambos who are no longer with us … a peaceful, contemplative space in which to remember those who have passed on. Loved ones are honoured with personalised, engraved, stainless steel hearts that adorn the walls of the garden. Enter through the beautifully crafted steel gates and relax in this place of solitude.'

That's what Isobel, Valerie and Mackay's surviving brothers Tommy and Frank did. Valerie said, 'There's a nice photo of myself and my dad's brothers on the bench. And another with us and mum.'

Spurs had already immortalised Mackay in their Hall of Fame and he remains the subject of floods of articles that emanate from the club. They also hosted the Mackay family's final visit to White Hart Lane on 15 March 2017. It was arranged by Spurs' senior tour guide John Jackson.

Derek said, 'It was an emotional day. John made it all possible. He's a lovely bloke, Spurs through and through. He arranged it just for the family to be on it with Alan Gilzean, Pat Jennings and his wife Eleanor, Cliff Jones and his wife Joanie. Spurs laid on a lovely spread for us at the end of the tour. It was a lovely day. We had extended family there too. My mum really loved what John did for us.'

Isobel said, 'It was so nice, and the last time we met Alan Gilzean [who passed on 8 July 2018]. Him and David were great friends, very friendly. I was glad he was there and didn't know he would be. Nor Cliff, Pat and their wives! That was lovely too.'

Mackay remains in the mind's eye at his clubs. Valerie said, 'Nobody at my Dad's clubs will forget him. It is lovely to think that, isn't it?'

Mackay was remembered inside the ground as Spurs said goodbye to White Hart Lane on Sunday, 14 May 2017, and also at the nearby No.8, a watering hole for our subject, team-mates and fans back in the day when known as the Bell and Hare.

Harry Kane netted the vital second goal as Spurs defeated José Mourinho's Manchester United in their final match at their home for 138 years before the £1bn Tottenham Hotspur Stadium replaced it almost exactly on the same site. Chas & Dave 'rabbited' to the crowd at half-time.

It was a prelude to the main event in my eyes. The finale was choreographed to perfection as Kenneth Branagh, the esteemed actor and Spurs supporter, provided the commentary on a pre-recorded video shown on the screens, featuring Mackay and other Lane legends.

Then the stars of yesterday were introduced to the crowd by Paul Coyte as the current players lined up on the pitch. Mackay's team-mates featured heavily, the likes of Cliff Jones, Terry Dyson, Les Allen, Terry Medwin, Phil Beal, Pat Jennings, Joe Kinnear, Jimmy Robertson and Alan Gilzean. They were joined by, among others, Glenn Hoddle, Chris Waddle, David Ginola, Graham Roberts, Ossie Ardiles, Ricky Villa, Teddy Sheringham, Darren Anderton, Micky Hazard, Justin Edinburgh and Ray Clemence. Steve Perryman, working at Exeter, Paul Gascoigne and Jurgen Klinsmann sent messages. They all illustrated the star-studded history of the Lilywhites who trod the turf of the club's traditional home.

And that emphasised the greatness of Mackay, considered the best of them all by so many. Valerie remembered how there was mention on television of the players and officials sporting Dave Mackay Club Ties in Tottenham Hotspur's white and navy blue. She said, 'All the players and officials had these new ties from the tie shop. We watched the finale on television and heard it announced our family ran the shop. That upset us.

'We loved the fact Dad was being remembered by getting a mention on the occasion of the last game at White Hart Lane. But it was a bit embarrassing because we have nothing to do with the business. People were perhaps thinking we were cashing in big time on the last day, when it was nothing to do with us. It was a bit awkward. Somebody asked me and I said, "No, it has got nothing to do with us."

'When Dad passed away, as a family, we were inundated with sympathy cards and letters of support from so many people, mainly sent to Mum's address, and via clubs Dad had played for. They were so heart-warming to receive.

'The confusion about the Mackay family being involved with the shop, we can just about handle, but what upsets us most is to think about not being able to read and respond to the many sympathy cards, letters and emails that we have been told were sent to the shop. We'd have loved to have read them all and had a chance to reply. Spurs fans, in particular, probably thought the family ran the shop, and they would have written lovely things in memory of Dad which we never received. We only saw three or four emails that were sent to the shop. It's terribly sad.'

The years since the passing of Mackay have been a test of resolve and faith for the family. As if they had not been through enough with the death of their much-loved patriarch, eldest son David Junior passed away aged 62 in 2018.

Isobel said, 'David Junior's passing suddenly, on 29 November 2018, was the saddest and most painful time of my life. Thank God, I have my faith which got me through the darkest hours. I am so grateful for the help and support of my parish priest, Father Joe Wheat; a great comfort to us, once again, at such a difficult time. His dad's passing has got easier, but I don't think it will be the same about young David. I look out, and still see him mowing the lawn and stopping to use his inhaler – he was asthmatic. It grieves me very much about David. He was so like his dad in so many ways; kind, loving and generous, always giving, wasn't materialistic in any way.

'During his dad's illness, his thoughtfulness and caring nature shone through. He was there day and night, a massive support for his dad and me. He was distraught when his beloved dad passed away. I watched that night as he stood alone by the hospital bed and sang a Scottish farewell song to him. I cried. David would have been so proud of him, as I was.

'David began looking after me and the family like his dad did; he couldn't do enough for me. The best son any mother could wish for. I felt blessed. He more than appreciated anything I did for him, and always said a big, "Thanks Mum!"

'I love the times we shared and our holidays together in Bonnie Scotland, all happy memories I will forever cherish. David is now at rest with his beloved dad, David.

'I remember we didn't have Sky at the time so David Junior used to go to Derek's close by to watch Spurs or Hearts versus whoever. And he used to take a gnome with him!

'Banter was always good between the Hearts and the Hibs. I'm a Hibs fan and so are my family, Grandad, my dad, uncles, aunts, they all went to Easter Road. But David Junior and Derek's dad-in-law on David's side were Hearts. Anyway, when Hearts v Hibs was on David Junior would get out the Hearts gnome, which was kept brand new indoors, to take round to Derek's, while the Hibs gnome stayed out in the garden getting dirty. One day, I said, "Right, I'm going out in the garden and bringing that poor Hibs gnome in!"

'We also had a Spurs gnome which David Junior took round to Derek's when they were playing. I used to joke that the Hearts gnome was modelled by John Robertson, a Hearts legend. We have laughed about it. Somehow, we don't have a lucky Derby gnome.'

Robertson said, 'Isobel and I had a fair bit of banter about the gnome along the lines of it being a life-size model of my good self!'

Derek noted, 'The gnomes used to be put on the television acting as lucky mascots.'

Valerie added, 'My brother David, when Dad was ill, was definitely his right-hand man to the end. Had an amazing dry humour. He was like an encyclopaedia for sport, football in particular, and music. He was great at quizzes too. We'll always miss him.'

Derek confirmed that his dad remains in the hearts and minds of Spurs fans when he attended the final trial game for the new Tottenham Hotspur Stadium on Saturday, 30 March 2019.

A Spurs Legends squad – featuring Paul Gascoigne, Dimitar Berbatov, Robbie Keane, Darren Anderton and David Ginola – were pipped 5-4 by Inter Milan Forever.

Derek, his wife Maureen, cousin Alan and his wife Lynne were in the eating and drinking area close to their seats when he recognised TV actor Jim Howick, who was with his wife Lauren, close by. Derek said, 'We got talking with him. When Alan told Jim that Dad was his uncle and that I was his son he couldn't believe it. He told me how he became a Spurs supporter because of his dad who was a big fan of Dad and the Double team and the side with Jimmy Greaves in it. A nice guy. It's so nice that Dad is remembered.'

42

'I was blessed'

THE IMMEDIATE family – Isobel, Derek, Valerie and Julie – remained settled in either Burton Joyce or its surrounds during the process of writing this book. There was plenty to keep them busy through dealing with health, work and personal issues. But they are all comforted by the memories given them by David Craig Mackay.

Valerie said, 'What was he like as a dad? I've already thought about it this morning. It gets me emotional. I don't mind. I can't really express how he was. I'm just looking at his photograph just now ... you just felt safe, special. You just knew you would be all right. It's hard to explain.

'He would always think of you. And others. A school friend of mine who lived near us in Enfield told me recently that Dad went up to pay a hospital visit to her husband when her husband was a boy and had broken his leg. My friend said her husband was thrilled to bits. At Easter, us kids were given so many Easter eggs by Spurs supporters that Dad took them to the Great Ormond Street Hospital. My brother David had spent so much time in there as a youngster. Dad never forgot anybody.

'I read something online recently about dad's generosity. This lad wrote that he recalled the time Dad came into a barber's shop in the High Road in Tottenham. A few punters were sitting around awaiting their turn and he bought them all a Mars bar.

'Rob Stiles, son of Nobby, said he deemed my dad the most respected man in football. That's lovely. Rob said his mum and dad had a glorious football weekend with Dad years ago. Rob's mum said it was one of the best weekends her and Nobby ever had, fun and laughter-wise.

'I remember at school when I was about ten this girl said, "Your dad's really famous but you never say anything." I didn't then. When you're young I suppose you don't want to sound like you are showing off. But, by God, I've made up for it since. I couldn't be any prouder. I remember the fans' faces light up when they came up for autographs after he retired. He'd obviously given them so much pleasure on the playing field.

'David, my brother who passed away, used to go to Spurs games with his best friend Nick Turner. Dad was just leading the team out one game as they sat at the front, Nick says. Suddenly Dad stopped, ran over to them with two programmes and ran back to his waiting team-mates to carry on running to the pitch.

'Paul Adcock, who with his parents [Peter and Wyn] and brother Steven made up the family where Terry Dyson had his digs, remembered watching Dad making a crunching tackle near where he sat, one he said was hard but fair. And Dad winked at him. Paul was delighted. Paul, who has passed away, sadly, and his brother idolised my dad. They grew up following his career. That's nice to know.

'It was lovely with my mum and dad. Mum was very supportive of everything Dad did, I suppose. Certainly, clothes-wise, she did all the choosing. He was happy for that. For the big decisions, it was probably a mutual thing. They trusted each other to do the right thing.

'All the family live in Scotland apart from us. We always missed seeing them of course, and still do. I remember saying to my brother when I was young that one day in the future we'd be able to see them at the same time as talking to them on the telephone, of course it has come true now! Our grandparents saw their other grandchildren all the time but not much of us because we were in England.

'But when they came down we got extra treats. I used to be one of the Bay City Rollers' biggest fans. I saw them in concert umpteen times, and I met them twice! Nana and Grandad Mackay took me shopping in Nottingham, and bought me these massive white platform shoes with tartan inset. I was on cloud nine, and couldn't believe they let me have them! I saw their lead singer Les McKeown in concert at a little Musselburgh theatre recently, the Brunton Hall.

'My dad's parents were amazing people. Every time I woke up when I stayed there it felt like Christmas morning. It was that exciting to stay because of Nana and my Grandad. Nana used to let me go through the sideboard drawers in their house. There were purses and compacts I took out.

'My dad used to bring presents for his mum and dad when he went away. A couple of times he bought Nana powder compacts. One compact in particular was gold and engraved "to mother from David". Nana used to say, "You can have that when I'm gone." I said to her, "Don't say that, I don't like you saying that." She died when I was 14 and it was a big shock. It was just horrendous. I got these compacts, a tartan purse, and the wedding ring as well. So she'd obviously told Grandad what she wanted me to have, which was lovely. I loved that. I idolised my Nana like I did Dad.

'I turned 60 in January 2021 and have a good memory for those days. As kids, myself and my siblings used to go up to Spurs' Cheshunt training ground in the holidays and had a great time. The players were all lovely. We'd hear the banter. You just felt welcome with Bill Nicholson and everyone. Bill would get us a bottle of juice each. I have brilliant memories of going to the club gym too. I went to games but not as many as my brothers.

'I remember I was good friends with goalkeeper Bill Brown's children Rosalyn and Beverley and lost touch when their family moved to Canada. I was asking Alan Gilzean on one of the last tours of White Hart Lane about them and he gave me a number. I've not rung it yet. I must do that.

'I went to Derby games in the holidays even though we still lived in London. Sometimes I stayed at the Midland Hotel.

'I have great memories of watching football at home, on *The Big Match*. A few times Dad would be on that in the studio, talking to Brian Moore. It was always a thrill to watch when we were kids.

'Dad was on *A Question of Sport* a couple of times as the mystery guest where they have to guess who it is. You just see parts of his face. One time he was eating an apple; another getting a drink out of a machine.

'It means something to me when I see a note written by him, and a photograph Dad has signed. I saw one on eBay. Someone asked Dad to autograph a photograph. He just wrote "sorry about the delay, Merry Christmas and Happy New Year". I didn't want it to go to a stranger so I bought it. I hang it on my Christmas tree as a decoration.

'Growing up was just wonderful. The big thing with Dad was his sense of humour, something he shared with colleagues.

'When I was about 16 I went down to Wembley for a big concert with musical stars. Dame Vera Lynn was there. Afterwards my friends and I were walking out when suddenly a luxury car appeared and she was in it. I waved – and she waved back. I put this on Facebook and Norman Giller, the journalist and Spurs supporter we know, replied, "I bet she was saying, 'Oh, there's Dave Mackay's daughter!'"

'Growing up was just wonderful with Dad's sense of fun. Everything was an adventure with Dad, always having a laugh, wanting the music on, and thinking of others by wanting them to enjoy themselves. He was very kids orientated – the pied piper. Kids would want to follow him and join in. When I used to stay at Glendevon Park, a bunch of kids would knock at the door saying, "Is Davie coming out to play?" And my dad was a grown man! He did go a couple of times, round the corner to the park. Jumpers for goalposts, and my dad's playing football. Kids would surround him when he was dropping me off for school when I was about nine.

'It was a great experience living in the family bungalow in Enfield. If I won the lottery I'd buy it. Such unforgettable memories and lovely neighbours. Recently I asked one of my old Enfield friends to send me some pictures of where we used to live. Her in-laws still lived in Enfield. She sent me a video. It got me to tears and gave Derek goosebumps. A lovely surprise.

'I remember it had a lot of greenery, and a huge lounge in which a ball was kicked about. I was a bit of a tomboy because of my brothers. They were older and their pals came round and used to join in. I probably got on their nerves. I played netball at school but remember playing tennis with one of my brothers. He was beating me and I was in a right huff. I was a bad loser, but I grew out of it.

'At Christmas I'd get a cowgirl suit with skirt, waistcoat and a little holster. But I really liked playing with my Sindy doll. So I was a mixture. I miss Enfield more than I thought I would. But I loved the house we moved into in Burton Joyce. You just get attached. A spectacular house, it really was. A special place, especially at Christmas.

'Mum and Dad agreed to have au pair Anneliese, a German girl, stay at The Glade. She wanted to learn English and was due to stay for a couple of weeks. She ended up staying two years and became part of the family and left with a Scottish accent!

'I just wish my dad was still here. You'll know with your mum [your author's mother passed in 2020], Mike, you miss them, picking up that phone to talk to them or visiting them. I've definitely not grieved properly, not as much as I thought I would, because the good stuff my dad has given me has been a comfort because it makes me feel happy and secure even though he's not here anymore.

'I lost my best friend six years ago to cancer. One of her two daughters had a baby after her mum had died. We just have to be glad we're here, alive.'

Derek said, 'My earliest memories are from when we lived at Enfield. It was in a bungalow in a street called The Glade.

'I remember playing football indoors there. Dad's friend Ricky Prosser and Ricky's son used to visit and we'd play in the lounge. It was only a little bungalow. All the rooms were standard, the bedrooms, the kitchen and that but it had this lovely big lounge. It was massive.

'It had these floor to ceiling windows with great big curtains. If you had the curtains shut you could play. It'd only be with a light, plastic ball. We'd smack it into the curtain like it was the back of the net. Sometimes Dad joined in the kick-about. Used to drive my mum mad! She'd tell us off. Fantastic growing up in Enfield. Had a great time.

'Dad had one of those white Jags [which, it is reported, he re-sprayed Hearts maroon]. He drove off in that when he was suited and booted going off to Spurs.

'He was an easy-going family man. The family meant a lot to him. He'd look out for everybody even when we got older and make sure you were all right.

'I was probably under five when Dad started to take me to White Hart Lane. I can't remember him playing but obviously I went to loads of matches. I remember going into the dressing room afterwards with the players laughing and joking. It was a great atmosphere. There's a picture of me, my eldest sister Val and eldest brother David Junior with Dad alongside when he had a plaster on a broken leg at one game. Sometimes we got to bring our school friends. And we went to see them training at Cheshunt on school holidays, which was great fun. Lots of pitches and green fields. Dad was great with the fans. I remember at Cheshunt, he was in his car after training and he'd make them queue up, saying, "Come on, get in line." He'd stay for ages and wouldn't go until they all had his autograph. A few of them used to say Dad was one of the best for signing.

'We went to a massive indoor gym. Dad used to give us a couple of balls and we'd go out and belt these balls about on the White Hart Lane concourse. My brother and sister Val and I used to run up and down the terraces. It was really good fun.

'After dad left to go to Derby, I stood on The Shelf and in the Park Lane end with my mates. I'm glad I did as the stadium was exactly the same as when he played. I've always got that memory. There was a big crush to get in.

'All us children got on really well with Bill Brown's family. The Browns used to live at Bush Hill Park but they moved to a new estate built near where we lived. It was just about the time Bill left for Northampton. His son Michael was my mate. We went to the same school. And Val was friendly with his daughters. We used to go to each other's houses.

'We know Cliffy Jones's son Steven. He was a fantastic footballer. I don't know how he didn't get professional. I used to have kick-abouts with him and I was amazed some of the things he could do. He played high amateur.

'I knew the late John White's son Rob and have seen him on several occasions through the years. A nice guy. Dad used to bring him to Derby County when he was a manager.'

Julie said, 'The first thing I think of when I think about Dad is his happy smiling face and a twinkle in his beautiful green eyes, loving, caring and always funny.

'He was amazing as a dad. My friends used to come to our house because Dad was cool and always played outside ball games with us, which was great fun, but there was always a competitive edge to it.

'What was he like as a person? The best. He had an aura about him. He was definitely a people person. He was easy to talk to and a great listener, always happy and his humour was second to none.

'We had a lot of good times with Dad. Parties were great. Dad would get everyone up dancing and having a good time. I loved them because my party piece was doing the jive with my dad.

'It was nothing different for me being the youngest of the children, really. We all got on as brothers and sisters.

'I can't really recall Dad playing, but what I've been told is that he's been many people's hero. And the footage that I've seen is amazing. He was so skilful. Precise tackling, always for the ball. His claim to fame was he was never sent off throughout his career.

'Dad was our dad to the end. He was always happy to see his loved ones with a double thumbs-up. Life hasn't been the same since he passed. I miss and think of him every single day.'

Isobel said, 'I just miss David so much since he passed. We'd been together 60 years. I can still hear his infectious laugh and always remember his big 'come-to-daddy' hug when things weren't going well. You never get over it, but you learn to live with it.

'He was more than just a footballer considered by colleagues and fans among the best to play for three clubs and his country, although he would have been too humble to acknowledge that.

'He was the best husband. I was blessed to have one like David. The best father to David Junior, Derek, Valerie and Julie. He had so much fun with the children. He was the best son-in-law and treated my mum like his own, while I couldn't have wished to have joined a better family. He was the best grandfather, and best great-grandfather at the finish although he had his illness problems. He was very much loved. So loving, kind and generous, to a fault.

'After David passed away, we heard stories about his kindness and generosity. That was the man he was but he didn't make a big thing of it.

'We were quite surprised by a lot of what people told us. I don't think his right hand knew what his left hand was doing sometimes, to be truthful. He would come home sometimes and he'd be missing a pullover or a coat. He'd maybe been in a pub. He just said, "Somebody just admired it so I just let them have it."

'When he went on a football tour he used to bring home presents galore. I used to call him Santa Claus. He always treated me well. He wasn't romantic in the way of buying me flowers and chocolates, but he'd always bring me gifts, like jewellery and perfume.

'He would give memorabilia away. Not long ago, a nephew of mine called Alan went into a menswear store called Ice Menswear in Loughton, Essex. He was looking at a jacket and got talking football to the two assistants. It turned out that one, a guy called Gary, was a Spurs supporter so Alan said, "My uncle played for Tottenham." When he was told who it was, the guy said that David had given his bookmaker grandad one of his international shirts. It happened when David and Jimmy Greaves came into the grandad's bookies one day.

'The guy told Alan he was left the shirt in his grandad's will and to come back in a day or two when he would bring it in. When Alan went back the guy had the shirt. I think it was from when David made his last international appearance after two leg breaks, telling him, "It's still got a plastic covering over it. It's never been washed." Alan said, "That's lovely."

'The guy said, "Go away and have a coffee and come back and see me." So Alan did and when he returned the guy said, "I've just been thinking, I should give the shirt back to the family." So he did. What a lovely gesture and the next time Alan saw me he gave me the shirt.

'We have got one or two things in safe-keeping. There's that watch he was given to commemorate winning the Double with Spurs. David gave it straight to his dad who wore it until the day he died and it was given to David Junior.'

Isobel pondered a question posed by Jimmy Greaves and the answer from our subject in *The Sun* during the 1970s.

Greaves had asked, 'With a gun to your head, who would you say was the most important influence on your career?'

Dave replied, 'Without question, my wife Isobel. She is the perfect football wife. Knows when to encourage and when to shut up. Without her, I would not have been half the player or half the manager. She is my strength and I'm not saying this only so she'll let me off the shopping tomorrow so I can play golf.'

Isobel said, 'I don't know how to take that. I was surprised to see that myself. He respected my opinion but I used to go to the games and never praised or criticised him.

'The only time I can remember saying something was when he was playing for Spurs against Leeds at White Hart Lane and got Billy Bremner by the neck. I was there and thought, "God, he's going to throw him over the stands! He'll be sent off!" I asked him what he said to Billy. He said to me with a smile, "You wouldn't want to know. Billy just said 'help'!"

'Generally, I knew when to speak and when not to speak. Going back to when he played for Hearts when the children were small, the family knew that he wasn't going to be very happy if he got beat. So we knew when to keep quiet and not ask any questions.

'The influence thing was a compliment considering people he knew in football like Tommy Walker at Hearts, Bill Nicholson at Spurs and Brian Clough at Derby. I suppose it is. I don't know how he would say that. Maybe because he loved me, I don't know.

'He was very humble, as I've said, about any of his achievements, but I've never heard any player that could be so successful at three different clubs, captain all of them, and captain Scotland. Just amazing. I don't know if he should have been honoured in some way. Sir David Mackay? I wouldn't go to those lengths. In my mind, he's the best.

'He worked very hard. He was a winner and hated losing at anything, even to me at dominoes or cards. He just had to win. Even with the children when he played football with them. That's what he was like. He wouldn't let them win. I used to say something and he'd say, "No, no. They've got to learn."

'Why was winning so important? He used to say when he was at school he was small in comparison to boys of his age. He had to prove he was as good as they were. He didn't like bullies. Sometimes he would see them fighting or calling other people names in school and he would stand in and deal with them even though he was small.

'I will never forget David. We had a wonderful life together in Scotland, England and the Middle East. Nor will the rest of our family – and we welcome new members in great-grandchildren Myles and Phoebe – and friends and all those in football who either knew or admired him.

'I've got both Davids' ashes in my bedroom and I speak to them often. Every morning and every night – and in between. It's like they are not away. It just helps. It's not easy. I'd say during the coronavirus issue, "I'm glad you are not here because there's a covid pandemic, oh my God. Things are not right." I wouldn't have liked it if they had become ill with the covid.'

The Beatles, one of Mackay's favourite groups, once sang, 'And in the end, the love you make is equal to the love you take'. The line has been interpreted by its composer Paul McCartney as 'the more you give, the more you get'. Perhaps Mackay gave more than he took.

It seems the Mackay family's 'Banner Man' and the public's 'Braveheart' would have been too self-deprecating to acknowledge such a thought before coming up with the distraction of a fun party sing-song and launching into the chorus of 'The Sideboard Song' by Chas & Dave

Peacock, 'I don't care, I don't care, I don't care if he comes round here, I got my beer in the sideboard here, let mother sort it out if he comes round here.'

Cheers, David Craig Mackay.

43

Legacy

DANIEL LEVY, a carrier of the Tottenham torch along with a myriad of other duties at the club in modern times, has told your author that Dave Mackay was a 'real gentleman' and 'will always be considered one of our greatest players'.

Levy oversaw a move from the Lane to the £1bn Tottenham Hotspur Stadium, negotiated transfers to bring in Gareth Bale (twice), Luka Modrić and Hugo Lloris, and appointed the likes of Glenn Hoddle, Mauricio Pochettino, and José Mourinho as manager to help maintain the club's high profile after succeeding entrepreneur Alan Sugar, destined for the House of Lords and TV's *The Apprentice*, as chairman in February 2001. Testament to his work was a first European Cup Final appearance, under Pochettino in 2019, regular Champions League qualification through top-four Premier League finishes, a best league position since Mackay's 1962/63 team of runners-up in 2017 and a 2008 League Cup triumph.

In the 2020/21 season, Levy remained at the helm as chairman while Spurs attempted to celebrate the diamond anniversary of the Mackay-inspired Double triumph with more glittering prizes with runs to the last 16 of the FA Cup and Europa League, and to the final of the League Cup against Manchester City at Wembley.

But not once did he lose perspective on what Mackay means to Spurs and indeed British football. He appreciated the Scot's legacy remains as strong as ever.

Levy, a businessman and Cambridge graduate who began supporting the club in the 1960s, said, 'Dave was an iconic figure for this football club during a golden generation in our history. Many will remember that famous image of him grabbing Billy Bremner's shirt during a match against Leeds United but our memories of him are far greater than that. I was fortunate to welcome him to a game at White Hart Lane. He was a real gentleman, someone with great presence who was hugely respected both on and off the pitch.

'He will always be considered one of our greatest ever players, as well as a legend in British football, someone who could inspire others with his intensity and will to win. We will never forget his contribution to our club.'

Mackay's former team-mate Cliff Jones said, 'Dave remains one of the best of all time. I can't speak highly enough of him and I'm sure I'm not the only one who has got that opinion. People up in Scotland, Derby County and Tottenham would say the same. He was the man.'

Pat Jennings said, 'George Best and I were team-mates from 1964 for Northern Ireland. George was a great player. Breathtaking and brave. Was he as good as Lionel Messi and Cristiano Ronaldo? They're brilliant, but I'm biased towards George. He was in a class of his own. But if I chose my favourite ever team Mackay would be the number one pick as captain and leader.

'When I look back now and Dave Mackay only played 22 times for Scotland, you just can't believe it. It was the same with Gillie [Alan Gilzean]. I think they had a problem with all the Scottish players who came down to England. They didn't look the same on them as they looked at the home players. They definitely cut their nose to spite their face.'

Mackay himself was asked if he had a modern-day equivalent in 2009. He said, 'One would be little Paul Scholes.'

Terry Dyson was unable to name any player in the second decade of the 21st century who compared to Mackay. He said, 'I can't think of anyone now who is as good or like him as he was. He had everything – class, strength, good skills. He got goals and was brave. An inspiration to me and everyone else. Spurs need someone like him. They try hard but lack a leader. Dave would lead them.'

Alan Mullery said on talkSPORT, 'I wish Dave had been English. We would have been far better than we were back in my day to have a Mackay in the team. We had a leader called Bobby Moore but he was not so influential to other players as what Mackay was. He gave that belief to lots of people. Today, probably when you see a sliding tackle and the ref blows up because he's come from the wrong side, Mackay did those every minute. There's nobody like him today. Contact in football has gone out of the game completely from what we played in those days.'

Steve Perryman added, 'To me there wasn't a weakness in his game. There was more to him than aggression. I want people to view him more as a technically gifted player and put that in a package with his all-round ability, character and manner.'

Ann Budge, who became Hearts owner in 2014, succeeding Vladimir Romanov, stated that Mackay has been viewed by 'many' as 'our greatest player'.

The Jam Tarts would have made the winner in Mackay proud by beating Edinburgh rivals Hibernian to reach the 2019/20 Scottish Cup Final, although they were ultimately pipped 4-3 on penalties by Celtic in the decider at an empty Hampden due to the coronavirus pandemic.

He would have been equally lifted by the 2020/21 promotion charge, which saw Hearts win the Championship and return to the top flight at the first attempt.

She said, 'As captain of Heart of Midlothian FC he guided the club to some of its greatest glories and his passing has been keenly felt by all of us at Hearts and beyond. The term "legend" is often used all too readily. However, this is a wholly fitting tribute in Dave Mackay's case ... one of the 'greats' immortalised in the famous "Hearts Song".

'A natural leader ... many would argue that he was our greatest player. There can be no doubt that football is a poorer place without him.'

Robbie Neilson, Hearts' manager during the 2020/21 season, said, 'Dave Mackay is probably the best player Hearts ever had. Hearts was a big part of his life but to be a legend at three different clubs is phenomenal. I had the pleasure to meet him at a couple of functions and he always came over as a nice person.'

Craig Levein, the former Hearts player, boss, director of football and, until 2020, advisor, has insisted Mackay is 'held in hero status'. The former Scotland manager, who attended Mackay's funeral, said, 'When you come into a club you quickly learn about its history and the famous players. And Dave was always mentioned in the same breath as the likes of Willie Bauld; held in hero status. I was surprised when I first met him just how humble he was considering all the things he has achieved in football. He was such a down-to-earth guy and for me that's almost as important as his record as a football player. Nobody lives forever. But if there's one guy you wish could have done, it would be Dave.'

John Robertson said, 'The legacy that Mr Mackay will always leave is that to be a legend at one club it utterly outstanding. For anybody to do that shows that he's had a good career. But to be a legend at each of three clubs and his national team as well! And in the Hall of Fame at Hearts, Spurs, Derby and Scotland. Couldn't have been too shabby, eh?

'I think when you talk to real football people, you take something from them all. What impressed me most of all about Mr Mackay was the clarity of his thoughts and ideas. Football is not a complicated game. You get players fit and organised and get them to express themselves. Make them do what they are good at, then you'll be successful. You hear about sports scientists, conditioning and coaches in the modern day but the basics of the game still remain the same.

'The thing for me, was his presence. He wasn't a big man. Solid but not well-built to intimidate anybody physically. But what Mr Mackay did do was intimidate with his natural presence, which you respected and admired. You can understand why he was successful on and off the pitch.

'Mr Mackay and, when I was in the Hearts commercial department, the players from the 1950s and 1960s seemed to be cut from the same branch of the tree. I got this appreciation being with them. It was a breeding thing. Working-class men who were earning a little bit more than other guys in skilled jobs like joiners, carpenters, plumbers and electricians but weren't pompous. They never lost sight of who they were. They were superstars in many people's eyes but they didn't act like superstars. You would look at football players today and they would drive past the fans in the street, whereas these guys would stop their cars and say, "It's raining, get in. Where are you going? I'll drop you off." They'd even be happy to go in and have a cup of tea if invited. As much as Mr Mackay was a giant of a player, he was a very, very humble man. There was a humbleness about all these players.'

Derby County have a lasting legacy to Mackay in the form of a giant white clock with his image imprinted at its centre hanging from a stand at Pride Park.

The Dave Mackay Clock was unveiled before Derby hosted Fulham on Boxing Day in 2015.

The Rams reported, 'The clock, which proudly displays a picture of the Derby legend in the centre, has been installed at the end of the north side of the Toyota West Stand, fittingly just outside the recently -refurbished Dave Mackay Suite.

'It has been produced by Paul Mordecai and his two sons Oliver and Alastaire – of As Time Goes By Limited – who are Rams season ticket holders and live in Southampton.'

As well as the 2015 unveiling of a statue outside the stadium, a giant banner with Mackay's picture on it was in the stands during the lockdown periods of the 2019/20 and 2020/21 seasons.

It no doubt reflects reasons why Mel Morris, who became Derby owner in 2015, rated Mackay so highly.

Morris said, 'Aside from possibly Steve Bloomer, Dave Mackay has to have been one of the most inspired, inspirational and impactful signings this club has ever made. His contribution was huge and ever present driving and inspiring those around him to achieve their best day in day out. A true leader.'

Sam Rush, president and chief executive at Derby from 2013–17, who attended the unveiling of Mackay's statue, said in the club's tribute matchday programme, 'The last man to manage a top-flight championship-winning team at Derby, Dave Mackay is a hero to people throughout football. We are proud of all his achievements which comfortably mark him out amongst the very best that have worn the shirt or led the team.

'His contributions to the history of this great club will never be forgotten … a man who achieved so much both as a player and a manager for Derby County.'

Roy McFarland, these days a club ambassador for Derby, said, 'It sounds crazy, I suppose, but I just loved the guy as a person. Forget the football. He was a great, great guy, and I'm privileged, like I say, to have known him, to be invited back to his house, to play with him and to be managed by him. If anybody talks about superstars I'm telling you now Mackay should be up there without doubt.'

John McGovern, who played with and then under Mackay at Derby, added, 'How did Dave compare to the best players? George Best was magical and there was Eusébio around. Dave was one of those great players. If you said Franz Beckenbauer was a great player – obviously he was outstanding – and had the ability to play the ball forward, I'd put Dave in that category. But obviously a stronger, more physical player, because he'd played a bit earlier. As good as that.'

Colin Todd said, 'A modern-day equivalent of Dave Mackay? You could look at Bryan Robson first of all. He was the type of midfielder that Dave was. He also had a go at management but found it difficult, but Dave managed to win championships as a player and manager. Paul Scholes was an aggressive midfielder who could play. Another who could combine that approach with skill and ability on the ball was Graeme Souness.'

David Moss, who played for Mackay at Swindon, said, 'As a player, I was too young to see him but if top players of his day put him high on their lists he was clearly a top player himself, definitely. He proved to be a successful manager too.'

Jimmy Robertson, a Mackay team-mate at Spurs and a player for him at Walsall, said, 'You don't get many like Dave in modern football. I see people and there's always been hard men in football, because it's a competitive game, but I don't see anybody with the combination of toughness and skill that Dave had. Bryan Robson, I think, would be near him. And Graham Roberts. Roy Keane is a good example. Keane was probably a more box-to-box player than Dave was in the modern day.

'Tackling has very largely been taken out of the [modern] game with referees blowing for fouls when his opponent hasn't touched him. Players are much better now on going down on first contact. If Dave was playing he would drag you to your feet. If you got an injury when you played with Dave – if you were down on the deck for any length of time – he would pull you up and put you back on your feet because he didn't want the opposition to see you weakened.'

Neil Martin, who was a Mackay opponent, player at Nottingham Forest and assistant manager in the Middle East, said, 'If you picked a world team, you'd put Dave in it.'

Les Robinson, who played for Mackay at Doncaster Rovers, agreed, 'As I've said, Dave Mackay is a legend in football.'

Ian Atkins, who played for Mackay at Birmingham City, reckoned Mackay a 'strong character', while team-mate John Frain recalled 'a humble man'.

Craig Brown, a Scotland manager involved in two World Cup campaigns and two European Championships, said, 'He would rate very, very highly on the world stage. In the Scottish pantheon of players I would put him at the very top. I was with the Scottish team with Alex Ferguson and saw first-hand Gordon Strachan, Murdo McLeod and Paul Lambert play. They were very good midfield players but I think Dave Mackay would be up there with the very best of them. If you took Strachan and Souness and combined them you'd get Dave Mackay.

'He had positive attributes. An ability to pass a ball, deliver a telling pass, read and control a game with authority. We've had good players in Scotland who've got more caps than Mackay. Paul McStay was wonderful but wasn't as strong as Mackay. Gary McAllister had a good pedigree in England winning the championship with Leeds and three other trophies at the end of his career. But Dave Mackay was tougher and more aggressive than him.

'The fact he was picked by several different Scotland managers – Ian McColl, Andy Beattie, Sir Matt Busby and Jock Stein – tells you he was obviously a quality player. You won't meet anyone with more admiration than I have for Dave Mackay.

'He was the perfect all-round player. He would get into any team today, any top European or international team. He had all the attributes and could do the lot. John McGinn [who moved from Hibernian to Aston Villa in 2018] could be that kind of player to be in the heart of everything in the middle of the park. He's the nearest player I've seen to Mackay in the last decade.'

Ian Ure, a Scotland team-mate, has similar views, saying, 'Dave Mackay is my favourite player of all time. He'd be a great player in ANY era.'

Denis Law, Mackay's team-mate friend, said, 'Dave is without doubt one of the best ever to play for Scotland.'

Sir Alex Ferguson, who eulogised Mackay at his funeral, wrote the foreword in the Scot's 2004 autobiography, *The Real Mackay*. He said, 'The better the footballers he played with the better he got ... everywhere he went he was the mainstay of the team.

'Dave is the player of his era, representing strength, dignity, fairness and value for money. The qualities of honesty, skill, leadership, industry and courage are perhaps rarer today, especially all rolled into one player but I see Dave in Roy Keane and Steven Gerrard, and a little while back in Bryan Robson. I think Dave sought those qualities in players when he became a manager. Archie Gemmill and Bruce Rioch spring to mind as footballers who excelled under Dave, and let us not forget the substantial success he had as a manager.'

Sir Alex Ferguson, Craig Brown and other colleagues and friends had fun picking their all-time world XIs during the national lockdowns necessitated by the coronavirus pandemic. It's safe to say that Dave Mackay was very much in the mix.

The family are comforted their patriarch's legacy is in such good shape, saying simply and with modest understatement characteristic of the man himself, 'It's good to hear.'

Postscript

DAVE MACKAY would have hoped to see Tottenham Hotspur add to the club's trophy cabinet for the first time in 13 years during the 2020/21 campaign. To celebrate the Diamond Jubilee anniversary of the season his fellow White Hart Lane history-makers became the first side to achieve English football's first Double – the lifting of the Football League championship and FA Cup in the same campaign – during the 20th century.

If we are talking diamonds, the League Cup – the last major prize to be won by the folk from London N17 – is considered a lesser gemstone of a prize to the priceless successes mined by Mackay and Co as they set the benchmark for the whole of football, let alone the Lilywhites. But that was what modern-day Spurs were left trying to win after championship, FA Cup and Europa League hopes dissipated.

Yet, nonetheless, Spurs followers would have welcomed the trophy being placed alongside the silverware housed at the Tottenham Hotspur Stadium, more or less on the site of the club's razed White Hart Lane ground. Frustratingly, Spurs were defeated 1-0 by Manchester City in the competition's final at Wembley on Sunday, 25 April 2021.

It was a Wembley showpiece overshadowed in the build-up by upheaval in Tottenham, Manchester and across Europe.

Spurs dismissed manager Jose Mourinho and left caretaker boss Ryan Mason in charge against Pep Guardiola's champions-elect, while the club were – along with City – lambasted for becoming a founding member of a European Super League without promotion or relegation before hastily withdrawing alongside the Blue Mooners within a couple of days after a public outcry against the proposal.

The so-near-so-far knockout cup run followed the Lilywhites falling at the last-16 hurdle in the FA Cup during a campaign which marked the centenary of when Arthur Grimsdell skippered Peter McWilliam's Tottenham to the trophy; winning the decider, coincidently, 1-0, against Wolverhampton Wanderers. And the 120th anniversary of the club becoming the first and only from non-league to secure the most famous domestic cup in the game; overcoming Sheffield United.

You wonder how Spurs would have fared in domestic and continental competition during 2020/21 had Mackay – with his zero tolerance for defeat and relish of the big stage – been in his pomp prompting and inspiring the likes of Harry Kane, Son Heung-min, Gareth Bale and Co.

The season proved a disappointing one for the other English clubs our subject graced as a player.

Derby County hoped the appointment of former England and Manchester United superstar Wayne Rooney as manager at the turn of 2021 would help sprinkle enough stardust to escape relegation into the third tier. But the campaign proved a constant struggle to escape the trap door. And they avoided the drop to the third tier by just a single point after a final-day 3-3 home draw against relegated Sheffield Wednesday. Meanwhile, Swindon Town, where Mackay closed the curtain on his playing career, slid into the fourth.

But Heart of Midlothian, where Mackay's professional career began, provided the taste of glory the Scot helped Tynecastle savour in the 1950s.

The efforts of manager Robbie Neilson and his Jam Tarts in sealing a return to the Scottish Premiership at the first attempt, and as champions, would certainly have earned Mackay's seal of approval.

Appropriately, it was a Mackay who shone on the day they collected the trophy. Gary Mackay-Steven scored twice in what was the last home fixture of the term, a 3-0 win over Inverness Caledonian Thistle; a result which ended play-off hopes for opponents managed by John Robertson, the former Jambo and Mackay pallbearer.

The last time Hearts secured the second-tier title, fittingly, of course, was in the wake of Mackay's passing in 2015. And Neilson, who had taken charge the year before, and his squad, as we know, attended our subject's funeral. Perhaps the Mackay legacy will spur further success for his hometown club and an upturn in fortunes for his old ones south of the border. Watch this space.

Appendix 1

Eulogy

Our Dad

The four of us truly and utterly idolised our dad. He was an absolute joy to be around. We had an idyllic childhood with our mum and dad, living in Enfield, and spending many school holidays with the rest of our wonderful family, up in Scotland. Later, living in Burton Joyce, the memories that stand out are of us all relishing family Christmases, and parties at home, with Dad always at the forefront of any celebrations and excitement, making them so much richer.

Dad cherished and protected all his family, and he adored all his buddies. He saw the good in everyone, and his constant positivity encouraged us in everything we wanted to do, reassuring us and giving us the confidence we needed. He loved us, and Mum, unconditionally, and my oh my did we know it.

He would do anything for anyone, nothing was ever too much for him. His kindness and generosity knew no bounds, and he constantly wanted to give, and to treat people, and make everyone happy, and ultimately for everyone to have fun. Taking after our amazing grandparents, and along with his brothers, Tommy, Frank and Ronnie, Dad had an extraordinarily loving and caring nature. Wherever he went, everyone in his company mattered, he made sure of that, and woe betide 'a bully'!

Similarly, with his six grandchildren, of course the number had to be six: Lisa, Daniel, Ria, Lois, Gregor, and Lucy. He was the pied piper of grandads; they all worshipped him, and he worshipped them all back, individually. He adored time spent with them all, the funny things they said, and he taught them so much, and so well. Come to think of it, he was the pied piper of all children anywhere near him, ever, at all, he just had that way with kids. As great-grandad, alias 'Noo Grandad', to Remae, three and a half years, and Lilly, two and a half, he shared a mutual true love and friendship, an inseparable bond which was enchanting and heart-warming to watch.

His fantastic and quick-witted sense of humour could be very dry, it was often very quirky, and he would have us, and many friends and other family members, in stitches with his jokes, and his antics. His laugh was so infectious, especially when it really got going; it would become high-pitched, with sporadic silent pauses in between, it was hilarious to see and hear.

Dad treasured the enthusiasm of football supporters, and he enjoyed all the banter. As we grew up, we proudly watched, and more than enjoyed, Dad's footballing prowess; along with our mum, we were his biggest fans. But we were also as proud as punch, over the years, at school, when our pals used to comment that our dad was 'trendy', 'cooler than cool', 'a little bit rock and roll'.

That is just how we felt about him too, and we always will. He lit up our lives, leaving us with the most amazing memories. Metaphorically speaking, whenever he walked into a room, people stood up, whether at home or elsewhere; his charisma was that alluring.

Most of all he loved music, and we are so grateful he introduced it into our lives, from a very young age. His music tastes included a bit of everything; in the early days, the Beatles and Dusty Springfield, later on Neil Diamond, to name but a few. In fact, almost anything in the charts over the years, with a good rhythm to it. Chas & Dave were great favourites, who we managed to 'see live' with him, in recent years. And wherever there was music he loved to dance, and his dancing was unique and spectacular, and we could've watched him dance for hours, as many people actually have done on social occasions! Daddy cool, right enough.

Contrary to previous reports, Dad did not have Alzheimer's; he knew us all right to the very end, and we are so grateful for that. On 14 November last year he enjoyed his 80th birthday celebrations at home with 'our piper', Stuart MacLaughlan, making it an extra special occasion. An apt description would be Dad was very much 'on the ball', in that room with us all, having a very special family gathering.

Thank you Dad, we are so lucky to have had you. You were 'double handsome'; we will miss your sparkling eyes, and your wonderful smile, your winks, your thumbs-ups, your riveting conversation, and your nods of approval. The comforting way you would pat us on the back, or the shoulder, your warm firm handshake, and your gentle embrace. We are so proud of you.

Now we raise a glass or two of Mateus Rose to you, our forever Banner Man; you were an absolute genius; a 'Genius Dad', and most comforting of all, we told you this a few weeks ago.

David Junior, Derek, Val and Julie

* Delivered by Tom Dixon at Dave Mackay's funeral service inside Mansfield Traquair Church in Edinburgh on Tuesday, 24 March 2015.

And delivered by Ninian Cassidy at Dave Mackay's memorial service inside St Stephen's Church in Bush Hill Park, Enfield, north London, on Thursday, 30 April 2015.

Appendix 2

Historians

DAVID SPEED, Heart of Midlothian club historian:

Dave Mackay was possibly the most complete midfield player that Scotland has ever produced. Dave was a tough ball-winner, an astute and skilful passer, and a regular goalscorer. He also had limitless energy and leadership qualities, and many of our senior supporters believe that it was his spirit and drive that turned the immensely skilful Hearts players of the '50s into winners. Dave was very much a local hero. His football potential was quickly apparent and he stood out from an early age.

Dave was a lifelong Hearts supporter and he was thrilled when he was recruited by manager Tommy Walker, possibly the best investment that the club has ever made. His skill and energy was then outstanding in the side that won the Scottish League Cup Final in October 1954 with a magnificent 4-2 victory over Motherwell at Hampden ... and created a group of unforgettable heroes, including Dave Mackay.

Dave never lacked the energy and enthusiasm to pull on a maroon shirt. In fact, he was once again a key man as Hearts won the Scottish Cup Final in April 1956, beating Celtic 3-1 at Hampden. That memorable Scottish Cup victory was soon followed by the record-breaking Scottish League championship success in 1957/58, when Dave was immensely proud to be captain of Hearts.

On a personal note, he won four under-23 international caps and played three times for the Scottish League. Davie also made the first of 22 full international appearances (four with Hearts, two of these as captain) against Spain in May 1957. In addition, he actually represented the Football League on three occasions after he moved down south.

Hearts' talisman became Scotland's Player of the Year in 1958 and Davie represented his country at the World Cup finals in Sweden. Not surprisingly, Everton wanted his transfer, but he remained in Edinburgh and in October 1958, Davie played in the Hearts side that won the Scottish League Cup Final against Partick Thistle, the Maroons winning 5-1 at Hampden.

However, to the dismay of the supporters, he was then transferred to Tottenham Hotspur in March 1959 for a fee of £32,000. Sadly, he never managed his hometown club but during his playing days at Tynecastle, Dave Mackay had thrilled the fans scoring 32 goals in 208 games, including the club's first European ventures. He had inspired Heart of Midlothian to unprecedented success and left a legacy of wonderful memories.

It was wholly appropriate that Dave Mackay was elected to the Heart of Midlothian Hall of Fame at the inaugural event in 2006. He was truly a legend and a man who will be sorely missed and well remembered.

DAVY ALLAN, Heart of Midlothian museum and collection manager: The *Evening Dispatch* headline read 'Super Hearts, Then Came Jitters' after their second successive loss in the Scottish Cup semi-final in 1953. Opinion pieces lamented that for all the brilliant play of the 'Terrible Trio' (inside-forwards Conn, Bauld and Wardhaugh) Hearts were missing something to make them winners.

The solution was found at the start of season 1954/55 when 24-year-old converted left-winger John Cumming at left-half was regularly paired with at right-half 19-year-old Davie Mackay. This partnership provided the missing steel in defence. It reaped instant rewards with the winning of the League Cup on 23 October 1954. Over the next four years they would anchor the side to the Scottish Cup, the league title and another League Cup. After Davie left to go to Spurs, John would win another title and two League Cups, making him the most successful player in Hearts' history.

JOHN FENNELLY, Tottenham Hotspur club historian: As a schoolboy on my lofty perch at the front of The Shelf, I had seen Dave Mackay play but must admit that my affection was a slow burn. I was just ten when I first made it to White Hart Lane and at that age was more interested in the young players making their debuts as Bill Nicholson set about rebuilding the side.

Thankfully, I was quickly educated about Mackay's value. Not just about Dave as a player but the inspiration he brought to the side that made other players better. Throughout my work as the club's programme and magazine editor, that appreciation has grown. Not just thanks to my own research but by the response of fellow supporters from that era.

Whenever I would opt for that forever-popular request and ask readers to pick their best Spurs XI – or even their top individual player of all time – Dave Mackay was always right up there. And that was true for all ages. Even those who had never seen him play. Their parents and grandparents had ensured that Dave's worth needed to be perpetuated. And for those of us fortunate enough to see him play, that admiration can never be exaggerated. He truly was that good.

He was the perfect balance to Danny Blanchflower in Bill Nick's great side and although Danny would understandably and naturally also always figure in the selections of Spurs fans, it was perpetually such a difficult pick that both would breast the tape together in any final analysis.

It was 1966 when my father first took me to White Hart Lane. But he only went the once. After that I would go with the families of friends and by 1967 I was a regular. But regularly on my own! My mates were fair-weather followers and the side had lost the consistency they craved and demanded at that age.

What they couldn't grasp was that watching home defeats by lesser sides is what being a Spurs fan is all about! And the ecstasy when the side finally put it together for 90 minutes and won against the odds was all the better for that negative experience! So little has changed in that regard over the years!

Fortunately, my pocket money just about covered the expense involved on a matchday. I could walk from home to Cheshunt railway station, pay the half-price return fare to reach either White Hart Lane or Northumberland Park and enter via the boys' turnstile in the East Stand. On reflection, how sexist was the title of that long-forgotten gate!

In those days, you could select and walk on to your favourite terrace, apart from the enclosure on the west side. That was more expensive. My choice was an early arrival – often waiting outside for the stadium to actually open – and a quick run to the front of The Shelf. My need was driven by my lack of height at the time – and even then it was hard in the early days to actually be able to peer over the fence – but I still look back on that position as probably the best standing view of a football match that I have ever had as a supporter.

Although the great days of the Double were still recent to the vast majority of the supporters at the Lane, it all seemed in the dim and distant past to a ten-year-old. Few of the stars from that special time were still in the squad – but the indomitable Dave was. We saw cameos from a few from that unique era, but Dave Mackay was always so much more than that.

As an avid reader of all things Spurs in Dad's *Daily Mirror* or the *London Evening News*, I had read about the doubts that Dave would return as his old self after those two broken legs. I had seen him working hard, often on his own and after many others had gone home – or for a swift one – on my regular visits to our old Cheshunt training ground.

I could walk to that Brookfield Lane site from our home in Flamstead End and the fact that entrance was free made it attainable. The deal was that you behaved. And we all did. There was just a rope separating us on the bank overlooking the pitches, but that looping barrier might as well have been a solid wall. You just didn't cross it.

There was much more laxity in the car park after training where you could obtain autographs. No selfies in those distant days. They hadn't been invented. And although a simple glance from Mackay terrified us youngsters, once you plucked up the courage to ask, and did it politely, he was always prepared to stop and oblige by signing whatever scrap of paper you proffered.

But the media kept saying that he was finished. And some even suggested that his midfield enforcer role would be taken over by Alan Mullery – although he had been brought in with the impossible brief to replace Blanchflower.

By the time I first saw Dave play it was alongside Mullery and the pair performed so impressively and consistently together in a Spurs side that Mackay was now clearly inspiring all over again. He was all about not taking prisoners or a step back, hard tackling, fist waving – and total confidence. A man at home in his own natural environment.

He was our captain. The team leader. Performing a crucial role. And that's how I saw him. Yet maybe I was taking that 100 per cent effort for granted. As I say, I took more interest in players almost half his age. And, looking back with less star-struck eyes, they probably also had half his talent.

My education came towards the end of that 1965/66 season as I took my usual place up above the halfway line. I had saved up to buy one of those old-fashioned wooden rattles but had only sounded it once when the man next to me – who had almost jumped out of his skin at that first crashing sound – pointed out to me that if I did it again, my rattle would be stuck somewhere that would make it difficult for me to walk home after the game!

Having realised that he was talking to a kid, he relented once his nerves settled and opted to engage me in conversation. It was the usual question to youngsters, 'Who's your favourite player, son?'

There were so many to pick from. Mullery was always special, showing touches of the real Mackay as their partnership developed in those early seasons. Terry Venables had just arrived and, for me, was up there with Greaves, Joe Kinnear and Cyril Knowles. My inquisitor could see where I was going with this. I was following the general belief that Mackay was a ball-winner whereas I responded to flamboyance. And after convincing me of Dave's respected and enduring playing abilities, he told me to watch him as the team took to the field.

As 'McNamara's Band' rang around the euphoric stadium, Dave led the boys out and immediately booted the ball into the air before performing that unique piece of control and skill that will certainly appear elsewhere in this book, and described far better than I can do it justice. But it instantly captivated me.

I probably hadn't noticed it before because I hadn't seen it! Because the crowd celebrations at that moment would have obliterated the view of a little lad clutching the top of the fence. But I didn't doubt the excellence of his all-round game after that. I had been educated about what a total and complete player the great man was.

He didn't let us down at Wembley in 1967 and I was such a Mackay fan by then that I was saddened when he left us for Derby the following year. He showed there that we had perhaps let him go too early. Particularly with how he adapted to a new central defensive role – and especially when he inspired the Rams to a 5-0 hammering of my favourites in 1969!

When I completed my apprenticeship as a journalist in 1977, I was offered the job of covering Spurs for the *Tottenham Weekly Herald*. By the time I arrived at my new office just down the High Road from the stadium, we were in the Second Division and Mackay's management career was well underway at home and abroad.

Our paths occasionally crossed when he was back in north London where he was always in demand to make personal appearances, lighting up the Q&A circuit, opening pubs and generally mirroring the affection that the supporters held for one of the greats. And his own love of his wonderful time at Spurs always shone through as he related the memories and inside stories that the Tottenham faithful queued to hear.

After a spell back in Fleet Street where I had started work as a trainee sportswriter straight from school, I took on the position of press officer at Spurs. They were the first top-flight club to create such a role when I received the call in 1984 and my office was just along the corridor from Bill Nicholson, who was back at the club in a consultancy role.

Bill clearly loved the honesty that a man of Dave's stature brought to the game. All done at full capacity, done with consistency, a born leader, a creative yet destructive force when he needed to be. He also had this cherished capacity to score important goals. So, we would chat about Dave and Bill would smile as he reflected on a man that was the complete player – but a player that could never be replicated because there were so many strands to his game. And Bill did search.

So many players are specialists at what they do – for Bill, Dave could do it all. Bill Nick was clearly delighted when he managed to sign Mackay from Hearts. Because, as he already knew, the man had it all – strength, stamina, power, energy, self-belief, calmness under pressure and a neat passing game.

Yet it was his infectious spirit that we needed when he arrived late in the 1958/59 season as he instantly played a massive role by lifting the players around him and helping to steer us away from the relegation zone. How different our history might have been if we had gone down in Bill Nick's first season in charge.

We were third the following season, then champions in 1961, wrapping up the title and then going on to add the FA Cup as the fabulous Double was brought home. And Bill needed no reminding of what Dave had gone through as our talisman at that time.

Bill searched for another Mackay throughout his own career as Spurs boss. But he knew he wouldn't find one. He found facets, potential and other traits but never the real deal. Realistically, Bill knew that there would only ever be one Dave Mackay.

I met up with Dave again when Bill died in 2004 and it was so clear that Mackay's admiration for Bill was mirrored with matching respect. When Dave passed on more than a decade later I travelled with the Spurs party for the funeral in Edinburgh where he was still treated with such affection that the cortege from Tynecastle saw the streets lined with supporters of all ages who had never forgotten the man who brought such great honour to their city with both Hearts and Scotland.

There were many ex-players there. Alex Ferguson recounted the terror of playing against the great man while Cliff Jones spoke about how special it was playing alongside him. This was the first time that I met Dave's charming wife Isobel who told me about his warmer side as a family man at home and left me with the complete picture of the real person behind the image.

He didn't revel in his hard man persona and hated that famous Billy Bremner photograph as it was seen by many to encapsulate a reputation that he repudiated. And that was something I too was guilty of but soon grew to realise how wrong I was. He was so much more than that.

I was honoured to be asked by Spurs to deliver the eulogy when we held a memorial service at Bush Hill Park soon afterwards. This enabled local fans to pay tribute to the great man and they came out in force to do so.

A day of reflection when you closed your eyes and there was the big, barrel-chested, buccaneering Mackay in his pomp. The pirate king of White Hart Lane.

ANDY ELLIS, Derby County club historian: At the end of Brian Clough's first season at Derby, although he reached the semi-final of the League Cup, the team actually finished lower in the league table than they had during the previous season.

Clough was starting to rebuild the team with younger and less-experienced players and needed an old head or two to direct the younger players in the team.

Mackay was leaving Tottenham, and had an option to return back to Hearts but Clough having got wind of this saw him as the ideal person to fill the gap, bringing an end to his six-month search. He was signed on 24 July 1968 and at 33 years old he still had lots to offer, even though he was older than his manager.

Clough wanted him to change position – no longer a wing-half, but to drop back to a sweeper and to be able to control the game and let the young players do the running around for him, allowing his experience to put him in the right position.

By the end of his first season, Derby had strolled to win the Second Division championship and Mackay was named joint Football Writers' Association Footballer of the Year, along with Manchester City captain Tony Book. The return to the First Division in 1969/70 probably went better than anyone had hoped. Finishing in fourth place would normally be good enough to qualify for a place in the UEFA Cup, but financial irregularities, one of which was Mackay being paid for his contribution to the match programme, saw the club receive a European ban amongst other fines.

It is unfortunate that the likes of Mackay, goalkeeper Les Green and Willie Carlin were deprived of a crack at European football in the twilight of their careers for non-footballing reasons. The start of 1970/71 saw the introduction of the first sponsored tournament in British football in the Watney Cup, with Mackay lifting the trophy following a 4-1 demolition of Manchester United in the final, in which he scored one of the goals.

At the end of his contract he had agreed to join Swindon Town as player-manager, with no thought that he would return within three years to manage the Rams.

Despite initial worries regarding whether he could play in the majority of games, he only missed four league matches during his entire three-year stay.

October 1973. Derby were in turmoil. Clough and Taylor had resigned, sparking supporter demonstrations in the town and players having evening meetings with the management pair to see what could be done to get them back. It was a difficult situation for any replacement to come into, but the only person with the respect of the players and fans was Mackay. Mackay was now manager just down the road at Nottingham Forest and needed little persuasion to come back to a town he knew and many players he had played with.

He had his own ideas on how he wanted the team to play and desired more attractive, attacking football with more powerful players than Clough had. Rod Thomas was the first to arrive, the Welsh international coming to take over the right-back position and helping secure a UEFA Cup spot at the end of the season. By the start of 1974/75 Clough had taken charge at Leeds United for his infamous 44-day stay. In that time he had taken Jimmy Gordon as coach and John O'Hare and John McGovern with him (both of whom he had known from his days at Sunderland and Hartlepool respectively).

Roy McFarland had been seriously injured whilst playing for England against Northern Ireland and that would leave him out for much of 1974/75. To fill the gaps, Francis Lee was signed on a two-year deal from Manchester City and Bruce Rioch from Aston Villa to complement the emergence of Roger Davies and Peter Daniel from the reserves. Daniel had been at the club since the early 1960s and was to take McFarland's place for most of the season, which in turn put added pressure on Colin Todd and Archie Gemmill as the senior, influential players.

Derby bowed out of Europe at the third-round stage, losing to Velez Mostar in controversial circumstances after an official complaint was lodged following crowd behaviour in the away leg.

Results went well for them and three results over Easter against Burnley, Luton Town (where Davies scored all five goals) and Manchester City set them up for the run-in. They won the title with a game to spare whilst at the annual awards night when Ipswich Town failed to win their match. Mackay now had won the First Division title as a manager as well as a player.

The annual season curtain-raiser saw Derby comfortably beat West Ham United in the Charity Shield with new signing Charlie George in the starting XI, and Mackay had an array of forwards to select from – Lee, Davies, Hector, Hinton and George. Leighton James was bought as a replacement for Alan Hinton on the wing.

Three famous matches that season were within a few weeks of each other. There was a 4-1 win over Real Madrid in the European Cup at the Baseball Ground that had a George hat-trick and probably one of the best goals you will ever see. Next was the usual bad-tempered affair against Leeds, in which Francis Lee had dived to get a Derby penalty before being sent off with Norman Hunter following a brawl on the field, and Davies scored a superb goal in the last minute. The third was the return game in Madrid in front of 120,000 fans. Derby were decimated by injuries and coupled with some very dubious refereeing decisions, they were beaten 5-1.

Elsewhere they had a run to the FA Cup semi-finals where they eventually were beaten by Manchester United at Hillsborough. A season-ending injury to George on a frozen pitch at home to Stoke knocked the stuffing out of the club as they were firm favourites for a league and cup Double. History shows that this game was the start of a slide in the club's fortunes over the next decade that saw them relegated twice and nearly go out of business.

By the start of the 1976/77 season, Derby were lacking in players, particularly strikers. Lee had retired, George was still out injured and recovering, Davies had been sold to FC Bruges, Hinton had emigrated to play in the NASL and Hector was ageing. Mackay was stubborn in that he wouldn't just go and buy any striker in the market and was wanting to wait for the right one. The odd freak result during the first few months (8-2 v Tottenham, 12-0 v Finn Harps) couldn't paper over the cracks and the board of directors were so impatient for a striker that eventually Mackay relieved of his position.

Mackay was fully justified in his cautious approach – Colin Murphy was promoted to be manager and quickly spent a huge amount of money on Derek Hales from Charlton, who was a steady scorer in the lower leagues. To prove Mackay's point, Hales failed to reproduce his form and so began a long line of managers and strikers, as the club dropped down the leagues.

Appendix 3

Fans

MICHAEL McNAMARA: I heard that Dave Mackay was to be signing his autobiography at W.H. Smith in Brent Cross one Saturday morning so decided to get my friend who was laid up after a car crash a get-well present – and a copy for my brother, as he'd never forgive me otherwise. When I arrived, the queue was predictably large and I found myself chatting to a female Arsenal fan who was buying the book as a birthday present for her father-in-law and only had the vaguest notion of who Dave Mackay was. Nice girl, for a Gooner.

The signing was well organised by the store staff and Dave was accompanied by a Scottish chap dressed in a startlingly orange-tinged tartan suit, looking for all the world as if he'd been ejected from The White Heather Club. He was, however, a very personable fellow, wandering up and down the queue chatting to everyone.

As I got closer to the signing table I remember agonising over whether 'get well soon' was a suitable phrase to have forever inscribed in the front of a book. I still can't remember what my decision was.

When asking who I'd like the signature made out to, Orange Tartan Man was suitably complimentary about my purchase of two copies; but, on hearing that neither were for me, he suggested that I obtain a third. I remember Dave chuckling all the way through that encounter.

I don't think I was too gushing when I told Dave that, as a kid, I'd seen him play a number of times, felt very privileged to meet him and was happy to see that he was looking so well but, as I was leaving, Orange Tartan Man patted me on the shoulder, thanked me and muttered a 'well said lad' into my ear.

As I made for the counter to pay for my purchases, I heard him, in a Shanklyesque voice, call out that Dave was going to take a ten-minute 'half-time break', but would be back signing again shortly.

Having completed the transaction I made to leave and glanced back to the table expecting, I suppose, the chair to be empty. But the great man was still sitting there, cup in hand, gazing into the middle distance. As I turned towards the exit I, rather self-consciously, raised my bagged-up books in his direction in a sort of half-wave, not really expecting any reaction.

What I got, however, was a hand raised in response and a lovely, slow smile. From Dave Mackay – to me.

It was only then as I left Smith's – passing some unaccountably blurred figures – that I became aware that I was having my 'Matthew Pinsent moment' and also realised that modern shopping malls don't have quiet corners where a grown man can find his handkerchief and pretend he's blowing his nose.

ROB WHITE (Tottenham Hotspur Supporters' Trust): For a lot of fans – and not just fans of a certain age – Dave Mackay epitomises what you might necessarily not think of as a Tottenham player, although I've talked to people like Cliff Jones and Terry Dyson and others about Dave. And he was a remarkable footballer. What a lot of people recognise was just the true grit, and determination to not give in. Every good team needs a leader. As Spurs fans, time and time again, we've had the flair players and sometimes a good defence and occasionally a good goalkeeper. But we are always missing that guy who has the determination to run through brick walls. When I think of that kind of player it is always Dave Mackay who comes to mind. I think Graham Roberts, to my mind, is the closest thing to that, although Graham himself would testify that he would not put himself anywhere near the class of Dave Mackay. Probably he had a similar 'heart' to Dave.

There's the image – which I know Dave hated because he felt it portrayed him as a bully, which is why I hesitate to talk about it – with him and Billy Bremner. To Spurs and football fans in general it is such an iconic picture. It embodies the spirit of Dave. I know that if there was one thing Dave wasn't it was a bully. He was absolutely fuming with Billy Bremner, basically.

For a lot of Spurs fans there is that big-hearted, barrel-chested player. When we look back at proper legends of this club there's no doubt – and I'm biased – but in my opinion he has to be right up there with the best all-time players who played for Tottenham. I always think my fellow Trust board members – I don't think there's any who saw him play – would be of an equal mindset.

I listened to an interview – and it was beautiful to hear him speaking again – when he was talking about managing Derby. He said basically every time he played he wanted to win. Every competition, every game he started he expected to win. If you put that mentality into a lot of football teams, the Spurs team in particular as it is something we could be criticised for lacking! Sometimes it is enough to be on the field showcasing your skills, getting to nutmeg somebody. But that wasn't enough for Dave.

I just had a memory of speaking to Terry Dyson when I was researching the book on my dad (former Spurs star John). Terry was saying about the five-a-sides they had in the gym at White Hart Lane. And Terry would say you always wanted to be on Dave's side. But if you were you always wanted to make sure you were never in front of him because you never knew when he might take you out as well as the opposing player to get the ball! No matter what level there's always somebody who needs to get the ball. One of the beautiful things his team-mates would say is that.

STEVE DOLMAN: Still the biggest thrill of my sporting life was seeing 'Rams Sign Mackay' on the back page of the local newspaper. I was in my last year of primary school, mad keen about the game and knew a lot about its teams and history. Everyone knew Mackay, the legend, the leg breaks. And he was coming to play for Derby County!

What a player he was. He oozed composure and class, chipping the ball from tricky defensive situations to a team-mate in the clear. Capable of thundering free-kicks, plenty of hand-clapping, shaken fists and a load of pointing. The younger lads – Webster, McFarland and Robson – did his running. He just told them where and when to run.

When Derby played Aston Villa, the visitors' tricky winger, Willie Anderson, had got past Ron Webster and was heading to the byline and an undoubtedly tricky cross for the Rams defence. Hurtling across from the middle of the area, as he cut in, was Dave Mackay.

Anderson pushed the ball just too far ahead of himself and Mackay was in with a sliding tackle that took the ball neatly away for a corner, but also looked sufficiently intimidating, as he slid in, to catch the man. He squealed as Mackay made contact, and those of us in the Osmaston Stand looked at one another and laughed.

Another time, Dad and I went to the BBG to get tickets for a cup game. It was midweek and, having got them, we walked past the players' entrance as Dave walked out. Dad and he spoke for ten minutes and then he saw me with my autograph book in hand and offered to sign it. Having done so, he ruffled my hair and asked if I would like those of other players. He took it back into the ground and emerged ten minutes later with the signatures of Kevin Hector, Alan Hinton, John O'Hare, Roy McFarland and more. He didn't need to do it and many wouldn't have. But it spoke volumes for the man who has been my hero ever since. I loved him as a man, manager and player.

'NOGBADVAN50': I've watched Derby since 1964 and Dave Mackay had a real presence about him when he joined us. At Spurs he was revered and absolutely outstanding under Bill Nicholson. He was coming to the end of his career when he joined us, similar to Wayne Rooney, but the players all looked up to him. I never forget watching midweek games at the old Baseball Ground and walking back to town with mates and having drinks with him and Willie Carlin in the Irongate Vaults, which is now the Slug and Lettuce. Try doing that now after a game! A great captain, hard as nails and kept every player on his toes. I read once he was voted in the top 20 players of all time. That's how good he was.

TONY HARRIS: Dave Mackay was the epitome of someone who never gave up. Coming back from two broken legs, for instance! There's that expression about more comebacks than Lazarus, isn't there? You could never write him off. You did that at your peril. You could never keep him down. I remember going up to the Baseball Ground as a Spurs fan to see him play for Derby and his team slaughtered mine 5-0. They ran rings round us. I was on my own and remember the Spurs fans on the train back kept pulling the communication cord and we got thrown off in this small place in the middle of nowhere. A lot of the fans smashed up a pub there. I was with another group walking to a bus stop and eventually got home about midnight. I was only 15 and it was before mobile phones. My parents had been going nuts!

'APACHE MAL': I would personally love a statue of Dave Mackay to be commissioned. The naming of a stand would be a fitting tribute too. It should probably have been done a long time ago. Can you imagine Dave Mackay's pride in having a stand named after him? He was the ultimate Hearts man.

'AMBITIOUS': Dave Mackay is obviously a Derby legend but it's strange for such an iconic player, looking back. Jesse Lingard has more caps for England than Dave Mackay did for Scotland. Scotland do have a long history of not giving as many caps as they should to super players. Davie Cooper and Alan Hansen fit that quite well and it's strange because even though England can be accused of the same thing, especially in the 1970s, it's not as though Scotland had the same pool numbers to select from.

CHAMBIE15: My dad was best friends with Davie Mackay's brother Frank. I was brought up on the anecdotes, the then recent memories and photographs of the great '50s and early-'60s team. An often unknown fact is that Davie, Frank and their other brother Tommy were ALL on Hearts' books at one time – probably the only time three brothers were all registered players at the club at the same time. This gave their dad Tom immense pleasure as the Mackays were – and are – Hearts men to the core. But they respected others who followed their own favourite teams, something we could all reflect on in modern football. Dignity and respect for others.

I had the honour of meeting Davie on quite a few occasions. My dad took me to see him play with Derby and Swindon, meeting up with him after the games. I also remember seeing him play in a testimonial game at Newtongrange Star who Hearts farmed him out to. The crowd that day was massive as there was the legendary Davie Mackay back strutting his stuff with the straight back, head high (always looking up) and the barrel chest to the fore. Nobody came within five yards of him that day.

I met Davie, Mr Mackay as I called him, a few times in social company when he was back home visiting his dad, brothers and old chums. Despite what he had achieved in the game of football, he was as humble, generous and gracious as any true gentleman you would want to meet.

Let's all remember everything that Davie Mackay achieved for Heart of Midlothian, what the club meant to him and the example he set to us all on how to follow your team. As others have said already, 'Hearts first. Always Hearts.'

CHARLES TOBIN: I remember meeting Dave Mackay at the main gate at White Hart Lane after Spurs had played the team I support, Manchester United. He looked dapper, wearing a Crombie overcoat. There was a bit of banter when he realised I was a United fan. He was a really nice, genuine bloke. I also met him at a meet-the-players evening at a small club in Colindale, north London. Pat Jennings and Ricky Villa as well as Dave were there. I was invited along and collected autographs for relatives who were Spurs fans. Dave and the rest of the players were cracking jokes all night. It was a good *craic*.

CHRISTINE TOBIN: I remember going with my dad and brother to White Hart Lane when Dave Mackay and Billy Bremner had their 'coming together'. Mackay was such a great player.

'WORLDCHAMPIONS1902': I had the privilege of meeting Dave Mackay at a Manchester Hearts Player of the Year night a few years ago. I remember telling my dad beforehand that Dave was on the guest list and my dad said to me, 'If you get the chance, tell Dave he was the greatest player I ever saw.' I had an opportunity to speak to the great man during the evening and he was very humble and dignified, saying that he was lucky to play in Hearts teams with great players.

NORMAN GILLER (Sports Journalists' Association): One of my great heroes. There has been no greater football warrior in my 70 years following the beautiful game. He mixed brain and brawn into a perfect cocktail, and it was his opponents who were shaken and his team-mates who were stirred. Jimmy Greaves, his Tottenham pal and partner on the pitch and at the bar, said, 'Dave made us try twice as hard to keep up with him. He was only just over 5ft 7in tall, but with that barrel chest of his he had the impact of a giant.' Braveheart.

'JAMBOX2': I grew up with my grandad telling me repeatedly how great a player Mackay was (and Gordon Smith, Wardhaugh, Conn etc.). But Mackay was the one he rated as superb. It must have been something to see in the flesh, that team he captained. A true club legend.

NICK EDWARDS: I just about crossed paths with Dave Mackay, thankfully viewing him from the stands not opposing him on the pitch! My first match at the Lane back in April 1968 was towards the end of his last season with Spurs before moving to Derby. As an 11-year-old boy, all the players looked like big men to me but the barrel-chested, burly figure of Mackay stood out as the most warrior-like of all the heroes I was seeing in the flesh for the first time that day. He embodied the very spirit of fierce competitiveness and as far as I recall didn't give the Southampton midfield much of a look in during our comprehensive 6-1 victory. He remains a club legend, as a force of nature who held everything together.

'GUESSTHECROWD': My friends and I had the great pleasure of bumping into Dave Mackay at the World Cup in 1982. We chatted away to him, and like everyone else, found him to be the perfect gentleman. We then mentioned casually who we'd been chatting to, to the travel rep, a real good-looking girl from the London area. Although she'd no real interest in football herself, it transpired that her family were Spurs fans, and she was utterly awestruck when she realised that the gentleman (her words) she'd been playing host to for the previous week was the one and only Dave Mackay, who was clearly a hero in her household. It dawned on me then that Hearts' best ever player was actually Spurs' best ever player too.

TIM McNAMARA: Regrettably, I was too young to have seen the great man play live so have had to rely on old, and mostly black and white, footage of him. But even in those brief, grainy images one can categorically see what a lion of a player he was. It's unsurprising then, that he is so often referred to as Tottenham's greatest ever player. I have always thought that one of the highest compliments that could have been paid to Dave Mackay was the fact that old team-mates, two each from Hearts, Tottenham and Derby County, were the pallbearers at his funeral.

JOHN DAVIES: Over the years we have probably all been asked, 'Who is the best Spurs player you have watched?' I know I have. My reply is instantaneous: Dave Mackay. Has there ever been a player who had such a determination to win in Tottenham colours? If there has been I'd like to know who. He backed up that determination with skill and bravery. The man was fearless. One match that still stands out in my mind is the 4-4 draw with West Ham United in December 1962. He was everywhere that day and scored a hat-trick.

'TAMBOJAMBO': My old man told me lots of great things about him. I hope the club will rename the Wheatfield Stand after him. Truly a Hearts legend and a very genuine and humble man. It would be a fitting memorial to a great Hearts man.

GLENN RENSHAW: I've been going to Tottenham since the late '50s (my dad took me then). Even though those early days are hazy, I will have to look to the '60s, where I have a better memory of him playing. I remember the time when Dave Mackay grabbed hold of Billy Bremner by the shirt and I was thinking, 'What the hell is he going to do?' For a boy of my age that was exciting stuff. I also met him on a few occasions. My dad knew most of the players because we used to get up to Tottenham early and eat in the same café that some of the players did on occasions. The players used to also travel on the buses in those days, and that was how I got to meet Bill Nicholson (that is another story). Today it is all different; you wouldn't catch a player on a bus now. His credibility would take a dive.

My dad used to chat to players like Greaves, White etc. And, of course, Mackay. Even though he came over tough or looking formidable, he was a nice chap, often ruffling my hair (which actually annoyed me). As for playing; he was something special. He would engage with the fans, and always had time for them. But to be fair, most of the players did then. On the field, he was spellbinding and always a joy to watch. I don't think he had an off-game.

When he tackled, he gave no quarter. He wasn't scared of anybody and wouldn't take any nonsense from the opposition. I often saw him reprimanding other Spurs players he thought weren't pulling their weight. I saw him lift the FA Cup in 1967 and remember jumping up and down. I was 11 at the time. I remember him being transferred to Derby County and how it affected me. Mackay was one of our greatest players and I was pleased to see him play. Over the years we've had some great players, but none matched the genius of Dave Mackay. A true legend.

'SMILER': My old man told me when I was a lot younger that Dave Mackay was the best player he's ever seen in a Hearts jersey. He told me today that he quite possibly still is. An absolute legend.

ALAN SWAIN: I can fondly recall the first time that I saw Dave Mackay wearing a Spurs shirt. It was a home game against Aston Villa in March 1959 when Spurs won 3-2. He had actually made his debut the week before in a 3-1 home victory against Manchester City, but I had not attended that game.

The game against Aston Villa was, as I recall, a Good Friday and we had heard good reports of the new signing Bill Nicholson had made from Hearts in Scotland. The Spurs side took to the pitch accompanied with the brass band playing 'McNamara's Band' and for the first time I sighted this relatively small, stocky yet barrel-chested player and the fans were not to be disappointed. He immediately displayed his ferocity in the tackle and his determination to win, a characteristic that he exemplified throughout all of his playing career at Spurs.

What a great signing he turned out to be as he performed such a vital role as the backbone in the Double-winning team of 1960/61. He formed such a great partnership with Danny Blanchflower, complementing his skill and elegance with his combative might. He was part of that fantastic Spurs side that won the First Division, the FA Cup three times, and two Charity Shields and got Spurs to the European Cup Winner's Cup Final.

His combative style will be remembered by any fan who got to watch any of his performances. Somehow, he managed to convey a delicacy of touch and sublime attacking play with power that made him a force to be reckoned with. This was accompanied with a great footballing ability that proved he was not just a hard man but also a really gifted player.

If there was one match that emphasised all of these traits then it was the semi-final of the European Cup played against Benfica under the floodlights at White Hart Lane in April 1962.

I had the good fortune to be there on that night and from the very first whistle it was Dave Mackay who led by example and drove the team on. Chasing a 3-1 deficit from the first leg, it was our barrel-chested hero who took control of the game and literally Spurred our players on. I shall never forget 'The Angels' dressed in white robes who had paraded around the pitch and one of their banners read 'Lisbon Greaves Tonight'. Although we won 2-1 on the night we lost on aggregate. How we failed to win that tie I shall never know. It was largely one-way traffic throughout the match and, despite Dave Mackay hitting the bar with a ferocious shot, his dynamic presence was not quite enough to see us over the line.

He is without doubt one of the greatest players I have ever seen play for Spurs.

'BROXBURN JAMBO': I started supporting the Hearts in the early 1960s and one of the reasons I did were stories that were told to me of the great '50s side and a great part of that legend was Dave Mackay.

PAUL SMITH (Spurs Odyssey): We Spurs fans have to accept that Mackay was not just our legend. The easy option to take when selecting an all-time Spurs team is to select the Double-winning side. Most Spurs fans of an age to have seen Dave Mackay would include him alongside Danny Blanchflower in an all-time team. Spurs were blessed to have had two such fine players and captains. I think of Dave Mackay virtually every time I watch Tottenham play. I think of the times he made a free kick anywhere inside the opponents' half a threatening situation, similar to a corner, and how he would swing the ball into the area, leading to many goals for those with heading prowess, such as Gilzean, or Bobby Smith before him. It frustrates me to see our team take a quick kick, with possession being the only objective, even if, as often happens, passing back to the goalkeeper is required. Oh for a player and a leader such as Mackay now.

'MIDLOTH_IAIN': A great wee tale:
For years the best players have valued how ball mastery and the ability to showboat is an intimidating psychological weapon in the armoury.

The night before Scotland played Spain in 1963, a talented squad sat in the Bernabéu watching Spain's training session. After ten minutes they were looking at each other in disbelief and ruefully muttering expletives.

The target of their cursing was a move being practised by Juventus's Luis del Sol, who hit five corners in succession with the outside of his foot.

Each cross was met by Real Madrid's great winger Francisco Gento, who ran into the box as fast as the Road Runner, dived forward, executed a perfect hand-spring and belted the ball past the goalkeeper with both his heels. They knew the Scotland players were watching and put on a show of such discipline, skill and arrogance that the Scots assumed, according to Frank McLintock, that it was 'largely to make us crap our pants'.

An hour before kick-off the following day, both teams were milling around on the pitch when Jim Baxter decided to show them not all British footballers were clod-kicking mugs. 'We all knew Dave Mackay's party piece,' says McLintock, 'and Baxter decided now was the right time to unveil it. Jim called over to his injured captain and shouted, "Hey Marquis, see if you can catch this!"'

With that he tossed a coin 15 feet up in the air and Mackay thrust out his right leg, bent at the knee, and caught the coin on his toe. He stood there for a second then flipped it back up in the air, caught it on his forehead, knocked it back up and caught it in his left eye socket then rolled it down his shoulder into his open blazer pocket and waltzed off back to the dressing room to thunderous applause. Scotland won the match 6-2, a victory put down to Mackay's ability to fight Spain's psychological warfare in kind.

SEAN DONOVAN: Dave Mackay was such a leader for Spurs. It would be a dream to have his ability, inspiration and plain will-to-win in our current squad.

MARK FRIEDLANDER: Dave Mackay was such a great player. I remember his barrel chest and how he fired up the Tottenham team. A tough cookie. Amazing how he came back twice from a broken leg.

DAVE HARLEY: Loved Dave Mackays long throws – first player I can remember seeing live at White Hart Lane.

* Contributions via interviews, emails, social media. Some submissions have been edited for clarity and length.

Appendix 4

Poets

The Real Mackay
by Billy Hunter

YOU can talk all night of Zola, with those magic twinkling feet,
Or hard man Dennis Wise, whose tough-guy tackling makes *ye' greet*,
Then there's 'pin-point passing' Beckham ... supreme among his peers,
Whilst we've got Gazza with his box of tricks ... and a crate
of local beers.

You've got Scholes of Man United, who can also stretch the net,
Vieira with his vision, one we never can forget,
Eric Cantona, the genius, who invented *impromptu*.
A timely *'megs'*, a swerving shot, and then the old Kung Fu.

In days of yore we'd Bremner ... a fireball of skill,
Jim Baxter, playing each game like he was in Brazil,
Bobby Murdoch of the Celtic, who laid on goals galore,
Big Greggie's reign at Rangers, with his rare *esprit de corps*.

The mention of these superstars may have you asking, 'Why?'
Quite simply, without dispute, we have the real Mackay!!!
The Marquis had all these qualities, and tonight we celebrate,
To Newtongrange to Tynie, down to London then Kuwait.
His spell at Derby County, when he played for Brian Clough,
And then became manager when Brian took the huff!!!

It started back in '51, when the Jam Tarts signed him up.
They didn't realise, that soon, he'd help them win the cup.
But first he went to Nitten, where the tough guys made him wince.
There was some old pros, and some miners, with their *heids*
full o' mince.

Surviving that, in '53, the Jambos called him in,
They had a premonition; Dave's middle name was – WIN.
Alongside Johnny Cumming, Andy Bowman, Alex Young,
Freddie Glidden, Jimmy Murray; how the names roll off your tongue.
Willie Duff, and Kirk and Thomson, two footballing full-backs
With Willie Bauld and Ian Crawford, they arrested cardiacs!!

The Hearts then won the Scottish League, the League and
Scottish Cup.
And at long last, gave Hearts' loyal fans, the chance to have a sup.
But all good things come to an end, and Dave Mackay moved south.
When 30 grand from Tottenham took him to their goalmouth.

The years with Spurs were Glory Years and it isn't hard to guess,
That once again the Marquis was the mainstay of success.
The Hotspur's 'push and run' style, was the plan of old Bill Nick
With Greaves, and Smith, and our own John White, it all just
seemed to click.

Although Dave had suffered two leg breaks, his move to
Derby showed,
In this old dog there still was life, not yet Madame Tussaud!
Then, finally, for 15 years, he roamed the desert sand.
He'd carved his name among the greats; Rob Roy to Genghis Khan.

For Dave Mackay, read Braveheart, a powerhouse de luxe.
When fights broke out, you'd find *oor* Dave, in the middle
of the rucks.
His leadership, without doubt, was Churchill at his best.
He could, because he had achieved, stick out that barrel chest.

And skill, let's see – even now he can on his instep or his toe
Catch a spinning coin, thrown in the air; don't bet, you'll
lose your dough.
The goals he scored from left-half back with boots submerged in *glaur*.
A hat-trick back in '57, the Bairns all screamed 'no more!'
Dave's passing too was unsurpassed, and whether long or short.
'*Jess gies* it back …it's mine …*no* yours,' the Marquis would retort.

He had it all, of that I'm sure, and on this gala night
Let's toast our legend, Dave Mackay, our man is outtasight!!!

* Billy Hunter (14 February 1940–4 August 2020) was a footballer who was in a Scotland squad with Dave Mackay and an inside-forward for Motherwell, where he was a member of the club's Ancell Babes. Craig Brown kindly supplied a copy of the poem.

* To quote the programme in which the verse appeared, 'This poem was penned especially for the Dave Mackay Tribute Dinner in the Sheraton Grand Hotel in Edinburgh and attended by former players from both Hibs and Hearts. Top table special guests were Andy Bowman, Alex Young, Jimmy Murray and John Robertson from the Hearts with Alan Wells and Jim Baxter completing a formidable cast.'

When I Think About The Good Auld Days

When I think about the auld days,
What went oan in Edinburgh toon,
Hearts gawn through a bad phase,
And looked like going doon.
God couldnae let that happen,
Or watch Auld Reeckie cry,
On speaking to his angels,
He sent Hearts Dave Mackay.

* AMERSHAMJAMBO wrote on the Jambos Kickback website, 'Don't know if this has been posted yet but sums up how important he was to Hearts.'

A Fine Goodbye
By George Dolbear Robertson

There were legends there of every hue
To say a fine goodbye to you
There were teardrops in each eye
As they said their farewell to Dave Mackay
A fine goodbye a fond adieu
As to the sky your spirit flew
The piper played and the reason
why
Was a fine goodbye to Dave Mackay
Men like you were rather rare
But some were there at Traquair
Goodbye Goodbye a final wave
To the Real Mackay the big man Dave

* Poem kindly supplied by John Robertson, brother of the poet

Appendix 5

Quite interesting

* Dave Mackay played 33 Hearts reserve matches, the majority before his breakthrough into the first XI; 28 at left-half rather than right-half.

* Mackay took nine penalties for Hearts, scoring five and failing with four. Two were saved and two were fired wide.

* A quote from January 1958, 'If you want to stop Hearts from scoring ... then you have to halt SIX attackers, instead of the normal five. For proof I offer the almost incredible record of wing-half Dave Mackay who has scored no fewer than nine goals in the last ten games.'

* He was booked once playing against St Mirren in a 2-2 draw on 15 September 1956 for 'trying to kick the ball out of goalkeeper Forsyth's hands'. Mackay put this down to not hearing the referee's whistle due to a hearing problem sustained when hospitalised after bangs on the ear during a match on Hearts' 1954 South Africa tour.

* Mackay cost a British record £32,000 fee for half-back when he signed for Tottenham in March 1959.

* Mackay made his Tottenham Hotspur debut against Manchester City at White Hart Lane on 21 March 1959. He helped Spurs to a 3-1 win.

* Mackay scored his first Spurs goal in a 5-1 victory over Manchester United at Old Trafford on 12 September 1959. Coincidently, it was the same scoreline when he netted his first goal at home a week later when he helped Spurs pulverise Preston North End.

* Jimmy Robertson was inspired by old Spurs team-mate Mackay after having his leg broken twice after they both had left the club. Like Mackay, Robertson made a successful comeback.

* Comedian and compere Jimmy Tarbuck hosted TV's *Sunday Night At The London Palladium* in the 1960s. On one show he singled out the 'great' Dave Mackay to a packed crowd at the prestigious venue in front of the cameras.

* TV contestant Harry, a 74-year-old accountant and football fan from Edgware in north London, did a short fist-pump after getting through to the final by beating Mark 'The Beast' Labbett on an episode of *The Chase* screened in November 2020. Host Bradley Walsh, a former Brentford footballer and Arsenal supporter, said the gesture reflected 'a touch of the Dave Mackays'.

* Dave Mackay was captain when Derby County established a record home attendance, 41,826 versus Spurs in 1969.

* Mackay was the first player to lift the Watney Cup, the first sponsored trophy in British football, in 1970.

* Mackay was the second and at the time of writing last manager to lead Derby County, one of the founder members of the Football League, to the English top-flight title. The 1974/75 campaign followed a first under Brian Clough in 1971/72.

* He was the manager when Derby County played in front of their highest ever attendance, 120,000 away to Real Madrid in 1975.

* Mackay also oversaw Derby's record victory, 12-0 versus Finn Harps in the UEFA Cup in 1976.

* Derby County unveiled lasting mementoes of Dave Mackay in 2015 following his passing that year, with a statue outside the stadium and a clock in one of the stands.

Compiled by Davy Allan (Heart of Midlothian museum manager), author Mike Donovan, and Andy Ellis (Derby County club historian).

Honours and career record

HEART OF MIDLOTHIAN

Scottish League Cup winner: 1953/54, 1958/59
Scottish Cup winner: 1955/56
Scottish League championship winner: 1957/58
East of Scotland Shield winner: 1953/54, 1954/55, 1955/56, 1957/58
Scottish Footballer of the Year: 1959
Scottish international caps: Four
Inducted into the Hearts Hall of Fame: 2006

1953/54	*Appearances*	*Goals*
	4	0

1954/55	*Appearances*	*Goals*
League	25	2
Scottish Cup	4	0
League Cup	7	1
Total	36	3

1955/56	*Appearances*	*Goals*
League	28	4
Scottish Cup	6	0
League Cup	2	0
Total	36	4

1956/57	*Appearances*	*Goals*
League	31	5
Scottish Cup	1	0
League Cup	6	0
Total	38	5

1957/58	*Appearances*	*Goals*
League	28	12
Scottish Cup	3	0
League Cup	6	0
Total	37	12

1958/59	*Appearances*	*Goals*
League	19	4
Scottish Cup	2	0
League Cup	5	1
European Cup	2	0
Total	28	5

TOTTENHAM HOTSPUR

First Division winner: 1960/61
FA Cup winner: 1960/61, 1961/62, 1966/67
European Cup Winners' Cup winner: 1963
FA Charity Shield winner: 1961, 1962, 1967 (shared)
Scottish international caps: 18
Inducted into Spurs' Hall of Fame: 2004

1958/59	*Appearances*	*Goals*
League	4	0

1959/60	*Appearances*	*Goals*
League	38	11
FA Cup	3	0
Total	41	11

1960/61	Appearances	Goals
League	37	4
FA Cup	7	2
Total	44	6

1961/62	Appearances	Goals
League	26	8
FA Cup	7	0
Charity Shield	1	0
Total	34	8

1962/63	Appearances	Goals
League	37	6
FA Cup	1	0
Cup Winners' Cup	6	3
Charity Shield	1	0
Total	45	9

1963/64	Appearances	Goals
League	17	3
Cup Winners' Cup	2	1
Total	19	4

1965/66	Appearances	Goals
League	41	6
FA Cup	2	2
Total	43	8

1966/67	Appearances	Goals
League	39	3
FA Cup	8	0
Total	47	3

1967/68	Appearances	Goals
League	29	1
Charity Shield	1	0
Total	30	1

DERBY COUNTY

Second Division championship winner: 1968/69
FWA Footballer of the Year (with Tony Book): 1968/69
Watney Cup winner: 1970

1968/69	Appearances	Goals
League	41	1
League Cup	8	1
Total	49	2

1969/70	Appearances	Goals
League	39	2
FA Cup	4	0
League Cup	6	0
Total	49	2

1970/71	Appearances	Goals
League	42	2
FA Cup	3	0
League Cup	2	1
Watney Cup	3	1
Total	50	4

SWINDON TOWN

1971/72	Appearances	Goals
League	26	1

SCOTLAND

Inducted into the Scottish Hall of Fame: 2004

Cap-by-cap
1: 26 May 1957: 4-1 defeat away to Spain in a World Cup qualifier.
2: 15 June 1958: 2-1 loss to France in World Cup finals in Sweden.
3: 18 October 1958: Mackay captain in 3-0 Home International Championship win in Wales.
4: 5 November 1958: Mackay captain in 2-2 home draw with Northern Ireland.
5: 11 April 1959: 1-0 loss to England at Wembley.
6: 6 May 1959: 3-2 friendly win over West Germany, crowd 103,415.
7: 3 October 1959: 4-0 win in Northern Ireland.
8: 4 November 1959: 1-1 home draw with Wales.
9: 4 May 1960: 3-2 friendly home defeat to Poland.
10: 29 May 1960: 4-1 defeat against Austria in Vienna.
11: 5 June 1960: 3-3 friendly draw with Hungary in Budapest.
12: 8 June 1960: 4-2 friendly loss against Turkey in Ankara.
13: 22 October 1960: 2-0 Home International reverse to Wales in Cardiff.
14: 9 November 1960: 5-2 victory over Northern Ireland at Hampden.
15: 15 April 1961: 9-3 defeat to England at Wembley.
16: 6 April 1963: 2-1 win over England at Wembley.
17: 8 May 1963: Captain in 4-1 friendly win against Austria at Hampden.
18: 4 June 1963: Captain in a 4-3 friendly loss to Norway in Bergen.
19: 12 October 1963: Captain in a 2-1 defeat by Northern Ireland in Belfast.
20: 7 November 1963: Captain in a 6-1 home friendly win against Norway.
21: 20 November 1963: Captain in a 2-1 home win against Wales.
22: 2 October 1965: Final appearance in 3-2 defeat to Northern Ireland in Belfast.

* Full international details gleaned from Alan Brown, Gabriele Tossani and Rec.Sport.Soccer Statistics Foundation.

MANAGEMENT

DERBY COUNTY
First Division championship winner: 1974/75
FA Charity Shield winner: 1975
FA Cup semi-finalist: 1976

AL-ARABI
Kuwait Premier League winner: 1979/80, 1981/82, 1982/83, 1983/84, 1984/85
Kuwait Emir Cup winner: 1980/81, 1982/83

ZAMALEK
Egyptian Premier League winner: 1991/92, 1992/93

QATAR
Under-17 World Cup qualification: 1995

Acknowledgements

A FOOTBALL figure such as Dave Mackay deserves to be remembered for posterity as a giant of the game and one of its strongest pillars. It was a daunting task to write a book that would do him justice as a professional, family man and a friend to so many, balancing his public and private persona and discovering what he meant to everyone. But the process proved, as I thought it would, a labour of love. And I did my best. To paraphrase the Beatles, one of Mr Mackay's favourite musical combos, 'I got by with a little help from my friends, plus his family, colleagues and friends'.

I have to start by thanking the wonderful Isobel, his wife of 60 years, and equally wonderful children Derek, Valerie and Julie for their time, support, contribution and encouragement. The same goes for Mr Mackay's brothers Tommy and Frank, plus Ninian Cassidy, Isobel's cousin and a close friend of the 'legend's legend'. They have all lent credence to the project and been the most crucial, fundamental source of information and insight in my journey to discover the 'real Mackay'. The family have also checked the manuscript and supplied photographs from their personal collection, for which I am grateful.

I appreciate the time and invaluable assistance of an almost countless number of interviewees, including many of Mr Mackay's colleagues and pals: Gordon Marshall, the last of the 1958 Hearts championship side; the Jambos' record league goalscorer John Robertson; Tottenham Hotspur Double winners Les Allen, Terry Dyson, Cliff Jones and Tony Marchi; Jimmy Greaves via his agent Terry Baker; Pat Jennings, Joe and Bonnie Kinnear, Mike England, Phil Beal, Jimmy Robertson, John Sainty, Steve Perryman, Rob White, Mike Rollo and Paul Coyte; Derby County trio Roy

McFarland, John McGovern and Colin Todd; John Duncan of Spurs and Derby; David Moss (Swindon Town); Les Robinson (Doncaster Rovers); Ian Atkins and John Frain (Birmingham City); Neil Martin (Nottingham Forest, Al-Arabi and Shabab); Craig Brown, who was wonderfully helpful; Ian Ure, Frank McLintock and Denis Law (Scotland).

Denis Law, a lovely, lovely guy and a close friend of our subject, also contributed a foreword along with Mr Mackay's son Derek. I am indebted to both for that. I appreciate the thoughts of Bobby Wishart, who played football with the child Mackay close to Glendevon Park and passed aged 87 on 3 December 2020, and the efforts of his daughter Carol Bonnie to pass them on.

I have also to thank club historians David Speed (Hearts), John Fennelly (Spurs) and Andy Ellis (Derby County) for providing pieces and, along with mentor Kevin Brennan, checking my written word. I have to pick out John for special mention for his continued help and encouragement. Thanks to Norman Giller, Mike Aitken, Alan Pattullo, Paul Morrissey, Alan Swain, Glenn Renshaw, Tom Loakes, all of the media departments of Dave Mackay's clubs, *The Scotsman* editorial.

Thank you Daniel Levy (Spurs) and Mel Morris (Derby) – and your staff – for tributes to Mr Mackay.

I am grateful to Andrew Hickie (Newtongrange Star), Davy Allan (Hearts Museum), Big Hearts Community Trust, Deborah, Val and all at the Bruce Castle Museum. Thanks to all Hearts, Spurs and Derby fans, contributors or otherwise. Paul, Jane, Graham, Duncan, Dean, Gareth, Alex and the rest of the team at Pitch Publishing who have, as always, been supportive, including exhausting the company printer by printing out 200,000 words on A4!

Also thanks to Mark, Tony, Dave H and Sue, Tilly, Mac, Caroline, Christopher and Rosanna, Tim, Kev, Pauline and Marc, Nick and Jan, Debbie, Jon and Sadie, Ray and Jackie, Graham and Penny.

Tony and Sue, Ade, Aaron and Maureen, Jean and Chris, Sally and Paul, Glen and Lynn, Dave M, Sean and Sandra, Chris and Charlie, June and family, Kate and Keith, Marc, Louise, Zachary and Lucas, Mick and Marg, Andrea and Clive, Joan and Morten, Peggy and Dave, Terry and Linda, the Bexhill Mob and Loughton five-a-siders. Any unlisted helpers who know who they are. John Donne had a point when his wrote in the 17th century, 'No man is an island.'

I'm feeling more and more humbled as I compile this list of assistants, but I cannot overstate how much I have appreciated all of their help.

Also, I am more than grateful for the memories of my mum and dad, who courted at White Hart Lane and loved Dave Mackay, and Mims. Finally, I would like to thank Rosemary, Matthew and Benny for their patience and understanding as I got the job done.

The Mackay family would like to say, 'Remembering, with thanks, everyone who has featured in Dave's life and made it so very special.'

Mike Donovan

Credits

Quotations

From sources beyond interviews undertaken by the author, plus Dave Mackay quotes from *The Real Mackay, The Dave Mackay Story* (Dave Mackay with Martin Knight, Mainstream, 2004), unless otherwise marked.

1: Ken Jones, 'He looked fitter and faster...'; Bill Nicholson, 'It's a three-quarter fracture...'; Frank Blunstone, 'I'm writing to Dave tonight...'; Alick Jeffrey, 'Watch as much football as you can...' (*The Daily Mirror*, 13 September 1964).

2: Dave Mackay, 'In cold print it may seem very uninteresting...' (*Soccer My Spur*).

3: Jim Hutton, 'I've grown out of my boots...'; DM, 'It was a look of love...'; Tommy Mackay, 'Now you'll find yourself playing with greater confidence...' (*Soccer My Spur*).

4: DM, 'I was able to use to the full my enthusiasm...'; 'Although I was surprised...'; ' I had a shocking game...'; 'A habit I had developed...'; 'Most Scots will tell...'; 'Although named only as a reserve...' (*Soccer My Spur*). DM, 'I was always like that...' (*FourFourTwo*). Johnny Haynes, 'Great fun and a thrilling overture...' (*It's All In The Game*).

6: DM, 'They were grand men...'; 'He taught me there was an urgency...'; 'I had attended many of their coaching courses...'; Duncan McClure, 'Why not become a professional...' (*Soccer My Spur*). DM, 'Yes I would have done...'; 'I was playing against grown men...' (Hearts tribute programme v Dumbarton). Jim Kelly, 'I was part of the Lochee Harp...' (24 December 2007); DM, 'All the older players...'; Andy

497

Morris, 'I… played in game v Loanhead…, (12 November 2010); Harry Powell, 'Having been brought up in Nitten…' (21 September 2013); (Newtongrange Star official website). DM, 'On the field…'; 'Believe me, we had to justify…' (*Soccer My Spur*).

7: DM, 'The crowd were enthusiastic…'; 'I lost my temper…'; 'Father pointed out…'; 'By accident I caused…'; 'For two seasons…' (*Soccer My Spur*). Laurence McIntosh, 'I don't think you'll ever make the grade…'; Nat Fisher, 'I played against Dave Mackay…' (*Scottish Daily Mail*, 2017). 'Playing wise… I find it hard…'; Sean Connery, 'I really wanted to accept…' (Scottish Junior FA).

8: 'I disappeared…'; 'I learned by using'; 'I like to think…'; 'I played a shocking…'; 'I felt washed out…'; 'In a matter…' (*Soccer My Spur*). 'No one ever told us…' (Hearts tribute programme).

9: DM, 'The League Cup win was very special…' (Hearts tribute programme). Freddie Glidden, 'To become part…' (Hearts TV). Davie McLean, 'It may take a little time…' (*The Hearts*). Tommy Walker, 'I'm a happy man…'; 'Bobby Parker, 'We're delighted…' (*Hearts The Golden Years*).

10: DM, 'For eight weeks I had to slog away…'; 'I lived only for the weekend…'; 'As a very raw Scottish footballer…'; 'A footballer has to discipline himself…'; 'As this happened in the early hours…' (*Soccer My Spur*). 'It was great because…' (Hearts tribute programme). 'The war was finished…' (*FourFourTwo*). 'I got off lightly…' (*The Sun*).

11: DM, 'We were always confident…'; 'I was too scared of losing the '56 final…' (Hearts tribute programme). TW, 'Walker said, 'It was the greatest day of my life…' (*The Hearts*).

12: FG, 'You would never know…' (Hearts tribute programme). DM, 'When a footballer is playing…'; 'Bobby Evans, a football-wise character…' (*Soccer My Spur*). 'I played for Scotland in vital matches…' (Great Tyneside Tales). 'We just knew…'; 'We just knew we'd scored…' (Hearts tribute programme).

13: DM, 'A lot better…' (*FourFourTwo*). DM, 'Dougie Cowie was a beautiful player to watch…' (*Soccer My Spur*). 'I would have been very happy to stay…'; 'Willie Bauld, Alfie Conn and Jimmy Wardhaugh: what players…' (Hearts tribute programme). AM, 'Hearts at once cheered…'

(Tottenham Hotspur). Gordon Marshall, 'It felt like…' (Hearts tribute programme). FG, 'He made quite an impression…'; Jimmy Murray, 'He was a true legend…'; Alex Young, 'He was a superb player…' (Hearts tribute programme). Sir Alex Ferguson, 'My own memories…' (*The Scotsman*).

14: Bill Nicholson, 'I saw enough of Mackay…'; 'Our deadline is Monday…'; 'Look, I am sure we can agree…'; 'Tommy [Walker] took me off to lunch…' (*Glory, Glory*). DM, 'Everything went right for me…'; 'Tommy Docherty…' (*Soccer My Spur*).

15: BN, 'I will always remember…'; 'I cannot overstate…' (*Glory, Glory*). BN, 'Mackay when he first came here…' (YouTube). BN, 'We trained every…' (*Football's Perfectionist*). DM, 'Everything went right for me…'; 'I will always believe…'; 'Once again…'; 'The Russian trip…' (*Soccer My Spur*). 'Whether I'm playing football…' (*The Sun*). John Motson, 'From north of the border…' (YouTube). Alan Leather, 'One day the players wanted boiled eggs…' (*Football's Perfectionist*).

16: BN, 'I tried to keep…'; 'It felt in 1960…' (*And The Spurs Go Marching On*). 'One of the best…'; 'We worked hard…' (*Glory, Glory*). DM, 'I naturally feel disappointed…'; 'I believe…' (*Soccer My Spur*). Keith Burkinshaw, 'That Double side…' (Tottenham Hotspur). DM, 'This is utterly untrue…'; 'Never was there a suggestion…'; 'I believe…'; 'One of the most important…' (*Soccer My Spur*), 'I was lucky…' (*The Sun*). 'It wasn't big…'; Ron Henry, 'Are you…'; Peter Shreeves, 'It's all right…' (*Football's Perfectionist*).

17: Phil Soar, 'Mackay, who seemed to play…' (*And The Spurs Go Marching On*). DM, 'That still hurts…'; 'Play? I didn't play…'; 'Our skilled players…' (*Soccer My Spur*)

18: DM, 'Well obviously the Tottenham team…' (*The Sun*). 'When I went to Spurs…' (*FourFourTwo*). 'Usually, I think…'; 'The players were just happy…' (*The Double*)

20: BN, 'I lost count…'; 'I was keen…'(*And The Spurs Go Marching On*). 'At a team meeting…'; 'When we played Ipswich…' (*Glory, Glory*).

21: Cliff Jones, 'With Dave Mackay…' (*And The Spurs Go Marching On*).

22: DM, 'I don't think Cantwell…' (Football's Perfectionist). 'I still well up…' (*The Sun*). 'The doctor said…' (FourFourTwo). 'I've never got over that…' (Cheshunt Q&A, 2007). BN, 'He sat for hours…', ' 'Well, Dave…' (*Glory, Glory*). Alan Mullery, 'I remember…' (Tottenham Hotspur).

23: DM, 'We had skirmishes…' (*FourFourTwo*).

24: Terry Venables, 'What stands out…' (*The Biography of Tottenham Hotspur*). DM, 'I was determined…' (TS). 'People ask me…' (*Tottenham Hotspur Football Book*).

25: DM, 'I went to Bill Nick…' (*FourFourTwo*). BN, 'There were many outstanding players…' (*Glory, Glory*). Alan Gilzean, 'Everybody talked about Dave Mackay…' (YouTube).

26: DM, 'I was all lined up to go back…' (*The Sun*). 'Hearts were going to…' (*FourFourTwo*). Julie Welch, 'The Man had much more to give…' (*The Biography Of Tottenham Hotspur*). Brian Clough, 'It gives a player incentive…' (*Derby County The Glory Years*).

27: AM, 'They did! Bill Nicholson was not amused…' (talkSPORT). DM, 'He picked on everyone else except me…' (*FourFourTwo*).

28: DM, 'I've been lucky to play under three of the greatest managers…' (*The Sun*)

29: DM, 'The hardest thing I found when I went to Nottingham…'; 'I didn't worry about the results to start with…' (*Goal*).

30: DM, 'Forget the troubles of last season…'; 'Brian Clough is a great manager but there are other great managers too…' (*Goal*). 'I'd been offered the job and was determined to take it…' (*FourFourTwo*).

31: DM, 'Forget the troubles of last season…'; 'I liked the way Clough did some things. There were others that I didn't like…' (*Goal*); 'Later, when I took over from Brian…'; 'It was fantastic…'; 'True. I knew Charlie George would rather not go to Spurs…'(*FourFourTwo*). 'Of course, he is a master…' (*The Sun*). Francis Lee, 'The trouble is that when you stop playing for England…' (*Goal*). Archie Gemmill, 'Dave and Des deserve every credit they get…' (YouTube), 'It was wonderful captaining Derby to the title…' (*Goal*). Bruce Rioch, 'It was exciting…' (*Goal*). Charlie George, 'Pull of Dave Mackay was too great…' 'I was a bit nervous…'; 'I feel people make a lot…'; 'Without being blasé…' (RamsTV).

32: Stuart Webb, 'Dave fell victim to some dirty work…' (*Derby Telegraph*). DM, 'I was beginning to lose interest anyway…' 'Tommy was a perfect gentleman…' (*FourFourTwo*). CG, 'I didn't think Dave should have been sacked…'; 'Thank goodness we didn't get relegated…'; 'I always respected Brian Clough…' (RamsTV). Alan Hinton, 'Dave Mackay took over and did a brilliant job…' (*Backpass*).

33: DM, 'Most of them [could] speak English…' (*FourFourTwo*).

34: DM, 'I'd had my fill…' (*FourFourTwo*).

36: DM, 'I decided it was time to use them…' (*Glasgow Herald*).

37: Harry Redknapp, 'Scott Parker was just amazing…' (BBC).

38: Sam Rush, 'Everyone at Derby County is truly saddened at the news that Dave Mackay has passed away…' (Sky). Craig Brown, 'He would be in my all-time greatest Scottish team…'; Tommy Docherty, 'He was a tremendous player, world-class…'; John Vicars, 'I'm delighted…'; Andy Edwards said, 'To play a part in this permanent tribute…' (BBC).

43 Ann Budge, 'As captain of Heart of Midlothian FC he [Mackay] guided the club to some of its greatest glories…'; Robbie Neilson, 'Dave Mackay, probably the best player Hearts ever had…'; Craig Levein, 'When you come into a club you quickly learn about its history and the famous players…' (Hearts tribute programme). Sam Rush, 'The last man to manage a top-flight championship-winning team at Derby, Dave Mackay is a hero to people throughout football…' (*The Ram* tribute programme for Derby County v Birmingham City, 7 March 2015).

Pictures
The Mackay family collection, Mike Donovan, Tom Dixon, Rob White; agencies Alamy, Getty and Colorsport.

Bibliography

Newtongrange Star Football Club Centenary Year 1890–1990 (A.C. Smith, Newtongrange Star Football Club, 1990)

Hearts The Golden Years (Tom Purdie, Amberley, 2012)

The Hearts (Albert Mackie, Stanley Paul, 1959)

Great Tynecastle Tales (Rob Robertson and Paul Kiddie, Mainstream, 2005)

Hearts – Greatest Ever Season, 50th Anniversary of 1957/58 (Mike Buckle, Black and White, 2007)

The Hearts – The Story of Heart of Midlothian FC (Albert Mackie, Stanley Paul, 1959)

Gritty, Gallant, Glorious – A History and Complete Record of the Hearts 1946–1997 (Norrie Price, Price, 1997)

Soccer My Spur (Dave Mackay, Stanley Paul, 1961)

Spurs' Greatest Games (Mike Donovan, Pitch, 2012)

Spurs' Unsung Hero of the Glory, Glory Years My Autobiography (Terry Dyson with Mike Donovan, Pitch, 2015)

Spurs Supreme – A Review of Soccer's Greatest Ever Side 1960/61 (Ralph L. Finn, The Soccer Book Club London, 1962)

London's Cup Final 1967 – How Chelsea and Spurs Reached Wembley (Ralph L. Finn, Robert Hale, 1967)

The Biography of Tottenham Hotspur (Julie Welch, Vision Sports, 2015)

Greavsie – The Autobiography (Jimmy Greaves, Time Warner, 2003)

Glory, Glory Lane – The Extraordinary History of Tottenham Hotspur's Famous Home for 118 Years (Mike Donovan, Pitch, 2017)

Bill Nicholson – The Master of White Hart Lane Revisited (Norman Giller, Norman Giller Books, 2013)

Glory Glory – My Life with Spurs (Bill Nicholson, Macmillan, 1985)

Bill Nicholson – Football's Perfectionist (Brian Scovell, John Blake, 2011)

Spurs – The Double (Julian Holland, The Sportsmans Book Club, 1962)

The Tottenham Hotspur Football Book No. 6 (edited by Peter Smith, Stanley Paul, 1972)

The Tottenham Hotspur Football Book No. 8 (edited by Peter Smith, Stanley Paul, 1974)

The Ghost – In Search Of My Father The Football Legend (Rob White and Julie Welch, Yellow Jersey Press, 2012)

Cliff Jones – It's a Wonderful Life! My Story (Ivan Ponting, Vision Sports, 2016)

Tottenham Hotspur Player by Player (Ivan Ponting, Guinness, 1993)

The Double – The Inside Story of Spurs' Triumphant 1960/61 Season (Ken Ferris, Mainstream, 2008)

The Spurs Alphabet – A Complete Who's Who of Tottenham Hotspur FC (Bob Goodwin, Robwin Publishing House, 2017)

Pat Jennings – An Autobiography (Reg Drury, Panther, 1984)

The Tottenham Hotspur Football Book (Dennis Signy, Stanley Paul, 1967)

Tottenham Hotspur The Complete Record (Bob Goodwin, Derby Books, 2011)

The Real Mackay – The Dave Mackay Story (Martin Knight, Mainstream, 2004)

The Glory, Glory Nights – The Complete History of Spurs in European Competition (Colin Gibson and Harry Harris, Cockerel, 1986)

Alan Mullery – The Autobiography (Alan Mullery with Tony Norman, Headline, 2006)

The Double and Before – The Autobiography of Danny Blanchflower (Nicholas Kaye, 1961)

The King of White Hart Lane – The Authorised Biography of Alan Gilzean (Mike Donovan, Pitch, 2018)

Spurs '67 – Revisiting the First Ever Cockney Cup Final (Norman Giller, Norman Giller Books, 2019)

And the Spurs Go Marching On …The First Hundred Years – The Official Story of Tottenham Hotspur (Phil Soar, Hamlyn, 1982)

Derby County The Complete Record (Gerald Mortimer, Breedon Books, 2006)

The Who's Who of Derby County, Gerald Mortimer, Breedon Books, 2004)

Clough – The Autobiography (Brian Clough with John Sadler, Corgi, 1995)

Derby County The Glory Years 1967–1976 (Simon Sharp, Max Media, 2018)

Swindon Town 1879–2009 A History in Facts and Figures, The Combined Volume (Paul Plowman, Footprint, 2009)

Nottingham Forest A Complete Record 1865–1991 (Pete Attaway, Breedon, 1991)

The History of Walsall Football Club 1888–1992 (Tony Matthews and Geoff Allman, Sports Leisure Concepts, 1992)

The Fall and Rise of Doncaster Rovers (Tony Bluff and Steve Uttley, Breedon, 2008)

Donny – The Official History of Doncaster Rovers (Tony Bluff and Barry Watson, Biddles, 1994)

Blues Insider – A Quarter of a Century with Birmingham City (Keith Dixon, Pitch, 2017)

Birmingham City A Complete Record (Tony Matthews, Breedon, 1995)

The King – My Autobiography Denis Law (Denis Law with Bob Harris, Bantam, 2004)

Joe Kinnear – Still Crazy (Hunter Davies, Andre Deutsch, 2000)

Bremner! – The Legend of Billy Bremner (Bernard Bale, Andre Deutsch, 1998)

Bremner – The Real King Billy; The Complete Biography (Richard Sutcliffe, Great Northern, 2011)

Keep Fighting – The Billy Bremner Story (Paul Harrison, Black and White, 2017)

Football: My Life, My Passion (Graeme Souness with Douglas Alexander, Headline, 2017)

No Half Measures (Graeme Souness with Bob Harris, Grafton, 1987)

It's All In The Game (Johnny Haynes, Arthur Baker, 1962)

Programmes

Hearts v Dumbarton, 14 March 2015

Hearts v Queen of the South, 28 March 2015

Spurs v Swansea City, 4 March 2015

Tottenham Hotspur v Manchester United, 14 May 2017

Derby County v Birmingham City, 7 March 2015

Newspapers
The Scotsman
Daily Mirror
The Guardian
The Sun

Magazines
Backpass
World Soccer
FourFourTwo
Goal
Shoot
Charles Buchan's Football Monthly

Online
Hearts TV
RamsTV
YouTube
BBC
ITV
Heart of Midlothian
London Hearts
Tottenham Hotspur
Derby County
Swindon Town
Nottingham Forest
Walsall
Al-Arabi
Shabab
Doncaster Rovers
Birmingham City
Zamalek
Qatar FA
Scottish FA
Scottish Hall of Fame
English Hall of Fame

National Football Museum
Rec.Sport.Soccer Statistics Foundation (prepared and maintained
by Alan Brown and Gabriele Tossani)
Wikipedia
Social media
Various fans' forums

Podcasts
The Spurs Show (hosted by Mike Leigh and Phil Cornwell)
Steve Perryman podcast

Other sources: Ken Bogle at the Local Studies Library in Loanhead
(Newtongrange Star).

Index

Aitken, Mike 120, 495
Al-Arabi FC 358-361, 363-366, 382, 391, 418, 495
Al-Mulla, Mohammed 358-359, 365, 418
Allen, Les 21-22, 177, 187, 197-199, 205, 209, 213, 217, 226, 234, 251, 275, 314, 318, 400, 435, 494
Anderson, Des 260, 314, 319, 325, 331, 341, 347, 351, 358, 365, 393, 395, 412, 423
Anderson, Des Junior 423-424
Anderson, Jimmy 159-160
Anderson, Lesley 423
Anderson, Viv 319, 321
Andrews, Eamonn 194
Ardiles, Ossie 17, 353, 420, 435
Arsenal FC 19, 145, 155, 162, 165, 192, 194, 198, 209-210, 214, 225, 237, 242, 250, 255, 269, 279-280, 299, 302-303, 317, 330, 341, 343-344, 354-355, 365, 368, 471, 487
Ashurst, Len 385
Attlee, Clement 61

Baily, Eddie 26, 33, 160, 208, 264, 283
Baker, Linda 175
Baker, Peter 28, 159-160, 167, 169, 194, 209, 251
Balgreen School 42, 44, 50, 55, 209
Banks, Gordon 206, 406, 408
Banner Man, The 426-427, 446, 460
Baseball Ground 277, 284-285, 288-290, 296, 298-300, 302, 307, 312-313, 323-324, 326-328, 334, 336, 338-340, 343-344, 346, 348, 350, 352, 424, 470, 474
Battles, Barney 58, 107-108
Battles Junior, Barney 58
Bauld, Willie 58-59, 69, 85-86, 88, 91, 96-97, 100, 119-120, 123-124, 128, 136, 139, 147-150, 154, 428, 450, 462, 483, 498
Baxter, Bobby 42, 85
Baxter, Jim 196, 233, 238, 397, 481-482, 484
Beal, Phil 28, 274, 276, 314, 420, 426-427, 435, 494
Beatles, The 11-12, 190, 224, 239, 265, 336, 387, 433, 446, 459, 494
Beattie, Andy 123, 172, 184, 454
Bernabéu Stadium 130, 343, 480
Best, George 10, 19, 31, 251, 253, 255, 271, 299, 301, 341, 397, 408-409, 418, 421, 449, 452
Birmingham City FC 112, 195, 217, 224, 240, 260, 262, 314, 336, 374-377, 380-382, 418, 420, 453, 495, 501, 504
Blackwood, Bobby 91, 103, 135, 148
Blanchflower, Betty 175
Blanchflower, Danny 13, 25, 117-118, 121, 146, 159-161, 167-169, 171, 175-177, 181-182, 185-188, 190, 192-194, 197-198, 201, 204-210, 213-215, 220-221, 223, 225-227, 231, 234, 236, 239-240, 245-246, 251, 266, 272, 279, 287, 301, 397, 431, 463-464, 479-480, 503
Blues, George 365, 385
Blunsdon House 314
Book, Tony 291, 468, 491
Bowyer, Ian 322
Boyd, James 109
Brown, Bill 22, 137, 144-145, 176, 190, 198-199, 202-203, 209, 227, 235, 238, 240, 242, 246, 250, 253, 276, 397, 440, 443
Brown, Craig 83, 182, 419, 454-455, 485, 495, 501
Bloomer, Steve 352, 452
Bremner, Billy 10, 27, 255-257, 275, 320,

370, 373, 404, 419, 445, 449, 467, 472, 476, 478, 482, 504

Brevett, Rufus 369, 371, 373

Brydon, Sir Donald 65, 151, 408

Budge, Ann 83, 423, 425-426, 450, 501

Burgess, Ron 248, 250, 278, 402

Burton Joyce 12, 35, 52, 321, 358-359, 365, 367, 374, 386, 392, 395-396, 405, 410, 412, 438, 441, 458

Busby, Sir Matt 31, 74, 113, 143-145, 165, 179, 225, 240, 242, 283, 307, 312, 340-341, 397

Butler, Bryon 287, 397

Cantwell, Noel 22, 27, 241-243, 254, 499

Carlin, Willie 277, 288-289, 293, 295, 302, 468, 474

Cassidy, Ninian 6, 34-35, 254, 398, 402, 414, 423, 425, 432, 460, 494

Celtic FC 71, 74, 99, 108, 112, 117, 119-121, 123-125, 127, 140-142, 149, 153, 155, 168, 187, 202, 207, 254, 268, 319, 340, 384, 424, 426, 450, 461, 482

Chalmers, Matt 63, 66-68, 122, 137, 139, 205, 209

Charles, John 271, 397, 408

Charles, Mel 162, 214

Charlton, Bobby 114, 225, 241, 255, 271, 299, 341, 397, 408

Charlton, Jack 255, 257

Chas and Dave 12, 387

Cholorton, Frank 347

Clarke, Harry 160, 167, 248, 376

Clough, Brian 5, 10-11, 14, 19, 129, 271, 284-291, 295-296, 298, 302-307, 311-313, 322-323, 325-330, 332-336, 338-340, 342-343, 346-348, 350-352, 396, 398, 402, 409, 411, 446, 467-469, 482, 487, 500-501, 504

Coleman, Eddie 165

Collins, Bobby 121, 129-130, 145, 187, 255, 365

Conn, Alfie 85, 88-89, 96-97, 100, 119-120, 122-124, 128, 136-139, 153-154, 402, 428, 462, 477, 498

Connery, Sean 73-74, 89, 498

Cooper, Terry 255, 376, 381

Coyte, Paul 401, 405, 435, 494

Cowie, Doug 498

Currie, Duncan 109

Crawford, Ian 117, 119, 121, 123-125, 128-129, 135-137, 147-148, 222-223, 483

Cumming, John 77, 88-89, 92, 98-100, 119, 121, 123-125, 135-137, 139, 147, 149, 154, 156, 169, 183, 462, 483

Dalglish, Kenny 76, 334, 397

Daniel, Peter 336-337, 469

Davies, Roger 323, 330, 336, 346, 395, 469

Deane, Brian 369, 371

Derby County FC 9-11, 14, 19, 33-34, 84, 98, 118, 129, 152, 271, 284-292, 295-307, 311-313, 315, 318, 321, 323, 325-330, 332, 334-337, 339-348, 350-352, 354, 360, 371, 374-375, 391, 395-396, 398, 402, 404, 409-411, 414, 416-421, 423-424, 426, 428, 433, 437, 440, 443, 446, 449, 451-452, 457, 465, 467-470, 473-475, 477-478, 482-483, 487, 494-495, 500-501, 503-504

Di Stéfano, Alfredo 63, 130, 132, 193, 220

Ditchburn, Ted 160, 167, 176, 208, 248

Dixon, Tom 35, 398, 460, 501

Docherty, Agnes 244

Docherty, Tommy 132, 143, 145, 169, 172, 175, 244, 252, 263-264, 266, 344, 351-352, 354, 406, 419, 499, 501

Dolby, Peter 23-24

Downs, Greg 376

Doncaster Rovers FC 6, 26, 35, 367-372, 374, 418, 453, 495, 504

Dyson, Kay 1752

Dyson, Terry 17, 27-28, 159-160, 167, 169-170, 173, 175, 181, 185, 187, 190-191, 197-199, 203-204, 206, 208-209, 213-215, 220, 226, 230-233, 235-236, 240, 242-244, 247, 251, 272, 383, 398, 430, 432, 435, 439, 449, 472-473, 494, 502

Duff, Willie 66-67, 69, 98-99, 121, 124, 128, 483

Duncan, John 278, 495

Edinburgh 14, 31, 35-39, 41, 44, 46-49, 51-54, 56-60, 64-73, 77, 89-90, 94-95, 101-102, 106-109, 111-112, 115-116, 118-119, 122, 124-126, 133-136, 146, 150, 152, 155, 163, 166, 174, 211, 213, 233, 271, 283-285, 395, 405, 408, 421-423, 430, 432, 435, 450, 460, 462, 467, 484

Edwards, Duncan 104-105, 113, 131, 165, 169, 182, 271, 397, 419, 428

Ellis, Andy (appendix) 487, 495

Ellis, Ernest 109

Elms, Charlie 69, 74-77

End (Beatles), The 446

England, Mike 14, 254, 257-258, 260-261, 263, 266, 271, 273-274, 298, 314, 426-427, 494

European Cup 1958/59 146, 148, 151

European Cup 1961/62 28, 219, 221, 247

European Cup Winners' Cup 1962/63 229, 238–239, 268
European Cup Winners' Cup 1963/64 240, 242, 246
Eusébio 10, 31, 220-222, 228, 271, 323, 453
Evans, Alun 354-355
Evans, Bobby 123, 125, 130-131, 172, 184, 498
Everton FC 18, 49, 117, 135, 154, 159, 161, 165, 183, 187, 192, 236, 255, 291, 326, 336, 344, 349, 354, 462

Fahd, Sheikh 359
Ferguson, Sir Alex 10, 14, 19, 31, 66, 253-255, 272, 366, 386, 397, 422-423, 426, 428, 454-455, 499
Flavell, Bobby 63-64
Frain, John 377, 379, 453, 495
Fennelly, John 397, 426, 431, 495
Fontaine, Just 144
Footballer of the Year (Scottish) 1958 152
Footballer of the Year (English) 1969 291
Ford, Fred 312
Forever In Our Hearts 433
Fraser, Doug 319-320, 353
Fresco, Monte 27, 255-256

Gaffer, Farouk 294, 384
Gemmill, Archie 302, 337, 339, 345, 455, 469, 500
Gento, Francisco 130, 220, 481
George, Charlie 333, 341, 346, 349, 351, 469, 500
Gillies, Matt 315, 319
Gilzean, Alan 14, 33, 53, 83, 240, 244, 251, 253, 255, 261-262, 264, 268-269, 271, 278, 298, 314, 428, 434-435, 440, 449, 480, 500, 503
Glade (Enfield), The 5, 52, 92, 212, 304, 322, 371, 441-442
Glendevon Park, Edinburgh 36-40, 43, 54, 58, 61, 63-64, 66, 69, 75, 77, 85, 99, 101, 103, 112, 115-116, 127, 133, 137, 153, 163, 205, 217, 238, 422, 441, 495
Glidden, Freddie 69, 79, 91, 95-96, 98-100, 119, 121, 123, 125, 127, 135-136, 149, 153, 169, 483, 498
Gracie, Tom 109
Graham, George 255
Greaves, Jimmy 10, 14, 17-18, 27, 31, 33, 42, 83, 132, 165, 178, 195, 206, 209, 214, 216-217, 220, 226, 229, 231, 234, 236, 238, 241-242, 247, 250-251, 255, 257-258, 264, 268, 270-271, 273, 280, 291,

298, 300-301, 383, 393, 397-398, 406, 408, 432, 437, 445, 476, 494, 502
Green, Les 287, 292, 294, 302, 468

Hall, Terry 17, 174
Hamilton, Johnny 117, 129, 136, 149
Hamilton Academical FC 84, 91, 117
Hampden Park 22, 57-58, 60, 95, 119, 149, 155, 183, 268, 421
Harkness, Jack 126, 156
Harland, Stan 314
Harmer, Tommy 161, 167-168, 176-178, 402
Harris, Allan 384
Harris, Ron 17, 257, 263
Harvey, John (Johnny) 59, 85, 91, 98, 123, 148, 152, 283, 285
Hateley, Mark 423
Hateley, Tony 263
Haynes, Johnny 60-61, 73, 104, 129, 195, 213, 397, 497, 504
Heart of Midlothian FC 450, 501-502
Hearts FC Blind Party 126
Hector, Kevin 284, 287, 289-291, 293, 326-327, 336-337, 342, 347, 469-470, 474
Henderson, Willie 19, 234, 424, 426
Henry, Ron 159-160, 169, 189, 206, 209, 216, 250, 499
Hibernian FC 44, 67, 77, 90, 106, 146, 421, 450, 454
Hickie, Andrew 76, 78-79, 495
Hinton, Alan 288, 291, 294, 330, 337, 342, 345, 469-470, 474, 501
Hollowbread, John 176, 209
Houseman, Peter 290
Hoy, Chris 22, 66
Hunt, Roger 255
Hurst, Sir Geoff 17, 255, 301, 362, 398, 406
Hutton, Jim 43, 55-56, 497

James, Leighton 344, 347, 469
Jeffrey, Alick 26
Jennings, Eleanor 434
Jennings, Pat 17, 22, 28, 244, 246, 249-250, 253, 255, 258-260, 262-263, 267-268, 270, 272, 298, 314, 355, 397-398, 420, 424-425, 427, 430, 434-435, 449, 476, 494, 503
Jones, Cliff 13, 17, 28, 113, 146, 159-160, 162, 165, 168-169, 173, 177-179, 181, 191, 194-195, 197, 199, 202-203, 205-206, 209, 214-216, 220-221, 227, 236, 241, 246, 250, 254-255, 258, 260, 271,

280, 295, 383, 397-398, 400-402, 405, 407, 420, 424-425, 429-430, 434-435, 449, 467, 472, 494, 499, 503
Jones, Ken 21, 23, 26, 198, 497
Jones, Joan 175, 398, 406

Kane, Harry 206, 244, 405, 420, 434, 457
Keane, Roy 19, 437, 453-454
Kilgour, Nicol 151, 162, 165
King, Alex 119
Kinnear, Joe 28, 33, 35, 244, 252, 258, 264, 314, 359, 363, 368, 370, 398, 435, 465, 504
Kilmarnock FC 59, 136-137, 139, 148
Kirk, Bobby 117, 119, 121, 135-137
Knowles, Cyril 14, 244, 251, 258, 262, 264, 271, 298, 314, 370, 465
Kopa, Raymond 144
Kubala, Laszlo 130, 132
Kumars, The 379-381

Laing, Davie 88, 92, 98-99
Lampard Junior, Frank 342
Law, Denis 5, 12, 15, 31, 145-146, 183-184, 196, 238, 242, 253, 255, 259, 271, 278, 300, 340, 387, 397, 408, 422-423, 454, 495, 504
Leather, Alan 174, 208, 499
Lee, Francis 335, 338, 340, 343, 346, 349, 469-470, 500
Leicester City FC 168, 176, 194, 199, 202-207, 209, 214-215, 224, 228, 250-251, 279, 302, 319, 327, 331, 336, 354, 414
Levy, Daniel 10, 31, 495
Longson, Sam 289, 325-326, 333, 348, 350, 398

Mackay Junior, David 51, 52, 116, 163, 175, 196, 211
Mackay, Derek 5, 12, 54, 66, 211, 230, 248, 267, 280, 501
Mackay, Frank 49, 55
Mackay, Isobel 7, 14, 17, 19, 26-27, 31-32, 35-36, 52, 55, 65, 90-92, 103, 112, 114-116, 122, 144, 151, 163-164, 172-174, 191, 196, 208-209, 211-212, 216, 230, 233, 243-246, 248, 256, 280, 285-286, 300, 303-304, 321, 333, 337, 356, 359, 362-364, 371, 383, 387, 391-394, 398, 400, 402, 405-406, 409-411, 413, 418, 423-424, 427, 430-434, 436-438, 444-445, 467, 494
Mackay, Julie 425, 501
Mackay, Louis 45, 64, 101
Mackay, Tommy 55-56, 65, 425, 497

Mackay, Ronnie 10, 37, 39, 46, 49, 69
Mackay, Valerie 267, 428
Manchester City FC 15, 19, 70, 167, 170, 178, 191, 195, 240, 270, 287, 291, 335-336, 400, 448, 456, 468-469, 479, 486
Manchester United FC 13-15, 19, 21-22, 26, 28, 36, 49, 74, 105, 113, 143, 155, 160, 165, 169, 177, 185, 192, 194, 218, 225, 237, 240, 249, 251, 253-255, 259, 268-269, 278-279, 283, 299, 302, 326, 340, 343-344, 353, 366, 369, 386, 419, 428, 434, 457, 468, 470, 476, 486
Mansfield Traquair Church 460
Marchi, Tony 167, 195, 199, 209, 215, 217, 220, 222, 231-233, 235, 247, 494
Marshall, Gordon 31, 98, 128, 135-136, 147, 149, 152, 402, 424, 427, 494, 499
Martin, Neil 78, 319, 355, 358, 360, 365, 393, 424, 453, 495
Moore, Bobby 237-238, 255, 301, 303, 306, 342, 397, 408, 449
Mourinho, Jose 18, 32, 434, 448, 456
McCartney, John 109, 446
McLaren, Bob 119
McLeod, Don 86, 102, 123, 454
McClure, Duncan 68-69, 497
McColl, Ian 130-132, 454
McCrae, Sir George 85, 109
McDonaugh, George 54
McFarland, Roy 31, 284, 287-288, 291, 293, 300-303, 305, 307, 323, 329-330, 332-333, 335, 337, 339, 342, 351, 393, 395, 410-412, 424-425, 428, 452, 469, 473-474, 495
McGovern, John 287, 292, 295, 300, 302, 305, 307, 327, 332, 335, 352, 410, 424-425, 452, 469, 495
McKenzie, Tam 98, 117, 135-136
McIntosh, Laurence 64-65, 79, 86, 88-91, 498
McLintock, Frank 205, 209-210, 255, 279, 303, 423, 426, 430, 481, 495
McKenzie, Duncan 319
McPhail, John 140-141
Medwin, Joyce 175, 398
Medwin, Terry 146, 160, 167-169, 175, 178, 194, 197, 209, 226, 242, 383, 398, 406, 435
Midland Hotel, Derby 293, 300, 440
Mido 382
Mirk, James 119
Moore, Bobby 237-238, 255, 301, 303, 306, 342, 367, 397, 408, 440, 449
Morgan, Roger 33
Morris, Mel 452, 495

Moss, David 315-317, 453, 495
Motherwell FC 84
Mullery, Alan 14, 33, 210, 244, 246, 248, 251, 255, 258, 261, 264-265, 267, 269, 271, 298, 313, 397, 417, 420, 426-427, 449, 464-465, 500, 503
Munro, Robert 109
Murray, Jimmy 69, 135, 137, 139, 143-144, 146, 149, 153, 402, 483-484, 499

National Service 111, 113-116, 128, 132, 135, 176
Newton, Henry 326-327, 329, 337, 354, 410, 412
Newtongrange Star FC 68
Nicholson, Bill 10, 14, 18-19, 21, 25-26, 33, 100, 104, 141, 159-167, 169-171, 173, 175-181, 183, 185-188, 194, 198-199, 203-204, 207-208, 210-212, 214-215, 217, 219, 222-224, 226-227, 230-232, 235-236, 241-248, 251-254, 257-258, 260, 264, 267, 269-270, 272-275, 279, 283-285, 290, 299-300, 307, 311-313, 323, 336, 343, 350, 397, 409, 421, 431, 440, 446, 463, 466, 474, 478-479, 497, 499-500, 502-503
Nish, David 323, 335, 342
Noble, Peter 314, 316
Norman, Jacqueline 175
Norman, Maurice 159-160, 162, 169, 190, 199, 205, 207, 209, 234, 238, 240, 250, 275, 401

O'Hare, John 284, 287-288, 292-293, 332, 335, 395, 469, 474
O'Neill, Martin 319, 322
Orange Free State 93
Osgood, Peter 263-264, 341

Paisley, Bob 335-336
Palais de Danse 89
Parker, Bobby 98-102, 121-122, 134, 136, 498
Parry, Ray 61, 178
Partick Thistle FC 149-150, 170, 462
Pelé 271
Perryman, Steve 17, 277, 398, 426, 428, 435, 450, 494
Peters, Martin 17, 255, 271, 398
Portsmouth FC 202, 261, 313, 354
Poynton, Cecil 166-167, 204, 216, 236, 241, 244
Pride Park 395, 420, 433, 451
Purdie, Tom 106-108, 502
Puskás, Ferenc 220

Qatar Youth 362, 385-387, 391, 418
Queen's Medical Centre, Nottingham 411
Queen's Park FC 136, 138, 140, 155, 268
Quigley, Johnny 261-262, 365, 370

Ramsey, Sir Alf 179, 196, 222-224, 254, 376
Rangers FC 70-71, 88, 90, 95-96, 100, 117, 119-120, 127-128, 133-134, 139, 141-142, 146, 148-151, 155, 233-234, 299, 384, 406, 421, 423, 426, 482
Raschid, Mousa 358
Redknapp, Harry 34-35, 398, 400, 403, 406, 501
Revie, Don 121, 255, 335
Richardson, Jock 162
Rioch, Bruce 330, 333, 337, 340, 342-343, 345, 347, 349, 352, 455, 469, 500
Robertson, Jimmy 28, 244, 251, 265-266, 275, 278, 354, 430, 435, 453, 487, 494
Robertson, John 284, 292, 294
Robinson, Les 368, 371-372, 453, 495
Robson, Bobby 199, 327, 337, 377
Robson, Bryan 257, 408, 453, 455
Robson, John 199, 226, 257, 284, 292, 294, 327, 330, 337, 377, 408, 453, 455, 473
Rogers, Don 314-315
Rollo, Mike 400-401, 405, 426, 432, 494
Rowe, Arthur 19, 159-161, 180-181, 224
Russian Tour 1959 173–174

Sadler, John 347, 504
Sainty, John 22-23, 28, 276, 423, 426, 494
Salah, Mo 382
Saughton School 44, 55, 57-58, 63-64, 66-67, 69, 71, 85-86, 101, 201, 425
Saul, Frank 209, 215, 260, 262, 264
Scotland (international) 78, 87, 107, 123, 206, 264, 340, 353-354, 397
Scott, Sir Walter 37, 106, 111, 122, 126, 403, 406, 433, 501
Setters, Maurice 113
Shabab FC 359, 495
Shaw, Hugh 67
Sideboard Song, The 427, 432, 446
Shankly, Bill 179, 237, 269, 299, 335, 397
Scholes, Paul 449, 453, 482
Slateford Athletic FC 66, 71, 73, 98
Smith, Bobby 17, 24, 27, 159-160, 162, 167-169, 178, 183, 187, 190-191, 195, 197, 199, 202, 204, 208-210, 213, 215, 219, 221, 226-227, 233-236, 238, 243, 245, 251, 275, 398, 401, 480
Smith, Eric 112, 121, 123
Souness, Graeme 33, 56, 257, 453, 504

Souness, Jim 98
South African Tour 1954 92–94
Speed, David 68
Speed, Jimmy 109
St John, Ian 25, 255, 424, 426
Stein, Jock 121, 253, 340, 397, 454
Stiles, Nobby 194, 257, 438
Swindon Town FC 118, 291, 311-318, 321, 323, 327, 330, 333, 399, 418, 423, 453, 457, 468, 475, 495, 504

Taylor, Peter 284, 290-291, 325, 329, 340, 350
This Is Your Life 194-195
Thomas, Rod 314, 317, 330, 337, 395, 469
Tighe, Terry 56, 66-67, 69-70, 76, 201
Todd, Colin 302-303, 305, 333-335, 337-338, 342, 351, 360, 453, 469, 495
Tottenham Hotspur FC 6, 9-10, 13, 17-19, 21-23, 26, 34-35, 70, 98, 108, 116-117, 151-153, 159, 163-164, 166, 168, 173-174, 177, 179-181, 185-186, 188, 190-191, 197, 208-210, 212-213, 217-218, 220-222, 225, 234-235, 240, 243, 247-248, 250, 252, 255, 257-259, 261, 263-264, 266, 268, 270-271, 274, 276-280, 287, 291, 295-296, 298, 300-301, 305, 316, 319, 336, 341-342, 359, 362, 369, 371, 393, 397-398, 400, 406, 412, 414, 416-421, 423-428, 430-431, 434-435, 437-438, 444, 448-449, 456-457, 462, 466, 468, 470, 472-473, 476-478, 480, 483, 486, 494, 499-500, 502-503
Tottenham Hotspur Stadium, The 10, 18, 185, 434, 437, 448, 456
Trautmann, Bert 178
Tynecastle 32, 37, 42, 44, 53, 56, 58-59, 63-64, 66-69, 83-85, 88-91, 97-99, 101-102, 104, 107-109, 116, 118-120, 125, 127-128, 131, 133-134, 136-139, 142-143, 145, 147-150, 153, 155, 162-163, 165-166, 283-284, 402-405, 420-422, 425, 427, 433, 457, 462, 467, 502
Tully, Charlie 125

Ure, Ian 155, 254, 279, 454, 495

Venables, Terry 10, 252, 256, 260, 262, 264, 274, 465, 500

Walker, Bobby 108
Walker, Dan 409
Walker, Tommy 58, 64, 67, 69, 85-86, 93, 97, 100, 118-120, 122-123, 128, 132, 134-137, 139-140, 145, 151, 154, 161, 163-164, 166, 257, 284, 307, 312, 343, 350, 446, 461, 498
Walsall FC 353, 355-356, 358, 361, 374, 377, 418, 423, 453, 504
Wardhaugh, Jimmy 88, 92, 96, 98-99, 119, 135-136, 148-149, 154, 284, 498
Warriston Crematorium 427
Wattie, Henry 109
Wheldon, Ken 353, 356, 358, 374-375, 377, 380
White, John 13, 22, 25, 73, 92, 138, 154, 173, 175, 177, 181, 183, 190, 195-196, 199, 203, 205, 208-210, 215, 219, 226-227, 231, 234-235, 238-240, 244, 246, 248, 251-252, 271-273, 276, 280, 383, 397, 443, 483
White Fund, John 22, 248
White, Rob 403, 422, 426, 494, 501, 503
White, Sandra 175, 406
White Hart Lane 7, 10, 21-22, 61, 146, 151, 159, 166, 176, 185, 187, 192-193, 197, 202-203, 213, 219, 222-223, 225, 233, 247-248, 250-251, 255, 270, 274, 278, 285, 316, 323-324, 336, 355, 399-401, 405-406, 411-412, 417, 420, 431-432, 434-435, 440, 442-443, 445, 449, 456, 463, 467, 473, 476, 479, 486, 496, 502-503
Whitecraig 52, 90, 116, 166, 173, 245, 321
Whitehouse Way, Southgate 174, 211, 392
Williams, Danny 318
Wishart, Bobby 7, 38, 53-54, 63-64, 66, 85, 104-105, 117, 278, 495
World Cup 1958 143–145
World Cup 1966 32

Young, Alex 68-69, 76, 79, 96, 117, 121, 123, 129, 135-137, 148-149, 152-153, 155, 183, 187, 196, 397, 402, 483-484, 499
Young, George 130, 132

Zamalek FC 237, 382-385

Also available at all good book stores

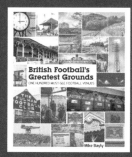

9781785316470

9781785313929

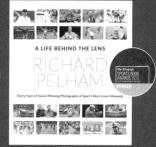

9781785315466

9781785317576

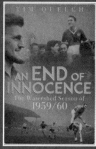

9781785317583

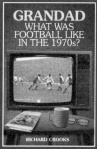

9781785312632

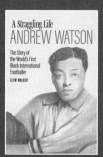

9781785318207

9781785318825

9781785317699

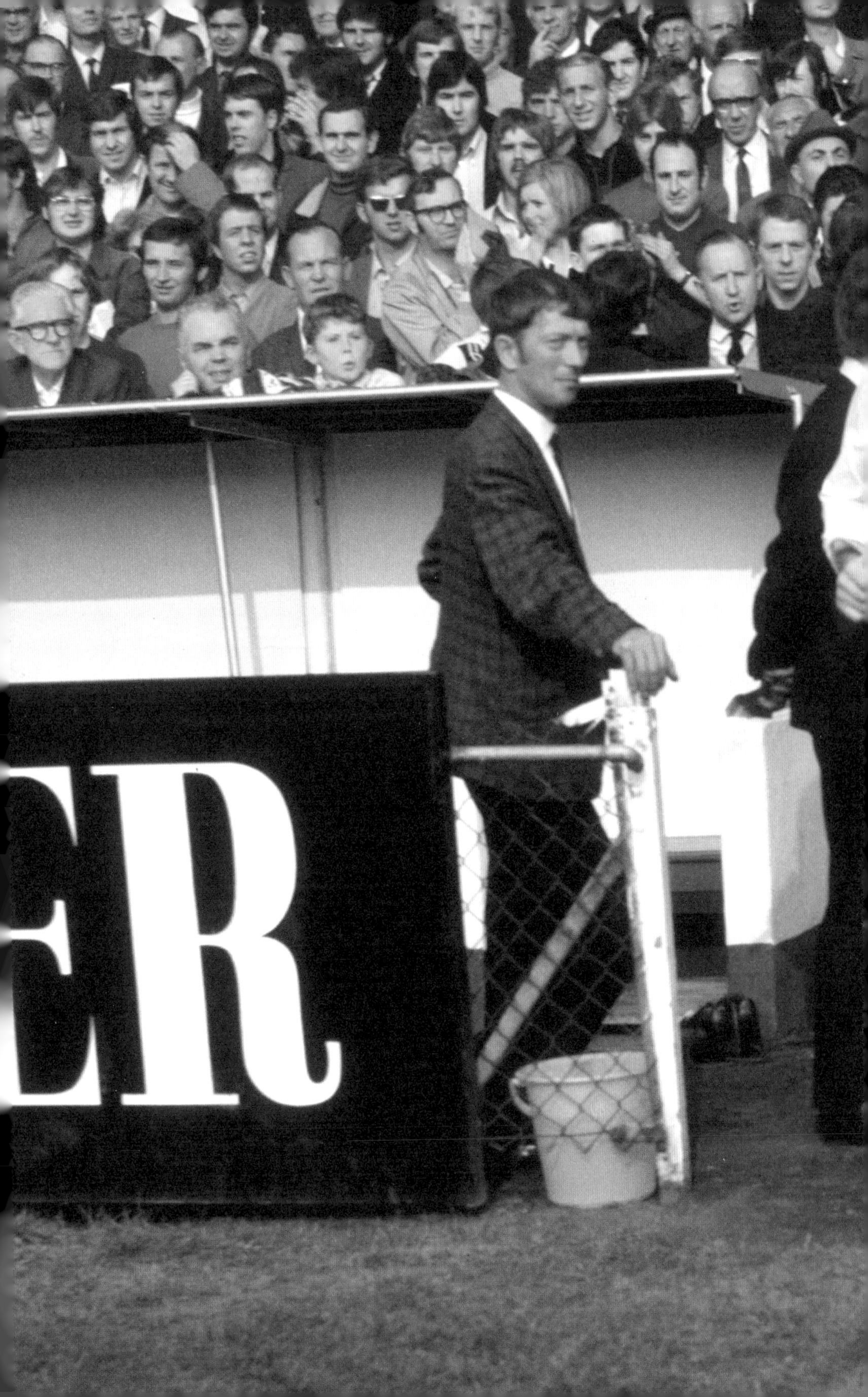
ER